Rocking Around
the Clock

E. ANN KAPLAN

Rocking Around the Clock

MUSIC TELEVISION, POSTMODERNISM, AND CONSUMER CULTURE

Routledge
New York and London

First published in 1987 by
Methuen, Inc.
Published in Great Britain by
Methuen & Co. Ltd
Reprinted 1988 by Routledge,
11 New Fetter Lane, London EC4P 4EE
29 West 35th Street, New York NY 10001

Reprinted 1989

Typeset in Great Britain
by Boldface Typesetters, 17a Clerkenwell Road, London EC1
Printed in Great Britain
by Richard Clay Ltd, Bungay, Suffolk

Library of Congress Cataloging in Publication Data

Kaplan, E. Ann.
  Rocking around the clock.
  Bibliography: p.
  Includes index
  1. Rock videos — United States. 2. MTV Networks.
  1. Title.
  PN1992.8.M87K36   1987   791.45'75'0973   86-33113

ISBN 0 416 33370 2
     0 415 03005 6 (pbk.)

British Library Cataloguing in Publication Data

Kaplan, E. Ann.
  Rocking around the clock: music television,
  postmodernism and consumer culture.
  1. MTV
  1. Title
  384.55'56'0973   HE8700.72.U6

ISBN 0 416 33370 2
     0 415 03005 6

Contents

ACKNOWLEDGMENTS   vii
INTRODUCTION   1

1   MTV: advertising and production   12
2   History, "reading formations," and the televisual
     apparatus in MTV   22
3   MTV and the avant-garde: the emergence of a
     postmodernist anti-aesthetic?   33
4   Ideology, adolescent desire, and the five types of
     video on MTV   49
5   Gender address and the gaze in MTV   89
6   Conclusion: MTV, postmodernism, and the televisual
     apparatus   143

AFTERWORD   154
NOTES   160
VIDEOGRAPHY   171
BIBLIOGRAPHY   181
SELECT GLOSSARY   186
INDEX   191

Acknowledgments

My very first thanks go to my daughter, Brett Kaplan, who first introduced me to MTV, although she has since moved on to other music. Interviews with Brett, Leo Margolf, and their friends, as well as with Paul Charney and his friends, helped me to understand how MTV was being received by some teenagers in 1984–5.

I next want to thank my good friend, Allon White, for the wonderful discussions during his visit to Rutgers University in 1983; many of my ideas for this book were generated in the course of our talks.

Martin Hoffman has been a constant source of encouragement and support in the writing of this book; he has borne many an hour of videos when he might have preferred other things, and helped me think ideas through when I came to an impasse.

I want to thank for their useful comments the Rutgers students who participated in seminars where MTV was briefly touched on. Gene Sobzchak was particularly helpful. Thanks also to the many students and faculty who came to all the talks on Music Television that I have given over the past few years; their thought-provoking comments, criticisms, and questions made me rethink some positions.

Peggy Phelan has been a thoughtful reader of various papers written as I was developing my ideas, and, in bringing MTV as a critical object to the attention of her graduate students at New York University, she has helped to develop interest in the area. She has also been invaluable in helping me locate specific videos and letting me borrow her tapes.

I want to thank music video director Eddie Barbarini for an illuminating interview, and both he and cameraman Bob Lechterman for allowing me to watch a video being made. Dr York, the producer of that video, also deserves thanks for being interviewed on the set.

I would like to thank the following book and journal editors for permission to reprint, in revised form, articles of mine that they published: first, Philip Drummond and Richard Paterson, editors of *Television in Transition* (London: British Film Institute, 1985) for "A postmodern play of the signifier? Advertising, pastiche and schizophrenia in music television"; the editors of *Journal of Communication Inquiry*, vol. 10, no. 1 (Winter 1986), for "History, the historical spectator and gender address in music television"; the editors of *The Oxford Literary Review*, vol. 8, nos 1–2 (Summer 1986), for "Sexual difference, visual pleasure and the construction of the spectator in music television"; and finally Deidre Pribram, editor of *Cinematic Pleasure and the Female Spectator* (London: Verso, 1987) for "Whose imaginary? Text, body and narrative in select rock videos."

I would have liked to be in a position to thank MTV Publicity for talking to me about their side of things, but unfortunately my calls were never returned. I therefore had to rely on secondary sources in making my comments.

My thanks to the various publicity departments of record companies (under whose labels videos were produced) for their patient supplying of information I needed; I also want to thank the Music Department at *Rolling Stone* magazine for helping out with missing details for my Videography.

I want to thank the following rock stars and record companies for permission to print stills from the following videos: Madonna and Warner Bros Records for stills from "Material Girl" and "Papa Don't Preach"; Bruce Springsteen for stills from "Born In The USA," "Glory Days," and "I'm On Fire"; Motley Crue and Elektra Records for stills from "Smokin' In The Boys' Room" and "Home Sweet Home"; Tina Turner and Capitol Records for stills from "What's Love Got To Do With It" and "Private Dancer"; John Cougar Mellencamp and Riva/Polygram Records for stills from

ACKNOWLEDGMENTS

"Authority Song" and "Hurts So Good"; Pat Benatar and Chrysalis Records for stills from "Love Is A Battlefield"; Elektra Records and The Cars for stills from "You Might Think"; Peter Gabriel and Geffen Records for the still from "Sledgehammer"; Tom Petty and the Heartbreakers and MCA Records for the still from "Don't Come Around Here No More"; Artists Against Apartheid and Manhattan Records for the still from "Sun-City."

I want to thank John Kline (New York Department of Photography) for his work photographing stills for "You Might Think," "Smokin' in the Boys' Room," "Home Sweet Home," "Sledgehammer," "Born in the USA," "Glory Days," "I'm On Fire," "Hurts So Good," "Authority Song," "What's Love Got To Do With It?," "Don't Come Around Here No More." Other stills photographed by Patti Sapone (Blakely/Sapone Productions).

Finally, my thanks to those people in video departments of record companies who tried patiently to track down dates when videos were released. Mark Rodriguez at Capitol Records was particularly helpful, as was Catherine Berclau at Atlantic Records.

Introduction

STRUCTURE AND CONTENT OF MTV

This book is concerned with rock videos as exhibited through Music Television – MTV – as an institution. What I have to say about rock videos only applies directly to their presentation within the MTV context. The textual analyses naturally stand on their own to a degree, and points made in those parts of the book have implications beyond MTV as an institution. But the larger arguments about postmodernism and spectatorship only make sense within the discussion of MTV as a commercial, popular institution, and as a specifically *televisual* apparatus. I will briefly address both issues, whose full implications will emerge as the book progresses

MTV is a 24-hour, non-stop, commercial cable channel, beamed via satellite across the United States and devoted to presenting rock music videos around the clock. Originally owned by Warner Amex Satellite Entertainment Company (WASEC – the station has recently been purchased by Viacom International), MTV is an advertiser-supported, basic cable service for which subscribers do not pay extra. As of Spring 1986, the channel reached 28 million households[1] (it is available wherever there are cable systems to hook it up). The brain child of Robert Pittman, WASEC's then Executive Vice President,[2] MTV was begun in 1981 for an initial cost of $20 million. MTV earned $7 million in ad revenue in the first eighteen months, and in May 1983 the station already had 125 advertisers representing 200 products including Pepsico and Kellogg, that bought air time

1

for spots from 30 to 120 seconds at a cost of from $1500 to $6000.[3] By 1984 the audience had grown to 22 million, aged between 12 and 34, and ad revenue had reached one million a week.[4] By the end of 1983 the channel had $20 million in ad revenue, and figures for 1984 show more than one million a week in ad revenue, with an audience of 18 to 22 million.[5]

In August 1984, MTV became a public corporation and announced that it had agreements with four record companies for exclusive rights to new videos. It was in response to Turner Broadcasting Company's announcement that it would initiate a competing 24-hour music television station that MTV opened its second channel, VH-1 (intended for what Robert Pittman called "an untapped new audience," namely that between the ages of 25 and 49), for an initial cost of $5 million.[6]

Pittman's genius was in imagining, and then implementing, the concept of a 24-hour station devoted entirely to rock videos. For, while rock videos existed before MTV, they were largely tapes of live performances, played on late-night television and mainly used for publicity purposes (the Beatles' "Strawberry Fields" video made in 1967 is an exception in anticipating the contemporary surrealist/ fictional tape). Some Top Twenty programs also featured videos, but it is only since the invention of MTV that regular channels like NBC and ABC have featured rock video programs (e.g. NBC's "Friday Night Videos" and ABC's "Hot Tracks") and other cable channels, like Channel 3 in New York, have put on programs like "Video Box" and "Video Soul," which, like "Hot Tracks," feature mainly black artists. Since MTV, Feature Film Cable channels like HBO also run rock videos between films (HBO has a spot called "Video Jukebox") and USA Cable Network runs videos on its "Night Flight." The recent home VCR boom has now brought increased access to rock videos through the cassette market. A new cable channel – U-68 – is recently available in the East Coast area, featuring videos considered too "avant-garde" for MTV (this channel recently abandoned its rock video format). The Apollo Entertainment Network has produced a series of taped concerts from the renovated Harlem Apollo Theatre, filling in the gap in airplay time for black bands.

These other television sites for video music, then, attempt to remedy the gaps left by MTV's particular "format" – as Bob Pittman calls it when questions are raised. MTV essentially duplicates FM Radio's white rock focus, although FM has perhaps more variety than the cable channel. Clearly Pittman is pleased with the mix of heavy metal, new wave, and pop that he has managed to produce, but people predict that there will be a series of specialized channels in the future, including a jazz-blues channel and a black pop/funk channel, to fill in the gaps. MTV Networks have already begun the trend in their second channel, VH-1, that features "pop" as against "rock" music – a broader category that permits black artists to get airplay. (These issues will all be discussed in more detail later on.)

If MTV is enmeshed in discourses about rock music, it is the insertion of these discourses in the specifically *televisual* apparatus that produces a result drastically different from prior organizations of rock. By "televisual apparatus" I mean: the technological features of the machine itself (the way it produces and presents images); the various "texts," including ads, commentaries, and displays; the central relationship of programming to the sponsors, whose own texts – the ads – are arguably the *real* TV texts;[7] and, finally, the reception sites – which may be anywhere from the living room to the bathroom.

Research on individual aspects of this apparatus has already begun. For instance, scholars may focus on problems of enunciation, that is, who speaks a particular TV text and to whom it is addressed; or look at the manner in which we watch TV (who *controls* the set when it is watched) and at the meanings of its presence in the home; or they may study the so-called "flow" of the programs, the fragmentation of the viewing experience even within any one given program, and the unusual phenomenon of endlessly serialized programs; or, finally, scholars may investigate the ideology embedded in the forms of production and reception, which are not "neutral" or "accidental" but a crucial result of television's overarching commercial framework.

One of the as yet unresolved issues in such research is that of the degree to which theories recently devised for the classical Hollywood cinema are pertinent to the very different televisual apparatus. One striking way that the televisual differs from the filmic apparatus is in the prevalence of programs that are "serials"

3

in one form or another – that is, continuous segments to be viewed daily or weekly. The most obvious are soaps or prime-time dramas, but, stretching the idea a bit, we should also include the news (regularly slotted and so highly stylized as to be "drama"[8]) and the game shows, which are equally stylized. All of these programs exist on a kind of horizontal axis that is never ending, instead of being discrete units consumed within the fixed two-hour limit of the Hollywood movie or, like the novel, having a fixed and clearly defined boundary.

In a sense, TV has neither a clear boundary nor a fixed textual limit. Rather, the TV screen may be conceived of as a frame through which a never ending series of texts moves laterally; it is as though one turned a film strip on its side and pulled the "frames" (episodes on TV) through a strip projector that way instead of vertically. Peggy Phelan presents an alternative metaphor of Foucault's Panopticon, in which the guard surveys a series of prisoners through their windows. She sees the TV producer as the "guard" and the individual TV viewer as the "prisoner who watches in a sequestered and observed solitude."[9]

The "guard" metaphor also works well for the spectator's relationship to the various episodes (serialized programs of various kinds) that represent, in Foucault's words, "a multiplicity that can be numbered and supervised." For the spectator has the *illusion* of being in control of the "windows," whereas in fact the desire for plenitude that keeps him/her watching is, in this case, forever deferred. The TV is seductive precisely because it speaks to a desire that is insatiable – it promises complete knowledge in some far distant and never-to-be-experienced future. TV's strategy is to keep us endlessly consuming in the hopes of fulfilling our desire.

MTV's programming strategies embody the extremes of what is inherent in the televisual apparatus. The channel hypnotizes more than others because it consists of a series of extremely short (four minutes or less) texts that maintain us in an excited state of expectation. The "coming up next" mechanism that is the staple of all serials is an intrinsic aspect of the minute-by-minute MTV watching. We are trapped by the constant hope that the next video will finally satisfy and, lured by the seductive promise of immediate plenitude, we keep endlessly consuming the short texts. MTV thus carries to an extreme a phenomenon that characterizes most of television. The "decentering" experience of viewing produced by the constant alternation of texts is exacerbated on MTV because its *longest* text is the four-minute video.

Later on in the book, I will be extending this discussion so as to clarify precisely the nature of the televisual "imaginary" as against the filmic one. I will be arguing that MTV reproduces a kind of decenteredness, often called "postmodernist," that increasingly reflects young people's condition in the advanced stage of highly developed, technological capitalism evident in America. As an apparatus developed only in recent decades, TV may be seen as at once preparing for and embodying a postmodern consciousness. MTV arguably addresses the desires, fantasies, and anxieties of young people growing up in a world in which all traditional categories are being blurred and all institutions questioned – a characteristic of postmodernism.[10]

WHY WRITE A BOOK ON MUSIC TELEVISION?

In one sense, my writing a book on MTV requires no explanation: I have long been interested in popular culture, focusing particularly on the classical Hollywood film but also on women's popular fiction and commercial television. And MTV, as a new popular phenomenon, would seem to warrant study as much as anything else.

However, as it is many years since I last studied adolescent or youth culture, a few words of explanation may be in order. I first became interested in youth culture when teaching in a further education college in London in the early 1960s. At that time, of course, there was not much youth culture proper, this being prior to the explosion of the Beatles and the proliferation of a very clearly defined adolescent and young adult group whose various cultural innovations and political activities would become news headlines for more than a decade.

Bobby Duran, Adam Faith, and Cliff Richard (sometimes seen as a tame British Elvis Presley) more or less represented the music interests of our students in those days. Well-dressed, clean, and conservative, these rock singers did not represent much of a rebellion to the status quo. The Teddy Boys alone, with their well-oiled hair and suits modeled on Edwardian dress, suggested any oppositional culture. We had in all this only a glimpse of the mid 1960s and 1970s youth culture explosion, in which rock and roll was to play a central, often subversive, role that has been well-documented.[11]

At Kingsway Day College, London, following the approach worked out by Paddy Whannel and Stuart Hall, we tried to indicate the disparities between the trivialized experiences of this early British pop music and commercial film, and the more complex possibilities of what we still called "great art."[12] But this was carried out with enormous respect for the commercial works our students were drawn to, and usually involved understanding, and helping them understand, the bases for their interests rather than attempting to turn them toward the canon. Mostly we tried to interest them in the new working-class culture of the period, represented by the plays of Arnold Wesker, John Osborne, and John Arden; the novels of Alan Sillitoe, David Storey, and John Braine; and the films often made out of these novels by Tony Richardson, Lindsay Anderson, John Schlesinger, and Karel Reisz.

However, this lesson in realism was rather bleak and humorless, just like the works themselves. Only so much could be said about the banal, boring working-class lives of the protagonists, and texts did not seem to offer a way out. No wonder the British Youth responded with glee to the Beatles, who finally introduced joy/exuberance/fun into the traumatized post-World-War-II British landscape. But by then I had left England.

It is a far cry from the early steps toward a youth culture in Britain briefly sketched in here to the full-blown, heavily commercialized youth phenomenon that MTV represents. In the 1960s I was part of the politicized youth culture, although we all kept up with the Hippies, the Flower Children, and the rock and roll culture, especially as represented by the Beatles, the Stones, the Grateful Dead, the Doors, Led Zeppelin, Janis Joplin. But in the 1970s I dropped out to become an adult, only vaguely keeping track of punk, new wave and heavy metal — largely through my daughter.

Obviously these "developments" partly paved the way for MTV. Perhaps the subject attracts me because it contains remnants from the first ten years of the youth culture that I had known, together with the less familiar – to me – 1970s. But MTV also attracts because it seems to embody aspects of contemporary youth culture that signify a new era. It attracts, that is, by its very combination of similarity to, and *difference* from, my own various youth cultures; and by seeming to be an index of a new stage of things, a different kind of consciousness. I will be suggesting what this new consciousness involves, using postmodernism and psychoanalysis to illuminate it. More than much previous popular culture, MTV makes evident its address to adolescent desire, to the spectator's imaginary repertoire, which now takes precedence over any obvious political stance toward dominant culture. Obsessed like much popular culture has always been with sexuality and violence, rock videos nevertheless represent these in new ways.

This new consciousness is perhaps partly the result of the Cold War, nuclear technology, multinational corporate capitalisms, star wars, advanced computer and other high tech developments, as well as, on a more mundane level, being produced by highly sophisticated new marketing strategies, building upon ever-increasing knowledge of psychological manipulation. In other words, MTV seems to embody what Jameson and others have been calling *Postmodernism*.

I am concerned with postmodernism on a number of different levels. The first level, already briefly touched on but to be fully developed later, presents the televisual apparatus as itself postmodernist, with MTV carrying this characteristic to an extreme; second is the more strictly aesthetic level, to be addressed in Chapter 3, where the technical, formal strategies of MTV videos are seen to generally embody postmodernism; third is the postmodernist "ideology" or "world view" as it emerges from in-depth analysis of specific videos, a project to be undertaken in Chapters 4 and 5.

The effort to find a label to indicate a new stage of things in itself reflects the nature of the crisis. People of older generations sense that the old categories will no longer serve, and yet can do no better than to come up with a term that includes the prefix "post" attached to what was a familiar category, namely "modernism."[13] By this strategy, one hopes to indicate a connection with what was, with the familiar, while at the same time noting the difference, the new, the unknowable.

ROCKING AROUND THE CLOCK

Now MTV obviously is connected with past developments, as my analysis will reveal. But that connection may not quite be what the "post" prefix suggests: that is, what is important is the sort of use made of the past by contemporary youth culture rather than *the fact that* the past is used. The manner of use suggests a drastically Other consciousness for which a completely new word may well be better than "postmodernism." But we have not yet made a sufficiently clear break with the past, nor with the concept of historical evolution, to arrive at a new word. And for my purposes, the notion of the postmodern is helpful in providing a method of conceptualizing what is *different* about the new phase. One cannot think without a shaping framework: it seems to me that the only way to understand a new phenomenon must be through understanding why one's current categories do not fit. Working dialectically, then, we can move beyond current categories to new ones in a way impossible without *moving through* the old ones.

Clearly, since each generation enters the stream at a different point, the same phenomenon will take a different shape if studied by people with different starting frameworks. Someone looking at MTV from the position of growing up in the 1970s is bound to bring to it frameworks other than mine, and come up with different results. Indeed, someone like Greil Marcus might argue that I cannot possibly write about MTV since I did not grow up with it, and have not belonged in a network of teenagers who "lived" rock music daily, and for whom this was a silent common bond.[14]

I do not agree with the notion of rock music as a kind of mystique that someone outside the specific generation cannot understand. But reading Marcus made me aware of how different MTV is from previous rock cultures in terms of its address. For Marcus, 1960s rock was something that bound his small circle together in a largely non-verbal way; they shared the common, secret bond of enjoying the same songs, all of which represented a certain stance toward the establishment, a shared set of mildly subversive values. This is something that I will be exploring later, so let me merely note here that the very fact that MTV addresses itself to a broad, generally youthful section of the American public that ranges from 12 to 34 on up distinguishes it from earlier rock cultures, which addressed much more homogeneous groups, clearly defined in terms of values, age, and social status.

But the point about looking at MTV from different conceptual frameworks raises a problem that confronted me in setting out on my project, that is, what use to make of rock history in my text. As will be clear in a later chapter, MTV situates itself in a special way vis-à-vis past rock movements, and must be positioned outside of what has become a familiar linear history of rock developments.

Like most history, that of rock music has now developed its own narrative pattern, repeated from text to text. One of the earliest histories was Nick Cohn's *Rock From the Beginning* (1969), whose basic linear model has been taken up by later histories (such as Jahn's *From Elvis Presley to the Rolling Stones*).[15] Let me briefly rehearse this narrative, if only to indicate a historical sequence that now seems to have run its course. By this I mean that trends set in motion originally by black musicians have possibly gone as far as they can, as is arguably the case with modern art developments. Part of what we call the postmodern is precisely this phase of a movement that seems to have reached the end of its line.

MTV arguably emerges at this historical moment just because such an impasse in popular rock music has been reached. The historical "line" goes pretty much as follows: Everyone sees the 1950s as the great founding moment of rock music, which has its origins in black Rhythm and Blues, and in the Country and Western music that itself drew heavily on black music. Most historians comment on the way that white imitations of black songs were acceptable whereas the black originals were not. Billy Haley and Elvis Presley are central to everyone's story as setting the stage for all that happened subsequently. Presley, with his extraordinary mixture of pop and blues, foreshadows later rock developments. Early 1960s rock is viewed as a product of both Rhythm and Blues and of 1950s rock: the Beatles are credited with revolutionizing sound with their new instruments, new combinations, and new use of Indian forms and musical themes.

Historians vary somewhat in the degree to which they see late 1960s so-called "acid" or "protest" rock as innovative; most agree that the "hippie" music did introduce new sounds and new instruments, and that the advances possible through new musical technology (especially the capacity to increase volume) did have a big impact. Most writers agree, too, that this period represents the high point in recent rock history, and honor the original contributions of the Rolling Stones, the Beatles, the Who, Led Zeppelin, and the Kinks (among others) from Britain; and of Bob Dylan, the Grateful Dead, Janis Joplin, Jimi Hendrix, the Doors, and the Jefferson Airplane, from America. The important "protest" element is generally agreed upon, although the actual political significance of the stances taken by late 1960s rock musicians in their lives and lyrics is debated.

The narrative generally sees the 1970s as representing a decline in American rock, which had led the way in the late 1960s. Continuing the story of mutual back-and-forth influencing between England and America, historians now see the British moving in to fill the gap with their new wave and punk rock bands that gradually revitalized the American scene in the mid 1970s. Punk and new wave took on a different tone and style in America: already well on their way to postmodernism, it took the peculiar nature of the 1980s political scene in America to move the trends over into a full-blown postmodernism.

In this recurrent "dialogue" between America and Britain, MTV may be America's latest contribution. If postmodernism really does herald a new era, requiring totally new historical and aesthetic paradigms, it may signal the end of the kind of historical processes that rock history texts decribe. That is, we may no longer be looking for "pendulum" swings but for something else.

Whether or not MTV can be considered as in the mainstream of rock history, or an altogether different development, it seems necessary to link it, however tenuously, with the past.[16] I will argue that rock and pop forms from the past thirty years or so are currently being used to express a new sensibility that has been labeled "postmodernist." As we'll see, MTV uses themes, motifs, and forms from rock and pop history indiscriminately and without recognizing what it is doing, or making distinctions between rock "proper" and its popularized forms.[17] It cannot therefore be said either to represent a reaction to what went before or to foreshadow what will come hereafter. It is precisely those sorts of linear progressions that it violates in not situating itself within their parameters.

10

INTRODUCTION

Let me remind readers that this book addresses itself not to rock videos in general but to their incorporation in the institution that is MTV. Rock videos have their own history as an art form (a history being documented as of writing in an unprecedented Museum of Modern Art exhibition),[18] and are exhibited in a variety of different contexts. In most European countries there is no 24-hour channel like MTV devoted to videos; there, videos have half-hour slots on the different channels, a kind of visual "Top of the Pops." Often there are merely short clips from the videos in the count-down. Videos can be seen on a home VCR, since the cassettes are available, but one usually has to rent an entire tape by one artist. While the individual analyses of rock videos in this book should be interesting, my argument about rock videos and postmodernism depends on their exhibition in the 24-hour, continuous context.

Much of MTV's particular institutional form can be accounted for by looking at its links to a mode that at first seems to be the antithesis of rock music, namely advertising. It is to the wedding of rock music and aesthetic visual forms drawn partly from advertising that I now turn.

1

MTV: advertising and production

It was the sometimes extraordinary and innovative avant-garde techniques that first drew the attention of the critical establishment to MTV. It was tempting to view these devices as serving similar functions to those they served in what is now "traditional" modernism; but as we'll see in the next chapter, this is not so. In any case, the devices masked the promotional and commercial aspects of MTV that are evident in the contexts of production and exhibition.

But before I discuss the similarities between rock videos and ads, as specific texts, let me note how in its overall, 24-hour flow, MTV functions like one continuous ad in that nearly all of its short segments are indeed ads of one kind or another. If it is true that commercials constitute the *real* TV dramas in the case of series programs like soaps[1] then how much more true is this of a channel like Music Television that contains little else *but* ads of various kinds. As I'll show toward the end of this chapter, the various ad-segments, whether they be rock videos, a Levi or Cooler commercial, or promos for MTV itself, all have come to look more and more alike. It is for this reason that MTV, more than other television, may be said to be *about* consumption. It evokes a kind of hypnotic trance in which the spectator is suspended in a state of unsatisfied desire but forever under the illusion of *imminent* satisfaction through some kind of purchase. This desire is displaced onto the record that will embody the star's magnetism and fascination.

ADVERTISING AND PRODUCTION

The rock video idea was originally an advertising idea; in fact, a better name for rock videos is really "rock promos," since they are widely seen as promotional tools for the record companies.[2] The word "promo" is also appropriate because it indicates the videos' links to advertising evident in their style and manner of production. Their short, four-minute span originally suited a promotional context, while the illogical image-change and generally "avant-garde" techniques mimicked those long customary in many ads. The reliance on freelance crews, the omission of production credits and the financial tie-in to the record companies all duplicate the production situation of ads.

Interestingly, the promotional videos, which have hitherto been provided free by the record companies on the model of companies giving radio stations free records, are now in competition with one another for space on the channel. In the near future, record companies may have to pay to have videos on MTV. Given the already considerable cost of producing a video (from $35,000 to $50,000 at least), which is usually shouldered by the record company, this would be taxing. Several directors in a *Variety* interview suggested that record companies would be happy to be rid of the need to produce videos, for which they have "no clear-cut recoupment." Others, however, pointed out MTV's function in promoting songs not on the radio charts and in keeping songs in circulation that would otherwise have died. All seemed to agree, however, that a good video could not make a smash out of a "mediocre" song.[3] The huge success of Jackson's "Thriller" evidently convinced record companies of what videos could do, and interested several of them in the longer format (but so far as I can see, only David Bowie has taken advantage of extra time).

Exactly how any particular video was produced (who financed it, what artists were involved) is unclear to the viewer, since no credits of any kind are given (the rock group, the title of the song, and the record it comes from are the only clues). Full credits are given only for each week's video that is Top of the Countdown, and for those that make it to the MTV Awards ceremony. Directors differ greatly in the degree to which they demand or receive artistic freedom, though undoubtedly some see a tension between the record companies and themselves which is exacerbated by the fact that the companies are responsible for the financing.[4]

13

Rock videos differ from ads in the degree of concern for artistic elements. In this sense they are a hybrid form, in between the ad and the pop culture text. Directors themselves are a mixed bunch, drawn from a variety of backgrounds. Those coming from commercials think about a video very differently from those coming from independent filmmaking. Ken Walz is concerned that videos are becoming increasingly commercial, with record companies demanding "a more scientific approach to writing, producing and directing . . . videos." He fears that the more commercial directors get into the scene, the more they will feel comfortable with such restrictions and the less creativity there will be.[5] Other directors in the group interviewed have not yet felt the restrictions of commercials and apparently see themselves free to create what they want. All agree that there is often tension among the three main groups involved in production – the performers, the artists, and the record company. Directors believe they are the ones who know what has to be done and who can best come up with suitable ideas, but often performers or company people think they know best. Some directors find the record companies at a loss because the rock video is such a new form, and only too glad to leave things up to the person they have hired. The possibility for creativity in music video production is evident in the big name film directors (Brian de Palma and John Sayles have already made videos) now becoming interested in making videos just because of the greater freedom than Hollywood that videos offer.

An important problem mentioned by the directors interviewed is that usually the song is written first, and therefore takes priority over the visuals, limiting visual possibilities. The creativity of the film director has to be subordinated to that of the song-writer and performer. One director suggested that a rock star should begin working with a director at the point of conceptualizing the song but this is clearly impractical.[6] Others are concerned that videos may begin to affect the music negatively. August Darnell, organizer and chief composer for a band (Kid Creole and the Coconuts), is quoted as saying that "The attention that used to be devoted to content and song form is now being given over to the videos."[7] How things are finally resolved in the current set-up varies from case to case.

A second source of conflict is that between the groups producing the video (usually the director and the performers) and MTV as an institution. Because videos are more than *merely* ads (they are, as it were, ads plus), artists and bands have already, in MTV's short history, been in conflict with MTV management and with the record companies. There is a built-in contradiction, familiar from Hollywood, between the interests of the artists and performers and of those creating a profitable enterprise. In a predictable cycle, the more tapes were adapted to what would please the largest audience, the more successful the channel, and the greater the urge to censor material. Wary both of parental objections to the cable and of white audiences in racist parts of America, MTV at first censored black bands and explicit sex (e.g. Frankie Goes to Hollywood's *Relax*).

The motivations for both kinds of censorship were probably mainly commercial, but Dr York, one of the American black artists who has had trouble getting videos shown on MTV, is convinced that it is the difficulty of finding sponsors for the channel when black artists are featured that has kept them off MTV. According to Dr York, advertising strategists find the market for blacks hard to predict and unreliable, and thus are wary of committing money for promoting the music of black artists.[8]

As a result of objections raised by well-known stars like David Bowie, who refused to have videos on MTV if the situation continued, things improved somewhat in 1984 – 5. Predictably, changes have been merely in line with what the establishment could tolerate; that is, videos by black artists like Prince and Michael Jackson who have obviously "made it" are played from time to time, but black bands are still by far in the minority in the regular MTV run.[9] Prince is featured regularly only when he has a hit (like "Purple Rain" or "Raspberry Beret"), but was rarely represented until his recent, mildly scandalous "Kiss" video that (perhaps because of its explicit sexuality) did not remain long in circulation. Now that Michael Jackson is out of the news, his videos are also only rarely seen. Until the recent advent of Whitney Houston, Tina Turner was the only female black singer featured regularly, and even so, her videos are few and far between. Aretha Franklin's "Freeway of Love" was played frequently when it got into the top twenty, but we have mainly seen her since then co-starring with white artists (see below); the Pointer Sisters' "Neutron Dance" was only their second video since "Jump" to be shown, and their newest video appeared only

15

recently. Black artists who are not well known cannot get a video on MTV in the way that a similarly obscure white rock musician can, and rightly feel discriminated against by the channel; they have to content themselves with appearances on the weekly programs on other channels already mentioned, or on cable slots.

As of writing, one solution for black artists who want to get on MTV is to make videos jointly with white artists. Phil Collins and Phil Bailey paved the way with their successful "Easy Lover," and the video perhaps still represents the most playful and thoroughly integrated of joint videos. Hall and Oates made a successful video with David Ruffin and Eddie Kendrick, played constantly in September 1985. Most recently, Robin Clark has appeared with Simple Minds in their successful "Alive and Kicking" (top of the countdown for several weeks in 1986), and again in their "All The Things She Said" (she is apparently becoming a staple of their act); Aretha Franklin is given homage in Whitney Houston's "How Will I Know", but appears most dramatically with Annie Lennox in their powerful "Sisters Are Doin' It For Themselves", discussed in Chapter 5.

The other use of black artists – namely as back up choir and/or dancing figures (as in Young's "Everytime You Go Away" or Sting's successful "If You Love Somebody, Set Them Free") still seems somewhat exploitative, but perhaps better than nothing. The September 1985 MTV Video Awards broke new ground in having Eddie Murphy as the host and including more black artists than ever before. Perhaps because of this, in combination with the space that Channel Three has been providing especially for black artists (in the Video Soul and Video Vibrations slots), in Summer 1986 lesser known black artists, often relying on rap and reggae music that MTV has hitherto claimed was not their province,[10] appeared more frequently. A striking example of this is the recent success of the rap group Run – DMC's "Walk This Way," which has been in the countdown several times and has been frequently cycled on the channel. This success will no doubt pave the way for more rap groups, such as Whodini, to get on MTV. Janet and Jermaine Jackson, possibly because of their famous connection, and Jermaine Stewart, are currently paving the way for others.

Censorship of sex seems to be relaxing, but again this is a mixed blessing. Homosexuality is not addressed directly (I will be discussing

16

bi-sexuality and androgyny in their constricted forms later on), and relaxing of sex censorship has merely permitted degrading images of the female body (not that dissimilar from some pornography) to emerge (see John Cougar's "Hurts So Good," etc. discussed in Chapter 5, Prince's "1999," or his recent "Kiss" video mentioned above). Some of the most sexist heavy metal bands, such as Ozzy Osbourne, Motley Crue, Judas Priest, Alice Cooper, and Twisted Sister, have recently become popular and are now featured on MTV regularly (heavy metal bands were earlier censored), particularly in the weekly "Most Requested Videos" slot. (As of writing, there is a special "Heavy Metal" slot on the channel, presumably as a result of popular demand.) Twisted Sister's extraordinary video "Leader of the Pack" details, in comic mode, the incredibly violent adventures of a proper middle-class girl en route to union with one of the awesomely endowed band members parading huge biceps, broad chest, and hair down to the waist. Ozzy Osbourne's "Shot in the Dark" similarly shows the transformation of another middle-class girl into a zebra-like seductress through Osbourne's initiation rites; while Alice Cooper's "(He's Back): He's the Man Behind the Mask" this time has a middle-class young *male* terrifyingly inducted into the Alice Cooper nether world.

Artists and performers are naturally implicated in the contradictions because the increased success of the channel means their increased exposure and sales. They cannot help being involved because of their status as mediatory objects between a private and a public sphere. The artists' subjectivity is constructed for them through their involvement in the public sphere, changing their relationship to society. Although personally they may object to racism, since their success depends on exposure on MTV they are brought to acquiesce.

Here the similarity between ads and videos is central, for, as Stephen Levy notes, "MTV's greatest achievement has been to coax rock and roll into the video arena where you can't distinguish between entertainment and the sales pitch."[11] The "sales pitch" has two objects, first that of selling the MTV station itself, second that of selling the band and their song/album. In both cases, videos function like advertising, in which the signifier that addresses desire is linked to a commodity. The signifiers used to sell the MTV station

17

address the desire for (1) power and virility, and (2) nurturance and community, neatly combining appeals to both male and female spectators. Power and virility (and, one might suggest, patriotism) are signified by the huge rocket plunging into outer space, followed by images of men on the moon exploring new territory. (Interestingly, this logo has remained constant since MTV's inception, attesting presumably to its expression of an appeal basic to the channel.) Another logo, now dropped, used to show a TV monitor, scrawled with the letters MTV, into which a globe dropped (MTV *is* the world!), but has been replaced with logos insisting that, with its 24-hour flow, MTV is LIFE!, and with an image of a gleaming, stream-lined subway train coming to a halt. The idea is clear: MTV equals the men exploring outer space in its breaking of new territory, and also equals new technologies, the future. MTV claims also to encompass all that the young adult needs – it is the World as well as Life. One logo references the Aztec culture, showing its monuments being toppled over. MTV is a "civilization" greater than the Aztec.

Interestingly enough, in 1986, an MTV logo began to reflect the various debates about MTV and rock videos generally (like, for instance, those started by the parents against rock (PMRC) organization). The logo cleverly seeks to co-opt objections by satirizing them: one logo shows a man watching MTV for 24-hours, taking its own ad literally; he becomes increasingly dishevelled and ill, until a voice-over says that MTV is *bad* for you. Another logo consists of interviews with people describing the evil things that go on on MTV; the *appeal* now is to the illicit, but it is in fact obvious that all is quite innocent.[12]

There used to be a vivid signifier for nurturance, namely the plaintive, child-like voice of Pete Townshend or Mick Jagger (both attentive early on to the possibilities of MTV) saying "I want my MTV!" (i.e. "I want my Mommy, my milk"), but this is no longer played. The station now relies on its trusty veejays (Martha Quinn, Mark Goodman, Alan Hunter, and J.J. Jackson) to create an appeal essential for the success of the station, that is the creation of a casual, intimate ambience. (In 1986, some new veejays (like Chuck Slick Kanter) were added, and older ones phased out or given less time.) After intensive marketing research, Robert Pittman hit upon the desire for a pseudo, rock and roll "family," very much along the lines of that deliberately created in programs like *Good Morning America* to appeal to adults.[13] But in this case, the "family" was to be a family of peers, very deliberately lacking adults. The supposedly informal, easy, and relaxed style of the veejays was intended to conjure up the natural ambience of teenagers gathered in a room to listen to music with their peers. (My sophisticated sources tell me that the ambience is far from being convincingly "natural," seeming rather deliberately fake to these viewers, and indeed MTV is all pre-recorded.[14] They resent the forced attempt to be one with the audience.[15]) The decision not to include any news except that relating to music further ensured the absence of adult authority figures. MTV thus constructs a false sense of addressing a unified teenage rock "community," fulfilling young people's desire to belong in a world without parents.

But in addition to selling itself, MTV also sells the music and the bands featured in videos. Here the signifiers that address desire (for sex, violence, freedom, love) are fastened onto the commodity that is, in this case, the band and their music contained in the purchasable album. The desire is displaced onto the album, which then promises to satisfy it, in the familiar manner of advertisements.

Videos differ in the degree to which they feature the rock star in performance and other members of the band playing their various instruments. But those that do clearly show traces of the tapes of live performances that preceded MTV, and of live transmissions. Performers and managers here rely on the star phenomenon, promoting an identification with band members that will bring teenagers out to live concerts and persuade them to buy not only albums but also all the paraphernalia (T-shirts, jackets, hats, etc.) related to the stars. (Interestingly, the directors in the *Variety* interview by and large thought performance videos boring, and were annoyed by the insistence of performers and record companies on the stars being seen in the videos. Several would have preferred to make videos entirely without featuring the stars, but the hard-sell aspect demands their presence.) The 1985 ad for a look-alike Michael Jackson coat shows the way that the phenomenon can be capitalized on by firms outside of the record companies and band managers and, as of writing, a big selling campaign for look-alike Madonna "Susan" jackets is underway. The recent look-alike rock star contests (in which teenagers compete for the best imitation in synch sound of a rock star's look, performance-style,

19

dress, and movements) encourage teenager identification with the stars, increasing their dedicated close listening to, and watching of, the stars' voices, actions, movements, and clothes. The gimmick is yet one more piece of evidence for the centrality of advertising to the whole MTV institution and mode of operation.

At first, MTV was watched mainly by young people within the privacy of their homes. Many teenagers report concentrated watching as a relaxation, particularly if they do not have cable and see MTV at a friend's house. The experience is then often a group one, people responding loudly to their likes and dislikes as part of the fun. Often, however, the program provides the background for casual partying rather than being watched concentratedly by teenagers. While some teenagers report watching the program alone, many evidently use it as background music (not attending to the visuals) while doing homework, much as they would use the radio.[16] Others match the visuals to music they prefer.

The visual dimension, however, obviously sets certain constraints upon sites of consumption. (Given the current stage of technology, people could, but do not yet, carry around small TV sets as they do small radios since the cost is prohibitive. The Walkman phenomenon, moreover, allows people to *listen* to music in many more contexts than they can *look* at videos.) But still MTV is "consumed" in a variety of settings, ranging from the lounge or cafeteria of the college student center (where MTV may be either piped in live or students operate a pay-per-video machine), to the dance club scene in cities – where TV screens dot the various floors above and behind the dancers, to the large department store where the TV set playing MTV may be seen in the youth clothes sections.

MTV, then, exists in a variety of sites of reception, although the home is still presumably the largest. The channel consists of a variety of things, including the veejay's comments and introductions to videos, their specific Music News and Concert Tour Information sections, their advertising of MTV promotional items like T-shirts, and their interviews with various stars, usually pre-taped. There are also music competitions, winners getting prizes such as a weekend with one of the rock stars or a flight to London and a screen appearance, or a rock star's special car. There are weekly events, such as The Friday Night Video Fights, the Saturday Night Countdown, the

ADVERTISING AND PRODUCTION

MTV Feature Event (consisting, in Spring 1986, of skits by the Monkees), or the late night weekend live concerts.

Interspersed with all this material are the ads by companies spon-
soring the station. Usually in groups of four at a stretch, these are
predictably geared to the young adult audience, and are increasingly
themselves extremely short rock videos. This is so much the case that
the uninitiated viewer cannot at first tell whether a TV-segment is
going to be an ad or a rock video.

According to random sample hours documented in June 1985, the
proportion of videos to other material is now almost half.[17] This
proportion may vary at different times in the 24-hour flow, but the
point is that there is significantly more promotional material other
than regular ads and the videos than when MTV started in 1981 – a
fact that attests to the increasing commercialization of the channel
as it has succeeded. At the end of 1986, MTV began to imitate radio
rock stations in their new "four in a row" strategy, which cuts into
ad time in those 30-minute sections. It is the mechanism of identification which advertising relies on, and which is central in MTV
videos, that I want now to discuss.

2

History, "reading formations," and the televisual apparatus in MTV

At the end of the last chapter, I began to address the issue of spectator identification with MTV rock stars as encouraged by the station's management in order to involve teenagers even more with the channel, and thus increase consumption. But the issue of identification raises all the larger ones about the way any individual (i.e. historical subject) receives a popular text; this involves the codes that govern such a spectator, and affect response, making him/her receptive to appeals like that of the "look-alike" contests (to be discussed later on). The related issue of the kind of spectator positions that MTV videos construct or, perhaps better, *offer*, will be dealt with in a later chapter. But both issues involve attention to the specifically *televisual* (as against filmic) apparatus, since both the historical and hypothetical or model spectator (the latter "constructed" through textual strategies) are differently positioned in television from in film.

Here I want to deal with the *historical* televisual spectator, and it may be useful to set up the discussion by briefly summarizing theoretical positions as they have been developed in relation to film. In the early 1970s, contemporary film theory replaced the old notion of history as the "truth of past experience and the truth of present accounts of it"[1] with two main concepts, influenced by semiology and psychoanalysis, that located history in the register of signifying practices. In other words, the notion that "To learn lessons from the past, it is necessary only to unlock this truth''[2] was shown to be invalid in the light of new understandings about the way discourses, past and present, function.

First, Emile Benveniste's distinction between history and discourse represented a major influence in reconceptualizing the old notions of history as truth.[3] Christian Metz used Benveniste's categories to distinguish the classical realist Hollywood film from the avant-garde text. History, as a concept, was removed from the terrain of knowledge about social events to that of "fiction," analagous to any classic text. History and the classical film were alike in being present to the reader/spectator, "but only as something which is already past and which has already a fixed resolution for the problem it evokes.''[4] Or, in Metz's words, "The 'story' as system makes it possible to reconcile all, since history, in Benveniste's terms, is always (by definition) a story told from nowhere, told by nobody but received by someone (without which it could not exist).''[5] Discourse, on the other hand, in foregrounding the source of enunciation suppressed in history, describes the avant-garde address, always eager to comment on its own processes.

The second set of concepts that located history in the register of signifying practices rather than of ontological "truth" was initiated by Foucault, who used a very different notion of discourse in looking at power as displayed through institutions. For Foucault, history became the study of discursive practices, which, like texts, function to construct and position subjects in their lived experiences. That is, people's daily lives are shaped and governed by institutional discourses outside of their control, which the historian can rediscover by looking at documents (that contain the discourses) as evidence. Foucault's work was important in combining Althusserian Marxism with Lacanian ideas about the constitution of the subject through language, so as to theorize the subject in history.[6] Against the project of a "continuous history," with its "indispensable correlative of the founding function of the subject," Foucault proposes "An enterprise by which one tries to measure the mutations that operate in general in the field of history . . . an enterprise by which one tries to throw off the last anthropological constraints; an enterprise that wishes, in return, to reveal how these constraints could come about.''[7]

ROCKING AROUND THE CLOCK

Under similar intellectual influences, Roland Barthes shifted the emphasis from the *text's* strategies, that had preoccupied semiologists like Umberto Eco, to the function of the subject in creating the text. But, if the text cannot exist without the subject, the subject, for Barthes, also cannot exist without the text. As he put it, "The reader is the space on which all the quotations that make up a writing are inscribed without any of them being lost; a text's unity lies not in its origin but in its destination . . . (The reader) is simply that someone who holds together in a single field all the traces by which the written text is constituted."[8] Metz developed similar notions in relation specifically to the film, noting that "In watching the film, I help it to be born, I help it to live, since it is in me that it will live and it was made for that, to be seen, i.e. to come into existence only when it is seen."[9] The subject is thus as much constructed in the process of reading a text as, in the Lacanian model, it is constructed in the process of the entry into language and the symbolic.

As a result of these theories, the historical subject was written out of film theory, first because we could know nothing about any such subject, and second because the subject was in any case fixed into the position constructed for him/her by the institutional practices or the filmic/literary text. Neither Foucault nor Barthes were interested in the empirical level of things: Foucault, for instance, did not try to find out how far any actual historical subjects resisted the positioning that institutional discourses constructed for them. Feminist historians, on the other hand, often provide information about women that shows their local resistance to dominant discourses; only then these positivist historians have not researched the resistance in terms of over-arching institutional discourses, or shown any interest in the complexities of subject construction. It seems to me that ideally we need historians able to work on both fronts at once.

In relation to literary and film texts, both certain Marxists and feminists have objected to the way that the historical subject has been all but written out of critical discourse. The few empirical studies that existed (such as David Morley's on the British TV program *Nationwide*)[10] were marginalized, suspect because the information could only be "subjective impressions," of no general or scientific value. The common objection has been that the theories sketched in above constructed a monolithic, a-historical spectator,

24

not distinguished in terms of race, class, gender or *context* of reception.[11] A further objection is that the spectator has also not been differentiated in terms of historical *time*, i.e. the time of the text's production and original exhibition, and the time of the subject receiving it. The codes governing the historical subject in each case will be different, and thus the "reading" of the text will have to be different.

Stephen Heath, always mindful of the historical subject and of the issues in relation to him/her, is important in initiating corrective work, but seems ultimately to return to a position whereby the historical subject is unable to resist textual construction. In his important essay, "Film performance," Heath begins by recognizing the historical subject.[12] He notes that while "the individual is always a subject in society, the place of social and ideological formations," he/she is always more than simply "the figure of that representation, is in excess of such placing formations" (p. 126). He goes on to note that the crucial element of ideological systems is "the number of machines (institutions) that can *move* the individual as subject, shifting and tying desire, realigning excess and contradiction, in a perpetual retotalization – a remembering – of the imaginary in which the individual subject is grasped as identity" (p. 127). Heath here, and in the following discussion, seems to elide the historical subject, that he *does* recognize, with the subject constructed through representations, through what he calls the "novelistic" process. For Heath, cinema "occupies the individual as subject in the terms of the existing social representations and it constructs the individual as subject in the process, in the balancing out of symbolic and imaginary, circulation for fixity" (p. 127). Heath does not allow for the possibility of two conflicting subject constructions; rather, he sees cinema as an institution *completing* the subject, as "the translation of plurality into a *certain* history, the single vision" (p. 128). Like Barthes, then, Heath ultimately sees the fictive text as necessarily constructing the subject in the processes of reception. As he puts it, "What moves in film, finally, is the spectator, immobile in front of the screen. Film is the regulation of that movement, the individual as subject held in the shifting and placing of desire, energy, contradiction . . . The spectator is *moved* and *related* as subject in the process and images of that movement."

ROCKING AROUND THE CLOCK

Recent Marxist theorists like Tony Bennett and Keith Tribe, and various film historians like Robert Allen, Janet Staiger, David Bordwell, and Kristin Thompson, have begun to address the problem regarding the historical subject as outlined in the above theories.[13] Bennett has usefully attempted to differentiate theoretically the hypothetical or model spectator that texts construct or offer (and this is an important distinction) from the historical subject. Building on the work of Ernesto Laclau and Michel Pêcheux,[14] together, perhaps, with that of Marxist Formalist Eikenbaum, Bennett argues that the relationship is best conceived of as dialectical. According to Ron Levaco, this was a perception already to be found in embryo in Eikenbaum's work. As Levaco, summarizing Eikenbaum, puts it:

> From this Marxist viewpoint, what is important is that while the text of any artwork may appear patently static, it must be understood that its meaning is dialectical, a reciprocal expression of society and culture, situated and understood by auditors at a particular moment in history. . . . And that the events of history and the advances of technology can and do transform the signification of the artwork for any human subject situated in history.[15]

Bennett's theory allows, not for *individual impressions* as unique experiences relying on some essential subject, but rather for the subject's coming to the text with already coded perceptions of the world that he calls "reading formations":

> By reading formations, I mean a set of discursive and intertextual determinations which organize and animate the practice of reading, connecting texts and readers in specific relations to one another in constituting reading subjects of particular types and texts as objects to be read in particular ways.[16]

An individual's reading formations may have been shaped either by the same dominant codes as govern the popular text being read/viewed, in which case there will be no tension; or by some sub-culture – such as feminism, trades unionism, Marxism, Moral Majority thinking, homosexuality, identification with minorities, etc. – in which case the spectator may refuse the offered position, resist the positioning he/she is experiencing. With a popular text made at an historical time different from that of the spectator, there may be, as Eikenbaum already saw, an ideological discrepancy, such as around race or gender.

Keith Tribe, meanwhile, usefully distinguished an *anti-history* position from an *anti-historicist* one. He argued that "history" is something perpetually constructed in a specific conjuncture and that it is necessary always to question historical discourse about the arguments it supports, about what it does. History is always the result, not of a revelation of the past, but of "determinate relations in a given conjuncture."[17] But many have been limited by the psychoanalytic paradigm to a focus on the a-historical psychic mechanisms that position the spectator. Building on Laura Mulvey's pioneering essay,[18] feminist theorists have been exploring the complexity of what it means to be a female spectator, but have tended to ignore the issue of *historicizing* that spectator.

Her focus on narrative has, however, recently led Teresa de Lauretis to insert the female historical spectator. De Lauretis argues that theorists have ignored, in favor of gaze-image dichotomies, a second set of identifications involving identification with the "figure of narrative movement, the mythical subject, and with the figure of narrative closure, the narrative image." This leaves room for "a double female desire (for the Father and for the Mother)" that will be useful in understanding gender address in some MTV.[19]

Nevertheless, although De Lauretis does insert the historical spectator, her theory still assumes, in accord with the psychoanalytic paradigm, a female spectator undifferentiated in terms of race, class or reading formations. Just because it is a special kind of art form, as we've already seen, involving different kinds of gender address, a 24-hour continuous flow, song-image format, MTV is a useful terrain on which to explore issues about history, the historical spectator, and gender. I will address the specificities of gender address in Chapter 5, but want here to deal more generally with two issues: first, how far even the modified theories developed in relation to film (i.e. the distinction between a model and a historical spectator) apply to the different televisual apparatus; and second, the degree to which MTV may be seen once again to embody in extreme form what is inherent to television generally.

27

ROCKING AROUND THE CLOCK

Regarding the first question, does a similar distinction between a model and a historical spectator arise in the television situation? The distinction certainly makes some sense given the filmic apparatus, although once we make the comparison to television, one realizes the far greater *textual* construction of the spectator in film. What Heath says about the spectator, "immobile in front of the screen," ultimately being all that moves in film ("moved and related as subject in the process and images of that movement") highlights the different relationship of the TV spectator to the screen. While we saw the necessity to point out the existence of the historical film spectator, that spectator is usually overwhelmed by his/her textual construction.

The relationship between the historical and model spectators in television is different on both sides of the screen, as it were. For the spectator is not as monolithically constructed, as a result of the fragmentation of the viewing experience; but he/she is paradoxically also less the separate historical spectator as well. While the film spectator is drawn into the filmic world through structures that appear to satisfy the desire for plenitude and for the unification of split subjectivity, the TV spectator is drawn into the TV world through the mechanism of consumption (i.e. constant unsatisfied desire, the constant hope of a forthcoming but never realized plenitude). It is the endlessness of the series of TV texts – a continuous strip, as noted, that is always available to the spectator even when the set is off – that produces this different effect. For the subject is always a potential viewer at the flick of the switch, as is not the case for the film spectator, who pays for and consumes a delimited "text" in a fixed space and amount of time.

This means that the TV world is more like the actual world of the TV viewer in that it goes on and on, 24 hours a day, and is always "available." The historical spectator is more inside the TV world than is the film spectator who knows that he is "dreaming." The distinction between "fiction" and "reality" is less obvious to the TV spectator just because, as Robert Stam has argued, the *reality-effect* is greater and the regression to the dream state far less.[20] There is thus less *cause* for the historical spectator to resist his/her textual construction since the relationship relies less on that kind of construction than on the *simulation* of an *object-relationship,* of a

kind of one-on-one intimacy that Jane Feuer and Charlotte Brunsdon, in different ways, have analyzed.[21]

The historical spectator, in his/her specificity, is also far more
important in the televisual than in the filmic situation, which adds to
the need to bring him/her into the apparatus. He/she is crucial to
the mechanism because of the sponsors who pay for the programs
and whose strategies are ultimately responsible for situating the
viewer as endlessly consuming, endlessly in the state of an about-to-
be-filled desire.

This state furthers one's televisual sense of existing in some timeless present: neither texts nor the institution of television itself is historically situated. MTV in particular blurs distinct separations and
boundaries including that between past and present. As will be more
clear in Chapter 3, MTV simply takes over the history of rock and
roll, flattening out all the distinct types into one continuous present.
The teenage audience is now no longer seen as divided into distinct
groups addressed by different kinds of rock music but is constituted
by the station as one decentered mass that absorbs all the types
indiscriminately – without noting or knowing their historical origins.

But this "present" is one that often looks uncannily like a future,
postholocaust world, drawing as it does upon imagery from the
science fiction film, creating ever greater dislocation of the time
dimension. The result is the construction of a decentered,
a-historical model spectator that mimics the cultural formation of
contemporary teenagers appearing to live in a timeless but implicitly
"futurized" present.

But let me now, as Tribe suggests, ask what "the determinate relations" of my own discourse are. First, my discourse is historical in
that I am setting up a point of enunciation outside of MTV, from
which I examine how its institutional practices construct subjects to
the tune of 28 million (as of April 1986). While the relations between
MTV as institution and the subjects it constructs do not involve the
same kind of power as Foucault's mental, penal, and educational
institutions, the station deliberately creates, for its own profit, subjects who would not otherwise exist. I am both a subject positioned
by MTV as viewer, and a subject using a critical meta-language to
distance myself from, and to explain, that positioning.

Second, then, as this last point suggests, my discourse emerges from academia; it is situated within an institution whose function is, partly, to produce scholarship. My meta-critical discourse belongs in the academic tradition of cultural studies, and is inevitably shaped by that context.

Third, as a feminist, I bring to MTV a set of reading formations that lead me to resist the gender positions that MTV offers. Other resistances come from the generational gap between myself and the white, middle-American teenager or young adult that MTV addresses (a gap I partially addressed in the Introduction), and who brings to reception far different cultural formations around sex and politics, especially race and class, from mine.

Finally, as this last point implies, we have a situation where the mass of the MTV audience brings to reception reading formations that by and large coincide with those that shape MTV texts. As a commercial form, it is MTV's ability to address current adolescent desires and wish fulfilments, inscribed in an idiom familiar to teenagers, that guarantees its success.

What are some of the cultural codes that structure the majority of MTV programs? How far can we say that these in fact duplicate the reading formations of the station's spectators? To begin with, MTV appears symptomatic of Reagan's America in its unquestioning materialism. Videos for the most part assume an upper-middle-class ambience (note the sleek, modern design settings, the emphasis on luxury items – big cars, fancy clothes, jewelry, contemporary furniture). Only a few videos (and these belong in a special "critical" category, as we'll see) show working-class settings and consciousness.

Another thing that strikes the uninitiated is the frequency of either settings that recall earth prior to civilization or those that suggest a futurist, post-holocaust world. In either case what we have is depersonalization. In the futurist videos, there is an uncritical over-valuing of the machine that is arguably a product of the nuclear age in which teenagers live. (This tendency is evident in the many popular science fiction movies geared to the teenage market. Significantly, the feature of the simulacrum, most common in these movies – viz. *The Man Who Fell to Earth*, *Blade Runner*, *Brother From Another Planet* – is not often evident in MTV tapes, presumably because, for commercial reasons, the focus has to be on the live body of the star. But the kind of drugged out, alienated, androgynous doubling found in a film like *Liquid Sky* is present in MTV videos.)

Further, in terms of reading formations, there is the new openness toward sexuality that has been part of this generation's cultural experience. The 1970s and 1980s have witnessed the irruption into consciousness (and often into the daily experiences) of young adults of all varieties of sexuality – bi-sexual, homosexual, sado-masochistic, transvestite, etc. This has evolved partly through the emphasis of the 1970s Women's Movement on sex-roles and female homosexuality and partly through the increasing male gay rights movements and general loosening up of rigid male/female sex-roles, providing a variety of positions for both genders not possible before. Finally, there is the racist aspect of MTV discussed in the Introduction and that reflects aspects of Reagan's America. The largely white, middle-American audience to which MTV gears itself are uninterested in black bands, and this we must attribute to cultural codes that shape this group in Reagan's America.

Nevertheless, as I hope to show later on, MTV's peculiar form means that management cannot contain all the positions shown: the short four-minute texts embedded within a continuous 24-hour flow, leave gaps for some alternate positions. In recent months, following the inspiration of the USA for Africa and Bob Geldof's Live Aid events, there has been a significant increase in videos with working-class settings and social commentary. The Farm Aid and anti-apartheid rock events of Fall 1985, the powerful "Sun-City" video, Cougar-Mellencamp's farm-related "Rainbow Man" video, and feminist videos like Pat Benatar's "Sex As a Weapon" and the Annie Lennox/Aretha Franklin "Sisters Are Doin' It For Themselves," suggest a continuing social concern on the part of rock musicians of all types. However, as we'll see, the placement of the videos within the 24-hour televisual flow often eliminates any possible effectiveness; and there is the further issue of a new kind of "radical chique" around the large fund-raising events that mitigates their oppositional aspects.

As will become evident, beneath this set of sociological "reading formations" lies the address to adolescent desire already noted, which involves the level of the unconscious. Values, narratives, images are organized thematically according to these reading formations, but they are inflected always to satisfy unconscious fantasies, wish fulfillments, and adolescent ideal-ego formations in the imaginary. This register, in its televisual specificity, will be explored in a later chapter. Let me note merely that the linking of materialist and cynical values to the adolescent imaginary repertoire makes teenagers vulnerable to absorption of these values if they do not already hold them.

This critique, however, addressed as it is from within the humanist, sociological discourse, may ultimately miss its mark. The categories of the discourse, arguably, are irrelevant to MTV if we view it as a postmodernist phenomenon. It is here that the specificity of the televisual apparatus becomes important, since television may itself be seen as a postmodernist phenomenon in its very construction of a decentered historical spectator, and its obliteration of hitherto sacrosanct boundaries, such as those between "fiction" and "reality," or between the space of the viewing-subject and that within the TV screen. In other words, part of the reading formation for MTV (and possibly the greater part) is its belonging within a postmodernist discourse that structures not only the psychic and social lives of adolescents but also their dominant entertainment experience, namely watching TV. It is to this postmodernist discourse as evident in the aesthetic forms and themes of MTV, as also in the very structuring of desire in the videos, that I will now turn.

3

MTV and the avant-garde: the emergence of a postmodernist anti-aesthetic?

In this chapter I address the second of the various levels of discourse about MTV and postmodernism, namely that of the ways in which the technical and formal devices of the majority of videos on MTV may be seen to constitute a postmodernist "anti-aesthetic." I will explore first the generally avant-garde techniques of videos on MTV which have led the casual critic to celebrate their subversive aspects. But are the deconstructive, apparently "modernist" devices in fact subversive? How are we to explain them, given MTV's commercial context of production?

Let me briefly survey the techniques that *appear* avant-garde. There is, first, the abandonment of traditional narrational devices of most popular culture hitherto. Cause—effect, time—space, and continuity relationships are often violated, along with the usual conception of "character." Even in videos that seem to retain a loose sort of story, editing devices routinely violate classical Hollywood codes of shot/counter-shot, the 180 degree rule, the 30 degree angle rule, eye-line matches, etc. (See the detailed analysis of Madonna's "Material Girl" in Chapter 5.)

The violation of classical codes is paradoxical in "Material Girl" since the film pastiches Howard Hawkes's *Gentlemen Prefer Blondes*, as will be clear later on. Here "Material Girl" typifies what one first notices about rock videos, namely their frequent reliance on classical Hollywood film genres, whether it be incorporation, parody, pastiche, or ridicule of representations from mainstream cinema that is going on. Many videos early on seemed to take off from standard genres (the most brilliant and complete early example was Michael Jackson's famous video "Thriller," that both used and parodied the gothic/horror genre, as, later, his near-perfect "Billie Jean" did the spy film). Videos like Bonnie Tyler's "Holding Out for a Hero," which relied on the Western; Berlin's "No More Tears," relying on the crime film (specifically *Bonnie and Clyde*); Rockwell's 'Somebody's Watching Me" (depending on the horror film); or, most recently, The Rolling Stones' colorful "Harlem Shuffle" (a cross between Walt Disney and the Broadway musical), stand in a special relationship to the classical cinema and are inconceivable without knowledge of Hollywood. Recently, directors have taken to incorporating certain stars' images in videos (the Romantics' "Talking in Your Sleep" includes images of Marilyn Monroe; Carnes's "Bette Davis' Eyes" takes off from another star), or inserting swift, unmarked clips from Hollywood movies. A recent example of the latter technique is Ratt's "You're in Love," which mocks the whole concept of romantic love as depicted in classical films from Fritz Lang's *Metropolis* to the present, and including clips from Walt Disney, Ingrid Bergman and Peter Lorre movies, and from films with Lucille Ball and Groucho Marx (themselves already in the satiric mode). In between, we have shots of the heavy metal band wearing typical lurid and androgynous outfits in hectic performance in a strobe-lit arena, dramatizing the distance between the largely innocent and romantic Hollywood world and their own contemporary nihilist one. An even more recent example of this use of Hollywood clips is Elton John's "Heartache All Over," which, like the Ratt video, isolates movie love-shots. However, the video takes clips from even further back in the Silent period than did the Ratt one, and here the band are also imaged within a frame, highlighting their awareness of their status as "representations," on the same level as the movie-clips.

Second, videos are routinely, and increasingly, self-reflexive. For instance, we may see the video we are watching being played on a TV monitor within the frame; or the video sets us in the production room in which a rock video is being made that turns out to be the one we are watching (viz. the Rolling Stones's "She Was Hot," Rick

MTV AND THE AVANT-GARDE

Springfield's "Someone to Love," Human League's "Don't You Want Me Baby?"). In different ways, two Phil Collins videos, one with Phil Bailey, offer the most extended commentary on video production. The entire narrative of "Easy Lover" (made with Phil Bailey) deals with the tape being made. We are let into the intricacies of the filming, and see the large 35mm camera in the foreground, its video monitor relaying the framing to the camera man; in the rear we see Collins and Bailey rehearsing their act, then being made up, getting properly dressed for the actual filming, taking a lunch break, etc.

Phil Collins's recent "Don't Forget My Number" belongs in a group of videos whose theme is parody of video production as an institution rather than commenting on, and including, the technical processes involved. The thematic parody is carried further than that familiar from Hollywood film commenting on the Hollywood world, but the type is not truly self-reflexive in the manner of videos discussed above. "Don't Forget My Number" begins with Collins's agent leaving him with the pompous director who has been hired to make his new video. The two men compete to see who knows most about popular culture and then try out various ludicrous scenarios for the video, including a mock Western set-up not at all appropriate for Collins. Some of the scenarios tried out parody not only classic film genres but other popular MTV videos, such as the award-winning Cars' "You Might Think," Elton John's videos, or David Lee Roth's successful "California Girls."

David Lee Roth's "Just Like a Gigolo" in a similar vein, begins with a parody of agents, video producers, and directors fawning over an exhausted Roth at the conclusion of what they see as a successful video. Lee Roth however clearly disagrees, and proceeds to imagine the video he would make if left to his own devices. Predictably, the fantasy video is full of surprising events and sexy girls. Steve Perry's "O Sherrie" also begins with a parody of agents, directors, and groupies trying to get the protagonist ready for a video set in the medieval period. Fed up, the hero refuses to comply, and he finally runs off with his girlfriend, leaving behind his exasperated money-and image-conscious entourage.

Dire Straits' "Money For Nothing" comments baldly on MTV itself, and on the alternate blandness and sensationalism of videos shown (as the director, Steve Barron, has noted).[1] The video is already famous for its extraordinarily innovative techniques (Barron had already experimented with "rotoscoping" in the equally famous and creative A-ha video "Take On Me"). Sung by robot figures in the image of working men installing microwave ovens, the video shows them monotonously moving fridges and colour TVs. In the course of their work, they watch rock stars on MTV; as they sing about their tasks, we have images of huge TV screens playing MTV videos and featuring, from time to time, the Dire Straits band. From the robot-workers' point of view, "Playing a guitar on MTV/That ain't working" but "Money for nothing/Chicks for free."

In other videos, the text foregrounds some aspect of the technology involved in video production, again drawing attention to the fact of the text's construction and to the processes of spectatorship. An interesting example is the lively, well-edited, and humorous Mick Jagger/David Bowie "Dancing in the Street" because the first version did *not* include shots of the camera filming the duo. The later one includes a number of such shots, and reveals what the device does; in this case, the effect is to situate the dancing by making the narrative that of filming the dance. Thus the self-reflexivity here paradoxically enhances the "reality-effect" by providing an audience for whom the pair are performing. It is true that the spectator is also made aware of the processes of the text's production, but the two levels become blurred.

In Glen Frey's "The Heat is On" the video is apparently what a man is watching on an editing machine, since the tape begins and ends with the monitor image, while in other videos, like Peter Gabriel's "Shock the Monkey," there is a projector present and running throughout. In this case, the device is disturbing precisely because it is not narratively located or *explained*, as in some of the other cases. A familiar image, direct from Godard and the avant-garde film tradition, is the clap-board being closed in front frame, coming down on the action about to be filmed, and foregrounding production. (A recent example is the start of Tom Petty and the Heartbreakers' "Make It Better.")

Another prevalent deconstructive image is that of a man with a camera taking hidden photographs of a woman (see Eurythmics' "Here Comes the Rain Again" and Rod Stewart's "Infatuation"). A recent Eurythmics' video, "Sexcrime" (in the news because of censorship), imitates Hitchcock's *Vertigo* in the image of a huge close-up of the human eye, inside which we see a camera clicking away. The eye is no longer, as with Vertov, a metaphorical camera but a literal one; the camera-eye has become the camera-I. Even more recently, Duran Duran's "A View to Kill," the video promo for the movie, takes as its entire theme the idea of photography, focusing on the objectification of the female body through the camera lens. Instead of Hitchcock, its dedication is to James Bond (whose logo also seems to imitate *Vertigo*). Voyeurism, always an implicit theme in commercial movies, has recently become an explicit one, especially with a director like Brian De Palma, who is much influenced by Hitchcock. Like *A View to Kill*, his *Body Double* plays with and comments upon the camera's voyeuristic properties, much as do the videos, as I'll show in detail later on.

A new related phenomenon is the representation of the production of the music in the sense of showing the different components and technology of the band that produces the music itself. The video "General Lee" not only pastiches old movies but also shows the band's equipment being assembled. Again, we find an analogue in a contemporary film like the Talking Heads' *Stop Making Sense* (the title itself is significant, as we'll see), which starts with David Byrne standing alone on an empty stage with a cassette recorder, and proceeds to show us the band assembling itself bit by bit with a corresponding increase in and complexity of sound, until it reaches its deafening full strength. David Bowie's "D.J." illustrates the "behind the scenes" aspect of radio, rather than video, while betraying the anarchic, nihilist element of the postmodernist video that I'll discuss later. Bowie's "Blue Jean" comments not only on video production but on the whole rock star phenomenon.

Videos often focus on photographs of the protagonist as a child or in the present, or set up the image in a series of photograph-like frames. Def Leppard's "The Photograph," as its name implies is a classic of the type, but the device is used in many other videos, such as John Cougar's "Jack and Diane" and his successful "Small Town," or Real Life's "Send Me An Angel," where the video is set up as a series of slides being projected onto a screen.

All kinds of framing within the frame are now common; one video sets up a proscenium arch type of frame, with perspective, the image played out on all sides of what is essentially a box. Dateline News, Channel 4, recently picked up the device for its evening news spots, and Aretha Franklin and Annie Lennox's "Sisters Are Doin' It For Themselves" ends with such a box on which are displayed various images from the video. Videos increasingly use a large screen within the screen, set up above or behind the performers' heads and on which we see not only the greatly enlarged images of the players, but also the narrative involved, confusing and destabilizing the spectator/screen relationship. Duran Duran's "Reflex" explicitly plays upon disrupting the spectator/screen relationship when, after seeing the figures of the performers on the huge screen behind their heads, a wave fills the screen and then spills over onto the fans watching the performance.

A variation of these devices may be found in a Bryan Adams video where the performer stands on stage facing the audience of TV sets and has behind him another series of sets containing his own image. Or the video mise-en-scène can consist entirely of TV sets piled up on one another, on which the performer's image is displayed in varying ways as in Asia's "Only Time Will Tell," or Outfield's "All the Love in the World." Daryl Hall and Oats use all kinds of inventive visual devices in their "Out of Touch," including play with a huge screen on which we see the performers imaged while at the same time they are present in front of it. Motels' "Shame On You" has a dialogue between a bored woman trapped in a traditional relationship and a woman on a large ad board outside her window, who suddenly comes alive in various guises in response to the woman's distress. Don Henley's "Boys of Summer" opens with the forlorn hero apparently calling up a movie of his former happiness with his lover. This movie plays behind his head, but then the viewer is taken up into it as it becomes the narrative, only to be later repositioned as a spectator of the movie within the fictional world.

The sanctity of the image of illusionist texts is completely questioned by these devices. But in another set of videos specific violation is done to the image, so that no representation is stable or solid for very long. One of the early videos to play with the image was Yes's "Leave It" (famous for its many versions): here the image was

The Cars, "You might think"

This shot exemplifies the common destruction of illusionism: the band first enter
the round photograph of the heroine's dressing table, where they are seen playing;
the hero then takes his place beside the heroine in the square photograph, having
first removed her old lover.

This image shows the common play with old Hollywood films: here the hero
mimics King Kong, in the old movie, hanging onto the Empire State Building with
one hand while cradling the heroine, now miniscule, in the other.

turned around as a flat, two-dimensional surface and then swept off into space. In Cyndi Lauper's "Girls Just Wanna Have Fun," the image is scrunched up into balls, each with a girl's image on it, that then circle around in space, splitting into many pieces in the process. But perhaps the most outrageous and daring play with the illusionist image is the Cars' now classic video, "You Might Think," in which all manner of surprising and unexpected operations are performed with the image, very much in the style of the French Surrealist painter and sculptor, René Magritte. (This video won the first MTV Academy Award in Fall 1984, presumably for its ingenuity.)

In Emile Benveniste's terms (discussed in Chapter 2), many MTV videos are "discourse" rather than "history" in that they foreground their sources of enunciation and comment on their processes of production. Yet these devices do not go along with an ideologically subversive stance toward dominant culture as in the "proper" avant-garde text of Benveniste's model. The aesthetic discourse dominant in western culture from the late nineteenth to the mid-twentieth century has polarized the popular/realist commercial text and the "high art" modernist one, making impossible a text that was at once avant-garde and popular. And yet this is what MTV apparently is.

The discourse of contemporary film theory has continued the distinctions basic to dominant aesthetic discourse, if for different reasons. The classical Hollywood text has been conceived as producing the "reality effect" specifically through effacement of the means of production. That is why both Metz and Geoffrey Nowell-Smith, as we saw earlier, categorized the classical text as "history" — the "story told from nowhere, told by nobody but received by someone, without whom it would not exist." Devices like shot/counter-shot, continuity editing, the 180 degree rule and so on, give the spectator the illusion of creating the images, suturing him/her into the narrative flow. Theorists have claimed that it is the very "reality-effect" produced through these devices that ensures the texts remaining safely within dominant ideological constructs. Avant-garde texts, on the other hand, have been seen as able to embody ideology subversive of bourgeois hegemony because their aesthetic strategies are set up in deliberate opposition to classical realist forms. The self-reflexivity of modernist texts together with the self-conscious play with dominant

Table 1 Polarized filmic categories in recent film theory

The classical text (Hollywood)	The avant-garde text
Realism/narrative	Non-realist anti-narrative
History	Discourse
Complicit ideology	Rupture of dominant ideology

forms often included (at least in the *political* modernist text) a critique of mainstream culture (see Table 1).

The above polarized categories obviously do not fit MTV, and it is this very blurring of hitherto sacrosanct conceptual boundaries and polarities, in terms of both aesthetic forms and critical categories, that marks the station as a postmodernist form. The short, four-minute span, the origin of the form in advertising and the song-image format (which defies many Hollywood conventions) as we already saw seems to require different critical conceptions. But if we add in the prevalence of deconstructive devices, we clearly need new theoretical formulations to explain what is going on.

The main differences between MTV and the classical Hollywood film arise from the structuring of the station as a 24-hour continuous flow with its three- to four-minute texts (often non-narrative or non-Oedipal narrative), and from the song-image format. First, a word about the structure that offers a decentered position for the spectator, far different from the sutured, Hollywood film spectator mentioned above: on the one hand, there are the constant interruptions caused by the ending of one video and the start of the next, by the veejay's comments, introductions, interviews, and by the ads; on the other, there is the absence of the cause—effect narrative of the Freudian "family romance" type that film theorists have described. Together, these elements prevent the kind of regression to Oedipal primary processes possible in the cinema through the prolonged narrative identification, and through the devices of shot/counter-shot, etc., mentioned earlier. The whole construction of the cinematic apparatus, with the projection in a darkened room and the voyeuristic play of the lit screen with larger than life figures upon it, encourages in the cinema regression to Oedipal childhood processes (particularly the voyeuristic/fetishistic gaze) much discussed by film theorists.

The cinema has also been theorized as re-evoking the Lacanian mirror phase, particularly for the male spectator. Because Lacan's theories of the way the subject is constructed in a patriarchal language order have been so influential in recent film theory, and since the model clearly needs adapting to the television context, let me briefly outline aspects of his theory that will be central to my discussion here and elsewhere in the book. It is Lacan's distinction between the imaginary and the symbolic, in which woman is relegated to the position of absence, or lack, that has preoccupied film theorists.

For Lacan, the imaginary *proper* lacks specificity – or rather, it brings both genders into the feminine through the illusory sense of being merged with the mother. What Lacan calls the "mirror-phase" (the moment when the child first sets up a relationship to its image in the mirror) marks the awareness of the illusoriness of oneness with the mother. The child, that is, begins to be aware of the mother as an object distinct from itself (the mirror contains an image of the mother holding the child); it also recognizes its "mirror" self (which Lacan calls an ideal imago) as an entity distinct from itself.[2] The subject is thus constituted as a *split* subject (i.e. both mother and non-mother; this side of the mirror and within the mirror). It is important that the ideal ego constructed during this mirror-phase is not entirely on the side of the imaginary in that the child introjects the image of the mother as *another image*; it begins to symbolize thus its own look as that of the Other, and to set in motion the desire for the mother (displaced as we'll see into a desire for what she desires) that will persist through its life.

This symbolization of the mother as the Other is for Lacan a universal experience and one that is essential for the human-to-be to in fact become *human*. The individuation that the level of symbolizing involves is a necessary development; the mother—child dyad must be interrupted by the language order if the child is not to remain down in the level of the imaginary. The mirror-phase thus prepares the child for its subsequent entry into the realm of the symbolic (by which Lacan means the language and other signifying and representational systems, such as images, gestures, sound, etc.), in which the child takes up its position as a "sexed" being (it recognizes various subject positions such as "he," "she," "you," "it").[3] Because signifying systems are organized around the phallus as the prime signifier, for Lacan the woman occupies the place of lack or absence. The boy and girl child thus find themselves in vastly different positions vis-à-vis the dominant order once they enter the realm of the symbolic.

The problem for the girl is in being positioned so as to identify with the mother, which means desiring what the mother desires, namely the phallus. This desire has nothing to do with anything essential or biological about the girl but everything to do with the way that the symbolic is organized. Lacan's system, in fact, frees us from the tyranny of the biological.[4]

Roland Barthes has, perhaps better than anyone, described the nature of the "lure" of the film image that he equates with the "lure" of the infant's mirror image:

> The image is there before me, for my benefit: coalescent (signifier and signified perfectly blended), analogical, global, pregnant; it is a perfect lure. I pounce upon it as an animal snatches up a "life-like" rag. Of course, the image maintains (in the subject that I think I am) a miscognition attached to the ego and to the imaginary. In the movie theater . . . I glue nose, to the point of disjointing it, on the mirror of the screen, to the imaginary other with which I identify myself narcissistically.[5]

Barthes shows how the cinematic viewer tries to recover the original illusory plenitude that precedes the mirror phase, and that is temporarily duplicated during the mirror phase in the misrecognition of the infant's image as him/herself, but more perfect. But the televisual apparatus, as described earlier, is not the kind to produce this sort of effect. This means that the MTV text cannot be viewed in the same way as the dream text that the film spectator imagines she/he is producing. Nor, as we'll see, can we talk of MTV being geared to the same kind of male voyeuristic/fetishistic gaze that film largely relies on. (The whole issue of gender address will be discussed in Chapter 5.) In terms of the Lacanian paradigm outlined above, MTV, like most television, rather positions the subject at the moment of discovery of split subjectivity that follows the stage of

43

illusory miscognition of unity with the ideal image. The aesthetic devices of many videos evoke not plenitude but precisely split subjectivity (the images in all those TV screens or movie screens within TV screens); but the very evocation of split subjectivity calls up the desire for plenitude which we somehow hope to achieve by continued consumption which keeps us at least from lapsing into emptiness.

Or does it? Are "fullness" or "emptiness" still relevant terms? Baudrillard, for instance, has argued that the televisual apparatus manifests a new stage of consciousness, which he calls the "universe of communication," in which all we have are "simulations," there being no "real" external to them. This means that we have a universe in which "fiction" and "reality" coalesce in a realm of "simulacra." The universe replaces the old one in which people *believed* that "fiction" copied some original that was "real."[6] The new postmodern universe, with its celebration of the look – the surfaces, textures, the self-as-commodity – threatens to reduce everything to the image/representation/simulacrum. Television, with its decentered address, its flattening out of things into a network or system, the parts of which all rely on each other, and which is endless, unbounded, unframed, seems to embody the new universe; and within television, MTV in particular manifests the phenomena outlined by Baudrillard.

Perhaps most relevant to our discussion of the postmodernist devices in MTV videos generally is the blurring of distinctions between a "subject" and an "image." What seems to be happening in the play with the image of the various kinds discussed is the reduction of the old notion of "self" to an "image" merely. Television in this way seems to be at the end of a whole series of changes begun at the turn of the century with the development of modern forms of advertising and of the department-store window.[7] A second major change was the invention of the cinematic apparatus, and television has produced the last round of changes; its screen now replaces the cinema screen as the controlling cultural mode, setting up a new spectator—screen relationship that is evident in the plethora of devices described above. This will I think be more clear in the detailed analyses in the next chapters.

To the degree that MTV is still a narrative form, we have a new *kind* of story that reflects this changed relationship of image to self.

MTV AND THE AVANT-GARDE

It makes little sense to talk about the self-reflexive devices of MTV defying dominant ideology through a deliberate undercutting of illusionism, since that discourse and its language I have argued is irrelevant to the new MTV phenomenon. MTV videos embody a new story about what the machine can do, and within that story it abandons traditional illusionism by blurring the "fiction/reality" distinction.

Modernism is itself partly responsible for this: its strategies have become assimilated into the dominant culture, so that the spectator cannot be shocked any more in the old ways. The representation of a representation is no longer inherently subversive as in modernism. And it is in the very effacement of previously distinct boundaries and separations, particularly those between high and popular forms that we have been discussing, that MTV reveals itself, arguably, as a postmodernist form.

In a well-known essay, "Postmodernism and consumer society,"[8] Fredric Jameson has defined postmodernism negatively. He is concerned about the "disappearance of the sense of history" and the living in a perpetual present which, following Lacan and Baudrillard, he associates with the schizophrenic state. For Lacan, as for Jameson, schizophrenia is an effect of language, the refusal to enter the realm of the symbolic. Instead of signifiers and signified in postmodernist texts being coherently organized in a comprehensive chain, the flow of words or images is such that the reader/spectator cannot associate any meaning or recognize boundaries and differences, past and present. She/he rather is coaxed into what Jameson calls the postmodernist, schizophrenic stance – that of being fixated on the detached signifier, isolated in a present from which there is no escape.

This return to an eternal, undifferentiated present is an attempt to return to the realm of the imaginary in which there was no self and Other, merely an illusory, timeless continuum. Louis Sass has provocatively tried to link clinically defined schizophrenic states with modernism;[9] while this is interesting, I think it more correct to see the schizophrenic stance as a *postmodernist* phenomenon. For modernism, as Jameson points out, still retains a position from which it speaks. It attempts to critique bourgeois culture through the creation of a unique style that was "subversive and embattled" in its time. Jameson cites "Abstract Expressionism, the great modernist poetry of Pound, Eliot or Wallace Stevens; the International Style (Le Corbusier, Frank Lloyd Wright, Mies); Stravinsky; Joyce, Proust, Mann . . . '' (p. 111). Thought to be ''scandalous or shocking to our grandparents,'' these are now, ''for the generation which arrives at the gate in the '60s – felt to be the establishment and the enemy – dead, stifling, canonical, the reified monuments one has to destroy to do anything new'' (p. 112).

Postmodernism is partly defined by its reaction to earlier modernist models, but it uses pastiche in the place of the modernist parody. Modernism often parodied the increasingly industrialist and consumerist society in an attempt to position it critically; but postmodernism, according to Jameson, is precisely fascinated by what modernism tried to take a stance against, namely ''the whole landscape of advertising and motels, of the Las Vegas strip, of the late show and the Grade-B Hollywood film, of so-called paraliterature with its airport paperback categories of gothic and romance, the popular biography, the murder mystery and the science fiction or fantasy novel'' (p. 112). While modernism often parodied such things, postmodernism merely uses pastiche, a ''neutral practice of mimicry . . . without that still latent feeling that there exists something *normal* compared to which what is being imitated is rather comic'' (p. 114).

If one accepts Jameson's argument, then MTV's preference for pastiche reveals its lack of orienting boundaries; in this case, like much postmodernist art in Jameson's view, rock videos incorporate, rather than quote, other texts, ''to the point where the link between high art and commercial forms seems increasingly difficult to draw.'' MTV refuses any clear recognition of previously sacred aesthetic boundaries: images from German Expressionism, French Surrealism, and Dadism (Fritz Lang, Bunuel, Magritte, and Dali) are mixed together with those pillaged from the noir, gangster, and horror films in such a way as to obliterate differences (see The Cars' ''You Might Think''). Indeed, the constant reference to Hollywood film genres, particularly the western, film noir, the detective film, the science fiction film, is pervasive, as noted earlier (i.e. Bonnie Tyler's ''Holding Out for a Hero,'' and Devo's ''Whip It'' (the western); Mama's Boys' ''Mama, We're All Crazy Now'' (Hitchcock); Sting's ''Fortress Around Your Heart'' (detective); Sammy Hagar's ''V.O.A.'' (spy film)).

46

MTV AND THE AVANT-GARDE

For Jameson, such eliding of forms indicates the end of any critical cultural position, a dangerous lack of the ability to speak from a particular place and to make distinctions. While there is some justification for this kind of concern, it seems to miss possible positive aspects of the effacement of hitherto sacred boundaries. Jameson's Marxist critique retains the notion of history as a discourse that speaks from a perspective of "truth," and this, as we've seen, is problematic. It may prevent Jameson from seeing how the very defiance of a historical positioning may be progressive. In the case of MTV, video artists are often playing with standard high art and popular culture images in a self-conscious manner, creating a liberating sense by the very defiance of traditional boundaries. Images from both high and low art are now arguably cliché, threadbare, archaic in the computer and space age. Rock videos may be seen as revitalizing the dead images by juxtaposing and re-working them in new combinations that avoid the old polarities. This may be the only strategy available to young artists struggling to find their place in society and to create new images to represent the changed situation they find themselves in.

MTV's construction of a decentered spectator indicates recognition of the alienated world teenagers confront. Nevertheless, individual videos themselves often construct a brief "centered" effect, intended to mediate the overall possibly unpleasurable decentering and to keep the spectator watching. The overall commercial framework of MTV (as of all television) requires, as we've seen, locking the spectator into the hypnotized state of *impending* satisfaction; "centering" must take place for short periods if the requisite consumption mechanism is to work. In the case of MTV, the "centering" effect is produced by the song-image format and the constant return to the lip-synching face of the rock star who is being "sold" in any particular video.

This particular song-image format represents one of the main differences between the rock video and the classical Hollywood film. Not even the Hollywood musical is useful here as a model. I will deal with this issue in detailed analyses of particular videos in the next chapters, so let me merely note here that in the rock video, we find images evoked by song words (obviously arbitrary, quixotic even), and relayed through the voice and face of the rock star and band members. Most often, as already noted, there is no narrative proper (there may be loosely linked narrative suggestions), and nothing corresponding to the Hollywood conception of "character." It is the return to the human face that prevents the disconnected image-series from becoming unpleasurable in the manner of the truly avant-garde text. The dominant construction in videos replaces the Hollywood suturing of the spectator in the images through shot/counter-shot with a constant return to the centering close-up of the lip-synching face of the singer. This, together with the musical rhythm/tones/sounds and the rock star's voice, holds together otherwise disparate images and incoherent signifieds.

But the "gaze" involved in the brief "centering" moments is far from the monolithic one of the classical Hollywood film, largely because the televisual apparatus, with its arrangement of a series of short, constantly changing segments (in place of the two-hour continuous film narrative) enables the production of a variety of gazes. In the next chapter, I will outline the main kinds of "gaze" that occur within the 24-hour MTV televisual flow in the video segments, but will leave full discussion of gender address in the gaze until Chapter 5. There, bearing in mind Baudrillard's theory of the televisual apparatus, we will see the new kinds of narrative as they deviate from the old, classical Oedipal ones. Chapter 4 will focus mainly on themes in the socially conscious video.

4

Ideology, adolescent desire, and the five types of video on MTV

If Lacan did not actually use the term the "social imaginary," this is implied by his general discussion of the imaginary/symbolic polarity in the sense that every child apparently moves through the *same* imaginary and enters the *same* symbolic (i.e. the langauge and other representational orders). But both the imaginary and the symbolic are social in a more specific sense – a sense that involves particular historical and cultural context. The cultural/historical embeddedness of the symbolic is obvious in the post-structuralist era, but less obvious may be the social nature of that imaginary that continues alongside the symbolic, enmeshed with it in the manner of secondary with primary processes, and which harnesses the insatiable desire instituted at the moment of individuation. While the infant's early, pre-symbolic psychic experience (the mother–child dyad) may vary rather little from one culture or historical period to another, the post-symbolic imaginary is surely inflected by cultural and historical specificities.

What I am calling the post-symbolic imaginary combines Lacan's notions of the subject split at the moment of entry into the symbolic with Althusser's conception of Ideological State Apparatuses. It is the splitting of the subject into an entity both mother and not-mother; this side of the mirror and within the mirror that sets up the structure of the ideal imago that will remain after entry into the symbolic. The subject, that is, will forever yearn, unconsciously, for the illusory state of plenitude that it experienced before the mirror phase. The symbolization of its own look as that of the Other that takes place in the mirror phase makes the subject vulnerable to subjection to a transcendental Subject which Lacan identifies as the phallus, Althusser more generally as "ideology." According to Althusser, this ideology interpellates individuals as subjects: all ideology, he says, is "speculary, i.e. a mirror-structure, and *doubly* speculary: this mirror duplication is constitutive of ideology and ensures its functioning."[1] In ideology, the absolute Subject occupies the centre, interpellating individuals around it into subjects "in a double mirror-connexion such that it *subjects* the subjects to the Subject, while giving them in the Subject, in which each subject can contemplate its own image (present and future), the guarantee that this really concerns them and Him" (p. 180). For Althusser, that is, ideology turns individuals into subjects by "hailing" them, and is thus a necessary part of human social organization.

But the specific form of that ideology will vary from culture to culture and from one historical period to another since, for Althusser, "Ideology is a 'representation' of the imaginary relationship of individuals to their real conditions of existence" (p. 162). The specific *kinds* of ideal imagos that predominate in any concrete cultural context will obviously vary and they will change as, on a level of which the individual is not aware, his/her "real" conditions of existence change.

One of the Ideological State Apparatuses that Althusser mentions but does not examine is television. Writing in 1969, Althusser was not yet aware of television's specific cultural impact, of its role in developing what Baudrillard has called the new, "cold" universe of communication with its profound changes in the relationship of subject to image suggested in the last chapter. We saw that while the movie screen harnesses the subject's desire in terms of subjection to a transcendental Subject, appearing momentarily to provide the longed-for plenitude, the TV screen rather keeps the subject in the position of discovery of split subjectivity before the mirror and of the actual ensuing *decenteredness*. The TV screen's constantly changing "texts," of whatever kind, provide the constant *promise* of a plenitude forever deferred.

Baudrillard takes things a step further, arguing that the TV screen symbolizes a new era in which "The Faustian, Promethean (perhaps Oedipal) period of production and consumption" has given way to "the narcissistic and protean era of connections, contact, contiguity, feedback and generalized interface that goes with the universe of communication."[2] By this, Baudrillard means that the whole earlier "intimate" universe (in his words, "projective, imaginary and symbolic" (p. 126)), with its domestic scene, interiority, private space-time correlative to a public space – all this is disappearing. "Instead," he says, "there is a screen and a network. In place of the reflexive transcendence of mirror and scene, there is the nonreflecting surface, an immanent surface where operations unfold – the smooth operational surface of communication" (pp. 126-7). He concludes that "with the television image – the television being the ultimate and perfect object for this era – our own body and the whole surrounding universe become a control screen."

For Baudrillard, this entails a dramatically different relationship of the subject to objects: for him, people no longer project themselves into their objects in the old ways of getting psychological gratification out of them. If the psychological dimension can still be marked out, "one feels that it is not really there that things are being played out" (p. 127). We have instead a "tactic of potentialities linked to usage." Baudrillard is here talking about the automobile, but what he says applies equally to the television set, to which we likewise relate in terms of "mastery, control and command, an optimalization of the play of possibilities" rather than as "an object of psychological sanctuary" (p. 127). (See Table 2.)

I quote at such length because Baudrillard's predictions are

Table 2   Chart summarizing Baudrillard's and Callois's scheme

Old "hot" universe		New "cold" universe	
Investment			Ecstasy
Desire	Expression	Hazard	Obscenity
Passion	Competition	Chance	Fascination
Seduction		Vertigo	Communication
Processes of hysteria (female) and paranoia (male)		Processes of schizophrenia, elimination of boundaries, exteriorization of the interior	

significant enough to warrant examination in relation to MTV, the channel par excellence where the phenomena he outlines would be taking place. How true is it that "we no longer live in the drama of alienation" (Marx's world) but rather in that of "the ecstasy of communication" (p. 130)? How true is it that the old "hot, sexual obscenity" (the world of Freud) has been succeeded by "the cold and communicational, contractual and motivational obscenity of today" (p.131)?[3]

This has important implications for understanding the issue of "ideology" in MTV: given its roots in blues and jazz, it is not surprising that rock music has traditionally (and especially since the 1960s) embodied a liberal or left humanist position. If the televisual apparatus manifests a new stage of consciousness in which that liberal/left humanism no longer has a place, this implicates the roots of rock.

The social imaginary that I will explore in MTV (in this and the next chapter) has been constructed through the contradictory post-1960s historical moment in which rock videos arise as a mass popular culture form. It is the mapping in the 1980s of the new 1960s discourses about politics, sex, and romance onto the increasingly high-tech stage of an already advanced capitalism that produces the extraordinary MTV imaginary. MTV partly exploits the imaginary desires allowed free play through the various liberation movements, divesting them, for commercial reasons, of their originally revolutionary implications, reducing them largely to the "radical chic" and the pornographic; but its chosen non-stop, 24-hour format of short, four-minute texts inevitably enables expression of positions critical of the status quo not necessarily favored by the institution. But, given Baudrillard's conceptualizations above, we need to analyze how far these "alternate" positions in fact have anything behind them – any on-going alternate politics in the realm of the social formation. How far do the left/humanist positions have referents? How far are they, like much else on MTV, mere simulacra, with nothing *behind*, mere representations, images?[4]

Obviously, the specifically commercial nature of MTV is relevant to this question: the main aim of the channel is consumption, as we've seen, and it thus follows that the overall address cannot be on the level of ideas or values per se, but of what "look" will *sell*. The level of any one text's production – in which individuals might have artistic ambitions and an aesthetic (or even an anti-aesthetic) end in mind – is completely irrelevant once a video is accepted by MTV. For then, the video becomes a commodity to be circulated in a particular fashion by the channel's personnel. It is completely out of the hands of the original producers and of the performers as well.

In MTV, then, we have an altogether different and more encompassing level of commercialization of rock than hitherto. Earlier promoters at least manipulated live bodies, who could resist in certain ways; but now the "materials" that are manipulated, positioned, circulated in a certain fashion are *simulations* which begin to *replace* the "real." The situation is further complicated by the subversive roots that historically shaped rock and roll and that in the 1960s had "referents" in the social formation. Are these radical traces evident on MTV? What is MTV's relationship to the history of rock and roll?

The 24-hour flow is partly responsible for effacing the original address to specific, delimited youth rock audiences. MTV gathers up into itself the history of rock and roll, rendering the originally distinct subject positions merely nostalgic reflection on earlier periods. (This is most clear in the nostalgic return to 1950s styles and sounds, epitomized in the Ramones' "Rock and Roll High School" video.) The relationship of MTV as text to the historical discourse of rock and roll constructed by critics such as Jahn and Cohn, or more recently by Lawrence Grossberg, is interesting in terms of the uses it makes of that discourse in *its* discourses. The three recent phases of rock and roll that critics have identified—1960s soft-rock, 1970s punk and acid rock (often critical of the establishment), and 1980s heavy metal, and new wave rock (nihilist, anarchic) have each been seen historically as addressing distinct teenage communities, distinguished by dress and stance toward the establishment. MTV takes over this discourse, reproducing all of the three main types (there are of course many sub-types that do not appear on MTV, such as reggae or funk), but popularizing and trivializing them into a common "pop" dimension; and then flattening them out into one continuous present of the 24-hour flow, eliding the basic historical addresses. Even the old 1960s and 1970s groups who are still featured (e.g. the Stones, Supertramp) or band members from those decades now going out on their own (e.g. Phil Collins of Genesis,

John Fogerty of Credence Clearwater, Joe Walsh of the Eagles, Pete Townshend of the Who, Eric Clapton, or lesser known returning stars, like Huey Lewis) are simply inserted along with all the rest, without any positioning. In similar fashion, the teenage audience is now no longer seen as divided into distinct groups addressed by the different kinds of rock, but is one decentered mass that absorbs all the types without noting (or knowing) their historical origins, for these have been all but erased, traces remaining only in some aspects of dress and, occasionally, in relation to 1950s mock revivals, in black and white photography.

The erasing of the specific historical address inevitably involves a corollary diminution of specific political or ideological comment. Videos do not even manifest the phenomenon of youth culture searching for a position from which to speak, or concluding that there is no position from which to speak. We rather have the displacement of what we earlier *called* ideology into the new era of the "look," "style," "self-as-commodity," all of which suggest postmodernism. In any case, the effort of MTV managers to bring rock into mainstream culture entails a dilution of originally oppositional stances, or even, as we've seen, censoring of groups, like punk or black bands, that stand too far toward the edges of dominant culture. (If one looks only at MTV one might conclude that rock is dead, or that it has come to the end of its line. In fact, innovative and important music is being developed outside of this "mainstreaming," but is only heard or seen by those aficionados who make efforts to follow developments.)

In exploring further the issue of what specific *kinds* of ideologies we find on MTV, or indeed of whether or not the word "ideology" has any meaning in a postmodern universe, at least of the Baudrillardean variety, I want to distinguish five different types of video that dominate the 24-hour MTV flow. As always, the point in establishing any categories is first to make manageable what is, at least in this case, a huge and unmanageable mass of material, and second to establish a few broadly defined types which are archetypal rather than anything else. That is, rather few videos may actually fit precisely the specific types; but those types offer a schema to which nearly all the videos can be related. They *approximate* rather than *embody* the types. (See Table 3.)

Table 3 Five main types of video on MTV

Modes
(all use avant-garde strategies, especially self-reflexivity, play with the image, etc.)

Predominant MTV themes		Romantic	Socially conscious	Nihilist	Classical	Post-modernist
	Style	Narrative	Elements varied	Performance Anti-narrative	Narrative	Pastiche No linear images
	Love/Sex	Loss and reunion (Pre-Oedipal)	Struggle for autonomy Love as problematic	Sadism/masochism Homoeroticism Androgyny (Phallic)	The male gaze (Voyeuristic fetishistic)	Play with Oedipal positions
	Authority	Parent figures (positive)	Parent and public figures Cultural critique	Nihilism Anarchy Violence	Male as subject Female as object	Neither for nor against authority (ambiguity)

I also want to historicize my own development of this schema: when I began this study in 1982, MTV was far less "postmodern" than it now is. The "socially conscious" video, for instance, was prevalent and had still "behind" it a kind of 1960s politics. Some of the videos I will now put under that heading raise all the issues of the new "radical chic" and of the Baudrillardean "simulacrum" mentioned above. There have been corresponding changes in the romantic video, which I will explain, and in addition changes in the frequency and regularity of cycling of various types over the years. The postmodern video, for instance, seems to extend further and further into the channel in 1986, threatening to take over as the dominant kind.

There are five basic types of video on MTV, three of which seemed, when I first developed the scheme, to correspond roughly to the three types of rock music that have been developed over the past twenty years as noted above (p. 5). I have thus labeled three types "romantic" (i.e. looking back to 1960s soft rock, popularized); "socially conscious" or "modernist" (deriving vaguely from rock groups in the 1960s and 1970s that took oppositional stances); and "nihilist" (deriving from heavy metal, here watered down). That is, in 1982 I felt that these videos still had some special kind of relationship to the (then) recent history of rock music. As we move further away from the 1960s and as the postmodern universe seems increasingly here, so these types begin to reflect merely a different "look" rather than specifically to embody what we may loosely call different "ideologies."

The fourth kind I call "classical" because it adheres more than the others to narrative codes (not necessarily following Hollywood strictly), often being set in realistic environments and eschewing the usual play on the figures of the performing band members. Once again, this type also seems increasingly self-conscious about what it is doing so as to fall into a postmodern "pastiche." In other words, all of what earlier seemed to reflect distinct modes of address now seem ultimately to fall under the "postmodern," which is a term that I had earlier reserved for a specific type of video that even then refused to position itself vis-à-vis what it showed. I still keep the postmodernist video as a separate type, embodying in an extreme form what many videos now evidence.

56

THE FIVE TYPES OF VIDEO

The terms along the top of Table 3 distinguish videos in relation to their overall style and tone: music, words, visuals all create a mood that categorizes the video. Underneath the word "mode" are listed the various techniques that characterize all videos, such as avant-garde devices (self-reflexivity, play with the image), pastiche, the foregrounding of performance, the use of choreographed dance that links some videos with the Hollywood musical. While any of these devices may be found across the three modes, generally the romantic and classical videos use a degree of narrative and less focus on musical instruments and the band in performance (their gender address differs markedly however); the postmodernist videos, at the other extreme, use more pastiche, less self-reflexivity and are characterized mainly by their refusal to take a position toward what they show; their positioning in the realm of *simulacra,* with no gestures toward a signified, sets them apart from other videos.

In between, there is the nihilist video, usually featuring heavy metal bands and often giving most screen time to images of the performers on stage (live concert footage is spliced together, sometimes with other interspersed shots away from the stage); and the "socially conscious" type, defined more by its surface themes than specific visual devices.

Along the side of Table 3 are the themes that dominate all the videos, but the words in the box indicate the differing treatment of the themes in each video type. As will be clear, discussion of "themes" assumes a text's involvement in a signified, and what I have been suggesting is that there is less and less assumption being made about that signified. Thus we have to take the word "theme" as a mere counter for discussing videos that continue to construct stories in which events take place. The same applies to psychological dilemmas portrayed, and for which I have used Freudian terminology in the table; i.e. we must also take these terms as "counters" rather than as having literal application. As Baudrillard noted, despite the psychological level being there, things often seem to be played out *somewhere else.*

Implicit in the table is that MTV, arguably like television as a whole, includes a wide range of gazes with different gender implications in contrast to the (largely) monolithic gaze of the Hollywood film. The televisual apparatus is not gender specific in its modes of functioning, as arguably the filmic apparatus is. Across the various ad-segments we find a variety of "gazes" that indicate an address to a certain kind of male or female imaginary. I will argue that there is frequently a genderless address, and that people of both genders are able to undertake multiple identifications, although this will vary from video type to video type.

As a preliminary, let me say something brief about each kind of video and then proceed in this chapter to analyze the ideological "imaginary" in select videos. I will look here at political meanings in some "socially conscious" videos and then in Chapter 5 study the markedly different kinds of "erotic" imaginary in videos figuring male and female stars. As should be obvious, I am not imputing any authorial control to the historical star subjects being discussed here, since how much control a star has in any one case is unclear; my focus is on *texts* rather than stars. Videos produced for stars in no way attempt to construct an image constant from one text to another; a star's image will depend on what seems most marketable at the particular moment, and on the general style/tone/image of the single, or the record from which the single comes. Since selling the record is the base-line, that will control the "look" of the video being made for sale of the song and its record.

The romantic type, as noted, looks back to the 1960s soft rock, now popularized and sentimentalized. A year or so ago, this type was largely the province of female stars, like the Cyndi Lauper of that time, and tended to address the female spectator. Lionel Ritchie, with his poignant, haunting "Hello," was an exception. The type as a whole was not frequent on the station, nihilist, classical, and alternative types predominating.

In the past years, important changes have taken place: first, in 1983-4 the romantic video increased in number, while the nihilist one declined. Second, male stars took over the romantic type, which routinely headed the MTV Top Twenty Charts (viz. Phil Collins's "One More Night," Foreigner's "I Want to Know What Love is," Paul Young's "Everytime You Go Away"). Currently (mid-1986), the romantic video is generally on the decline, the nihilist and postmodern on the increase, while there are profound changes in both the classical and socially conscious types.

It is the overall nostalgic, sentimental and yearning quality that

58

defines the romantic video. A love relationship, usually male/ female but it can be parent/child or parent-substitute (viz. the 1983 videos, Denise Williams's "Let's Hear It For The Boy," or Lee Carey's "A Fine, Fine Day"), is presented as central to the protagonist's life, something that would "solve" all problems. The address is to the absent or lost loved one, or the video plays out the pain of separation, as in Cyndi Lauper's "Time After Time." Occasionally, the romantic video shows celebration of a love union (as in Pat Benatar's "We Belong," or Stevie Nicks's "If Anyone Falls in Love").

Usually in romantic videos the images are linked in a narrative chain that reproduces the song lines about love, loss, reunion. But it is a weak narrative chain, the main focus being on the emotions of loss or reunion rather than on the causes, conditions or effects of such loss. Cyndi Lauper's "Time After Time" has an unusually complicated narrative, beginning as it does with a typical moment of pastiche as the heroine is inspired to leave her lover by the poignant, bitter-sweet parting on the television screen of Dietrich and Gary Cooper. Before she leaves, the heroine recalls her past with her lover, and we have scenes of his distaste for her wild outfits, of her longing for her working-class mother's comfort, which in turn evoke happy memories of their times together. Catching her in the act of leaving, Lauper's lover takes her to the station, the heroine stopping by to wish her mother farewell before the poignant parting scene at the station. (Lauper's other well-known early video, "Girls Just Want to Have Fun," takes a different stance, and will be discussed under the "socially conscious" type. Most recently, her work falls into the nihilist category, if "Money Changes Everything" is typical of what she will do. Perhaps a bitter comment on her own success, this performance video shows an angry Lauper, shouting out her words and storming around the stage in sneakers, kicking oil drums and twisting and turning in an undirected rage.)

The close, overtly stated mother—daughter bonding in "Time After Time" is significant in foregrounding what I think has increasingly become a sub-text of the romantic video by both male and female stars. Videos in this category idealize parent—child relationships, manifesting pre-Oedipal, bisexual yearnings in the urge to merge with the loved one and recapture infant mother—child closeness. In the early versions of the type, however, close parent—child relationships were usually mother/son (cf. Denise Williams's "Let's Hear It For the Boy") or father/son (cf. Lee Carey's "A Fine, Fine Day," where the close father/son bonding is set off by images of a cold, inadequate mother). Paul Young's video, "Every Time You Go Away," which will be analyzed in detail shortly, arguably exemplifies an interesting genderless address, although the video may be seen as falling into the traditional male yearning for the lost mother object, as we'll see.

As might be expected, the music in these videos is tuneful, melodious, lyrical. Instrumentation is light, often focused on one instrument (like Phil Collins on the piano), and the melodious, main theme is frequently repeated. In the background there is usually a reassuring, steady beat. The star's voice is in the foreground, leading the instruments, and a choir may be pulled in for echo effect. Drums, if used, are soft-pedalled, muffled.

The nihilist video, meanwhile, retains some of the originally anarchic positions of recent punk, new wave and heavy metal bands. On MTV, the type is represented mainly by the heavy metal bands, punk being a sub-group largely censored as too far to the cultural margins. Lawrence Grossberg has focused on the negativity of punk and heavy metal: "It reveals," he notes, "a self-reflexive affirmation of difference, a decathexis of any affirmation."[5] But what impresses me is the paradoxical linking of an overall vitality and creativity (evident in the musical compositions, the visuals, and their combination) with a nihilistic ideology.

Most, but not all, nihilist videos show their origins in live concerts by retaining the performance set-up. The camera focuses on the figures comprising the band, seen playing their instruments in often hectic style on the stage, while we see fans' arms waving in front of the image or else at the rear of an image shot from the performers' point of view. These videos differ from the romantic ones in their aggressive use of camera and editing; wide-angle lenses, zoom shots, rapid montage, typify devices used. In the non-performance type, one image rarely has much to do with the next, and lighting techniques in all of them derive from film noir and German Expressionism. As in those film genres, the world of these videos is unstable, alien. A common image is the sudden, unmotivated explosion, shattering the filmic world and underscoring the violence that lurks beneath (e.g. David Bowie's "D.J."). The stage is often made to look like a strange, deserted landscape simply through lighting devices, or is translated into a disorienting space, as in Ozzy Osbourne's "Shot in the Dark" or Motley Crue's "Home Sweet Home"; but sometimes the performers are seen in non-stage expressionist environments, hanging as it were in outerspace, in a shadowy, undefined, hazy place (as for example in Scorpions' "Rock You Like a Hurricane," analyzed in detail later on, or their recent "No One Like You").

The intensity and concentrated shock effects of these videos produce images that violate those in dominant culture, especially in the area of sexual representation and gender address, which I'll discuss shortly. But the music is equally disorienting and disturbing. Instrumentation is here complex, varied, unmelodious. Drums often roar, while the electric guitars are made to screech and scream and wail. Musical themes often work against each other, and in opposition to the usually screaming voice of the star. The rhythm is driving, relentless, apparently almost out of control at times. Deafening sounds drive out the words, and the performers leap violently about the stage, often bashing about their instruments and microphones. (See Billy Idol's "Rebel Yell," Scorpion's "Rock You Like a Hurricane," Van Halen's "Jump," Police's "Synchronicity," AC/DC's "For Those About to Rock, We Salute You.")

In nihilist videos, the love theme turns from a relatively mild narcissism and a focus on the pain of separation, to sadism, masochism, androgyny, and homoeroticism; while the anti-authority theme moves from mere unresolved Oedipal conflicts to explicit hate, nihilism, anarchy, destruction.

The nihilist video thus has (at least hitherto) taken up an angry, iconoclastic stance, making clear its position. The same has been true of the so-called "classical" video that is partly defined by its employing the traditional Hollywood "male" gaze toward the female figures. These are the videos that rely more than most others on narrative situations and that do not necessarily show band members performing with their instruments at all. The videos are however mainly "classical" in retaining the voyeuristic/fetishistic gaze toward woman as object of desire that feminist film theorists have spent so much time analyzing in relation to the classical Hollywood film.

These arguments are too well-known to be rehearsed here, and I will be returning to specific examples in the next chapter. But, briefly, these videos set up the female image as object of an obsessive male desire and are positioned in the male protagonist's viewpoint. There are numerous examples of this kind of video, but Rod Stewart's "Infatuation," John Parr's "Naughty Naughty," The Romantics' "Talking in Your Sleep," John Cougar's "Hurts so Good," The Rolling Stones' "She Was Hot," are familiar, oft-played examples. I'll be commenting later on the deliberately self-conscious stance toward their own voyeurism evident in these videos. (The Stewart video deliberately foregrounds the voyeurism in imaging the protagonist constantly photographing the desired woman, but the feature is perhaps at its most extreme in the popular David Lee Roth "California Girls" and "Just Like A Gigolo/I Ain't Got Nobody".) It is this self-consciousness that sets them off somewhat from the voyeurism in the classical film.

A second main "classical" type is that which derives largely from certain Hollywood film genres. Especially prevalent recently have been videos deriving from the horror, suspense, and science fiction film types. The type began relatively innocently with Jackson's famous "Thriller," but has lately gotten more ominous, as in Peter Gabriel's "Shock the Monkey," White Wolf's "Shadows in the Night," or Yes's "Owner of a Lonely Heart." In the Gabriel and White Wolf videos, some kind of alien presence inserts itself in the filmic world; in the first, it is a monkey that seems to cause the protagonist's strange alternation between his regular business self and a savage, totemic other self; in the latter, an alien presence enters the forest and frightens the young people away. The Yes video remains within the gangster tradition, as the protagonist is swept out of the mass of the people by rain-coated men in dark glasses, who submit him to a variety of tortures, physical and psychological. Duran Duran's "Wild Boys" also tends toward the science fiction mode: a group of men in some wrecked, post-holocaust world, tied to planks on a revolving wheel, seem to exist on the margins of civilization.

Powerful images of entrapment and unexplained descent evoke deep psychological fears in the viewer. While these are familiar from classical Hollywood genres, there is an important difference that again suggests the sliding over into postmodernism. For in most of the Hollywood genres mentioned here the mystery is ultimately resolved; we are given explanations (even if they involve "belief" in the possibility of extraterrestrial beings or in spirits/ghosts, etc.) for the events shown, so that the viewer leaves the cinema secure that he/she is living in a rational world. This is not the case for most of the videos described above: we never know why certain things happen, or even precisely what *is* happening. We are forced to exist in a non-rational, haphazard universe where we cannot expect any "closure" of the ordinary kind. On this level then, these so-called "classical" videos also gesture toward postmodernism.

What characterizes the postmodernist video is its refusal to take a clear position vis-à-vis its images, its habit of hedging along the line of not communicating a clear signified. In postmodernist videos, as not in the other specific types, each element of a text is undercut by others: narrative is undercut by pastiche; signifying is undercut by images that do not line up in a coherent chain; the text is flattened out, creating a two-dimensional effect and the refusal of a clear position for the spectator within the filmic world. This leaves him/her decentered, perhaps confused, perhaps fixated on one particular image or image-series, but most likely unsatisfied and eager for the next video where perhaps closure will take place.

Ambiguity of the image and frequency of pastiche is most evident in postmodern videos. These videos, which sometimes have loose narrative elements, are disturbing in not manifesting a position from which they speak; Motley Crue's "Too Young to Fall in Love," for example, has the trio – bizarrely dressed in tight leather pants, studded leather straps over bare chests, leather boots, and wearing their hair very long and straggly – involved in a James Bond-style oriental crime plot. With much macho maneuvering and improbable sword play, they rescue the beautiful young oriental girl from the clutches of her stolid fat captors. But it is impossible to tell whether or not this video intends to comment upon, and thus critique, the clichéd Bond conventions. Is it merely employing them for its own ends? Are we supposed to find interest in the contrast between the Bond mise-en-scène and the Motley Crue stars in their outlandish attire? Does the video merely want us to delight in the stars' wonderful, athletic bodies so highlighted by their clothes, and in their dazzling macho feats?

ROCKING AROUND THE CLOCK

Queen's "Radio Ga Ga" is similarly difficult to read. In this case, an argument could be made for Queen self-consciously playing with images from Nazism and Germany in the 1930s, setting off Fritz Lang's version of the future (in footage taken from *Metropolis*) against futurist Star-Trek imagery. The intent then could be to link Lang's foreboding of fascism with the present. Supporting this view is the fact that the radio is recalled nostalgically as an instrument that pre-dated the dangerous proliferation of "spectacle" that Nazism so exploited and that contemporary youth celebrates in its very fascination with rock videos.

On the other hand, this reading is sophisticated and only possible within the framework of knowledge about Fritz Lang and fascism in 1930s Germany. The video does not itself construct a position for the spectator or even seem to raise questions about its own use of fascist imagery. It does not say whether it is for or against fascism, hedging along that line (mentioned above) of not letting us know what we are to do with images of proto-fascism. The rally scenes pastiche Leni Riefenstahl's *Triumph of the Will*, the figures looking like a cross between those in her film and in *Star-Trek*. The easy, regular beat of the music, with its haunting tune uncharacteristic of the postmodern type, is perhaps deliberately in opposition to the potential violence of the images, but the average spectator would not notice this ironic juxtaposition and is merely swept along in a way that is pleasurable rather than disjunctive or questioning. If there really *is* irony rather than pastiche, it takes work to grasp it.

The same is true of their recent "Princes of the Universe," which seems at once to parody and celebrate machismo and male acts of violence and destruction. The title might refer ironically to heads of powerful nations in the world, whose self-proclaimed omnipotence in fact leads to pathetic destruction (viz. the image of the child electrocuted as he hangs onto a bar). This is one of the videos with a futurist "look" that resembles a nuclear holocaust, and is packed with images of explosion and destruction. Yet the stars themselves appear to parade their power and virility as they withstand the onslaughts of their world, and seem to triumph over it. Again, the pastiche/satire boundary is blurred.

I have left the "socially conscious" video until last because I wish to focus on this type here. When I first started this work (and in some already published papers), I used the category to distinguish those videos which made social issues their specific theme from others which, following Althusser, are necessarily in ideology but do not have explicit ideological *content*. The "socially conscious" video is arguably the closest we have to one modernist tradition in western culture that deliberately positioned itself against the dominant bourgeois society. The great nineteenth-century novel produced one level of critique of bourgeois culture, followed by the post-romantic, modernist kind of critique. Although the category "modernism" is now under debate, it can still stand for a type of art that is in deliberate reaction against what are perceived as dominant, established forms. As a counter-art form, modernist texts defined themselves against what they opposed; this strand of modernism, then, was a largely *political* art, looking from a critical position, whether to the right or the left of the establishment.

From 1982 to 1985, one could find videos that still seemed ideologically linked to various forms of 1960s left and liberal humanism, i.e. that had behind them political signifieds embodied in on-going movements of certain kinds. These videos found their way onto MTV arguably because the station could not quite contain all positions shown during the 24-hour flow. So these "socially conscious" videos were there, albeit largely drowned out by the ongoing flow of the other types, and not usually cycled with any regularity.

In this sense, of course, the channel was not risking much in allowing the occasional video with politically liberal messages. Yet it is important that the format of short, four-minute texts permits gaps through which a variety of enunciative positions are possible. I am thus able to temporarily "stop the flow," in order to concentrate on representations other than the dominant postmodernist fixation on surfaces/textures/style/self-as-commodity that dominates the channel's offerings. But this is with full awareness that these isolated moments are overridden by the plethora of surrounding texts, and that this sort of focus only occurs within an academic discourse. These various possibilities for "seeing otherwise" are worth exploring in terms of understanding what popular culture *can* do, despite the fact that the average viewer will in fact have little opportunity for such alternate "seeing."

In the early 1980s, three themes dominated the "socially

John Cougar Mellencamp, "Authority"

In this "socially conscious" video, the protagonist is victimized by representatives of authority.

conscious" video, all of which involve moments of disruption, conflict, rejection, and alienation. There were first the anti-parental, anti-authority videos, revealing adolescent disillusionment with, and distaste for, parental, work-related, or state authority. Protagonists are sometimes shown as painful victims of authority, as in John Cougar's "Authority Song" video, where the protagonist is victimized by all representatives of social authority; or that which equates Friday liberation from the work week with an escape from prison. Here, secretaries are imaged in chains that tie them to the desk, the boss (always fat and ugly) is bound up in ticker-tape by the liberators. The performers, in their anti-establishment punk clothes, are imaged as freedom fighters who destroy the office and the oppressors, releasing the employees.

The British have been most active in expressing a generalized, anti-establishment attitude that continues a tradition in British counter-culture dating from John Osborne's *Look Back in Anger* (1956) and embodied in the "Angry Young Man" movement that followed. Jo Boxer's "Just Got Lucky," which contrasts the happy-go-lucky band in their working-class men's clothes and box-cart, with a stuffy, overweight and quarrelsome parental couple in their swanky car, was a typical early example of the type, as was also Stray Cats' "Look At That Cadillac." More explicitly anti-parental than anti-bourgeois, Mama's Boys' "Mama, We're All Crazy Now" shows a typical British working-class mother, busying herself doing housework for her son, suddenly catapulted into her son's rock and roll world when he arrives with his friends and starts loud, wild playing that nearly brings down the kitchen roof. The transition from the mother in the kitchen to the mother immersed in rock 'n roll is ironically conveyed through a Hitchcockian filmic moment, when we see only the mother's bedroom slippers creeping silently up the stairs to a certain kind of death.

Tears for Fears' "Mother's Talk" (in its third video version in 1986) operates on two levels simultaneously; it is again explicitly anti-parental (and anti-family), although the mother seems the most repressive figure in keeping with a long representational tradition.[6] But it makes this critique in the context of the sudden outbreak of nuclear war; that is, we see the pathetic/stupid reactions of a working class family (circa early 1950s), with Moma at the ironing board, head-cloth and apron in place, Dad reading the paper, boy on the floor watching a TV set on which images of a hydrogen bomb exploding (the start of the nuclear holocaust) alternate with those of the band in performance. Mother is seen berating boy, who ignores her, when suddenly the father realizes from watching the TV what is happening, and begins to dismantle doors and to paint over the windows in an effort to build the "inner refuge" the TV demonstrates. The mother, meanwhile, tries to hoover up the father, increasing his rage. The video ends with the onset of a nuclear war and the family packing all their belongings; they wave to the camera, from their obviously inadequate "refuge," as the video ends.

The Kinks' imaginative and poignant "Do It Again" and Wham!'s more aggressive "Bad Boys" exemplify the kind of video that has been coming from England recently, as does also the Dream Academy's "Life in a Northern Town," with its poignant, nostalgic look back at the 1960s and John F. Kennedy and the Beatles. The videos all have an explicit working-class identification and a clear anti-middle-class point of view: the political codes that structure the position within British society are evident, and provide a kind of referent *behind* the text.

Some American bands picked up the stance in 1985, but partly because class codes function very differently here from Britain, and partly because by 1985 there was already a sliding over into the postmodern stance in which social themes exist *merely* as representations and lack any political referents any more, the results are startlingly different. Sammy Hagar's "I Can't Drive at 55," and Motley Crue's "Smokin' in the Boys' Room" are representative of what is going on in America. Let me briefly analyze this latter comic video so as to provide some sense of the "new" anti-authority position.

"Smokin' in the Boys' Room", in pastiching a 1974 Brownsville station song, is a postmodern version of the socially conscious video. Its comedy works through the relationship between song and image, and through play with a kind of Bakhtinian notion of the carnivalesque, particularly as this has been discussed recently by Peter Stallybrass and Allon White.[7] Like much of MTV, the usage of past modes is superficial – textural rather than fully ideological; but, in Bakhtin's words, Motley Crue's video does celebrate "temporary liberation from the prevailing truth of the established order," and marks "the suspension of all hierarchical rank, privileges, norms and prohibitions." For Bakhtin, "Carnival was the true feast of time, the feast of becoming, change and renewal, it was hostile to all that was immortalized and complete."[8] Certain American bands like Motley Crue (one could also include Twisted Sister, Ozzy Osbourne, Kiss, and others) play with the carnivalesque in their anti-establishment videos, perhaps replacing political protest against the established order with a kind of "licensed release" arguably characteristic of the carnival.[9]

"Smokin' in the Boys' Room" carries us quickly and efficiently through the establishing narrative (the hero loses his homework, is sent to the Principal and whipped and retires to the boys' room to recover). The musical instruments – and sound effects, such as the dog's growl, the slamming doors, the rushing noise as Jimmy approaches the Principal, the sound of the whip, etc. – effectively underscore the humorous camera work used for Jimmy and the teachers (wide-angle lenses, high angle shots, extreme close-ups, etc.). Jimmy looks into the mirror and, echoing the Principal (who had bemoaned the fact that Jimmy was "Never able to see *our* side of things"), wonders why "Somebody can't see *my* side of it."

At this point, Jimmy suddenly sees the images of the four Motley Crue band members in the mirror; one of them pops his head out, and tells Jimmy that they have found a way of getting out of the world of authority. Combining the carnivalesque tradition outlined by Bakhtin with more recent 1960s concepts, this world, when viewed from the "other" side of the mirror, is now seen to be "crazy." Values are turned upside down: what was before "rational" authority is now exposed as repressive and inhibiting. The band members pull the boy across into the world of the grotesque in which all bourgeois restraints are released. From here, Jimmy looks out at the school world transformed into madness and horror from the alternate, carnivalesque position.

To begin with, the band's own clothes are a total (and radical) violation of normal male dress clothes. Three of the band members (the drummer remains seated throughout) are dressed in even more outlandish get-ups than usual: the point seems to be to shock the establishment by the blurring of the usual male/female dress barrier – a familiar element in the carnival. Motley Crue all have very long

Motley Crue, "Smokin' in the Boys' Room"

Motley Crue, "Home Sweet Home"

The point is to mock the establishment by blurring usual male/female dress codes.

hair, elaborately styled, faces made up to look like women, with long eyelashes, heavy lipstick, mascara, rouge, etc.; they wear earrings and necklaces and have painted nails. Their clothes are also feminine, one of them wearing a one-piece suit, with dots on it, golden epaulettes and wide sash; another, white sequined pants, shiny necklace, a huge sequined belt, amulets, bracelets, a low-cut sleeveless top, and patches over crotch and rear; a third wears short leather pants and high leather boots, and a leather jacket with cut pieces, *gamin* style. Halfway through the video, they change clothes, one now wearing a white and black striped imitation of coat-tails, another a long leopard-skin coat and boots. The clothes in themselves are enough to disrupt the "straight" world on the other side of the mirror; far more than the 1960s "hippies," Motley Crue draw upon traditions of the medieval and renaissance clown, as well as upon more recent conventions of the transvestite.

But the group have other telling secrets to reveal: from the other side, the regular classroom looks like a jail, with a Nazi-style lady warden in charge (shades of Lina Wertmuller's Commandant in *Seven Beauties*); the students are all hooked up to machines, their faces and eyes fastened so that they have to look directly at a bright light (one recalls Plato's cave allegory here). Since students might manage to use one eye to look elsewhere, the warden patrols the machines, controlling all with a huge gear on which the word "Conform" is written in large letters.

Meanwhile, Motley Crue reveal the stupidity and inanity of the Principal, who is associated with a look-alike puppet. The band disrupts the ever-vigilant video camera, which, like Foucault's Panopticon, allows students to be seen without themselves seeing. The band first put a picture of their Other Side world in front of the camera, but then allow their own images to appear on the Principal's multiscreens, much to his dismay. They walk Jimmy into the auditorium, where the music teacher is performing, push him off the stage, and take over, to the wild delight of the students.

After a liberating and hectic performance, students dancing madly to the music, Motley Crue return Jimmy to the boys' room whence they took him. The Principal offers an apology, now scorned by Jimmy, who winks at his friends in the mirror, and pulls off the Principal's wig, revealing his ugly, egg-shaped head.

ROCKING AROUND THE CLOCK

The inventive music track for this video, together with the group's extraordinary appearance, enables the whole to transcend its narrative clichés. The musical sounds in the opening section used to indicate the brutality and inhumanity of the school are effective, and throughout the instruments create a hard-driving, heavy metal sound that perfectly suits the comic turns of the plot. The band's music defines the "other side" as much as anything else, and seems to embody the carefree, iconoclastic stance of the rebels. But the visuals also add a good deal: the idea of contrasting the straight and subversive worlds through the device of the mirror is imaginative and effective. It provides a graphic visual correlative for the concept, and permits a constant play with the notion of "seeing" and "being seen," but in far different terms from the standard Hollywood shot/counter-shot cutting sequence. The rebels look out onto, and thereby manage to control, and ultimately conquer, the world of the establishment. The video supports the idea that "liberation" lies through rock sounds and through refusing to conform to essentially moribund (if not corrupt), stuffy, bourgeois values. But, unlike the genuine Bakhtinian carnival, the protest remains superficial: mere play with oppositional signifiers rather than a protest that emerges from a powerful class and community base.

These generalized anti-establishment videos seem largely the province of male stars, and rarely even include reference to women, unless they are of the fat/ugly types to be ridiculed (as in "Smokin' in the Boys' Room"). Motley Crue's feminized appearance seems rather to mark the absence of women as something desirable. They have incorporated the feminine, as it were, making its actual presence superfluous. The band takes the place of women in Jimmy's life, while vicariously providing the semblance of the feminine. This sort of androgynous address, common in nihilist videos, will be more fully explored later on.

It might also be noted, briefly, that the American anti-establishment videos differ from the British ones in their clichéd ridicule of generalized (not class-marked) authority figures. The British seem rather to follow the tradition (immortalized by the Beatles) of exposing the pathos and banality of the routine, daily bourgeois life that people are tracked into without their being aware of what is happening to them. Sometimes the British try to show such people as stupid (as in the Kinks' video referred to), but often they will be empathetic. Sometimes they delight in being different, but are just as likely to express a certain poignancy about their alienation from the crowd. At any rate, by and large, the British anti-establishment videos are not so aggressively machismo as many of the American ones.

Perhaps the best socially conscious videos of a general kind on the American scene are the rare ones that fit into what we might call the "art" or "avant-garde" video. (That this type is finally being recognized as such by the channel is evident in the creation of a new slot, "The New Video Hour," perhaps inspired by the Newark-based Channel U-68.) The well-known Polish video director, Zbigniew Rybczynski, often produces videos of this type, as for instance in his "Close to the Edit" for Art of Noise, or his "Sign of the Times" for Grandmaster Flash. He is best known, perhaps, for his work with Simple Minds. For their recent "All the Things She Said," Rybczynski used a digital disk video recorder that allowed him to shoot and

Peter Gabriel, "Sledgehammer"

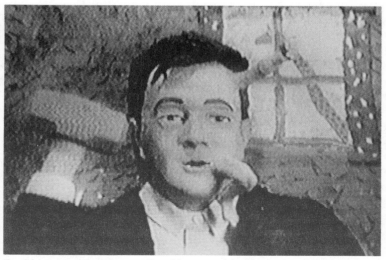

In this extraordinarily creative video, no objects remain what they seem for long: the video is constructed around the idea of *transformation*.

73

edit simultaneously. This breakthrough in video technology made possible a continuous flow of 112 separate takes, all slightly different. Also interesting are experimental videos by Sly Fox (another black and white team) called ''Let's Go All the Way''; or any by the extraordinary artist Grace Jones. Peter Gabriel's disturbing ''Sledgehammer'' is yet another example of a creative use of the video form. Here Gabriel's face is filmed in stop-motion technique to produce a disorienting, jerky series of images, and the instability of objects becomes the norm; one thing is transmuted into another, often grotesque, form, until at the end even the human body turns into a series of shapes that dissolve into the cosmos, there now being merely an infinite, boundless, and inhuman universe. The Art of Noise's ''Paranoimia,'' featuring as it does the computerized man, or ''simulacrum,'' similarly addresses the confusion of boundary between human/non-human of an advanced technological era.

But the Talking Heads' ''Burning Down the House'' and Laurie Anderson's rarely shown ''Language is a Virus'' are both more obviously socially conscious examples. The creative use of metaphor in ''Burning Down the House,'' and the aesthetic intelligence underlying the video's construction, typify much of David Byrne's work. Here the trope of ''house'' can be taken in the senses of both the historical subject and of the public sphere; it works on both levels at once, suggesting the archaism and inadequacy of the family as an institution, while also implying that the State no longer has the ability to create a meaningful society. The symbolic sub-urban house dominates the video as an image constantly returned to; its side wall (facing the camera) functions like a screen on which different images are projected (Byrne's haunted face, blown up large; flames; the concert audience with the search light panning across them, suggesting hostile authority over people). The performers themselves symbolize family members, Byrne's child self alternating with his adult one. At one point the various faces of the family members superimpose themselves on one another, representing the aim of family life to shape its members in one mould, ''Everything stuck together,'' as the lyric notes. At another point, the band members mimic the burden family members impose on one another by climbing on each other's backs while the words on the track note, ''I don't know what you expect of me.'' The final images suggest isolation and fragmentation, as we see Byrne's back, apparently facing emptiness rather than people; and his disconnected face superimposed over a panning shot of an empty road. Throughout, the staccato words and the deliberately mechanically orchestrated beat, together with the blank faces and robot-like movements of the performers, convey the sense of a world devoid of, and disillusioned with, earlier familiar comforts.

Laurie Anderson's "Language is a Virus" constructs an equally alienated environment; Anderson relies on staccato phrasing and robot-like gestures not unlike Byrne's.[10] In addition, at times her musicians wear stocking-masks over their faces, and strange, lamp-like headgear. Godardian fashion, Anderson uses words floating across her image to underscore and add meanings, and the whole is well-edited on movement and music beat. Taking her theme from a William Burroughs quotation, "Language is a virus from outer space," Anderson uses a combination of cinematic images, avant-garde theatre, computer graphics, play with the TV and cinema screens, all held together by her own half-talking voice, commenting on the abuses of language that in turn lead to exploitation (particularly of woman by man, it seems).

A second theme in "socially conscious" videos has been more specific allusion to foreign policy or specific social injustices, such as poverty. Again, the British bands lead the way, and they alone retain much of the genuinely political era of rock and roll (1967-70). These explicitly resisting videos are, however, very rarely shown on MTV. Frankie Goes to Hollywood's powerful "Two Tribes" video, which makes a bitter comment about East—West relations with specific reference to Ronald Reagan and the Soviet leader — we see the two aging men wrestling in a circus ring — was shown very infrequently, but it makes just the kind of ironic comment likely to reach viewers. The Clash and other rebellious British bands get scant attention from the channel.

Perhaps influenced by the British, there has recently (1986) been a significant increase in the explicitly political video on MTV. Let me deal with four examples in some detail. First, there is the sort of generalized critique of an America seen through the eyes of a Vietnam veteran, as in Bruce Springsteen's "Born in the USA." This represents a genuine outraged reaction to social conditions and the

Vietnam War, and the political referents are obvious. Second, there is the less politically explicit and more visually experimental stance of a band like Midnight Oil, whose "Best of Both Worlds" is an ironic comment on the state of things, in the general mode of Frankie Goes to Hollywood. Third, I want to attend briefly to a heavy metal band, Sammy Hagar, whose "V.O.A." indicates that the right can also make political videos, if again veering off in the postmodernist direction. Finally, there is the recent spate of videos inspired by the "USA/Africa" event/video, which has been influential in making concern for the starving fashionable. While Springsteen was influential in this as in the related "Sun-City" video to be discussed below, he should not be seen as responsible for the, perhaps, postmodernist result of these efforts. Springsteen is personally unusual in the American rock scene in seeming to retain genuine identification with the working class and the generally "oppressed" of this world.

Springsteen's hard-driving video, "Born in the USA," reflects the

Bruce Springsteen, "Born in the USA"

Springsteen's "ironic" patriotism: here the star turns his head away from the (suggested) American flag

76

bitter irony common to many songs on the "USA" album. The first part of the video focuses mainly on Springsteen himself, in performance, yelling the song words into the microphone. His deep, husky voice and angry, rebellious face and body mimic the hard-driving, loud, repetitive beat of the music. The camera stays close-in on his face most of the time, revealing his 1960s style bandana, long hair, and army jacket. Occasionally, we pull back to his full figure, with arm raised in angry protest, fans' arms also waving in front frame. The words, shouted rather than sung, tell how the hero "Got in a little hometown jam" and was sent "to a foreign land to go and kill the yellow man." This is followed by a long series of repeated lines "Born in the USA," while the visuals show largely different close-ups of Springsteen's face.

The next section of the song and video tells of the return home to work in a refinery and of the Vet Man's inability to help. There are images here recalling the hero's happy childhood in a working-class neighborhood; he is seen at a birthday party, in a high school photo, on his bike, going off to a wedding.

We cut back to Springsteen on stage where again we have close-ups of his face as he repeats the "Born in the USA" lines again several times. This dissolves to images of fairground cars, followed by two possible "adult" cars – a fancy, sleek car and an old, decorated car, "For Sale." This is followed by a similar series of ironic contrasts that reflect American life – the welfare men standing outside a "Checks Cashed" place; a young man firing a gun at a fairground, which dissolves to American soldiers in a jungle in Vietnam surrendering to the enemy; followed by a close-up of a vet with one blinded eye, to other vets with tattoos on the arm, which dissolves to images of soldiers fighting in Vietnam, and again dissolves to pick up a tiny Vietnamese child walking on a street. As the music blares, Springsteen's voice rises to a cry, and the child-image dissolves into a fast-moving camera panning the rows and rows of white graves at Arlington Cemetery, ending in a dissolve to Springsteen's screaming face on the stage. We cut to images of men working in a welding factory as the long-held screaming note continues. On a flare of light in the factory, the video returns to the stage, to pick up Springsteen's band members – the drummer, the guitarist, hectically playing on that same high note, the fans screaming away in audience.

77

Bruce Springsteen, "Glory Days"

Bruce Springsteen, "I'm On Fire"

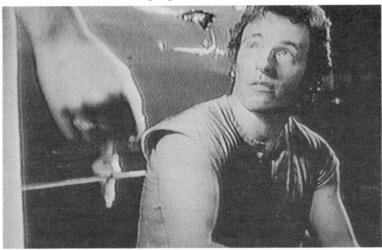

Springsteen's social consciousness is evident in other videos: "Glory Days" images the star in a working-class bar; "I'm On Fire" stresses the class discrepancy that inhibits the romance. The absence of the woman's face, and her fragmented body indicate her Symbolic status as lack, absent desire.

78

THE FIVE TYPES OF VIDEO

The video ends on a quieter, but still ironic note, showing images of young people – a young girl hard-hat, a girl on a bike, black performers, a man drinking coke, school girls walking home, men playing baseball – that is, shots of daily American life that still goes on, heedless of the meaningless pain and death in Vietnam. It is in fact the ironic juxtaposition of images that makes the song's already powerful statement even more so. Springsteen's musical score, in turn, reinforces both visuals and words in its loud, angry, rebellious sounds; it is as if the instruments are screaming out their rage at the way things are, echoing the hero's rage. Being "Born in the USA," that is, means being born to a senseless killing and to involving oneself in battle, injury, and death that belies happy childhood hopes and fantasies. Springsteen's recent "War" video, from his new *Live* album, reinforces and takes further themes in "Born in the USA."

Midnight Oil's "Best of Both Worlds" is in a vein rather similar to the Springsteen video, only perhaps with more humor in the bitter irony. The band present themselves in quite unconventional manner, the lead having a totally bald head, and the others dressed in various working-men's clothes. The video again consists of intercutting between the band in concert and images taken from newsreel footage, but there is a third space in this video – that of the outerspace from which the men look back on, and comment upon, doings on earth.

The first section shows the men in concert: the stage is dark, and they are lit in film noir fashion, so that they loom as spots in amongst the shadows. The music is hard-driving, unmelodious and, like Springsteen, the members shout rather than sing their words. As the music starts, we get shots of the men leaping about the stage in slow motion; there is quick intercutting between different band members, the film footage merely superimposed on the sound, and the camera is often so close in that we are not sure what we are seeing. As the song starts, the lead is filmed with an outerspace background, in which worlds are seen turning around. The first theme lines, "Times are tough/We got the best of both worlds," are repeated as we get a series of newsreel footage images – a rocket going off, a third world child dying, an image of Reagan's cheerful face, an image of a third world adult in the throes of death – first the body, then facial close-up; a shot of soldiers firing, a shot of the

ROCKING AROUND THE CLOCK

United States of America with major towns lit up, a shot of prisoners behind barbed wire, shortly juxtaposed ironically with a shot of fans' arms waving in a manner similar to that of the prisoners; a shot of another rocket taking off, and then of women and children on a third world, war-torn street.

We return to a sequence of shots of the band members, still singing the lines "Times are tough/We got the best of both worlds," followed by a repeat of war images and the rocket already seen. The next section changes somewhat to show the leader of the band floating in outerspace, from where he comments on the "real" world not being as good as it could have been. The music reaches its most loud, insistent, angry heights as these latter words are sung, over and over. The final image takes a comic stance, showing the band members on the moon, trying to catch the sausages they've cooked that constantly float away.

Both these videos make demands on the spectator not usual in rock videos on MTV. They do not construct an easy position for the viewer, and rely on viewers bringing certain reading formations to reception. For instance, how/where is the viewer supposed to identify? The stars are in so angry, rebellious a mood that identification with them is difficult, although I think this is what the spectator has to do; the newsreel footage moves fast, and the precise images can only be grasped on repeated viewings (stopping and pausing to get the full shot). The viewer is being barraged with information which is, however, imprecise. The decoding is not easy. The full meaning of the videos can only be understood if one deliberately thinks about what has been shown, which is not necessary for instance in the other types to be examined in the next chapter. The various pleasurable kinds of gaze that I'll also discuss there do not come into play here; one is forced, Brechtian style, to the more distanced position of watching and listening and thinking about what is going on. It is possible, however, that the insistent beat of the music, the energy, vitality, and clear commitment to express something considered important, can simply sweep the viewer along. The images and the music move fast, so that one's sensory organs are kept busy, even if one does not have time or inclination to think about what it all means.

A very different relationship to the status quo, this time from a heavy metal group, can be found in Sammy Hagar's "V.O.A." (i.e. "Voice of America"). Someone seeing the video from the perspective of liberal-humanist reading formations might be tempted to read the video as parody, but ultimately it is clear that it is closer to propaganda for "Voice of America" than a comic critique. Although there is comic play with both the standard Hollywood James Bond-style spy movie, and the international manipulations of the CIA, the video ends up celebrating "terrorist-style rockers" who are really vigilantes.

Hagar and the band members represent themselves as macho-style terrorist "rockers" aiding in CIA international dealings. The video begins with Hagar telling the enemy diplomat whom he has kidnapped, in no uncertain terms, that "We got to fight/Let's make that clear/If you push too hard/You're going to fall"; as these words are sung, we cut to shots of a gun battle between men in the hero's car and the pursuing enemy. Throughout the video, Hagar shouts rather than sings his words, and the heavy metal music keeps up a fast, loud pace; drums figure largely in the composition, while the guitars whine and scream as if to underscore the angry, patriotic stance of the protagonists, who, full of boundless energy, are determined to win.

As Hagar screams "We got fifty million rockers/All with guns," we cut to shots of men in black outfits, firing their guns from an open truck. At this point the group sing the macho-style lines, "We don' like it/We won't take it/Let it rock," that are repeated at intervals. The next section, in Damascus, shows the CIA and the Russians trading secrets, as Hagar sings "We're trying to strike/Everybody knows." As the music plays, we see Hagar avoiding capture because his group, in disguise, open fire and save him. We cut to Hagar looking through the film he's taken from a camera inside a false tooth, as he tells us "When we're together/We're the best/We think as one/There's no contest." Hagar claims "We got the power/They know the score," just before, ironically, he is finally captured and thrown into a rat- and insect-ridden cell. The words now cease as the music takes over for an interlude that shows the complexity of the composition and the skillful use of instruments to make interesting and fitting sounds. The sequence of the enemy's dragging Hagar to the electric chair and trying to make him talk is cut so as to coincide with the rhythm of the music; the sounds furthermore parallel what we see going on in the images, reaching their height at the moment of Hagar's attempted electrocution. In fact, he magically breaks free, runs off, and is next seen driving his car. His voice picks up the musical line on a long-held scream "No-o-o-o-o-," before the band chime in with the refrain, Hagar's voice rising above with the same "No-o-o-o."

In the final sequence, the music rises to fever pitch as we return to the opening car gun-battle, some images repeated from the earlier scene, and witness the protagonists' triumph over the enemy. The group now chant "Voice of America" several times, to underscore their patriotism. The last images are of the car blowing up in a huge explosion. Flames fill the screen as the camera follows the smoke up into the sky.

The vigilante violence evident in this video is a disturbing sign of the times. In other words, one can no longer assume that "rockers" are liberal humanists. The violence and anarchism of the nihilist video is here meshed with patriotic vigilante ideology involving direct action for the establishment in a united front. The political "referents" are here clear, although the comic mode still suggests a certain distance on Hagar's part toward what he is proclaiming.

None of these videos, whether from the right or the left, are frequently cycled on MTV and, except for the Springsteen, the stars are less well known. This has partly to do with MTV's commercial concern to keep things politically "safe"; but there is also the general Reaganite American climate that the channel addresses because that is where its audience is at. As John Orman notes, in a recent book on *The Politics of Rock Music*, the Gallup Youth Survey of 1977 "captured the sad state of rock in music by surveying 1069 teenagers in a random sample."[11] The list of top twenty artists selected by the teenagers in 1977 did not include "a true political rocker among them." According to Orman, "Rock had grown lazy and tame in all of its overblown opulence; it was hardly on the cutting edge of society change. Rock stars had to pay for their homes on the West Coast, the drugs, the limousines, and the good times. American popular culture easily absorbed the rock star into its class structure."

In the 1980s, Orman evidently conducted his own small survey and found little correlation between a person's favorite rock star and political attitudes. His sample (from a private Jesuit institution) all ranked USA, Jesus Christ, Catholics, and Martin Luther King, Jr, high; communists, homosexuals, blacks, the USSR, low. Of the fans, grouped into three based on their choice of Jackson Browne, Bruce Springsteen or punk/new wave music as their favorite kind, the punk/new wave were the least conservative, the Jackson Browne the most, with Springsteen in between.

A recent *Newsweek* article suggests the same general conservatism among rock fans and points out the irony of Bruce Springsteen's vast following, evidently not lost on Springsteen himself. According to *Newsweek*, Springsteen is imaged as an "all American guy" – a "kind of American archetype." He is "rock and roll's Gary Cooper – a simple man who expresses strong beliefs with passion and unquestioned sincerity. He is rock and roll's Jimmy Cagney as well – streetwise and fiery, a galvanic mixture of body and soul." Leery of being an icon, Springsteen sees such hero worship as antipathetic to rock's originally rebellious stance. Ironically, fans evidently take Springsteen's "Born in the USA" as "an exultant anthem for Reagan-era America."[12]

It would be impossible to mistake the message in a rare anti-Vietnam video which used newsreel footage from the war to expose the suffering and extreme youth of the men involved. Or that of The Firm's "Live in Peace," which implicates all nations in continuing hostilities that seem to be leading to world-wide destruction. Aside from the gratuitous imaging of evil in the clichéd forms of woman and snake, the video makes its point about the gap between government and ordinary people, who simply want to live in peace, well. Equally direct and earnest is John Cougar Mellencamp's "Rain on the Scarecrow" made in direct response to the plight of farmers in spring 1986, who were increasingly forced by desperate economic plight to give up land that had been in their families for generations. Jackson Browne's "For America," very much in the Springsteen mode, at once celebrates the high democratic American ideal – America's rhetoric about freedom – while deploring the failure to live up to the ideal. "The freedom I found," he sings, "Wasn't quite as free when the truth was known." The lyric and the images express at once loyalty and love for America, and profound disillusionment and distress at the automatic "my country right or wrong"

83

stance of many, and at America's having lost its conscience. The greatest and the most ignoble images of America's recent history are spliced together in an effective documentary-style montage.

But these videos are rare on MTV, only played at best a few times; otherwise, the closest MTV videos come to anything like a political referent are those like Don Henley's "All She Wants to do is Dance." Set in a guerrilla-warfare context, the focus of this video, despite the setting, is on the craziness of a young, perhaps shell-shocked girl, who, disregarding the street fighting going on around her, only wants to dance. (The sexist assumption that the girl cannot get involved in the political scene is typical of "political" videos.)

From this perspective, the recent USA Africa event/video, followed by the International "Live Aid" effort that brought together rock stars from America, Britain, Europe, and even the Soviet Union in a joint project to raise money for people starving in Ethiopia, seemed an encouraging sign of youth's concern with anything going on in the public sphere. While not exactly a radical cause, the two projects apparently demonstrated that rock stars could put aside their narcissistic interests in the service of something larger than themselves. The video and the Live Aid live transmission gave spectators a sense of being part of a community brought together around a moral cause unrelated to direct self-interest. The events incited a moral feeling in young people in an unusual way, and this can only be to the good. In addition, the fact that the Live Aid event (which involved thousands of young people at all-day-long concerts in London and Philadelphia) came off without any violence or disruptions showed a far different climate from that of the early 1970s, when rock had gone sour and when events like Altamont took place.

Further fundraising and consciousness-raising events around social issues followed those directed at poverty in Africa: the "Sun-City" video (in which again Springsteen played an important role) tackled the apartheid issue, on the heels of student campus protests, making a strong anti-apartheid statement; there was a Fashion Video event geared toward victims of Aids and several videos were made about the deadly disease (although they did not appear on MTV, as far as I am aware). Most recently, there was a Farm Aid Event in which rock, jazz, and folk stars participated. As noted, John

THE FIVE TYPES OF VIDEO

Cougar Mellencamp has made a striking video about the plight of the farmers near his home town, "Rain on the Scarecrow." It begins with a documentary-style interview with farmers describing their losses, and then moves into a visual essay on the pitiful conditions to which many American farmers have been reduced.

These events are interesting precisely because they took place within MTV's overarching commercial framework. Within that framework, one could obviously not expect in-depth political analysis to accompany events or to be embodied within the videos. It is certainly meaningful that young people are taking any kind of moral stand for those less fortunate than themselves. But what interests me about the videos and the events is the way that the organizers' genuine and committed intentions are taken up in the televisual apparatus and turned, inevitably, into something else. That is, it was hard to prevent these events turning into *media* events, hard to stop the televisual apparatus itself becoming the *event*. In the Live Aid event particularly, focus was on the awesome technological achievement of cross-Atlantic and inter-continental transmissions at the expense of the *cause* behind the events.

Likewise, it was hard to prevent events from becoming showcases for the stars – for *who* was to be there taking precedence over *why* everyone was there. Emphasis slipped over into the self-sacrifices the stars were making in time and money to be at the events (much, for instance, was made of Phil Collins's physical feat in performing first at the Wembley Stadium in London and then flying Concorde-speed to play in Philadelphia), and while this provides a useful model of moral behavior generally, it does not particularly publicize the problems of poverty and starvation, or give us better understanding of the political issues involved.

The question is complex in that indeed the stars' presence did attract millions of people and result in millions of dollars of donations. But the narcissistic elements were inevitably there on the part of both stars and audience. One cannot say that one gave one's money more for the stars than for the Ethiopians, but it is that very intermingling of issues, that blurring of boundaries between narcissistic desire and disinterested concern for the Other that seems postmodern.

Baudrillard has addressed this issue in his essays "In the Shadow of the Silent Majorities," and " . . . Or the End of the Social." In the first, Baudrillard notes that "Immense energy is expended in mitigating the tendentially declining rate of political investment and the absolute fragility of the social principle of reality, in maintaining this simulation of the social."[13] This notion is picked up and developed in the second essay, where Baudrillard talks of the "task of all media" as that of producing the "real, this extra real (interviews, live coverage, movies, TV-Truth, etc.)" (p. 84). For Baudrillard, the collapse of the distance between the real and its representation "puts an end to the real as referential by exalting it as a model" (p. 85). The real is "trapped in its own 'blown up' and desperate staging, in its own obscenity" (p. 85).

As always, Baudrillard seems to be onto some truth but, carried away by the force of his own rhetoric, to take it too far. Yet an occasional video, like Jimmy Barnes's "Working Class Man," would seem to fit his sense that actual political referents no longer exist: this video images so-called "working-class" men of all nationalities, taking off (presumably) from people like Springsteen and Mellencamp, but without situating the workers in any specific way. The video seems to bemoan the raw deal that working men get, yet there is no explanation for why they are so positioned. They are, then, reduced to mere signifiers, with which the video plays, and are not linked to any signifieds that would make a coherent statement.

In addition, the Live Aid and other media events, such as the "Hands Across America," suggest the effort to "simulate the social" of which Baudrillard talks. In this light, it is perhaps not surprising that "USA Africa" got the most airplay of all social issue videos, since it permits viewers at once to experience an unspecific, sentimentalized feeling of pity for the poor, together with an uplifting sense of wanting to be part of making "a better world," *and* to delight in close-up shots of their favorite stars. The video elicits the response "Oh, so-and-so's over there," or "Look at Michael Jackson who dressed up anyway," or "Isn't Bruce *fantastic*?" The song's catchy tune was important in bringing in the viewer and in making the experience pleasurable, but any specific information about poverty – even in dramatic images – was entirely absent.

The anti-apartheid video was rather different because, as in the case of the later Farm Aid Event, the politics behind the event were more

THE FIVE TYPES OF VIDEO

Artists Against Apartheid, "Sun City"

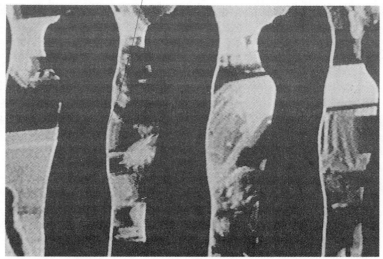

This video makes a strong anti-apartheid statement, sometimes by using graphics and posters.

specific. By the time of the "Sun-City" video, young Americans had become quite involved with anti-apartheid activities, persuading universities to give up their stocks in South African corporations (or ones investing in South Africa) through dramatic demonstrations and the erection of "shanty-houses" on campuses. Perhaps because of this, the video focused much more than did "USA Africa" on the politics involved, at least in the sense of the abuses of apartheid. The contrast between the pleasure-seeking white ruling classes and the poor, ill-housed blacks, deprived of many basic rights, is illustrated through the swift montage sequences of shots, some still photographs, interspersed among images of the rebellious, angry crowd demonstrating against apartheid. Springsteen's image is captured, but not obsessively so. In this video, the focus is deliberately on the people, not the stars.

The final theme in the socially conscious video is women's oppression and the possibilities for female solidarity. Since Chapter 5 will deal with the ideology of gender in select videos by male and female stars, with the representation of the female body and with the various kinds of "gaze" videos construct, it seems more appropriate to include the so-called "feminist" videos in that discussion.

5

Gender address and the gaze in MTV

As we have already seen, the very existence of different gazes and gender address on MTV, arising as they do from the specificities of the televisual apparatus already discussed and from the cultural codes governing America today, is part of what marks MTV as a postmodernist phenomenon. Thematically and aesthetically the videos gather up into themselves the previously distinct art modes, with their corresponding iconography, world views, myths, ideologies, specific techniques; they create out of western cultural history a kind of grab-bag to dip into at will, obliterating historical specificity. Correspondingly, the channel refuses to construct just one dominant gender address as did previous art movements and genres. It rather constructs several different kinds of gender address and modes of representing sexuality, several different positions for the spectator to take up in relation to sexual difference.

As we also saw earlier, one of the still unresolved issues in Television Studies is the degree to which film theories can apply to very different televisual apparatus.[1] Since feminist film theory has emerged from a study of the classical Hollywood film, it is important for women approaching television to consider how far that theory is relevant to the different apparatus that television is. We need particularly to explore how far theories of the "male gaze" apply to watching television: if the apparatus itself produces certain inevitable "narrative" effects, such as in film the forced identification with the (arguably male) look of the camera, we need to know how the televisual apparatus constructs the female body, and how bound by the limits of the apparatus are the images of women on TV.

MTV once again provides an ideal site for studying such questions since it carries to an extreme, as already noted, the linear flow of relatively short text-segments of different kinds inherent to the televisual apparatus. The apparatus, as a result, seems not to be gender specific in its very mode of functioning in the manner of the Hollywood film. Across its various segments TV in general, and MTV in particular, constructs a variety of gazes that indicate address to a certain kind of male or female imaginary. I will argue that there is sometimes a genderless address, and also that people of both genders undertake multiple identifications, depending on what particular video is being shown.

The plethora of gender positions on the channel is arguably linked to the heterogeneity of current sex roles and to an imaginary constructed out of a world in which all traditional categories, boundaries, and institutions are being questioned. The androgynous surface of many star images indicates the blurring of clear lines between genders characteristic of many rock videos, and which I'll address later on. All of this is linked to what I have been calling the increasing movement of rock videos into the postmodern stance, in which it is unclear what position a text is taking toward what it shows. This has implications for gender in that one often cannot tell whether a male or a female discourse dominates, and because the attitude toward sex and gender is often ambiguous. As I already mentioned, even in the category that I call "classical" because of its voyeuristic male gaze, there may be a studied self-consciousness that makes the result quite different from that in dominant commercial cinema. For instance, one finds oneself not quite knowing whether a video like John Parr's "Naughty Naughty" or Cougar Mellencamp's "Hurts So Good" is virulently sexist or merely pastiching an earlier Hollywood sexism.

In order to situate the forthcoming discussions, let me summarize briefly what feminist film theorists have argued about the cinema. According to these theories, the cinema as an apparatus at once evokes, and then attempts to resolve, original traumas around the Mother as sexual object. For the male spectator, arguably, it is at once the illicit desire for the mother and the fear of sexual difference (her castration) that the classical Hollywood film seeks to bring under control. But in so doing, it first evokes the original illicit erotic pleasure in sex with the parent.

In this theory, then, the female image on film functions rather as sign for something in the male unconscious than as anything to do with the historical female subject. The cinematic gaze is largely a *male* gaze, relying on Freud's twin mechanisms of voyeurism and fetishism as devices for the male spectator to avoid the threat that woman offers. "Woman" is then figured in three main ways: first, as ideal asexual mother, transcendent and nurturing the hero; second, as fetishized object, when the woman is given phallic attributes to lessen her threat (virtually presented as non-male rather than as "female"); or, third, woman is degraded by a voyeuristic gaze, her body set up as mere object of sexual desire, having no intrinsic meaning.[2]

Limited aspects of Lacan, as was discussed earlier, further created an analogy between the mirror and the screen; film-going was now seen as producing a regression to the Lacanian mirror phase, when the child saw a more perfect body than he in fact possessed, creating a split-subjectivity. This ideal imago is reproduced for the male spectator in the male heroes who dominate the landscape and control the narrative in the main male film genres.

Much of this work is now being modified, both in terms of paying more attention to the female spectator's position, and of realizing that gender address is far more complicated than the original model implies. Scholars have begun to work on the idea that multiple identifications take place for both male and female spectators through the narrative process, and on the notion that the pre-Oedipal as well as the Oedipal phase may be important in film spectatorship.[3]

But even so, theories have to start from the mechanisms of dominant classical Hollywood cinema that, as we've seen, rely on suturing the spectator into the image-sequence, on shot/counter-shot constructions, on the 180 degree rule, etc. If modifications to the theory are nevertheless necessary in film, this is far more true of rock videos which are embedded within the different televisual apparatus.

Partly because this apparatus manifests what Baudrillard has called the new "universe of communication," many videos do not evoke the pre-Oedipal and Oedipal configurations of the classical Hollywood film that belonged in the earlier "intimate" universe. We saw in the last chapter how Baudrillard characterizes this universe as "projective, imaginary and symbolic," as against the world of the "non-reflecting surface, an immanent surface where operations unfold – the smooth operational surface of communication." We will see the implications of this new, post-Oedipal world for the representation of women shortly, when I discuss videos by female stars. But the post-Oedipal world is, of course, manifest in the postmodernist video, and exists in some of the classical type that appear rather to play with Freudian voyeurism and fetishism than to take those gazes seriously.

Interestingly enough, the earlier Oedipal mode is evident in both the romantic and nihilist videos, although it emerges in ways rather different from that in the Hollywood film. I will begin by comparing and contrasting a romantic and nihilist video figuring male stars in order to show the ways in which rock videos take up parts of the Oedipal scenario other than the classical male gaze, and then further contrast these with a postmodernist male video. The second half of the chapter will then be devoted to a detailed analysis of the various kinds of gaze manifest in select videos by female stars. Let me again note that in providing in-depth analyses of individual videos I am rather unnaturally "stopping the 24-hour flow" for the same reasons as in Chapter 4, and with the same risks of assuming more impact than there really can be within that flow to the subject positions analyzed. The whole point about MTV is that the experience is defined by the flow of texts; in its very structure, this embodies Baudrillard's concept of "an optimalization of the play of possibilities" as against texts representing objects "of psychological sanctuary." Nevertheless, if we do "stop the flow," we can find texts that remain from the "old" universe and that do arguably rely on Oedipal processes.

The romantic and nihilist videos, then, as individual texts still work out of the Oedipal scenario. But, significantly, they are structured around aspects of that scenario rarely dealt with in the classical Hollywood film or indeed other major narrative forms that tend to rely on voyeurism and fetishism. Also, interestingly enough, each stresses an aspect of the psychic familial constellation at the opposite extreme from the other. The nihilist, heavy metal video involves adolescent male Oedipal identification with the phallus as signifier. This is a more deliberate and excessive identification than that involved in the voyeuristic gaze, and is more violent than the normal fetishistic one to which it *is* linked. Instead of seeking to find the phallus in the woman, the nihilist video seeks to appropriate the feminine to the phallus through the device of the masquerade.

Let me dwell on this a moment since the use of the masquerade here represents one kind of androgynous address in MTV videos. This form of masquerade, often accompanying the parade of virility (cf. the Brazilian Festival where men routinely dress up as women), seeks to control the feared feminine, the feared difference, by possessing it, incorporating it within the self. A Bakhtinian reading of this might argue that the adoption of female traits and clothing manifests a beneficial carnivalesque gender reversal. But while the carnival process *may* be at work for some stars (Motley Crue), something else is going on in those analyzed here. If I possess the feminine myself, it seems to say, then I no longer need to satisfy the desire for woman *outside* myself, thus avoiding the terror of so doing. Significantly, this is a very different function of the masquerade than that outlined by Mary Ann Doane when, following Lacan, she talks of women "operating a performance of femininity, a masquerade, by means of an accumulation of accessories . . . all designed to mask the absence of a lack."[4] The male masquerade uses a similar adoption of feminine accessories to different ends. That is, here the accessories do not *stand in* for lack (the male has the phallus), as with the female masquerade, but are used in an attempt to deny that there *is* any separate sexual difference that would necessitate accepting the possibility of lack. The strategy renders the feminine non-male rather than Other, as in the parallel strategy of "disguising" woman in masculine dress (viz. the many 1930s and 1940s films involving stars like Dietrich, Hepburn, Russell, and Crawford, which show women stepping into the male public sphere).

The nihilist video thus, seeks to eliminate or to master the mother, displacing desire for her into sadistic possession. The romantic video, by contrast, involves precisely the pre-Oedipal, dyadic and illusory oneness with the mother. Far from annihilating the mother, these videos, as we'll see, inscribe her gaze into their very aesthetic structure as much as the nihilist video inscribes the phallic gaze. The distinction between these gazes corresponds to that between Freud's scopophilic gaze and that of Lacan's mirror phase. While film theory often evokes the screen/mirror analogy in a general way, the differences between the Freudian, Oedipal and phallic gaze – relying on identification with the father, and the pre-Oedipal Lacanian mirror gaze – that involves merging with and separation from the mother, have not been developed. The fact that rock videos incorporate the mutual mother—child gaze at all is significant in revealing a certain opening up within popular culture of a terrain largely absent from the classical Hollywood film.

Let me briefly elaborate the differences between these two gazes within the Lacanian paradigm. As noted in Chapter 3, the mirror gaze represents the transitional phase between the pre-Oedipal and the phallic phases. It represents the start of realizing subjectivity (which is really a *split* subjectivity) as the child at once clings onto the illusory oneness with the mother in the world of the imaginary *and* begins to be aware of the mother as an object distinct from itself. The imaginary unitary self (whether a mother-self Self or a mirror-self Self) is now split into two objects: mother and self; mirror-image and self.

This process is only possible through the child's recourse to the world of the symbolic. Paradoxically, and despite Lacan's notorious scorn for object-relations psychoanalysis, the child's situation at the moment of entry into the symbolic involves an object relation (i.e. the relation to the mother or its image) that is in the process of being replaced by the word/image/representation as the device for enabling subjectivity and separation from the mother to take place.

This is perhaps most clear in the oft-discussed "fort"/"da" game occurring at approximately the same time as the mirror phase and also involved with the constitution of the unconscious.[5] There the mother is clearly replaced by the cotton reel that, as a symbol which replaces her, enables the child to conceptualize her absence and return. The child's subjectivity begins to be constituted, as we saw earlier, through the relation to a *representation* of the Other, just as in the mirror phase, subjectivity is constituted by the gaze of the Other.

The use that Lacan makes of the object relation is naturally different from that of the analysts he opposes, who are concerned with issues of bonding and attachment after the entry into language; for Lacan, the object-relation rather *ends* with the onset of the phallic phase and the entry into the symbolic. The unconscious is formed at this point, as the child enters the sphere of desire (desire being precisely that which cannot be fulfilled). From this point on, everyone in the Oedipal triangle will take his/her position from the phallus as signifier: objects are henceforth what Lacan calls "petit objects à," constituted through language and unavailable otherwise, in contrast to the "real" objects with which people supposedly interact in the object-relations schools.

The romantic and the nihilist video take their respective gazes from these two early childhood phases. The romantic video functions in the pre-symbolic dyadic terrain between the illusory merging with the mother and the phallicism that follows the mirror phase. Also important here is an even earlier pre-Oedipal phase (from birth to about six months) in which (as recent mother—infant interaction studies by Stern and Fraiberg have shown) the gaze at the mother's face provides a pleasure crucial in development.[6] In this phase, the child, still not aware of the mother's face as separate from itself, views it, like other objects, as a continuation of an undifferentiated world.

Many romantic videos manifest an unusual preoccupation with the human face, in constant close-ups and lap-dissolves that suggest regression to the moment when the mother's face represented plenitude, oneness, non-Oedipal pleasure. Since representation cannot but take place within the symbolic realm, we have an attempt to approximate the earlier imaginary and dyadic phase through technical devices that mimic the mutual mother—infant gaze.

Before looking at Paul Young's successful "Every Time You Go Away" as an example of this kind of gaze, let me make a comment about gender as it relates to the pre-symbolic. In pre-dating the construction of sexual identity through the acquisition of sentence structure and the grammatical "he"/"she" identifications, the pre-symbolic phase represents a libidinal, genderless reaching out in all directions. It thus differs markedly from the later phallic phase, which is firmly rooted in socially constructed sex difference identifications. Romantic videos are interesting precisely because of a certain bi-sexuality, which must be distinguished from the androgyny of the nihilist video.

ROCKING AROUND THE CLOCK

By bi-sexuality, I mean that both genders, whether as performers or as spectators, position themselves (and are positioned) similarly. The basic structure is the mother—infant dyad, and in the pre-symbolic phase the biological sex of the child (the mark that will become defining once the child enters the symbolic) does not matter. Whether male or female, the child experiences merging, illusory oneness with the mother; and while from the mother's position the sex of the child may make a superficial social difference, in terms of the *structure* of her relationship to the child it is not significant.

Romantic videos thus position both the male and the female spectator in what has traditionally been the "feminine" (i.e. passive) position. Whether the performer is male or female, and whether a male or female is being addressed as the lost object, makes little difference. It is the narrative situation of merging, loss, and separation that governs identification rather than the gender-based gaze—image dichotomies of the nihilist and classical types.

Nevertheless, it is significant that recently more male stars have been creating romantic songs with corresponding videos. Earlier, as noted in Chapter 4, the romantic video tended to be the province of female stars like Cyndi Lauper ("Time After Time"), Stevie Nicks ("If Anyone Falls in Love"), Heart ("What About Love"), etc. The male star in such videos, like Lionel Ritchie in "Hello," used to be an exception. But in 1983-4 the type had been virtually taken over by the male star and is often top of the countdown. Besides Phil Collins's "One More Night," Foreigner's "I Want to Know What Love Is," and Paul Young's "Every Time You Go Away," already mentioned as in the top slot for several weeks, there was Bob Dylan's "Tight Connection to My Heart," Simple Minds' "Don't You Forget About Me," Julian Lennon's "Much Too Late," Paul McCartney's "No More Lonely Nights." It is less common to find current female stars singing about loss and separation, although about the time that she was pregnant, Pat Benatar did make a sentimental, romantic video, "We Belong," complete with angelic children in a church-like choir and artificial nature setting. (Eurythmics' 1985 "There Must Be an Angel" video is possibly a parody of the Benatar tape, set, as it is, in some kind of Grecian heaven where children flit around with deliberately artificial-looking wings.)[7]

In focusing on the desire for merging with the loved one and on the lost (mother) object, videos elicit regression to the mirror phase, i.e. to beginning awareness of subjectivity through the need to separate from the mother. At this point, castration and Oedipal rivalry are not issues, there being merely a wish to return to the period of illusory oneness. Significantly, the female figure, as lost object, is rarely set up as voyeuristic object of the male gaze (The Cars' "Why Can't I have You?" and the Eurythmics' "Here Comes the Rain Again" are rare exceptions to this). She is rather imaged with longing and tenderness (as in Foreigner's "I Want To Know What Love Is"), or simply not imaged at all, her being merely conjured up by the song words and the hero's longing (as in Collins's "One More Night").

Like the infant in the Stern and Fraiberg studies already mentioned, the MTV spectator is silent listener/gazer in a one-way process, relying on the close-ups of the performer's face and on the tone/pitch/rhythm of the music for stimulation. Unlike the baby, the MTV spectator can decode the verbal information of the lyric, but in practice rarely has time to do so, taken up as she/he is by the movement of the visuals and the flow of the music. What we have is a structure of interaction with the image not unlike that of the baby vis-à-vis the mother's face.

Before going on to demonstrate this more clearly by analyzing Paul Young's "Every Time You Go Away," let me clarify what I am trying to argue here. I am not denying that the male appeal to the lost mother object can be seen as merely a reassertion of the traditional patriarchal essentializing of woman as Ideal Mother; what I am trying to argue is that, given that MTV is working within the patriarchal symbolic, it is interesting to find emphasis on a basically *genderless* yearning for the mother (i.e. that place can now be occupied by *either* sex, whereas in traditional patriarchal conventions it is denied the girl – she is to long for the *father*). A second interesting point is that Young, as protagonist in the video, does *not* remain locked into the child position but is also seen to occupy the nurturing *female* position. It is precisely the multiple identifications in the narrative on the part of both protagonist and diegetic spectators that I find interesting. It is true that the mother is literally relegated to absence, but the video so inscribes her gaze as arguably to make itself more powerfully experienced than in the literal images (as in Lauper's "Time After Time," discussed later on) of other videos.

ROCKING AROUND THE CLOCK

Part of the much touted "British Invasion," Paul Young comes out of 1960s soul music, and his performance style was inspired by studying videos of 1960s soul singers like James Brown. He is quoted in a recent *New York Times* article as being as obsessed with performers as with singers, but not necessarily finding stars who combine both aspects in ways he admires. "Some of the best performers, like Mick Jagger and Adam Ant," he notes, "aren't my favorite vocalists. As a singer I admire Sam Cooke the most of all. His diction is incredible and, although I haven't seen a video, the presence that comes off his records is enough."[8]

The performance aspect of "Every Time You Go Away" betrays Young's enthusiasm for Jagger, at least. Rarely still for a moment, he is seen leaping about the stage, bandying the microphone pole like a lance, or in one shot rolling on the floor toward the outstretched arms of his fans. At one point, he takes off his shirt and sends it flying into the crowd; other close-up shots show him reaching toward the outstretched arms and hands of his fans.

This video represents an extraordinarily sensitive, virtually poetic interweaving of musical sounds, Young's voice, the words of Daryl Hall's ballad and the visual images. The overall effect is of sailing or floating – an effect produced by the device of multiple dissolves and superimpositions as the dominant mode of moving from one image to the next. While there are obviously some straight cuts, dissolves predominate; often the superimposition happens on movement either of the camera itself or of Young on stage. Meanwhile, the musical composition and instrumentation convey the same floating effect in the contrapuntal use of Young's flowing voice rising up against the soft, continuous drums, cymbals, and electric sitar (an instrument that Stephen Holden notes has been little used since the late 1960s).[9] The instrumentation is sufficiently complex and unusual to carry the repetition of the main theme lines, "Every time you go away/ You take a little piece of me with you," which always come as a relief after the preceding build up to "Can't you see/ We got everything," at which time the drums and cymbals get louder and more insistent, receding then down to the quieter, melodious tune of "Every time. . . ."

The visuals basically consist of intercutting between two sets of footage: there is footage from one or more live performances intercut with an abstract studio set, consisting of a floor with wavy lines

98

"Joy": taken from a mother—infant interaction study, this image shows the baby's ecstatic response to its mother's presence. Images from Young's video (easily identified) mimic this look but we were refused permission to reprint them.

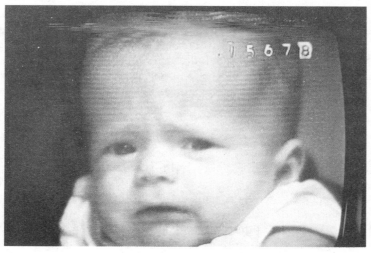

"Loss": taken from the same study, this image shows the baby expressing loss and anxiety at its mother's absence. Images from the Young video show a forlorn longing close to this look, but again we were refused permission to reprint them here.

on it, either to represent water or the lines on a section of an old tree trunk (but nature anyway). Young stands on this set, sometimes half enmeshed in a fishing net (the sea idea again), with fishing lamps behind him; sometimes his face in close-up is covered by water-like lines or we see these lines in back of the frame, creating a misty, tearful effect.

The stage shots focus heavily on Young's interaction with his fans. In an early shot, repeated later on, Young receives flowers from a fan; rarely is there a shot of him on stage that does not include the fans' arms in front or rear of the frame, or show them packed into the huge auditorium. He is tender and responsive to them, the image usually showing his back bending over the fans in a nurturing, loving fashion, leaning toward them and stretching out his hands. Occasionally we have close-ups of the fans' faces, when we are able to see their rapt, adoring expression; their gaze is fixed unwaveringly on him and on his every movement and their arms reach out to touch him in response to his gesture. In one shot, Young literally runs across the wide stage and rolls down on the floor among the delirious, caressing fans.

These images seem to evoke being held in loving embrace, being nurtured and cared for, as the mother cares for her infant. The fans love Young and he in turn loves them, and the video shows ecstatic expressions on everyone's part during their interaction. Meanwhile, the images intercut from the studio set focus more on loss and separation – on, that is, the mother's absence. Here the often extreme close-ups of Young's face show a forlorn, lost look such as the infant might have on discovering the mother's departure. The contrast between fulfillment and loss is stressed by the cutting: for instance, after an exuberant image of Young rolling on the floor with the fans (no words on the track), we cut to an extreme close-up of Young's forlorn face as, with eyes closed, he lip-synches the lines "Go on and go free/Baby you're too close to see" into the microphone (watery-lines in back of the image suggest tears). Another similar contrast takes place a little earlier in the video, where we go from an image of Young with his rapt fans, and another of him bending over the fans, to a shot of him in the studio set, caught behind the fishing net as he sings the lines "You take a piece of me with you."

Later on, the exuberance of a simulated plenitude with his fans on stage is intercut in rapid succession with the net image (obviously signifying emotional entrapment). These net shots are usually taken from a high angle, suggesting the hero's smallness and vulnerability, while the stage shots show him often in the foreground, looming large against the fans.

Towards the end of the video, we get a delirious, merged kind of sensation deliberately created through the play with the image. Young is on stage, when suddenly the image begins to turn around, dissolving to a bird's eye view of him on the studio set, still turning around, while a larger image of him appears on the right of the frame. This dissolves to a fast-moving camera sailing up to Young's figure in wide-angle in the center of the set, then to a very high angle of him small in frame, and onto his face in close-up superimposed on him performing as he sings "You think I don't care/But baby I'm with you everywhere." This leads into the final moments of the video in which we see images of Young reaching out to his fans, of the three-man chorus at the rear of the stage (who have been imaged from time to time, gesturing the "Me"/"You" positions in the song line "You take a piece of me with you"), the whole ending with a close-up of Young's face immersed in the watery-lines as his voice sails above the chorus singing the lyric against the instruments.

The total effect of this video is to leave the spectator with a pleasurable mixture of loss and fulfillment. Whether male or female, we identify with Young and his desire to merge with the lost mother object; we have vicarious gratification in the images of Young with his fans, when the ecstasy of momentary merging spills over to the viewer through the technical devices mentioned. Both the infant girl and boy long equally to merge with the mother, so that Young's being male does not prevent female identification with his urge. In fact, in the stage shots, he takes on the symbolic role of the mother, interchanging this with his role as the abandoned child in the studio images. The viewer thus plays out both positions along with the protagonist, getting a series of vicarious gratifications through so doing.

In contrast to this largely pre-Oedipal gaze in the romantic video, the nihilist type relies on the aggressive phallic gaze already referred to. This does not necessarily mean, however, that the address is exclusively to the heterosexual male, as it basically is in the classical category that derives from the voyeuristic gaze of the Hollywood film. A very complicated set of discourses structures the nihilist, heavy metal video, and the address is therefore also complicated — including homo-eroticism and female masochism in its appeal. Whereas the romantic video is structured around humanist notions of bonding and attachment, the nihilist one, in accord with its originally rebellious if often nihilist stance, deplores humanist solutions and speaks violence and destruction without compunction.

This address to violence appeals largely to young males, as is particularly evident in live performances and other shows involving live audiences. (At a recent heavy metal laser show in New York, for instance, the audience consisted almost entirely of groups of young men together. The few women there were safely in the company of two or more men. Deborah Frost in a recent *Village Voice* article did, however, note that more and more women were to be seen at heavy metal live performance shows, suggesting a shifting trend.[10]) But the androgynous aspects of the address, most evident in the performance video, complicate things. The address creates an energetic erotic appeal that is often violent and sadistic, and that consists in a split between a "feminized" outward appearance and "masculine" aggressive behavior. Significantly, most androgynous singers of this type are male (e.g. Duran Duran, Billy Idol, Motley Crue). Eurythmics' Annie Lennox is an exception, but even she belongs in a second, softer androgynous group in which I would put David Bowie, Michael Jackson, and Boy George. These are not so concerned to stress the masculine that lies beneath the feminized veneer, and are less obviously erotic.

In the main type of nihilist video that retains the stage setting, and often figures heavy metal or new wave groups, the male body is deliberately set up as object of desire: zoom shots pick up male crotches and bare chests in an erotic manner and instruments are presented as unabashed phallic props. The camera focuses aggressively on the performers' bodies as they stand front-stage, fans' arms stretching out toward them, often cutting in and isolating, deliberately garishly (effects made more strident by wide-angle lenses), crotches, buttocks, widespread legs. There are some facial close-ups and the performers still provide a centering focus for the incoherent images, but instead of evoking the gentle, mutual mother—infant interaction of the romantic video, these videos rather adopt a challenging, aggressive stance toward the fans and spectators. The camera focuses on the sexual/genital areas – the body rather than the face – and on the often outlandish, extraordinary costumes of the stars and band members. The camera often sways with the male bodies, and figures are filmed in slow motion, often jumping in the air, spread-eagled, as in Van Halen's "Jump." The aim is clearly to shock and to violate accepted social norms.

The female form is often simply absent from this type of nihilist video but, if present, she is usually also dressed in tight leather dress, high heels, sporting long, spiked hair. The iconography, like that of the males, suggests bondage and sadistic sexuality. Let me demonstrate some of these characteristics by looking at two nihilist style videos of rather different casts.

First, Billy Idol's "Rebel Yell," which was near the top of the MTV Countdown in Fall 1984. Very much in the tradition of American, as against British punk, Idol has fostered an image of snarling meanness, not unlike that of Sid Vicious of the British Sex Pistols but without Vicious's political base.[11] Idol's main stance is that of an angry, formless rebelliousness; his main aim, Nietzschean style, is to transvalue dominant ideology and to shock the bourgeoisie. Instead of kindness and helpfulness, he fosters hate, motiveless rage; instead of nurturing, he represents attack and hurt.

On first viewing, "Rebel Yell" appears to be one long, continuous scream; visuals, the musical sounds and rhythms, the song-words and Idol's use of his body, all conspire to construct an embattled spectator, on the receiving end of a boxing glove. The video remains for its entire length within the confines of the stage on which it is set, and the mise-en-scène is very deliberately designed to evoke the black, angry tone of the song. There is a heavy reliance on lighting devices familiar from German Expressionism and film noir; for instance, the spot-lights create pyramid-shaped panels of light, keeping to a blue and red color scheme, that are shed over the individual performers, isolating them in their own color-bound sphere. The stage is basically lurid and shrouded in smokiness much of the time. Its edges cannot therefore be seen so that one has the sense of an endless, timeless space that is No Place. In this murky space, the band members are variously highlighted as noted, but the lighting of course favors Idol. Usually, it is back-lighting, familiar from German Expressionism, that illuminates his short, punk-style blonde hair standing straight up. The lead guitarist, dressed in deliberate contrast to Idol in long leather jacket and pants, and sporting longer black hair, is often lit with a triangular slice of blue or red light that frames him behind Idol, the smoky swirls in the light providing a surreal effect. When we cut, twice, to the female pianist, scantily dressed in red, her blonde hair is also back-lit, giving a similar eerie effect. There are few long shots of the stage from the fans' point of view, as was common in the Young video, no corresponding long shots of the auditorium containing the fans either, and no studio shots away from the stage to provide an extended narrative context. Rather, the camera remains glued to Idol's face and body, or to those of his lead guitarist, with infrequent shots of the other band members or of the fans' faces at the edge of the stage. Often, the frame shows a rear shot of the fans' black-gloved hands and shadowed arms, mimicking Idol's angry fist/arm gesture, with Idol's figure facing the camera in medium close-up.

The result of this close-in camera is claustrophobic: the spectator simply cannot get away from the anger that is being directed often specifically at him/her. For instance, in one section, when Idol is not singing, the drums beat out a regular series of notes, and Idol punches directly at the camera with his lethal-looking, spiked, leather gloves and wide wrist band. He wields this "weapon" throughout, but usually directs it in medium shot at the fans, attacking and battling with them.

The claustrophobic effect is mitigated somewhat by the shifts in the mood and the rhythm that follow the phases of the song's moods. While these are within a narrow range, the changes do provide the spectator with a breathing space (and presumably permit Idol's own vocal chords a slight rest!). The video opens energetically and loudly with Idol screaming in his husky, throaty voice the main theme-lines of the song, oft-repeated: "In the midnight hour/ She cried more, more, more/ With a rebel yell/ She cried more, more, more." This is repeated several times, while the camera cuts between close-ups of Idol's face and spiked, gloved hand grasping the mike, and medium close-ups of his guitarists on either side of him. Idol here points his finger directly at the camera, punctuating

104

his deliberately articulated "More, more, more" with stabs at the viewer and the fans, his body meanwhile also moving up and down in time with the heavy, steady bang of drums and guitars. The shots of the lead guitarist focus on his guitar as a phallic prop, his side-angled body shot at crotch-level emphasizing the phallicism.

A quieter moment emerges with the words "She once said I'm bad/She's mean, she's bad," and the camera now closes in on Idol's face in wide-angle lens, as if for a confession. The tone remains quieter as he goes on to express his disgust at the woman's leaving, with "What set you free/I brought you to be with me, babe," rising in volume as he angrily screams his need: "I need you here by me/ Because [loudest now] in the midnight hour/She cried more, more, more/With a rebel yell/More, more, more."

This is followed by focus on the lead guitarist in front frame, very close-in to the fans, letting his guitar scream and whine as he brandishes it like a sword/phallus. Idol meanwhile is now positioned in rear of the frame, so that his muscular, bare-chested body with leather jacket open, legs astride in their leather pants and boots, is deliberately silhouetted. The guitarist then stops, Idol comes to front frame, and with snarls and grimaces he punches at the camera, timing his punches to the loud, steady drum beat. The drummer's image is intercut with Idol's a few times, and then with the guitarist when he enters the musical stream again.

The rhythm then slows, and Idol, at his most vulnerable in the entire video, sidles head down along the front row of fans and admits "I'd walk the wall with you babe/Then thousand miles with you babe/I'd dry your tears, babe/A million times for you, you, you/I'd sell my soul, soul, soul/For money to burn/For you, you, you." Here Idol acts more gently toward the fans, looking down at them, still pointing but less aggressively. The shot is longer than previous ones, the intercutting now ceasing temporarily.

But gradually, he works up to his anger again, screaming "I'd give you all because/In the midnight hour . . . " and so on, repeatedly, until the video ends on the same, loud, angry note with which it started. The intercutting between Idol and his guitarists resumes, and the camera angles move lower even than before, highlighting the crotches of both Idol and the guitarist as they stand astride in front of the now wildly waving and moving fans.

ROCKING AROUND THE CLOCK

This video, like other similar nihilist ones of its type, manifests the opposite psychic familial constellation to the romantic one by Paul Young. Instead of mimicking the mother—infant interaction as the moment of loss and separation, "Rebel Yell" voices the sadistic desire to master and possess the mother, to hear her cry "More, more, more." The hero will do anything for her if only she will succumb to him and worship his phallus as much as he does himself.

Iconographically, the video sets up Idol and his friends as signifiers for the phallus. Idol's carefully chosen name reinforces his self-fetishization; he takes his own body as a representation of what he wants to have, namely the phallus. And to *have* the phallus, it is necessary for the woman to *be* the phallus for him — hence the hero's need of her.

The self-conscious androgyny of a nihilist video like this one by Billy Idol, where we have images similar to those increasingly adopted by adult popular culture and by fashion and advertising, has far different sources and implications than the non-Oedipal, genderless gaze of the romantic video. There is an attempt to construct sexuality as undifferentiated, in opposition to the Hollywood construction of sexuality so as to emphasize difference; but while the new construction seems to attempt a transcendence of sex difference, does it really accomplish this?

One could rather argue that a video like "Rebel Yell" actually addresses both male and female desires as constructed within patriarchy — namely the male sadistic desire, the corresponding female masochistic one. In this reading, the female fans predominating in Idol's video signify female identification with the object of Idol's sadism, desiring to be desired, desiring also perhaps to be mastered. (It is significant that while the object of the protagonist's rage within the diegesis is not imaged, her "double" *is* represented in the bodies of the female fans that Idol addresses extra-diegetically.)

While the ambiguity in the sexual address in a nihilist video like this one typifies postmodernism, it seems likely that the androgynous address of many heavy metal videos reflects a restructuring of sexual difference so as to appropriate the feminine rather than a totally new sexual paradigm. However, it is possible that such restructurings are preparing for a new paradigm.

The hated female object *is* imaged in Idol's recent "White Wedding," where the nihilism structures the entire narrative, and where

106

the address seems unambiguously male. A desecration of the whole concept of "holy matrimony," the video turns marriage into an expressionist-style horror-show – a gothic funeral rather than an idyllic romantic ritual. Many of the assorted onlookers are dressed in black leather outfits, with chains, while the bridesmaid wears a black funeral veil. The bride's middle-class-looking parents are ridiculous in the "church" setting that looks like something out of Lang's *Metropolis*. The climax to the ceremony comes when Idol grabs the bride's hand, and, as he sings "It's a nice day to start again," rips the bride's finger with his barbed-wire ring. After a series of close-ups of the bride's screaming face, in slow motion, the assembly salutes the couple, Nazi-style. Bourgeois codes are symbolically finally violated as Idol smashes through a stained-glass window in a rain of glass shards. The bride is contrasted with three sinister looking blonde women in shiny black leather suits who dance behind Idol as they appropriate the "altar" after the bride has gone. The nihilist "message" is spelled out in the final scene, which has the bride dancing headily in a typical bourgeois kitchen, as all the normal household accoutrements explode; Idol, leering into the frame (in wide-angle lens), meanwhile sings, "There is nothing safe in this world/There is nothing pure in this world/There is nothing sure in this world/There is nothing left in this world." As if to underscore the point, the last image shows the "bride" (is she now a corpse?) covered in her white veil, like a mannequin, while Idol and his three black-leathered women dance in the front of the frame.

The second nihilist video that I'll discuss, Scorpion's "Rock You Like a Hurricane," also includes female representations and has a rather different sexual address. Made by a West German group, "Rock You Like a Hurricane" has a more complex heavy metal score than that in Idol's video. Consisting likewise of a large drum/cymbal unit and electric guitars, the instrumentation is more creative and imaginative and the voice is used contrapuntally in interesting ways. While loud and unmelodious in the manner of heavy metal, "Rock You" nevertheless manages not to overwhelm with relatively meaningless screaming sounds as in the Idol video. There is actually an inventive musical interlude half-way through the video where the instruments take over as against merely accompanying the voice as they do much of the time.

ROCKING AROUND THE CLOCK

In contrast to the two previous videos, there is a dramatic narrative situation here but it still permits the performance element to remain. Paradoxically, the precise narrative situation (which is anyway unclear) is less important than the interconnection between sounds and visuals. Both music and visuals take off from the idea of a hurricane and the resulting "rocking" (the whole perhaps a pun on rock music itself); the musical score mimics storm sounds, and the line of the music sweeps up and down like wind roaring. Meanwhile, the camera work duplicates the notion of "rocking" already present, consisting of very rapid cutting of single shots (sometimes almost too fast to capture in still frame), of extremely low and wide angle shots, and of sweeping movements around and along the bars of the cage in which the performers are trapped. The shots are mainly close-ups of the bodies of the performers and, sometimes, the women, creating a claustrophobic effect similar to that in Idol's video; but here there are a few extreme long shots, showing a high-angle view down on the entire cage, the women ranged around, and the white leaders (or whatever) in the rear.

The mise-en-scène is rather similar to that in the Idol video although, as noted, it does have a narrative dimension. The men are in some alien, science fiction otherwhere; they seem to be trapped first in long tubes and then (within the tubes? it is not clear) inside a cage. This cage "rocks," its walls moving in and out under the pressure of hordes of women locked outside the cage and evidently trying to reach the men within. The performers (especially the guitarists and the star singer) also rock their own bodies while they play or sing, so that at times the entire image is on the move. The atmosphere is murky, hazy, and generally unclear. There is a similar expressionist/noir mood to everything, here mixed with a sense of outerspace or of some other planet.

I am particularly interested in the representation of the women in this video since the situation is clearly an Oedipal one. To begin with, the men are subject to the Law of the Father, represented by the sinister, white-robed men, without proper faces, who stand around an alarming fire for which the men may be destined. On one level, there is a battle for power going on between the captives and these rulers.

But second, the men are evidently being seduced by the women in the community, whose situation vis-à-vis the rulers is unclear. The first woman we see, in close-up and attempting to seduce the hero, is dressed in skimpy sequined clothes (is she the Queen, wife of a ruler?) and has a mask over her eyes. But all the rest of the women are far more poorly dressed, although their eyes are still covered now by black make-up that looks like a blindfold. They have on primitive tops and mini-skirts and wear long black gloves which appear like snakes reaching through the bars to grasp the men.

The men seem to be in an impossible Oedipal situation, caught between the seductive mother and the castrating father. The women catch one of the guitarists through the bars and maul his head about before letting him go. In another shot towards the end, we see one of the women breaking through the bars of the cage and looming up, slow motion, toward the hero. The women are associated with fearsome imagery, since in the following shot we see them walk toward the camera up some mist-laden, tree-lined path, passing as they do so the agonized faces of men, crossed by thorns and sticks, who are bound in the woods. Finally, as the video ends, the men appear to have freed themselves, although they only have the same horrifying path to run along.

In contrast to the Idol video, this one embodies a more classical Oedipal scenario showing fear of the seductive mother. But interestingly, the mother is blinded, unable to see, and the fathers do not seem to have normal eyes either. The heroes thus emerge as both the ones who can see and who are virile despite their captivity. Shots again focus on the male crotches and guitarists use their instruments as phallic props as in the Idol video. Somehow, the heroes transcend their potentially passive "captive" situation through their sheer energy and inherent virility, evidently escaping the death that seemed to await them.

Even more than the Idol video, "Rock You" seems to close out any possible position for the female spectator other than identifying with woman as sign for something in the male unconscious. The male spectator may vicariously enjoy the representation of desiring women, but the female desire is merely symbolic. The women are more like automatons than living flesh, their gestures mechanical, perhaps ordered. They seem to lack any desire of their own, despite their narrative situation as trying to get into the cage. Once again, although via very different means, the video establishes an explicitly phallic gaze deriving from the Oedipal rather than the pre-Oedipal phase.

The second type of Oedipal gaze, that is the explicitly voyeuristic one, I have relegated to a separate category, the classical. This type lacks many of the qualities of the nihilist video, such as the blurring of genres, the sense of an alien, unstable world, the nihilism and androgynous address, etc. The type stays closer to the narrative style of the classical Hollywood film, although most do not adhere to classical cutting codes, eye-line matches, 30 degree rule and so on. In addition, the self-consciousness about what is being shown does position the videos in a different relation to the voyeuristic gaze.

Good examples of this type are Rod Stewart's "Infatuation" or the more recent John Parr's "Naughty Naughty." The first is "classical" in the sense of setting up a typical narrative situation of a young man spying on the beautiful faithless femme fatale being pursued by an older man, probably a gangster. Where the video differs from film noir is in its deliberate foregrounding of the hero's voyeurism by having him set up his camera in front of the window where the woman undresses. We have shots of him photographing her through the slots in the blind, the frame including both his body (front frame) and hers across the way, moving seductively to the music. We get close-up stills of the photos taken, and in one shot the hero dances in front of a huge blow-up of the woman in her skimpy bikini. Obsessed with her, he follows her around, constantly spying upon her through doors, windows, and from balconies.

A silent, distant figure, often in swimsuit and dark glasses, the woman merely stands in for something in the male unconscious, reflecting the theories that feminist film critics have developed in relation to the Hollywood film. Nevertheless, as noted there is a new self-consciousness about these voyeuristic videos that positions them differently from the unselfconscious classical Hollywood film. Stewart's words and gestures suggest rather a bored "déjà vu" than real anger that the woman is faithless and takes new lovers. "Oh, no, not again/It hurts so good, I don't understand," he says, repeatedly. There is a comic juxtaposition of the hero with his cat gazing into, and desiring, the goldfish in the bowl, suggesting an identification between the hero's and the cat's gaze. The video is lively, semi-comic and music and visuals keep up a fast, pleasing rhythm.

Parr's "Naughty Naughty" is in many ways more obnoxious because of the hero's arrogant, sneering attitude both in general and specifically in relation to women. The only thing that slightly lessens the video's strident sexism is, again, its apparent self-consciousness about the issues it treats. It opens with an arrogant hero giving up his job working on fancy cars because the boss catches him fondling the car enviously. The hero screeches out of the garage in his sports car, soon picking up a girl, whom he eyes possessively and then tries to seduce. Refusing to "be a girl like that" she jumps out of the car, throwing her necklace after it. The video next shows the hero happily in the midst of a cluster of sexy girls, all hungrily devouring his body. After this, he is once again on the road. The first girl has now evidently regretted her rejection of the hero, and allows herself to be picked up once again.

The video ends with them sailing off together in the car, the hero having his cake and eating it too! A far more deliberate and humorous parody of objectifying the female body is David Lee Roth's successful "California Girls." While I appreciate the parody of seaside postcard humor in this video, and the fact that it mocks tourists as much as anything else, the way the female body is (ab)used is disturbing. The video is built on the concept of voyeurism, which it laughs at without critiquing. The female bodies are set up as silent, statuesque entities for the camera and the tour guide to handle and gaze at without compunction.

Robert Palmer's "Addicted to Love" has a similar set of impassive female bodies, this time clothed like identical store-window mannequins in tight black mini-dresses: They surround Palmer as his musical accompanists and the camera freely plays with their eyes, heavily lipsticked mouths, and nude legs, rendering them passive objects of desire. The same is true of Palmer's recent "I Didn't Mean to Turn You On," which has this time *two* sets of women dressed identically, with whose sexy bodies the camera likewise plays, while the hero in the center has them all to himself!

The line of impassive female forms recalls a similar parade of the female body in the Romantics' "Talking in Your Sleep," where the hero walks through the lines of sleeping women who stand passively in their various, often sexy, nightdresses, and caresses their bodies with his flashlight, and sometimes with his lips. He is celebrating the fact that he has access to his lover's unconscious since she cannot keep her secrets from him because she talks in her sleep. We have here the ultimate voyeuristic fantasy of total male (in)sight into the female, with the resulting control and possession. "You tell me that you want me/You tell me that you need me/You tell me that you love me," he sings. A little later, he notes that "Don't you know you're sleeping/In a spot light" and the visuals show the hero scanning the woman's legs with his torch, revealing black stockings, suspenders, and the classic porn-style corset. This is immediately followed by a shot of the hero putting the finishing touches to the make-up on a large Marilyn Monroe poster, the image responding with seductive lip movements. The idea evidently is that the woman is to be a seductive little girl type, like Monroe. And indeed, many of the sleeping, passive figures are holding teddy bears!

The imagery here clearly looks back, somewhat nostalgically, to the 1950s, perhaps in an unconscious wish to return woman to that (mythical) passive position; a recent video by the Fabulous Thunderbirds, "Tuff Enuff," on the other hand, rather attempts to recuperate the image of the tough new "working woman" that is interestingly combined with the even more recent athletic female look. The deliberately spare, schematic set (it has a vaguely futurist look) suggests both a jungle-gym and a construction site; and indeed, the women who soon appear are dressed so as to connote both construction-site workers (they have on hard-hats) and women working out in the gym (sneakers, sweat-shirts, and shorts). But it turns out that the choreography intends to co-opt both suggestions, and return the women to the place (and status) of sex-objects. The women's movements, that is, increasingly move from those appropriate to construction work to those of the aerobics class, to those of the erotic dancer or the stripper. The band members arrive at the site on their phallic motorbikes and proceed to respond to the women's seductive movements. The climax (sexual, narrative) is achieved when the protagonist discovers the really erotic heroine, who explicitly merges the traditional erotic female with the new tough look as she swaggers in

John Cougar Mellencamp, "Hurts So Good"

Cougar Mellencamp's video plays with the recent interest in sado-masochistic imagery.

The play with voyeurism is evident in having the men face the camera and turn away from th women on stage in rear frame.

wearing high heels, fancy shorts, and a low-cut blouse, parading long, curly hair.

The choreography situates the originally distinct types of female bodies and movements along a similar signifying chain; women's bodies are made to signify sexuality no matter in what context they are being used. The video manages in this way to trivialize, or even negate, women's newly won efforts for entrance into traditionally masculine work spheres and their equally new interest in hitherto "male" athletics.

A less patronizing, more playful treatment of the female body, in a different mode, is John Cougar Mellencamp's recent "Hurts So Good." This video addresses recent interest in sado-masochism on the part of both young men and women; it is set in some kind of club, where a gang of macho-style motorbike men are gathered to watch two dancing women, dressed (classic porn style) in black skin-tight leotards, fishnet stockings, high-heeled shoes, and covered in chains and neck chokers. In a sense it is all rather harmless and unerotic. The video even plays with the classical voyeurism it first seems to endorse, since in one shot the men face the camera, looking *away from* the women dancing on the stage. But the video symbolizes the open address to sado-masochistic fantasies with women in the "victim" position.

A similar play with sado-masochistic imagery is evident in Prince's "1999." The futurist suggestion is ironic in that the imagery in fact looks back to Nazi sexual iconography, especially in the cut-aways from Prince, in his long black leather coat reminiscent of Nazism, to two blonde young women accompanists in short leather outfits and black military caps. Prince's aggressive, phallic stance is more show than meant seriously, however, and again the video manifests a kind of postmodernist play with this well-worn iconography, confusing the spectator as to an appropriate response.

In these more brutal videos, it seems that the sadistic component has taken precedence over the merely voyeuristic and fetishistic one of most videos in this category. While sadism is obviously involved in the latter drives, it is content to express itself through the gaze. Sadism proper, on the other hand, demands release on an object — it demands action. No longer prepared to work through the relationship to the mother via castration anxiety released in abusive visual objectification, it now seeks rather to displace the feared violence to the phallus onto fantasies of violence perpetrated on the female form. This prevalence of sexually violent and graphic material on videos has recently caught the public attention (cf. article by Kandy Stroud in *Newsweek,* May 6 1985), and the Parents' Music Resources Center (PMRC) are presently demanding that warnings be printed on records and cassettes with sexually explicit lyrics and images. (A recent ad by such a group ironically focused not on one of these sexist, sadistic videos by male stars but on Madonna's (possibly ironic but at any rate postmodernist) "Like a Virgin." The ad shows a little girl playing with a doll on a bed and humming "Just like a vi-i-i-r-gin." The voice then offers a warning about such songs.) I am not sure that censorship is desirable, viable or necessary, [12] particularly in the light of the self-parody of many of the videos objected to, but the fact that young teenagers who may not grasp the parody aspects are getting their first conception of an adult female identity through such videos is of concern.

Let me now turn to the representation of the female body and the gender address in videos figuring female stars. First, a word about the frequency of such videos and their cycling across the 24-hour flow, since these aspects are important for understanding the dominating kind of gender address on MTV. Both issues are further linked to the over-arching commercial framework of MTV in that only those female representations considered the most marketable are frequently cycled: and what is most marketable is obviously connected to dominant ideology, to the social imaginary discussed in Chapter 4 and to the organization of the symbolic order around the phallus as signifier.

According to a recent quantifying study of MTV, videos featuring white males take up 83 per cent of the 24-hour flow.[13] Only 11 per cent of MTV videos have central figures who are female (incidentally, the figure is even lower for blacks), and women are typically, like blacks, rarely important enough to be part of the foreground. Brown and Campbell assert that "white women are often shown in passive and solitary activity or are shown trying to gain the attention of a man who ignores them" (p. 104). Among those 11 per cent, the number of videos by women that *are* frequently cycled fall into the first type mentioned, namely those where the position is ambiguous, where what we might call a postmodern feminist stance is evident.

I will discuss what I mean by this "postmodern feminist" stance in a moment, but I want first to note the other kinds of female representations that do appear on the channel, if only rarely, and that I will by analyzing. There are, first, videos in the "socially conscious" category that make the kind of statement one could call "feminist" (e.g. Pat Benatar's "Love is a Battlefield" or her more recent "Sex As a Weapon," or Donna Summer's "She Works Hard for the Money"); these have quite conventional narratives, although they do not adhere strictly to Hollywood codes. Second, there are occasional videos that appear to comment upon the objectifying male gaze (as does arguably Tina Turner's "Private Dancer"), or that deconstruct an established American icon, as in Julie Brown's "The Homecoming Queen's Got a Gun." In these cases the visual strategies creatively embody the deconstructive aims. And finally, some videos attempt to set up a different gaze altogether, or to address some (possible) female gaze, as arguably happens in the recent Aretha Franklin/Annie Lennox "Sisters Are Doin' It For Themselves." Except for Benatar's "Love is a Battlefield," these videos only remained in circulation for a short period of time and then not at a high density rate.

It is important that the channel's format of short, four-minute texts does permit gaps through which a variety of enunciative positions are made available. I am then able to "stop the flow," as it were, in order to concentrate on constructions of the female body other than the prevailing "postmodern feminist" or various "male gaze" constructions. But this is with full awareness that these isolated moments in fact are overridden by the plethora of texts presenting other positions. The various possibilities for "seeing otherwise" in these different figurations of the female body are worth exploring as part of understanding what popular culture *can* do; but the ordinary MTV spectator will in fact get little opportunity for this kind of "seeing." For such female images do not fit into the prevailing desire for the rich sensation of glossy surfaces, bright colours, rapid action, or for the parade of bodies in contemporary clothing that the dominant videos offer.

Let me begin with a video, "Material Girl," featuring Madonna, the female star who perhaps more than any other embodies the new postmodern feminist heroine in her odd combination of seductiveness and a gutsy sort of independence.

"Material Girl" is particularly useful for discussion because it exemplifies a common rock-video phenomenon, namely that of establishing a unique kind of intertextual relationship with a specific Hollywood movie. Because of this, as well as the difficulty of ensuring the text's stance toward what it shows and the blurring of many conventional boundaries, I would put the video in the "postmodern" category in Table 3 (p. 55), despite its containing more narrative than is usual for the type.

As is well-known, "Material Girl" takes off from the famous Marilyn Monroe dance/song sequence in *Gentlemen Prefer Blondes*, namely "Diamonds Are a Girl's Best Friend." The sequence occurs towards the end of the film where Esmond's father has severed Lorelei (Monroe) financially from Esmond, forcing her to earn her living by performing. In this sequence, having finally found her, Esmond is sitting in the audience watching the show. We thus have the familiar

Tommy Noonan as Esmond in *Gentlemen Prefer Blondes*

Esmond's astonished gaze at Monroe from his theatre seat.

Marilyn Monroe as Lorelei in *Gentlemen Prefer Blondes*

Monroe surrounded by male suitors as she performs "Diamonds are a Girl's Best Friend."

Hollywood situation, where the woman's performing permits her double articulation as spectacle for the male gaze (i.e. she is object of desire for both the male spectator in the diegetic audience and for the spectator in the cinema watching the film). The strategy formalizes the mirror-phase situation by framing the female body both within the stage proscenium arch and the cinema screen.

During this sequence, which starts with Esmond's astonished gaze at Lorelei from the theater seat (presumably he is surprised anew by Lorelei's sexiness), Lorelei directs her gaze toward the camera that is situated in Esmond's place. The space relations are thus quite simple, there being merely the two spaces of the stage and of the theater audience. We know that the film is being made under the authorial label "Hawkes," that within the diegesis, Monroe and Russell are setting up the action, but that, despite this, the patriarchal world in which they move constrains them and makes only certain avenues available.

When we turn to the video inspired by the Monroe dance sequence, we see that the situation is far more complicated. First, it is unclear who is speaking this video, even on the remote "authorial label" level, since credits are never given in the usual run of things. Is it perhaps Madonna, as historical star subject? Is it "Madonna I," the movie-star protagonist within the "framing" diegesis? Is it "Madonna II," the figure within the musical dance diegesis? Is it the director who has fallen in love with her image and desires to possess her? If we focus first on the visual strategies and then on the soundtrack, you will see that we get different and still confusing answers to the question.

Visually, the director's (D) gaze seems to structure some of the shots, but this is not consistent, as it is in the Monroe sequence. And shots possibly structured by him (or in which he is later discovered to have been present) only occur at irregular intervals. The video begins by foregrounding (perhaps pastiching?) the classical Hollywood male gaze: there is a close-up of the director, played by Keith Carradine (the video thus bows again to the classical film), whom we soon realize is watching rushes of a film starring "Madonna I" with an obsessed, glazed look on his face. "I want her, George," he says; George promises to deliver, as we cut to a two-shot of the men, behind whom we see the cinema screen and Madonna I's image but as yet

119

ROCKING AROUND THE CLOCK

Madonna, "Material Girl"

A male desire, given birth through the cinematic apparatus.

hear no sound from the performance. The camera closes in on her face, and on her seductive look first out to the camera then sideways to the men around her. As the camera now moves into the screen, blurring the boundaries between screening room, screen, and the film set (the space of the performance that involves the story of the Material Girl, Madonna II), the "rehearsal" (if that is what it was) ends, and a rich lover comes onto the set with a large present for Madonna I.

This then is a desire for the woman given birth through the cinematic apparatus, in classic manner; yet while the sequence seems to *foreground* those mechanisms, it does not appear to critique or in any way comment upon them. In Jameson's terms, this makes the process pastiche rather than parody and puts it in the postmodernist mode. The blurring of the diegetic spaces further suggests postmodernism, as does the following confusion of enunciative stances, taking the visual track alone. For while the D's gaze clearly constructed the first shot-series, it is not clear that his gaze structures the shot where Madonna I receives the present. We still hear the

120

GENDER ADDRESS AND THE GAZE

Madonna, "Material Girl"

Madonna gazes at the camera, intent upon seducing the TV spectator.

whirring sound of a projector, as if this were still the screening room space; and yet we are *inside* that screen – we no longer see the space around the frame, thus disorienting the viewer.

We cut to a close-up of a white phone ringing and a hand picking it up, and are again confused spatially. Where are we? Whose look is this? There has been no narrative preparation for the new space or for the spectator address: the phone monologue by Madonna I (the only time in the entire video that she speaks) establishes the space as her dressing room. As she speaks, the camera behaves oddly (at least in standard Hollywood conventions), dollying back slowly to the door of her room, to reveal standing there the D. Was it then his gaze that structured the shot? At the moment of reaching him, the gaze certainly *becomes* his, Madonna I seen to be its object. The phone monologue that he overhears, along with the viewer, establishes that Madonna I has just received a diamond necklace, which

121

causes the D to throw his present into the waste basket that the janitor happens to be carrying out that moment. It also establishes that Madonna I is *not* the "material girl" of her stage role, since she offers the necklace to her (presumed) girlfriend on the phone.

We now cut back to the stage space that we presume is the film set; it is not clear, since the diegesis does not foreground the filming processes, and yet there is no audience space. Rather, Madonna II sets up a direct rapport with the camera filming the rock video, and therefore with the TV spectator, deliberately playing for him/her rather than for the men in frame. But the spatial disorientation continues: there is a sudden cut to the rear of a flashy red car driving into the studio, followed by shots of Madonna I's elegant body in matching red dress (knees carefully visible), of her rich lover bending over her, and of her face and apparently dismissive reply. Whose gaze is this? Who is enunciating here? As Madonna I leaves the car, we discover the D again, but the series of shots could not have been structured by his gaze.

We cut back to the stage/film set for the most extended sequence of the performance in the video. This sequence follows the Monroe "Diamonds" dance closely, and stands in the strange intertextual relationship already mentioned: we cannot tell whether or not the Monroe sequence is being commented upon, simply used, or ridiculed by exaggeration (which sometimes seems to be happening). Things are more complicated by the fact that *Gentlemen Prefer Blondes* is itself a comedy, itself mocking and exaggerating certain patriarchal gender roles. The situation is further confused by occasional play with the image in the video, destroying even the illusion of the stability of the stage/set space: at least once, a two-shot of Madonna II and one of the lovers is simply flipped over, in standard rock video style but in total violation of classical codes that seek to secure illusionism.

Since there is no diegetic audience, the spectator is now in direct rapport with Madonna's body, as she performs for the TV spectator. There is again no diegetic source of enunciation; the spectator either remains disoriented, or secures a position through the body of the historical star, Madonna, implied as "producing" the video or simply fixed on as a centering force. This is an issue to be taken up shortly.

GENDER ADDRESS AND THE GAZE

Most of the camera work in the dance sequence involves sharp images and either long shots (the camera follows Madonna II's movements around the stage) or straight cuts; but towards the end of the dance rehearsal, the style changes to superimpositions and deliberately blurry shots, suggestive perhaps of a heightened eroticism. The camera allows Madonna II's head to be carried by the men underneath itself, so that only her arm remains in view; after some "dazed" shots, the camera pans left along the edge of the set to discover brown stairs with the D standing by them, gazing at the performance. But once again, the sequence was not set up, as it would have been in conventional Hollywood codes, as his structuring gaze; the gaze is only discovered *after* the fact, thus allowing enunciative confusion.

The same disorientation continues in a shot (perhaps a flash forward, although that term suggests the kind of narrative coherence that is precisely missing here) that follows after another dance sequence. Here the D is seen bringing simple daisies to a now smiling and receptive Madonna I, clothed in white (a play on Hollywood signifiers for innocence?), in her dressing room. We cut to the end of the stage performance (there are repeated blurry shots as before, again signifying, perhaps, sexual delirium), before a final cut to the space outside the studio, where the D is seen paying someone for the loan of a car. As Madonna I walks seductively out of the studio, the D ushers her into his car. The last shot is taken through the now rain-sodden glass (inexplicable diegetically) and shows their embrace.

This brief analysis of the main shots and use of diegetic spaces demonstrates the ways in which conventions of the classic Hollywood film, which paradoxically provided the inspiration for the video, are routinely violated. The purpose here was to show how even in a video that at first appears precisely to remain within those conventions – unlike many other videos whose extraordinary and avant-garde techniques are immediately obvious – regular narrative devices are not adhered to. But the video violates classic traditions even more with its sound–image relations.

This aspect of the video brings up the question of the rock video's uniqueness as an artistic form, namely as a form in which the sound of the song, and the "content" of its lyrics, is prior to the creation of images to accompany the music and the words. While there are analogies to both the opera and to the Hollywood musical, neither form prepares for the rock video in which the song—image relationship is quite unique. The uniqueness has to do with a certain arbitrariness of the images used along with any particular song, with the lack of limitations spatially, with the frequently extremely rapid montage-style editing not found generally (if at all) in the Hollywood musical song/dance sequences, and finally with the precise relationship of sound – both musical and vocal – to image. This relationship involves (a) the links between musical rhythms and significations of instrumental sounds, and images provided for them; (b) links between the significations of the song's actual *words* and images conjured up to convey that "content"; (c) links between any one musical phrase and the accompanying words, and the relay of images as that phrase is being played and sung.

This is obviously a very complex topic – far beyond my scope here – but let me demonstrate some of the issues in relation to "Material Girl," where again things are far simpler than in many videos. We have seen that on the visual track there are two distinct but linked discourses, that involving the D's desire for Madonna I (his determined pursuit and eventual "winning" of her), and that of Madonna I's performance, where she plays Madonna II, the "material girl." These discourses are not hierarchically arranged as in the usual Hollywood film, but rather exist on a horizontal axis, neither subordinated to the other. In terms of screen time, however, the performance is given more time.

When we turn to the soundtrack, we find that, after the brief introductory scene in the screening room (a scene, by the way, often cut from the video), the soundtrack consists entirely of the lyrics for the song "Material Girl." This song deals with the girl who will only date boys who "give her proper credit," and for whom love is reduced to money. Thus, all the visuals pertaining to the D—Madonna I love story do not have any correlate on the soundtrack. We merely have two short verbal sequences (in the screening room and dressing room) to carry the entire other story: in other words, soundtrack and image track are not linked for that story. An obvious example of this discrepancy is the shot of Madonna I (arriving at the studio in the flashy car) rejecting her rich lover: Madonna lip-synches "That's right" from the "Material Girl" song – a phrase that refers there to her only loving boys who give her money – in a situation where the opposite is happening: she *refuses* to love the man who is wealthy!

In other words, the entire video is subordinated to the words with their signifieds that refer in fact only to the stage performance. The common device in the Hollywood musical of having the dance interlude simply an episode in the main story seems here to be reversed: the performance is central while the love story is reduced to the status merely of a framing narrative. Significant here also is the disjunction between the two stories, the framing story being about a "nice" girl, and the performance being about the "bad" girl: but even these terms are blurred by the obvious seductiveness of the "nice" girl, particularly as she walks at the end toward the car in a very knowing manner.

We see thus that the usual hierarchical arrangement of discourses in the classical realist text is totally violated in "Material Girl." While Madonna I is certainly set up as object of the D's desire, in quite classical manner, the text refuses to let her be controlled by that desire. This is achieved by unbalancing the relations between framing story and performance story so that Madonna I is overridden by her stage figure, Madonna II, the brash, gutsy "material girl." The line between "fiction" and "reality" within the narrative is thus blurred: this has severe consequences just because the two women are polar opposites.

In *Gentlemen Prefer Blondes*, on the other hand, no such confusion or discrepancy exists. From the start, Monroe's single-minded aim is to catch a rich man, and she remains fixed on that throughout. The function of her performance of "Diamonds Are a Girl's Best Friend" is partly simply to express what has been obvious to the spectator, if not to Esmond, all along; but also to let Esmond get the idea, were he smart enough. Lorelei sings a song that expresses her philosophy of life, but we are clear about the lines between the stage-fiction and the context of its presentation, and Monroe as a character in the narrative. Part of the confusion in the Madonna video comes about precisely because the scene of the performance is not made very clear and because the lines between the different spaces of the text are blurred.

The situation in "Material Girl" is even more problematic because of the way that Madonna, as historical star subject, breaks through her narrative positions via her strong personality, her love of performing for the camera, her inherent energy and vitality. Madonna searches for the camera's gaze and for the TV spectator's gaze that follows it because she relishes being desired. The "roles" melt away through her unique presence and the narrative incoherence discussed above seems resolved in our understanding that Madonna herself, as historical subject, is the really "material girl."

It is perhaps Madonna's success in articulating and parading the desire to be desired in an unabashed, aggressive, gutsy manner (as against the self-abnegating urge to lose oneself in the male that is evident in the classical Hollywood film) that attracts the hordes of 12-year-old fans who idolize her and crowd her concerts. The amazing "look alike" Madonna contests (viz. a recent Macy's campaign in New York) and the successful exploitation of the weird Madonna style of dress by clothing companies attests to this idolatry. It is significant that Madonna's early style is a far cry from the conventional "patriarchal feminine" of the women's magazines – it is a cross between a bordello queen and a bag lady: young teenagers may use her as a protest against their mothers and the normal feminine while still remaining very much within those modes (in the sense of spending a lot of money, time, and energy on their "look"; the "look" is still crucial to their identities, still designed to attract attention, even if provocatively).

In some sense, then, Madonna represents the postmodern feminist heroine in that she combines unabashed seductiveness with a gutsy kind of independence. She is neither particularly male nor female identified, and seems mainly to be out for herself. This postmodern feminism is part of a larger postmodernist phenomenon which her video also embodies in its blurring of hitherto sacrosanct boundaries and polarities of the various kinds discussed. The usual bipolar categories – male/female, high art/pop art, film/TV, fiction/reality, private/public, interior/ exterior, etc. – simply no longer apply to "Material Girl."

This analysis of "Material Girl" has shown the ambiguity of enunciative positions within the video that in turn is responsible for the ambiguous representation of the female image. The positioning of a video like "Material Girl," moreover, within the 24-hour flow on this commercial MTV channel, allows us to see that it is *this* sort of ambiguous image that appears frequently, as against any other possible female images, such as the ones mentioned earlier, which are only rarely cycled. That the video was directed by a woman, Mary Lambert, does not affect this argument. I would not collapse biological sexuality and ideological position. The post-feminist ambiguous images are clearly the ones sponsors consider "marketable", since they are not only most frequently cycled but also propagated in the ad texts that are interspersed among the video texts.

But let me, as I noted earlier, "stop the flow" and look briefly at other female representations with their different kinds of gaze and enunciative stances. It is significant that some of the female rock stars just preceding Madonna, such as Cyndi Lauper, Donna Summer, and Pat Benatar, came in on the coat-tails of the 1970s feminist movement. Interestingly enough, however, in the early 1980s they reflected different aspects of the "new" woman, Lauper often taking a woman-identified stance, Summer an explicitly "feminist" one, and Benatar embodying the "tough-woman" image.

In accord with a dominant strand of 1970s American feminism, all three stars attempted to "give woman the voice." The videos made from their lyrics fall broadly into the "socially conscious" category on my chart (see Table 3 on p. 55), and are most often made in a comparatively conventional narrative/realist style. The exception is Lauper's first video, "Girls Just Want to Have Fun," which comments playfully on young women's resistance to the confining traditional roles that their parents still demand, and employs all kinds of deconstructive technical devices in making its point. Part of the video's humor comes from the contrast between the extremely banal but tuneful pop music track and the imaginative visual devices.

This video embodies what was a common theme in the early 1980s, namely a strong anti-parental sentiment, often expressed in deliberate ridicule of adults. (Lauper's "Girls" in fact featured her own mother, filmed in Lauper's own home and evidently agreeing to be stereotyped.) Lauper's next, and highly successful, video, "Time After Time," belongs in the romantic category. It has a vague feminist angle in the heroine's decision to leave her boyfriend, evidently inspired by Marlene Dietrich's (first) refusal of her lover in *Morocco*. But more obviously feminist is the (in its time unusual) representation of a close mother—daughter bonding. The video intermingles the heroine's love for the man with her love for her mother, suggesting a pre-Oedipal quality to the love affair. When her boyfriend rejects her, she conjures up an image of her mother comforting her, which in turn evokes memories of earlier closeness with her mother (we have a shot of the two hugging in the obviously working-class kitchen). Insisting on leaving her lover, despite his pleas, the heroine stops to hug her mother once more on her way to the station and the mournful parting.

The problem with this sort of representation of the mother is that while it is gratifying to see close mother—daughter bonding in a video (there are increasingly few videos that deal with parents at all, let alone in any positive manner), the mother is presented in realist codes that cannot conceal her powerlessness. She comes across as an oppressed figure, pathetic, weak even. Peripheral to the narrative as usual, she cannot help her daughter, merely commiserating rather than taking control or bringing about change. (Paradoxically, some of the videos in the romantic category by male stars, such as Paul Young's "Every Time You Go Away," may open up new space precisely through avoiding any literal representation of the mother. Addressed as an absent figure, the mother-surrogate's gaze is nevertheless inscribed in such videos in a way that makes itself more powerfully experienced than in literal images.)

Similar problems beset the more explicitly feminist video by Donna Summer, "She Works Hard for the Money," shown in 1983. This hard-hitting video makes explicit its political message about woman's oppression. It focuses on a working-class woman's double jeopardy as single working parent, oppressed both within the home and in the job. The video's textual strategies are largely realist, except that the story is narrated rather untraditionally by Summer herself, in the position of "host," conducting the viewer through the heroine's daily life. Summer "shows" us how she has to work two jobs, do all the housework, and put up in addition with two quarrelsome, ungrateful kids. The images reveal the heroine in one appalling situation after another, there being no respite, while "Summer" as it were provides a didactic "reading" of the images as exemplifying woman's lot. The only mitigating aspects to the misery are our host's personal solidarity with the heroine (but since she is out-

Pat Benatar, "Love is a Battlefield"

Led by the heroine, the women in the bordello march out onto the street protesting their treatment. The "tough-woman" image is combined unselfconsciously with pleasurable aspects of the patriarchal feminine.

129

side the diegesis she cannot help her!), and the final scene in which all kinds of women, from different professions, gather together on the street to dance. It is a nice but utopian moment, resolving in a fantasized solidarity what in fact requires concrete *social* change.

Pat Benatar's far more successful and frequently cycled "Love is a Battlefield" embodies Benatar's tough-woman stance. (Benatar in an interview criticized most female stars for their self-denigrating romantic preoccupations, the "If you leave me, I'll die" syndrome; she herself prefers the "If you leave me, I'll kick your ass" stance. This explains, she noted, her finding male stars far more interesting than female ones!) Benatar's early video exposes the limitations of the nuclear family – the heroine is thrown out of her home at the start – and reveals woman's vulnerabilities in the big city. Ending up as a prostitute, the heroine nevertheless takes action against the male oppressing her friend; once again, the women side with one another, marching bravely out of the brothel to engage in a war-like, threatening dance on the street outside before going their separate ways.

The difference between these two "feminist" videos explains the relative success of the latter, as against the short cycling of the first. For the female representations in Benatar's video almost belie the strong woman-identified theme in their reliance on the standard "look" of the patriarchal feminine: the heroine, played by Benatar herself, is particularly glamorous, and the prostitutes' clothes, while somewhat unconventional, are colorful and fetching.

These videos are all important in offering alternate female narrative/thematic positions, if not alternate images. This distinction is important, since it reveals the limitation of a traditional liberal-humanist feminist politics expressed through fairly conventional filmic codes. Madonna's most recent video (August 1986), "Papa Don't Preach," is interesting in this connection, since it shows Madonna evolving a kind of postmodern feminist image that builds on, or combines, elements of the "new" woman that we traced in Summer, Lauper, and Benatar. This image, unlike her previous ones (of which "Material Girl" gives a glimpse), smacks not so much of post-modernism (although categories are still blurred in some ways) as of a combination of pre-feminist modes with ones we might call "feminist." In "Papa Don't Preach" (top of the countdown in America for a second week in August 1986, after having already

Madonna, "Papa Don't Preach"

Madonna keeps the virgin/whore dichotomy intact but reworks it in the body of a single protagonist.

Madonna's new *gamin* image

131

made the top in most European nations), the heroine is a determined, self-asserting teenager who, having fallen in love and become pregnant, insists on keeping her baby. Madonna's image is far removed from the bordello Queen/bag lady mix of her recent period; now svelt, almost gamin-like in her short hair cut, she struts confidently along in jeans and striped top as the video opens. These images of the home girl, *Daddy*'s girl indeed, it turns out, (the heroine seems to have been brought up by her father, there being no mother-image in the video), are intercut with images of the "bad" girl – although she is not really labelled as such – dressed in skin-tight black pants and 1950s-style black corset top, which sets off her blonde hair, white face, and bright red lips. She dances erotically in these scenes, and her words suggest the "bad" girl: "Papa don't preach," she begins, addressing her father, "I'm in trouble deep/I've been losing sleep/But I made up my mind/I'm keeping my baby." But it is precisely the blurring of the lines between the "virgin" and "whore" images that suggest a post-feminist stance; the heroine is *neither*, but rather a sexy young teenager, in love and pregnant, and refusing to conform to social codes and give up her baby (as her friends, she says, tell her to do).

But this postmodern feminist heroine still wants to be Daddy's girl: "Papa, don't stop loving me" she says. The last scene of the video involves the gradual reconciliation of father and daughter, the final shot being their embrace. It is important, however, that the reconciliation only happens because the *father* decides to relent, the heroine simply refusing to be what he demands; she insists on being herself.

As the video's rapid and broad success suggests, Madonna has here touched on issues confronting many teenagers today, particularly those in the lower classes, which her video (set as it is in a section of New Jersey facing New York City's skyline) obviously addresses. It shows a star evolving, perhaps maturing as a result of her own much-publicized recent marriage. Madonna is here far less seductive toward her audience, much more direct and forceful. She is at once strong and feminine, sexy and "innocent," offering an image that perhaps makes sense to young women growing up after the recent feminist movement.

Nevertheless, the video has some of the same problems as those by Summer, Lauper, and Benatar already discussed in that its (broadly)

132

realist strategies prevent any foregrounding of problems of female representation. Madonna pastes the traditional virgin onto the traditional whore, hoping to get rid of a polarity that no longer makes sense. But in not questioning the polarity's very terms, she runs the risk of keeping it intact. Perhaps because of their (essentially) liberal-humanist politics, these female stars have been less ready to experiment with aesthetic forms than have male stars. (It is significant that most of the prize-winning experimental videos have been produced by male video directors for male stars or groups such as The Cars, Dire Straits, Simple Minds, Phil Collins, David Bowie, Mick Jagger, Michael Jackson, Rush, The Power Station, A-Ha. This is not to deny the artistically innovative work of a Laurie Anderson or a Mary Lambert (or directors like Annabel Jankel or Tony Basil). It is a matter of what is given institutional acclaim. The list reflects the dominance of white male figures in the rock video phenomenon.

It is precisely women's position in the male order that is addressed in Tina Turner's effective "Private Dancer." This video, instead of presenting an explicit feminist message in the manner of Benatar's and Summer's videos, rather attempts to expose woman's position in the dominant male imaginary. It analyzes the structure of a male unconscious that reduces women to mere cyphers, signs in a male discourse, or instruments of pleasure shaped to satisfy male fantasies.

The video's enunciative strategies work to deconstruct the male imaginary: the heroine, played by Turner herself, is first seen in a realist image entering the high class bordello where she tells us, through the song lyrics, that she works as a "private dancer." Turner continues to speak this video as she moves from being a realistic character to a kind of female "metteur en scène," or a magician, conjuring up different aspects of the male erotic unconscious. Dressed now in elegant evening gown, Turner addresses the camera directly, in close-up or medium-shot, but the angles diminish fetishization of her form. She speaks here of the performer's own life and hopes – the need for money that brings her here, the wish for a family, home, and fun – the video aiming to construct a disjunction between "woman" and "male fantasy."

From this position, the heroine creates for the TV viewer the dream world of her clients, but in such a way as to highlight the oppressiveness of the fantasies imposed on the women in the bordello. The actresses and dancers participating in the fantasies are made to perform like robots or mannequins, reduced to mere mechanical embodiments of what men desire. Sometimes, the figures are seen to be operated like puppets, by ribbons tied to their limbs. They are seen to be at the command of the male customer, to produce the required image as would a machine.

The video's visual techniques produce the effect of a dream-space: one male fantasy, performed by the robot-like, mechanical figures, is made to merge into the next, the camera often floating in on a scene, watching it for a while until the image dissolves into another, when the camera will float out again. The effect is that of swooning, or of a dream-world in which anything can happen and in which one is not in control. The mise-en-scène adds further to the dream-like quality through the veils and netting that are draped across the image and through the claustrophobic sense of being in an enclosed, artificial space.

Tina Turner, "Private Dancer"

Turner uses her body to construct a meta-language for us to see *how* women are mere passive objects of male desire.

GENDER ADDRESS AND THE GAZE

Some of the fantasies conjured up involve the heroine herself, so that we get the double articulation of her narration outside of the male fantasies she conducts us through, and her positioning within those fantasies. The result is our understanding her physical/bodily ensnarement within the male imaginary, but experiencing her psychic detachment from it.

It is this representation of a psychic detachment that permits the exposing of the male erotic unconscious. The video constructs a kind of meta-language within which to let us see *how* the heroine's body is (ab)used, *how* women are mere passive objects of male desire, entrapped within a male fantasy world from which there is no escape. The blocking of woman's subjectivity and of her own desires is graphically depicted.

The video ends as it began with the realist image of the dance hall where clients and customers first meet. We have seen that this is a space controlled by the ever-watching Madame, making sure that her ''dancers'' are doing their job of pleasing the clients. The heroine is shot in close-up with her client and then, suddenly, seen to push him away and walk off the floor as the video ends.

This moment of negation of her role exposes the pathetic degree of resistance available to the woman. She cannot *change* anything, or free herself of the male constructions; she can only walk away from the scene, temporarily take herself out of the role.

While race is absent as any overt part of the narrative in ''Private Dancer,'' it perhaps accounts for the video's uncanny ability to present what is a predominantly white male imaginary. The only overt reference to race is perhaps the brief scene where a young beautifully dressed black boy and girl are seen dancing together; the little boy suddenly gets bored and walks away from the now-forlorn little girl. Perhaps the scene indicates the enmeshment of young black children in white codes; or the early vulnerability of the girl to seduction and betrayal? It is unclear.

This video is quite different from others produced for Turner, and its Turner-image is unusual. A number of videos were made from her very successful and remarkably staged London performance, where she unabashedly promoted her body as a sexual commodity. On the other hand, one can argue that in a video like ''What's Love Got To Do With It'' Turner attempts to gain control over her own

Turner and other black stars like Aretha Franklin initiated the "tough woman" stance being modified by new black singers. Here Turner comes between the heterosexual couple, "rescuing" the woman being seduced.

Turner appropriates the patriarchal feminine for herself as a strategy for retaining control over her desirability and keeping her independence.

sexuality through deliberately enticing male desire. Her short tight leather skirt with the slit up the side, her bestockinged legs and high-heeled shoes are in this case arguably used simply to assert control over the males by refusing them what her dress seems to offer. Turner here comes close to Benatar's "tough-woman" image, seeming to ask women to band together rather than giving in to male desire. But this is again merely a position taken up in the one lyric from which this video was made.

Turner's most recent video, "Typical Male," (August 1986) still assumes a "tough woman" image, but now Turner is poking fun at the intellectual male to whom she's attracted but from whom she cannot get "a reaction." She positions herself as trying to entice the male, with little success. The video plays off of the idea of Turner's enormous sexual desirability, rendering ridiculous the male who doesn't seem to notice it. Dressed in a strapless red dress and high heels, she parades about the set full of giant-size symbols of intellectuality (crossword puzzles, paper, pencils, chessboard, etc.) Her pleading position ("All I want is a little reaction/Just enough to tip the scale"; and "So put up your books . . . /Open up your heart and let me in") at once belittles her (she is literally pint-sized amongst the huge symbols of male intellect), and paradoxically emasculates and ridicules the reluctant (weak) male. The result is a strange mixture of the different kinds of address in the earlier videos discussed above.

Julie Brown's "The Homecoming Queen's Got a Gun," only shown a few times, deconstructs a staple of American mythology. This Homecoming Queen revolts against all that is expected of her, in the mode of a kind of black comedy. Bodies litter the house where she starts shooting, and of course, she is in turn shot by the police. The video's iconoclasm is powerful and disturbing, but the extreme rebellion against an oppressive female role perhaps prevented the video from being shown more often.

The last variation from the prevalent "post-feminist" female representation that I will deal with in my stopping of the 24-hour MTV flow is that evident in the recent Aretha Franklin/Annie Lennox "Sisters Are Doin' It For Themselves" video. The female images here are arguably different from those in either the feminist-message video or the deconstructive Turner video. At first glance, the Franklin/Lennox video looks like the feminist-message type, but on a closer examination the video attempts to move beyond the mere often romantic celebration of women's achievements that it does include.

There is first the amazing contrast between the images of the two star subjects themselves, who perform on a huge outdoor stage before crowds of ethnically mixed female fans. Franklin's image is embedded in discourses of the historically "strong" black female blues singer, as well as those of the black, no-nonsense matriarch. Her image is now frequent on MTV — as she appears in her own successful videos, as a co-star in this "Sisters" video; or as a homage-image in Whitney Houston's 'How Will I Know.'' Lennox, meanwhile, typifies the new androgynous rock-video discourse which is largely, however, a male phenomenon. Here she is resplendent in white male-style jacket, black leather pants, heavy boots, and short cropped blonde hair. Franklin, meanwhile, performs in a simple red gown. There is thus a bringing together of powerful, current, alternative female images and the past strength of black female discourses.

These different images of the female are also developed in the cut-aways from the two women performing and the montage sequences of shots of women spliced together. These intercut shots are of three main kinds: those showing women in non-traditional jobs, from presidents to construction workers; those showing women in the old patriarchal "feminine" rituals such as the traditional Indian marriage or the cheer-leader; and, finally, clips from silent films and those like Schlesinger's *A Kind of Loving* or Vidor's *Our Daily Bread* which show women as classic sex objects or idealized mother figures.

This montage sequence reminds the female viewer of where women have been and of where they have gotten to, but the inter-mixing of the various sets of images suggests the continuity of the old positions along with the new. There is thus an attempt to avoid the utopian element of the feminist message video by showing the series on a continuum rather than in a clear past versus present hierarchical ordering.

Most interesting perhaps is what the video does with the image of Dave Stewart played upon a huge screen that appears between the images of Lennox and Franklin on stage towards the end of the video. At first, one is perturbed at his presence at all in such a celebration of women's achievements; but it soon becomes clear that the video is using his image to say something about the processes of image-making already raised in the montage clips from male films. Here it appears that instead of the usual control of the female image by the male gaze, Stewart's image is being controlled by Lennox and Franklin as they stand on either side of the screen depicting his image. It is almost as if they are pulling some strings to make the image move in certain ways, much as the women in Turner's video were "operated" by the male unconscious. Stewart's figure is very much positioned as the object of the women's gazes, and further is reduced to a kind of mechanical object as it bounces about apparently uncontrollably within the screen.

Finally, there is an interesting attempt in the video to avoid making Franklin and Lennox direct objects of the camera's gaze. While there are inevitably some close-ups of their faces, for much of the time the camera catches them at oblique angles, so that their gazes do not directly meet the camera's. At times, this creates an unfortunate sense of their not-relating to each other, but this is in the service of avoiding an objectifying gaze as much as possible.

This video then appears to comment upon the problems of image-making and to foreground the notion that images are constructed rather than "natural." It processes old and new female constructions as if to warn us both of too readily assuming that old images have been abandoned and of the fact that women have currently been newly constructed as "liberated" or whatever. The present of the video, i.e. that of the concert where Franklin and Lennox are apparently performing, does convey a sense of female solidarity and celebration in the old utopian mode. However, there is a certain self-consciousness about this mode, as is evident in its presentation as yet one more "image." This is conveyed through the device of projecting, on a huge screen within the frame, images of Franklin and Lennox and the concert we are watching, intercut with images from the montage sequence of women shown earlier on in the video.

"Sisters" only got very short play on MTV, seemingly having made it that far merely because it was top of the British charts. As we resume the 24-hour flow, so such alternate female images once again recede into the background and the post-feminist image reappears.

As I noted earlier, the postmodern as an "ideology" has recently begun to shift all the hitherto quite distinct types in the same direction. So the fact that the post-feminist video is the dominant one in the flow is only to be expected. Nevertheless, there are videos that may be said to belong in a separate category, that may still be distinguished from the others as embodying in extreme form what they now merely show by an *inflection* into their hitherto specific type. Let me conclude this chapter by a brief look at some postmodernist videos which, unlike the majority of other types, seem to reflect Baudrillard's notion that, while the psychological is marked, "it seems to be played out somewhere else."

As we have seen, there are two main types of gaze – pre-Oedipal and phallic – in the other types of video. While the way these gazes function in at least two of the types differs markedly from the gaze in the classical narrative film, it nevertheless can still be usefully discussed within the psychoanalytic paradigm. This is not the case in the postmodernist video because of the refusal of the text to speak from any definite position. A video like Devo's "Whip It," for example, not only blurs distinctions between genres but refuses to reveal that it is speaking from a clear position. The issue of the gaze thus becomes confused: we have a sense of the text playing with Oedipal positionings but not really adopting any of them. The predominance of the pastiche mode makes it difficult to say that the video is taking the usual phallic pleasure in violence to women, although the surface imagery would suggest such pleasure.

The video sets itself back in the "mythic" West, toward which it takes a stand somewhere between pastiche and parody. There is intercutting between the band, dressed in extraordinary clothes that are a mix between children's television "Pot Men" and *Star-Trek* and standing in some obviously artificial TV garden plot, and a group of cowboys and cowgals, joking at the side of an open space. On this space stands what looks at first like a wax figure of a woman, dressed in old-fashioned middle-class women's clothes. As the band play and sing, the star whips the clothes off the woman, piece by piece. We see her body gradually becoming naked, the clothes flying off her as she is whipped; meanwhile, the cowboy group laugh at the display, and we cut to a fat/ugly Mom figure in a nearby house window, stirring her mixture and taking pleasure in her son's temerity. A comic-bubble out of her mouth has in it the words "Oh that Alan!"

GENDER ADDRESS AND THE GAZE

This video perplexes because the spectator is not provided with any clear place from which to identify. The pastiche element confuses: we want to believe that this is parody, but that is never made clear; if it is not parody, what is meant? Does the video want to have its cake and eat it too – that is, at once mock violence toward women while clearly itself quite enjoying what it shows? The female spectator has absolutely no position to occupy, torn as she is between disbelief and an unavoidable pity for the figure of the woman in the center. The representation of the fat/ugly complicit Mom further angers the female spectator, while at the same time she fears that she is being trapped by ''taking it seriously,'' when the video might be a comment on the macho nature of the West!

Tom Petty and the Heartbreakers, ''Don't Come Around Here No More''

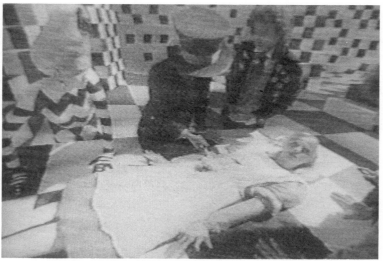

Like other postmodernist videos, this one refuses to speak from a clear position. Is the eating of Alice's body sadistic or a play with sadistic wishes?

Another video, with a similarly ambiguous pastiche mode, is Tom Petty and the Heartbreakers' ''Don't Come Around Here No More,'' which is based on the Alice story. A very imaginatively filmed tape, with fantastic set, creative camera use, costumes, and special effects (particularly the sudden size transformations of Alice and the Mad Hatter, and of objects like her tea cup), it is nevertheless chilling in its treatment of Alice and her body. The Mad Hatter has apparently turned into a sadist, with not a grain of humor; he is cruelly rejecting of Alice, briefly playing with her (making himself suddenly tiny, spouting mirrors like ears in which she sees her own image), and then sadistically taunting her. He has food brought to her, but then his servants steal it; he seats her at the table, but then rushes toward her and knocks her down; he sends a pram her way, only for her to discover an ugly piglet under the baby bonnet, and finally all but drowns her in his now huge tea cup, scaring her with the ringed faces of his servants peering down at her; the Hatter chases her around and finally he ends by cutting up her body, now mysteriously transformed into birthday cake, and eating it.

As with "Whip It," this video simply refuses to speak from any clear position. How are we to view the eating of Alice's body? It may seem "sadistic," but the rest of the filmic world does not really support such a reading. The events do not have the overall investment in a certain kind of desire that the sadistic narrative usually has. The narrative rather plays with sadistic wishes without really declaring them, leaving the viewer perplexed as to how to read the images.

Let me now discuss the similar kind of perplexity that an attempt to evaluate the channel as a whole produces and that seems particularly to indicate postmodernism.

6

Conclusion: MTV, postmodernism, and the televisual apparatus

In this book, I have tried to argue that MTV, as a 24-hour continuous channel, carries to an extreme, and thus lays bare for our contemplation, aspects inherent in the televisual apparatus. To summarize the main points in that argument briefly: first, the main force of MTV as a cable channel is consumption on a whole variety of levels, ranging from the literal (i.e. selling the sponsors' goods, the rock stars' records, and MTV itself) to the psychological (i.e. selling the image, the "look," the style). MTV is more obviously than other programs one nearly continuous advertisement, the flow being merely broken down into different *kinds* of ads. More than other programs, then, MTV positions the spectator in the mode of constantly hoping that the next ad-segment (of whatever kind) will satisfy the desire for plenitude: the channel keeps the spectator in the consuming mode more intensely because its items are all so short.

Since the mode of address throughout is that of the ad, then like the ad the channel relies on engaging the spectator on the level of unsatisfied desire. This remains in the psyche from the moment of entry into the Lacanian symbolic, and is available for channeling in various directions. Given the organization of the Lacanian symbolic around the phallus as signifier, it is not surprising that MTV basically addresses the desire for the phallus remaining in the psyche of both genders. This partly accounts for the dominance on the channel of videos featuring white male stars.

143

Second, we have seen how the fact that MTV calls into question hitherto sacrosanct aesthetic and critical polarities marks MTV as a postmodernist form. Its very status as a commercial form using avant-garde techniques has required a re-examination of previous critical categories.

Third, we have seen how the position that MTV takes toward history again marks its discourse as postmodernist. In a postmodernist fashion, MTV blurs previous distinctions between past, present, and future, along with its blurring of separations such as those between popular and avant-garde art, between different aesthetic genres and artistic modes. MTV, as a text, arguably makes a postmodernist use of historical discourses about rock and roll as constructed by rock critics.[1] We saw how there are four main phases of rock and roll — the beginnings in the 1950s with Bill Haley, Elvis Presley, and numerous other groups like Chuck Berry, the Platters, etc.; the 1960s "soft rock," often influenced by black "soul" music and jazz; the late 1960s so-called "acid rock," which for many represents the height of genuine rock and roll, with its inventive sounds and protest content; the 1970s search for new sounds in the wake of the collapse of youth and protest movements, leading in the 1980s to punk, heavy metal, and new wave rock and roll, with their loud, unmelodious sounds, their cynicism, their negative violence.

Each phase has been seen as addressing distinct historical teenage communities, distinguished by dress and by stance toward the establishment. MTV, however, simply sweeps up these discourses and distinctions into itself, calling upon all the separate traditions, re-shaping and re-using them for its own ends, flattening them out into one continuous present of the 24-hour video flow. MTV also effaces the boundary between past and present in drawing indiscriminately on film genres and art movements from different historical periods; and also in the often arbitrary use of settings and clothes from the Roman, medieval and other past eras. The stance of the texts is that there is one time continuum in which all exists: past, present, and future do not indicate major time barriers, but rather a time band upon which one can call at will.

Now what is interesting here is the way in which this timeless present often has a futurist, post-holocaust look, even when a video is not explicitly drawing upon science fiction, or using footage from

CONCLUSION

futurist films like Lang's *Metropolis*, *Star-Trek* or the more recent *Blade Runner*. We already saw this in some of the nihilist videos analyzed in detail (particularly "Rebel Yell" and "Rock You Like a Hurricane"), but the phenomenon is common across the types. Most often the rock video world looks like noplace, or like a post-nuclear holocaust place — without boundaries, definition or recognizable location. Figures are often placed in a smoky, hazy environment and, as already noted, the sudden, unexplained explosion is a common feature.

Marxist critics like Fredric Jameson and Lawrence Grossberg object to the fact — evidenced by this stance toward history — that postmodernist texts like MTV refuse to take up a secure critical position from which to speak. As critics who themselves retain a notion of history as manifesting a position of "truth" about the world, rather than yet one more discourse, they view contemporary youth culture as in danger because it does not take an explicitly critical stance toward on-going events.

Rock and roll is vulnerable to this objection because of some of the subversive roots (first from slave songs, then jazz, and finally 1960s protest rock) that form the basic traditions for all rock music. But elements of rock have long "sold out" to commercial entrepreneurs; the line between rock and pop has always been tentative, "pop" always attempting to bring the more rebellious "rock" into the mainstream.

But Jameson and Grossberg are correct in pointing out that a more fundamental change is taking place than the *mere* commercialization that MTV signifies. The stance toward history represents a new era, emblematic of the Baudrillardean "Universe of Communication"; for it is the televisual apparatus that is partly responsible for the kind of consciousness that no longer thinks in terms of an *historical* frame. That sort of "frame" involves precisely the kinds of boundaries and limited texts that television obliterates in its never-ending series.

In eliding history as a position from which to speak, rock videos fall into pastiche rather than parody, as we've seen, signifying a new lack of orienting boundaries, a tendency to incorporate rather than to "quote" texts. Without drawing the negative judgments about postmodernism that Jameson does, we can see that MTV is part of a contemporary discourse that has written out history as a possible discourse. What are the implications of this? To what degree is the cultural situation, as evident in MTV, progressive or dangerous, transgressive or regressive?

Marxist critics tend to draw negative conclusions: Jameson, for instance, is concerned about what he calls a new schizophrenic mode of relating to the world. Building on work by Lacan and Baudrillard, Jameson sees this as an inevitable product of the stance toward history. "The originality of Lacan's thought in this area," Jameson notes, "is to have considered schizophrenia essentially as a language disorder. . . . What we need to retain from this is the idea that psychosis, and more particularly schizophrenia, emerges from the failure of the infant to accede fully into the realm of speech and language."[2] This enables us to see schizophrenia as "the breakdown of the relationship between signifiers." Jameson notes that for Lacan, the experience of temporality – of past, present, and future – and of an identity that persists over time is an effect of language, produced through the fact that the sentence moves through time, linearly.[3] But since the schizophrenic does not recognize the time element in langauge, he/she does not have a sense of time as continuous. She/he, says Jameson:

is condemned to live in a perpetual present with which the various moments of his or her past have little connection and for which there is no conceivable future on the horizon. . . . The schizophrenic experience is an experience of isolated, disconnected, discontinuous material signifiers which fail to link up into a coherent sequence.[4]

Jameson goes on to note that "as temporal continuities break down, the experience of the present becomes powerfully, overwhelmingly vivid and 'material.'" What he means here is that because the schizophrenic cannot experience in words their larger contextual and temporal meanings, so she/he focuses in on their literality, their presentness, their sensory elements, not seeking to look beyond to broader signification.[5]

What is disturbing to Jameson about this is that the previous modernist movement at least retained a critical position vis-à-vis dominant culture, whereas society now takes into itself whatever

146

is produced from a counter-culture, such as punk rock and sexually explicit material. Far from this material being condemned by the establishment, it is rather made into a successful commercial commodity. Fashion, styling, advertising, etc., are all fed by postmodernism in an unprecedented manner. The problem with this, for Jameson, is the "disappearance of a sense of history" and the living "in a perpetual present and in a perpetual change that obliterates traditions of the kind which all earlier social formations have had in some way or another to preserve."[6]

While Jameson is concerned about the loss of any critical position from which to evaluate contemporary developments, Grossberg is obsessed with the negativity of recent punk rock music. He sees the despair and nihilism that stalks the music as representing the impossibility of youth to challenge, or hope to change, existing social formations from which they are, however, alienated. Rock and roll in the 1980s, Grossberg notes, "is no longer able to constitute itself a powerful affective boundary between its fans and those who remain outside of its culture. . . . Survival for this new youth seems to demand adaptation to and escape from, the hegemony rather than a response to the historical context in which they find themselves."[7] The moment leans dangerously deathward for Grossberg.

A more positive reading of MTV would involve linking it to a radical kind of postmodernism such as has emerged recently from theoretical developments in France. In its radical, Derridean form, postmodernism embodies an attack on bourgeois signifying practices. As a critical theory, postmodernism exposes how these practices, posing as speaking what is "natural" and "true," in fact set up a transcendental self as a point outside of articulation. But the practices conceal this point of enunciation, which is that of bourgeois hegemony, so that the spectator is unaware of being addressed from a particular position. The postmodernist critic and artist use radically transgressive forms in an effort to avoid the false illusionist position of a speaker outside of articulation. The "freeing" of the signifiers is in this case a kind of strategy – a way of preventing their usual linkage to mythic signifieds. The decentering of the spectator/reader then has a radical effect in releasing him/her from predictable, confining signifieds.

From this perspective, one could see the effacing in MTV of old boundaries between low and high culture, between past, present, and future, and between previously distinct art forms and genres as an exhilarating move toward a heteroglossia that calls into question moribund pieties of a now archaic humanism. The refusal of classical continuity editing, of the normal cause—effect narrative progression, of shot/counter-shot, of time—place unities makes new demands on the spectator, requiring a more active involvement; videos provide a whole variety of filmic worlds, as against the monolithic world of the classical realist Hollywood film. The creativity and energy of rock videos could represent a refusal to be co-opted into the liberalism that has brought America to its present crisis.

Far from the incoherent flow of images signaling a schizophrenic failure of language, the young adult's refusal to enter the realm of the symbolic could represent a healthy breaking of confining boundaries and dichotomies that were constructed originally to serve certain bourgeois ends at a particular historical moment. In this view, then, the vitality of rock videos shows the refusal of youth to be silenced or channeled in the old directions.

The very possibility of such contradictory readings of MTV is, again, part of what marks it as postmodernist. The institution is itself embedded in contradictions that are an inevitable part of its cultural context. There is some truth to the reading of MTV as a merely co-opted kind of postmodernism that utilizes adolescent desire for its own, commercial ends. The adoption of adolescent styles, imagery, and iconography by the adult fashion and advertising worlds, by TV shows like *Miami Vice* and by Hollywood films, does not necessarily signal a healthy acceptance of youth's subversive stances; it rather suggests the cynicism by which profit has become the *only* value – a cynicism represented by spies like Michael Walker trading secrets not for *ideological* but merely for monetary reasons.

We need to distinguish this co-opted postmodernism, which seeks to contain its possibly progressive decentering effects, from the radical Derridean kind. The Derridean decentering is ultimately unpleasurable because it refuses the plenitude and unity we all desire, and that makes us vulnerable to dominant commercial forms that tap into this need with their complicit ideologies. MTV at once addresses the American adolescent's consciousness of a decentered world,

148

CONCLUSION

while also providing a longed-for centeredness in the faces and bodies of the rock stars.

Contradictions abound in the representation of sexuality on MTV, as we've seen. As I have shown, the male gaze is not monolithic on the channel: here again, the televisual apparatus enables the production of a variety of different gazes due to the arrangement of a series of short, constantly changing segments in place of the two-hour continuous film narrative, or the usually single book-length or theatrical narratives. There is no possibility within the four-minute segment (others are shorter) for regression to the Freudian Oedipal conflicts in the manner of the classical narrative. What we rather have is a semi-comical play with Oedipal positions, as in the postmodern video, or a focus on one particular mode in the Oedipal complex in some of the other video-types outlined in Chapter 5.

The implications of all this for a feminist perspective need close analysis. Feminism has traditionally relied on a liberal or left humanist position, as was clear in my earlier discussion of major types of videos featuring female stars. If the televisual apparatus manifests a new stage of consciousness in which that liberal/left humanism no longer has a place, this implicates a majority of feminist positions. If Baudrillard is correct in seeing the TV screen as symbolizing a new era in which "The Faustian, Promethean (perhaps Oedipal) period of production and consumption" has given way to "the narcissistic and protean era of connections, contact, contiguity, feedback, and generalized interface that goes with the universe of communication," then feminism needs to address the changed situation. Gender has been one of the central organizing categories of what Baudrillard has called the old "hot" (as against the new "cold") universe, but this may be lost in the new era. Let me explore briefly what the impact of this might be for women and feminism.

Women's patriarchal functions have been constructed historically through the patriarchal institutions and social codes that Marx and Freud found in operation and around which they each, in different ways, constructed authoritative discourses in the late nineteenth and early twentieth centuries. One might think that the demise of the institutions that gave rise to these discourses would automatically benefit women. But this is not necessarily the case.

For, while the postmodernism that is partly produced by the

collapse of the old structures has some progressive aspects, it is a contradictory phenomenon for women. Contemporary feminism, as a political discourse, has developed a position from which to speak by attacking the old patriarchal theorists; feminists have both made use of and critiqued the powerful, often subversive, discourses of both Marx and Freud in their stance against dominant gender constructs. In other words, these discourses have provided the shaping framework for our work. If they are no longer relevant, on what ground does the feminist critique stand?

Second, as an aesthetic, postmodernism constructs a decentered, fragmented text; the breaking up of traditional, realist forms sometimes entails a deconstruction of conventional sex-role representations that opens up new possibilities for female imaging. Further, the fragmentation of the viewing subject perhaps deconstructs woman's conventional other-centered reception functions – women positioned as nurturer, care-giver – releasing new ways of relating to texts. Postmodernism offers the female spectator pleasure in sensations – color, sound, visual patterns – and in energy, body movement; it also opens up possibilities for expression of female desire.

On the other hand, one could argue that postmodernist culture primarily builds on and satisfies already dominant masculine qualities, such as violence, destruction, consumption, phallic sexuality, appropriation of the feminine in the non-male image. In postmodernism, as I've tried to show, often the domestic and the familial, especially the figure of the mother, are repressed; and these are modes that in the past offered some satisfactions to women. It is possible that the new "universe of communication" is precisely pleasing to males seeking relief from the old "Faustian, Promethean (perhaps Oedipal) period of production and consumption," just because women have begun, through their feminist discourse, to make and win demands within that system, thereby challenging male dominance there.

Is it possible that the postmodernist discourse has been constructed by male theorists partly to mitigate the increasing dominance of feminist theory in intellectual discourse? Could the discourse also partly remedy the gap in male theory resulting from the end of an era in French intellectual life, marked by the literal deaths of several of the great 1960s theorists — Jacques Lacan, Roland Barthes, Michel

CONCLUSION

Foucault and the withdrawal from the scene of Louis Althusser? I am not suggesting that the discourse does not accurately describe a new set of subject constructions produced by (and themselves producing, circularly) new technologies; indeed, my book has tried to show the links between one such new technology (i.e. television) and new subject constructions in rock videos. What I am suggesting is that certain theorists are drawn to postmodernism (rather than struggling against it) precisely because it seems to render feminism obsolete — because it offers a relief from the recent concentration on feminist discourse.

However this may be, it is important for feminists to confront the postmodernist challenge. Given television's role in the changed and still changing relationship of subject to image, feminists must analyze the implications of this postmodernist apparatus. The change involved began at the turn of the century with the development of advertising and of the department-store window; it was then further affected by the invention of the cinematic apparatus, and television has, we've seen, produced more changes. The television screen now replaces the cinema screen as the central controlling cultural mode, setting up a new spectator—screen relationship which I have begun to analyze in this book on MTV. For MTV constantly comments upon the self in relation to image (especially the TV image), to the extent that that may be seen as its main "content." The blurring of distinctions between a "subject" and an "image" – or the reduction of the old notion of "self" to "image" – is something for feminists to explore, even as we fear the coming of Baudrillard's universe of "simulacra."

The reduction of the female body to merely an "image" is something that women have lived with for a long time, and the phenomenon has been extensively studied by feminist film critics. But this study always somehow assumed an entity possible of being constructed differently. The new postmodern universe, with its celebration of the look, the surfaces, textures, the self-as-commodity, threatens to reduce everything to the image/representation/simulacrum.

Research is also needed on the impact of the televisual apparatus on other potentially oppositional discourses, such as those (like USA Africa, Live Aid, Farm Aid and, as of writing, Amnesty International) mentioned in Chapter 4. As one of America's powerful commercial apparatuses, television seems able to integrate and use any kind of potentially subversive counter-culture before it has even had time to identify itself as such. While this capacity of television (and, indeed, of American culture generally) may result in a certain humanizing of the dominant discourse – all to the good – it means that oppositional discourses are never given an opportunity to structure a community; once it existed, such a discourse shared by numbers of people might gain sufficient power to produce real changes in dominant discourses. (A good recent example is the "integration" of what had begun as an oppositional discourse about poverty in America, in the recent "Hands Across America" event, when Ronald Reagan finally agreed to let the line go through the White House and to stand in it himself.)

The loss of any position from which to speak – of mechanisms for critical evaluation of social structures and ideologies – that characterizes postmodernism is something to worry about even as we see the value of a radical postmodernism that moves beyond archaic humanism. While there may be a genuinely oppositional youth culture in some European nations, this is no longer true of America. What we have predominantly is a uni-dimensional, commercialized and massified youth culture, not really organized by youth itself but by commercial agents, that has absorbed into itself, and trivialized, all the potentially subversive positions of earlier rock movements. There are of course small sub-groups that are important but, just because marginalized and lacking access to the media, they are powerless. Any attempts at oppositional discourses struggle against their reduction to glamorous "media events," to the surfaces/textures/images of opposition rather than to its actuality as something that challenges the status quo.

Baudrillard sees the invasion of advertising into the social sphere as central in these sorts of change; taking over the public space, advertising, "no longer limited to its traditional language . . . organizes the architecture and realization of super objects." Adverts are our only architecture today, Baudrillard says, "great screens on which are reflected atoms, particles, molecules in motion. Not a public space or a true public space but gigantic spaces of circulation, ventilation and ephemeral connections."[8]

Much of what Baudrillard has to say about the absence of any

CONCLUSION

distinction between the private and the public space applies to MTV. This is yet one more distinction that postmodernism obliterates in its flattening out of things into a network or system, the parts all relying on each other. For Baudrillard, as we saw, the opposition between private and public has been effaced: "The one is no longer a spectacle, the other no longer a secret." The two have been submerged "in a sort of obscenity where the most intimate processes of our life become the virtual feeding ground of the media."

Some of the pleasures of the universe of communication mentioned by Baudrillard (no longer, he says, those of "manifestation, scenic and aesthetic, but rather of pure fascination, aleatory and psychotropic") are indeed those that MTV offers, and the flattening out of distinctions as we've seen puts the viewer in a kind of endless present not that dissimilar to the schizophrenic state. But I do not think we have yet arrived at Baudrillard's "cold universe." MTV rather signals a transitional period between the "hot" and the "cold" universes since, as noted, many videos still rely on Oedipal processes that belong to the old universe. Yet, on the other hand, MTV *does* manifest obliteration of the aesthetic distinctions that characterized the old, "hot" universe, and in this sense already looks toward the stage of the "ecstasy of communication" that Baudrillard envisages.

We cannot expect a commercial medium like MTV to resist the pressures of what may indeed be a deep cultural change. And as culture workers, we do not want to return to the error of insisting upon fixed points of enunciation labeled "truth"; but, as Tony Bennett and Ernesto Laclau have pointed out, we must continue to articulate oppositional discourses – recognizing them as discourses rather than an ontological truth that recent theory has cast doubt on – if we are to construct "new" subjects not totally defined by the reading formations of the postmodernist, "cold" universe. Important in this effort is more analysis of the televisual apparatus as it works to construct subjects unable any more to distinguish an "inside" from an "outside," "fiction" from "reality."

Afterword

Although writing this book on MTV has been an exciting experience, it has also been frustrating in various ways. There was first the difficulty of working in an area that was so new and had not been researched before; and second, of learning how to relate to the various managers, agencies, record companies, and the MTV management itself which became my only research sources and who were as unused to dealing with a cultural studies scholar like myself as I was to dealing with them. I have learned almost as much about MTV from my dealings with these institutions and their representatives as from anything I have ever read on the subject.

The lack of adequate research materials and particularly of any co-operation from MTV itself hampered my work. My only hope was to get the information from such sources, but this was where I often ran into problems. For example, trying to get dates for release of videos on MTV was difficult since MTV does not give out this information, for some unknown reason. I was forced to rely on the goodwill of people in the video departments of the various record companies, most of whom were pleasant and co-operative. However, I still could not verify release dates for every video, particularly for those made more than a year or so ago. There are as yet no reference books of any kind for MTV.

Another handicap was the sense of secrecy that surrounds a lot of the agents and managers, or their associates, whom one gets to speak to; I would confront a cagey, often wary voice on the other end of the line. People could not easily place me in a known category, often having as yet no experience with scholars writing about rock videos. Hence through nobody's fault I got shunted around a great deal, no-one seeming to know who could answer my questions about copyright, dates, permissions, etc. I often had the sense of dealing with vast interlocking networks, the parts of which did not always know about the others – a Kafkaesque experience of the whole organization being outside any one person's reach.

A different sort of frustration arose out of writing about something that was constantly changing. Even as I struggled to make generalizations, to codify, to formulate plausible theses and arguments, the channel would change and render a statement obsolete. In other words, the experience of writing the book was an experience of getting inside a postmodernist phenomenon. I was dealing with a body of material that would not stay the same, that was constantly transforming itself (like the image in Peter Gabriel's "Sledge-hammer") into something else even as I tried to grasp what it had just been. This phenomenon confirmed my sense of the relationship between constant transformation and the pressures of consumption that partly defines postmodernism.

This was most obvious in relation to the images of the stars that I was dealing with. In the past, with stars like Paul Anka, Elvis Presley, even the early Beatles or the Stones, the image that a star decided to promote remained relatively stable once a formula that produced commercial success had been found. If the image brought the fans out, and made them buy records and all the other star-paraphernalia, it would be exploited for a comparatively long time. But this is not the case with MTV stars who often undergo dramatic changes in the course of only months. For instance, Madonna, Pat Benatar, David Bowie, Prince, Tina Turner, Billy Idol, Motley Crue, to name only a few, have undergone major transformations over the past two years. Predictably, the stars making the more political videos (e.g. Bruce Springsteen, John Cougar Mellencamp, Tears for Fears), and who depend for their effect on a very personally committed and working-class appeal, on a stance in the world rather than on surfaces/textures/self-as-commodity, have not undergone such huge transformations.

155

ROCKING AROUND THE CLOCK

One can only theorize about the increased rapidity of changes in star-images: it has partly to do with the increased exposure that stars get today compared with in the past – an increased exposure produced largely through television. It is the very mechanism of a 24-hour channel that creates the need for rapid image changes; the consumption value of the old image is quickly exhausted given the intensity of its circulation on a 24-hour channel. If we take twelve videos an hour as a reasonable average, then 228 videos are shown every 24 hours. If we multiply this by seven, we get 2016 videos shown a week. And if a star has a video being cycled at the high-density rate, his/her image could be on the channel (and in viewers' minds) every three or four hours. Obviously, how often any particular viewer gets to see the same image depends on frequency of watching, but the point is that there is a high rate of market saturation in the new situation – far higher than in earlier historical periods. The stars evidently feel a need to keep changing their images in order to keep up their consumption. Viewers quickly tire of the same image, given its high rate of circulation, and there is constant demand for something new.

The case of Billy Idol here is pertinent, and also exemplifies the kinds of frustration that I experienced in relation to getting permission to reprint images from videos discussed in my book. Idol's agent had from the start been unusually co-operative and also unusually interested in my project. He asked me to send him the entire manuscript, which I did; he also requested that I send copies of the precise images I wanted to use, which I also did. The agent was even encouraging about Idol's being willing to let me put one image on the cover of the book – something that I could not get anyone else to agree to. But when I called for written confirmation of verbal agreements, I was told in no uncertain terms that I could not use anything since Billy was in the middle of changing his image; he was bringing out a new record and did not want anything to do with his old image in circulation.

This sensitivity about the star's image was pervasive; one agent (trying to be helpful) warned me that one had to be very careful when dealing with stars' images: *I* might think I had chosen an attractive video frame, but the star might see it quite differently and think the image ugly. Many agents indicated that the star in question refused to allow his/her image to be displayed in any way that he/she could not completely control. Images on a book cover were evidently viewed with great suspicion as being precisely an example of an image allowed to run wild, as it were. I was told that in the case of a book cover the stars would not know where their image was being displayed, and this they could not allow. An image on a book cover also presumably "fixes" an image for too long which, as I've noted, stars nowadays cannot afford.

I thus experienced firsthand what has been theorized about the circulation of the image and its ties to consumption. In the case of MTV, concerns take on a new dimension of urgency, since stars believe that they must make constant changes to remain desirable. If we look at the videos figuring Madonna in 1986, we can see extraordinarily rapid image changes. If the film *Desperately Seeking Susan* (its video was called "Getting Into the Groove") brings to full fruition an image Madonna had been working on in 1984—5, then 1986 reflected a series of efforts to abandon that image and replace it with something else. There was first the suddenly suave, serious, sleek image of the video "Live to Tell," again from a film; this was followed by the further transformation of the image in "Papa Don't Preach," where the figure is split between the Jean Seberg-style bejeaned teenager and the slick, sexy woman in black. Finally, right at the end of the year, a further dramatic change took place in the video "Open Your Heart," although perhaps it was a development of the sexy woman in "Papa Don't Preach." "Open Your Heart" is a daring critique of "carousel" porn parlours, such as proliferate on 42nd Street. In the course of this critique, Madonna not only figures as the girl inside the carousel who is being watched through windows that encircle her (the voyeur pays a certain amount for a fixed length of "seeing" time); but she also rescues an innocent young boy who has wandered into the carousel and wants to "play" Madonna. Madonna offers an uncharacteristic display of herself in traditional porn costume (black corset, suspenders, black stockings, high-heels, etc.), but at the end of the video, this sexy image is replaced by a kind of androgynous one: Madonna decides not only to run away from the parlor with the young boy, but to escape from sexuality into innocent boyhood (she is seen dressed like the boy in old-fashioned boy's clothes).

157

This sort of rapid change is increasingly demanded of the successful stars, whose images, just because of their success, quickly get saturated. As I tried to indicate throughout the book, the various types of videos that I outlined, from as early as 1982, also vary in popularity. For a few months the romantic seems to dominate, but then the nihilist type moves into the center; sometimes the socially conscious video (as in Summer 1986) comes to the fore, only to be followed by months when the postmodernist type becomes central. The one thing that has remained stable over the years studying MTV has been the five types I've outlined: the video technology has become more and more sophisticated, and production values for most of the videos now shown have gone up (videos are increasingly slick, professional, glossy, and using more and more elaborate, self-reflexive and deconstructive techniques), but the basic types remain the same. Perhaps, as I have tried to argue, the postmodernist aspects have begun increasingly to dominate videos of all types, but this has not yet reached a stage where the distinctions have become invalid (which I suppose could happen).

People often ask if I think that rock video and MTV are merely temporary phenomena which will be quickly exhausted. My sense is that the rock video is here to stay, although MTV as a 24-hour channel could change if competition from other such channels, or simply from the other sites of exhibition, increased so as to make their project unprofitable. It is possible that, like FM radio, TV channels could focus on one particular kind of rock video, or specialize in one type of rock/pop music. But so far there are no real signs to indicate this sort of change. For good or ill, MTV is most likely here to stay.

Any such change would emerge first from changes in what teenagers (and others MTV addresses) want from music video channels; and second from the receptivity of music television producers to changing audience tastes. As is clear from this book, I have not addressed myself to the level of historical viewers; I have been concerned with how MTV establishes itself as a production/consumption phenomenon rather than with how it is actually received by teenagers as historical subjects. MTV's postmodernist aspects may well be resisted or manipulated by such subjects in the viewing process. But research is needed to document this level of things. Theorizing the hypothetical or model spectator that a text constructs is compatible with studies of how historical spectators received texts. Different groups of teenagers no doubt use MTV in different ways according to class, race, and gender. However this may be, evidence of specific spectator behavior in no way invalidates the theory of MTV as a postmodernist form in its dominant modes of production, consumption, and exhibition.

Notes

INTRODUCTION

1 This figure was given to me by someone in the corporate office at Viacom.

2 Pittman is now President and Chief Executive Officer of MTV under Viacom.

3 Figures from unpublished paper by Gene Sobczak, "MTV, radio and unit sales," Rutgers University, June 1984, p. 12.

4 ibid.

5 *New York Times*, August 17, 1984, Section D.

6 ibid.

7 Cf. Sandy Flitterman, "The *real* soap operas: TV commercials," in E. Ann Kaplan, ed. *Regarding Television: Critical Approaches – An Anthology* (Los Angeles: American Film Institute, 1983), pp. 84-96.

8 Cf. Robert Stam, "Television news," in Kaplan (ed.), op. cit.

9 Margaret Phelan, "Panopticism and the uncanny: notes toward television's visual form," unpublished paper.

10 Cf. in particular *The Anti-Aesthetic: Essays on Postmodern Culture*, ed. Hal Foster (Port Townsend, Washington: The Bay Press, 1983).

11 There is already a quite formidable bibliography on the history of rock music. Perhaps the most solid sociological study remains Simon Frith's *The Sociology of Rock* (London: Constable, 1978), revised and updated in 1984. John Orman's recent *The Politics of Rock Music* (Chicago: Nelson-Hall, 1984) documents the subversive aspects of rock music in the 1960s, and the CIA's interest in rock stars, and ends up showing the increasing conservativism of rock stars and fans in the 1980s. John Eisen's uneven collection, *The Age of Rock: Sounds of*

NOTES

The American Cultural Revolution (New York: Random House, 1969) contains much discussion of rock's subversive aspects, while Nick Cohn's early *Rock From the Beginning* (New York: Stein & Day, 1969) takes a more cynical and skeptical stance.

12 Stuart Hall and Paddy Whannel, *The Popular Arts* (New York: Pantheon, 1965), especially chapter 2.

13 Cf. Stephen Melville, "Coda: The morning mail." Paper read at the Lacan Conference at The University of Amherst, Spring 1985. Some of this material has been incorporated into an article, "Psychoanalysis and the place of *jouissance*," *Critical Inquiry* (December 1986).

14 Greil Marcus, *Mystery Train: Images of America in Rock 'n' Roll Music* (New York: E.P. Dutton, 1975; rev. edn 1985).

15 Cohn, op. cit.; M. Jahn, *From Elvis Presley to the Rolling Stones* (New York: Quadrangle, 1973).

16 Students interested in the history of rock music should refer to the bibliography.

17 As of writing, there is a rich sub-culture of new rock sounds in major cities like New York. For reporting on the aficionado rock scene in New York, see Ron Cristgau's column in *The Village Voice*.

18 The exhibition presents what are seen as key examples of the rock video form. Titled "Music video: the industry and its fringes," the show has thirty videos by various artists. The form can be said to start with the Beatles' 1967 promos for "Penny Lane" and "Strawberry Fields," which exhibit the surrealist imitations so prevalent in current videos. Captain Beefheart's "Lick my Decals Off Baby," is already a classic, while Queen's "Bohemian Rapsody" was one of the first videos responsible for a song hit, and also prefigures MTV's interest in visual complexities. Cf. review by Jim Hoberman, *The Village Voice*, September 17, 1985, for more details.

1 MTV: ADVERTISING AND PRODUCTION

1 This is what Sandy Flitterman argues in "The *real* soap operas: TV commercials," in E. Ann Kaplan (ed.), *Regarding Television: Critical Approaches — An Anthology* (Los Angeles: American Film Institute, 1983), pp. 84-96.

2 Cf. the "Music Video Directors' Symposium," in *Variety*, Wednesday, March 14, 1985, especially p. 70, where Adam Friedman discusses how videos are becoming increasingly important to the record companies.

3 Cf. "Music Video Directors' Symposium," *Variety*, Wednesday, March 14, 1984.

4 Cf. Gene Sobczak, "MTV, radio and unit sales," Rutgers University, June 1984, p. 13.

5 "Music Video Directors' Symposium," op. cit., p. 70. Information was also obtained from an interview with New York Video Director, Eddie Barbarini.

6 John Rockwell early on suggested that this format would produce the most original results. Combining video with sound into something really new, he says, is the most innovative possibility. "Soon artists will begin to shape their aural imaginations to take account of the visual possibilities afforded them by the video medium, and will let the sounds in their heads affect the sights, abstract or realistic, that we see on the video screen." Cf. his "Rock is edging into video," *The New York Times*, July 29, 1979.

7 Ed Levine, "TV rocks with music," *The New York Times Magazine*, May 8, 1983, p. 43.

8 This material is taken from an interview with Dr York at a TV studio in New York, where Bob Lechterman and Eddie Barbarini were filming and directing (respectively) a video by the group "Petite" that Dr York was producing. Dr York indicated that one way for black artists to get accepted on American music channels like VH-1, MTV, U-68, or on the HBO and other slots on regular channels, was for them to have a record produced by a British record company. York believes the British market is far more open to black artists, and either has a large "quota" or no quota at all, as he thinks the American channels have.

9 Cf. discussions in popular articles, e.g. Steve Levy, "Ad nauseam – how MTV sells out rock and roll," *Rolling Stone*, December 8, 1983, pp. 36-7; comment by Arlene Zeichner in "Rock 'n Roll Video," *Film Comment*, vol. 19, no. 4 (July/August 1983), p. 45; Ron Gristgau, "Rock 'n roll coaster: the music biz on a joyride," *The Village Voice* (February 7, 1984), p. 43; Levine, op. cit: Levine notes here that Bob Pittman defends the few black bands by claiming that black and white pop music have always been separate – hardly any kind of justification for his practice!

10 The irony here, as Dr York pointed out, is that white musicians are using black forms in their rock; the Police and Sting play reggae, according to Dr York, while he characterized Wham!, Hall and Oates, and Madonna as playing "Blue-Eyed Soul."

11 Levy, op. cit, p. 33.

12 During 1986, there was a striking change in MTV logos: to begin with, the rocket logo was finally dropped altogether, ostensibly because of the Challenger disaster; but secondly, the logos now are immensely colorful, varied, and imaginative. There are animated, comic ones; abstract, patterned ones; the "MTV" letters are arranged in all imaginable ways that constantly engage one's attention. In addition, there are more direct ads for MTV in the form of interviews with people "on the street," saying what the channel means to them. It is as if the channel gave up trying to symbolize itself through the logos, and went instead for what would delight the eye.

13 Cf. Jane Feuer, "The concept of live television: ontology as ideology," in E. Ann Kaplan (ed.), *Regarding Television: Critical Approaches – An Anthology* (Los Angeles: American Film Institute, 1983), pp. 12-22.

NOTES

14 For an off-the-cuff look at the daily routine at MTV, including interviews with some of the Veejays and the pre-recording techniques, see Roberta Myers, "Behind the scenes at MTV," in *Careers*, Spring 1986, pp. 21-5.

15 The information reported here was gained by interviews with teenagers from The Bronx High School of Science, including Leo Margolf and Brett Kaplan, and from private schools including Paul Charney.

16 ibid.

17 Find below minute-by-minute outline of various MTV ad-segments (randomly chosen hours).

      (a) ONE HOUR ON MTV: TAKEN FROM 5:22 TO 6:22, JUNE 25, 1985

5:22	Ad: Crazy Eddie (½)
	Ads: Announcement series: Hans Kleper Corp
	Copy Quick
	American Lung Association
	Manhattanville Records
5:24	MTV logo (Mystery Man) (seconds)
5:24	Video: Eurythmics, "There Must Be An Angel"
5:28	MTV spot (seconds)
5:28	Video: Elton John, "Act of War"
5:32	MTV spot (seconds)
5:32	Video: Duran Duran, "A View To Kill"
5:36	Video: Rod Stewart, "People Get Ready"
5:39	Goodman/Piscope interview
5:40	Ad: Three Musketeers
5:40	Ad: Jordache Jeans
5:41	Ad: Sun Country Wine Cooler
5:41	Bryan Adams: ad of own upcoming appearance
5:41	Interview Goodman/Piscope
5:45	Video: Katerina, "Walking on Sunshine"
5:48	
5:52	Goodman – commentary on Gina; notes Adams' upcoming appearance; notes the "Let's make a music deal" award
5:52	Ad for movie, *Back to the Future*
5:53	Milk ad
5:53	Juicy Fruit ad
5:54	Ad: Merry-Go-Round Fashions
5:54	Soft-Dri ad
5:55	MTV ad for all-American rock and roll weekend (military iconography)
5:55	Video: "I Drink Alone"
6:00	MTV logo: Men on Moon; Quinn's voice re what's coming up
6:01	Video: Cyndi Lauper's "Goonies"
6:06	Video: Julian Lennon, "Valotte"
6:10	Martha Quinn with concert tour info

6:12   Ad for Columbia Pictures movie *St Elmo's Fire*
6:12   Ad: shorts
6:13   Ad: Levis
6:15   Video: Ratt's "Lay It Down"
6:18   Video: Madonna, "Getting Into The Groove"
6:21   Quinn, announcing the countdown Friday at different times; also the music competition game
6:22   Ads: the announcement series that came on at 5:22

(b) HOUR RUNDOWN FROM 5:11 TO 6:11, JUNE 26, 1985

5:11   Film ad: *Back to the Future*
5:12   Ad for rock and roll weekend and Friday night countdown
5:13   Video: Hooters, "All You Zombies"
5:17   Video: Journey, "Send Her My Love"
5:21   Veejay (Goodman) advertising MTV "Black Satin Tour" jacket; telling us Benatar tape coming up
5:22   Ad for Institute of Technology
        Ad for Calvin Cooler drink
        Ad for American Heart Association
        Ad for Calvin Cooler
5:23   New York State Bar Association ad: anti-drink and drive
5:23   Announcement ad for Carrot Top Pastries
5:23   MTV logo
5:24   Video: Hall and Oates, "Possession/Obsession"
5:28   MTV logo
5:28   Tape Collins/Bailey interview followed by their video, "Easy Lover"
5:32   MTV logo
5:32   Video: Benatar, "Invincible"
5:36   Video: Pete Townshend, "Let My Love Open the Door"
5:39   Veejay (Goodman): send away for the music deal
5:39   Ad: Snickers Bar
5:40   Ad: for Musicland Record Store
5:41   Ad: for Golden Champagne
5:41   MTV music news re Sting, Scorpions, Motley Crue
5:42   Clip of Motley Crue talking about themselves
5:43   Video: Talking Heads, "Once in a Life Time"
5:48   Video: Duran Duran, "A View to a Kill"
5:51   Veejay (M. Quinn) music news
5:52   Ad for film, *Emerald Forest* (struggle of father to find the son)
5:53   Ad for Alberto Mousse
        Ad for Country Wine Cooler
5:54   Ad for Merry-Go-Round Clothes
        Ad for Carefree Gum
5:55   MTV ad

164

5:59	MTV logo, Veejay (Quinn) voice over re the music competition
6:00	Video: Michael Jackson, "Beat It"
6:05	Veejay: music news
6:06	Power Slaties interview with veejay
6:07	Ad for milk
6:07	Ad for jeep
6:08	MTV ad re basement tapes competition (six new bands chosen)
6:09	Video: Robert Plant, "Little By Little"
6:13	Video: Chicago, "Along Came a Woman"

2 HISTORY, "READING FORMATIONS," AND THE TELEVISUAL APPARATUS IN MTV

1 Keith Tribe, "History and the production of memories," *Screen*, vol. 18, no. 4 (Winter 1977/8), p. 11.
2 ibid.
3 Cf. Emile Benveniste, *Problems of General Linguistics* (Miami: University of Miami Press, 1971).
4 Geoffrey Nowell-Smith, "A note on history/discourse" (Nowell-Smith's essay was a commentary on Metz's), *Edinburgh Magazine*, no. 1 (1976), p. 30.
5 Christian Metz, "History/discourse: a note on two voyeurisms," *Edinburgh Magazine*, no. 1 (1976), p. 24.
6 Foucault's *The Archaeology of Knowledge and the Discourse on Language*, trans. Alan Sheridan (New York: Pantheon, 1972) explicitly confronts the possibility of writing history. Foucault looks back on, and critiques, his own historical discourse in previous texts, while raising problems about the whole construction of academic disciplines themselves. A text like *The History of Sexuality, Volume I: An Introduction* (trans. Robert Hurley, New York: Random House, 1978), on the other hand, shows Foucault doing his kind of "history as discourse" work.
7 Foucault, op. cit., pp. 12-15.
8 Roland Barthes, "The death of the author," in *Image—Music—Text*, trans. Stephen Heath (New York: Hill & Wang, 1977), p. 148.
9 Metz, op. cit., p. 22.
10 David Morley, *The "Nationwide" Audience: Structure and Decoding*, BFI Television Monographs, no. 11 (London: British Film Institute, 1980).
11 Cf. Christine Gledhill, "Recent developments in feminist film criticism," *Quarterly Review of Film Studies*, vol. 3, no. 4 (1978), pp. 35-46. Reprinted in Mary Ann Doane, Pat Mellencamp, and Linda Williams, *Re-Vision: Essays in Feminist Film Criticism* (Los Angeles: American Film Institute, 1983), pp. 18-48.
12 Reprinted in Stephen Heath, *Questions of Cinema* (Bloomington, Ind.: Indiana University Press, 1981), pp. 113-30. Page numbers refer to this edition.

13 Keith Tribe, op. cit.; and Janet Staiger, "Mass produced photoplays: economic and signifying practices in the first years of Hollywood," *Wide Angle*, vol. 4, no. 3 (1980), pp. 12-28. Cf. also David Bordwell, Kristin Thompson, and Janet Staiger, *The Classical Hollywood Film* (New York: Columbia University Press, 1985).

14 Cf. Ernesto Laclau, "Politics and the construction of the unthinkable," unpublished paper, cited by Bennett; and his "Populist rupture and discourse," *Screen Education*, no. 34 (Spring 1980); and Michel Pêcheux, *Language, Semantics and Ideology* (London: Macmillan, 1982).

15 Ron Levaco, "Eikenbaum, inner speech and film stylistics," *Screen*, vol. 15, no. 4 (Winter 1974/5), p. 48.

16 Tony Bennett, "Texts in history: the determinations of readings and their texts," in Derek Attridge, Geoffrey Bennington and Robert Young (eds), *Post-Structuralism and the Question of History* (Cambridge: Cambridge University Press, 1986).

17 Keith Tribe, op. cit., p. 12.

18 Mulvey, "Visual pleasure and narrative cinema," *Screen*, vol. 16, no 3 (Autumn 1975), pp. 6-18. This essay has been reprinted several times.

19 "Oedipus interruptus," *Wide Angle*, vol. 7, nos 1-2, pp. 34-41.

20 Robert Stam, "Television news and its spectator," in E. Ann Kaplan (ed.), *Regarding Television: Critical Approaches – An Anthology* (Los Angeles: American Film Institute, 1983), pp. 23-43. Cf. also what Sandy Flitterman-Lewis has to say on this topic in her essay "Fascination in Fragments: psychoanalysis in film and television," in Robert Allen (ed.) *Channels of Discourse: Television Criticism in the 80s* (Chapel Hill, NC: University of North Carolina Press, 1987).

21 Cf. Jane Feuer, "The concept of live television: ontology as ideology," in E. Ann Kaplan (ed.), op. cit., pp. 12-22; and Charlotte Brunsdon, "Crossroads: notes on soap opera," in E. Ann Kaplan (ed.), op. cit., pp. 76-82.

3   MTV AND THE AVANT-GARDE: THE EMERGENCE OF A POSTMODERNIST ANTI-AESTHETIC?

1 Cf. Diana Frampton, "Pop promo man moves into ads," *Broadcast*, August 2, 1985.

2 Jacques Lacan, "The mirror stage as formative of the function of the I," in his *Ecrits: A Selection*, trans. Alan Sheridan (New York and London: Norton, 1979), pp. 1-9.

3 Lacan, op. cit., especially pp. 56-76.

4 For more discussion of the implications for women of the Lacanian model, see Kaja Silverman, *The Subject of Semiotics* (New York: Oxford University Press, 1983), especially pp. 149-93. For further understanding of Lacan in general, see Anika Lemaire, *Jacques Lacan*, trans. David Macey (London: Routledge & Kegan Paul, 1977).

NOTES

5   Cf. Roland Barthes, "Upon leaving the movie theatre," in Theresa Hak Kyung Cha (ed.), *Cinematic Apparatus: Selected Writings* (New York: Tanam Press, 1980), p. 3.
6   Cf. Jean Baudrillard, "The ecstasy of communication," in Hal Foster (ed.), *The Anti-Aesthetic: Essays in Postmodern Culture* (Port Townsend: Bay Press, 1983), pp. 126-33; and his essays in *Simulations*, trans. Paul Foss, Paul Patton, and Philip Beitchman (New York: Semiotext(e), 1983), especially pp. 30-48.
7   Cf. Rachel Bowlby, *Just Looking: Consumer Culture in Dreiser, Gissing and Zola* (London and New York: Methuen, 1985), especially pp. 1-17; and Peter Stallybrass and Allon White, *The Politics and Poetics of Transgression* (London and New York: Methuen/Cornell, 1986).
8   Fredric Jameson, "Postmodernism and consumer society," in Hal Foster (ed.), op. cit., pp. 111-25. Page numbers refer to this edition. A complete version of this essay appeared in *New Left Review* no. 146 (1984) as "Postmodernism, or The Cultural Logic of Late Capitalism".
9   Louis A. Sass, "Time, space and symbol: a study of narrative form and representational structure in madness and modernism," in *Psychoanalysis and Contemporary Thought*, vol. 8, no. 1 (1985), pp. 45-85.

4   IDEOLOGY, ADOLESCENT DESIRE, AND THE FIVE TYPES OF VIDEO ON MTV

1   Cf. Louis Althusser, "Ideology and ideological state apparatuses (notes towards an investigation)," in *Lenin and Philosophy and Other Essays*, trans. Ben Brewster (New York and London: Monthly Review Press, 1971), p. 180. Page numbers refer to this edition.
2   Jean Baudrillard, "The ecstasy of communication," in Hal Foster (ed.), *The Anti-Aesthetic: Essays in Postmodern Culture* (Port Townsend: Bay Press, 1983), p. 127.
3   For a full discussion of Baudrillard's ideas and their limitations, cf. André Frankovitz (ed.), *Seduced and Abandoned: The Baudrillard Scene* (New York and Glebe, Australia: Semiotext(e) and Stonemoss Services, 1984).
4   Cf. Jean Baudrillard, *Simulations*, trans. Paul Foss, Paul Patton, and Philip Beitchman (New York: Semiotext(e), 1983).
5   Lawrence Grossberg, "The politics of youth culture: some observations on rock and roll in American culture," *Social Text* (Winter 1983–4), pp. 110-11.
6   In a forthcoming book, *Motherhood and Representation*, I trace some of the history of mother images in film and literature – images that rock videos still draw upon.
7   Cf. Peter Stallybrass and Allon White, *The Politics and Poetics of Transgression* (London and New York: Methuen/Cornell, 1986), especially the introduction for a summary of Bakhtinian ideas of the carnival and of their critical uses, pp. 1-26.

8   Mikhail Bakhtin, *Rabelais and his World*, trans. H. Iswolsky (Cambridge, Mass.: MIT Press, 1968), p. 109. Quotes by Stallybrass and White, op. cit., p. 7.
9   Cf. discussion by Stallybrass and White, op. cit., p. 13.
10 As will be clear later on, videos by women stars are far fewer than those by male stars, and in the avant-garde category the imbalance is even greater. A recent series of programs of videos by female artists, going back to the 1970s, at Artists Space in New York (entitled "What does she want," and running from 2–27 November, 1985) demonstrated the range and creativity of much video work by women being done outside the mainstream. Laurie Anderson's creative "O Superman" was shown in that series; it is only because of her film *Home of the Brave* (given a short run at one New York theatre, The Bleecker Street Cinema) that her video made it to MTV.
11 John Orman, *The Politics of Rock Music* (Chicago: Nelson-Hall, 1984), pp. 164-5.
12 "He's on fire: America's latest rock-and-roll hero has the fans going wild about the boss," *Newsweek*, August 15, 1985, pp. 4-9.
13 Cf. Jean Baudrillard, *In the Shadow of the Silent Majorities . . . Or the End of the Social and Other Essays*, trans. Paul Foss, Paul Patton, and John Johnston (New York: Semiotext(e), 1983), p. 26. Page numbers refer to this edition.

5   GENDER ADDRESS AND THE GAZE IN MTV

1   For recent discussion of differences between the filmic and televisual apparatus cf. Sandy Flitterman-Lewis, "Fascination in Fragments: psychoanalysis in film and television," in Robert Allen (ed.) *Channels of Discourse: Television Criticism in the 80s* (Chapel Hill, NC: University of North Carolina Press, 1987).
2   Cf. summaries of recent feminist work, together with bibliographies in Annette Kuhn, *Women's Pictures: Feminism and Cinema* (London: Routledge & Kegan Paul, 1982): E. Ann Kaplan, *Women and Film: Both Sides of the Camera* (London and New York: Methuen, 1983); P. Mellencamp, Mary Ann Doane, and Linda Williams (eds), *Re-Vision: Essays in Feminist Film Criticism* (Los Angeles: American Film Institute, 1984).
3   Cf., for example, Teresa de Lauretis, *Alice Doesn't: Feminism, Cinema, and Semiotics* (Bloomington, Indiana: Indiana University Press, 1984); or Gaylyn Studlar, "Masochism and the perverse pleasures of cinema," in Bill Nichols (ed.), *Movies and Methods*, vol. II (Berkeley and Los Angeles: University of California Press, 1985), pp. 602-24.
4   Mary Ann Doane, "Woman's stake: filming the female body," *October*, no. 17 (1981), pp. 29-30.
5   Discussion of the episode is in Sigmund Freud, *Beyond the Pleasure Principle*, Standard Edition, XVIII, pp. 14-17.

6   Cf. Daniel Stern, "Mother and infant at play: the dyadic interaction involving facial, vocal and gaze behaviors," in M. Lewis and L.A. Rosenblaum (eds), *The Origins of Behavior*: vol. 1, *The Effect of the Infant on the Caregiver* (New York: Wiley, 1974). And Selma Fraiberg, *Every Child's Birthright: In Defense of Mothering* (New York: Basic Books, 1977).

7   In her more usual vein, Pat Benatar early on anticipated the recent "tough woman" look of many female vocalists. In 1981, Nick Wright quoted her as saying "I hardly ever listen to other female vocalists. It's the British male rock stars I admire most. . . . Low-keyed and laid back I'm not. A lot of women singers today seem to be saying 'If you love me and then hurt me, I'll die.' I say, 'If you love me and then hurt me, I'll kick your ass.'" Nick Wright, "Pat Benatar," in *The Year in Rock, 1981-82*, ed. John Swenson (New York: Delilah Books, Putnam, 1981), p. 16.

8   Quoted by Stephen Holden in "The pop life: a spicy new album by Carly Simon," *The New York Times*, Wednesday, August 7, 1985, C16.

9   Cf. Stephen Holden, "Review of Paul Young," *The New York Times,* Wednesday, August 7, 1985.

10   Cf. Deborah Frost, "White noise: how heavy metal rules," *The Village Voice,* vol. XXX, no. 25 (June 18, 1985), pp. 46-9.

11   Cf. David Fricke, "Heavy metal," in *The Year in Rock,* op. cit. According to Fricke, the Sex Pistols "embodied the seething anger and snowballing frustration of British youth faced with rising unemployment and a dead-end economy." Fricke goes on to note that "the recent riots in England, are, for the most part, Johnny Rotten's prophecy come true" (p. 20).

12   Cf. E. Ann Kaplan, "Pornography and/as representation," forthcoming in *Enclitic*; cf. also the Brief by Sally Law and Nan Hunter written for the Indianapolis Lawsuit about Censorship of Pornography.

13   Cf. Jane D. Brown and Kenneth C. Campbell, "Race and gender in music videos: The same beat but a different drummer," *Journal of Communication,* vol. 36, no. 1 (winter 1986), pp. 94-107.

6   CONCLUSION: MTV, POSTMODERNISM, AND THE TELEVISUAL APPARATUS

1   See notes to Introduction for relevant citations.

2   Fredric Jameson, "Postmodernism and consumer society," in Hal Foster (ed.), *The Anti-Aesthetic: Essays in Postmodern Culture* (Port Townsend: Bay Press, 1983), p. 116.

3   ibid., p. 119.

4   ibid., p. 119.

5   ibid., p. 120.

6   ibid., p. 121.

7   Lawrence Grossberg, "The politics of youth culture: some observations

on rock and roll in American culture,'' *Social Text* (Winter 1983-4), p. 111.

8 Jean Baudrillard, ''The ecstasy of communication,'' in Hal Foster (ed.), op. cit.

Videography

(Videos mentioned in the book)

AC/DC
"For Those About to Rock We Salute You"
For Those About to Rock
Atlantic Records, 1985

AC/DC
"Who Made Who"
Maximum Overdrive
Motion Picture Soundtrack
Atlantic Records, 1986
DeLaurentiis Entertainment Corp.

Bryan Adams
"Heaven"
Reckless
A & M Records, 1985

a—ha
"Take On Me"
Hunting High and Low
Warner Bros Records, 1984
Director: Steve Barron

a—ha
"Train of Thought"
Hunting High and Low
Warner Bros Records, 1985

Laurie Anderson
"Language Is A Virus"
Home of the Brave
Motion Picture Soundtrack
Warner Bros Records, 1986

The Art of Noise
"Paranoimia"
Invisible Silence
Chrysalis Records, 1986

Artists Against Apartheid
"Sun-City"
Manhattan Records, 1986

Asia
"Only Time Will Tell"
Asia
Geffen Records, 1983

Philip Bailey and Phil Collins
"Easy Lover"
Chinese Wall
Columbia/CBS Records, 1986

Bangles
"Manic Monday"
Different Light
Columbia/CBS Records, 1986

171

ROCKING AROUND THE CLOCK

Jimmy Barnes
"Working Class Man"
Gung Ho
Motion Picture Soundtrack
Geffen Records/Paramount
Pictures, 1986

Pat Benatar
"Love is a Battlefield"
Get Nervous
Chrysalis Records, 1983

Pat Benatar
"Sex as a Weapon"
Seven The Hard Way
Chrysalis Records, 1986

Pat Benatar
"We Belong"
Tropico
Chrysalis Records, 1984

David Bowie
"DJ"
The Lodge
RCA Records, 1983

David Bowie
"Modern Love"
Let's Dance
EMI/America Records, 1984

David Bowie
"China Girl"
Let's Dance
EMI/America Records, 1984

David Bowie
"Blue Jean"
Tonight
EMI/America Records, 1984

David Bowie
"Absolute Beginners"
Absolute Beginners
Motion Picture Soundtrack
EMI/America Records/Orion
Pictures, 1986
Director: Julian Temple

David Bowie and Mick Jagger
"Dancing In The Street"
EMI/America Records, 1985

Jackson Brown
"For America"
Lives In The Balance
Elektra/Asylum Records, 1986

Julie Brown
"The Homecoming Queen's Got a
Gun"
Goddess In Progress
Rhino Records, 1984

Kim Carnes
"Bette Davis' Eyes"
Mistaken Identity
EMI/America Records, 1984

Cars
"You Might Think"
Heartbeat City
Elektra Records, 1984

Cars
"Why Can't I Have You"
Heartbeat City
Elektra Records, 1985

Phil Collins
"One More Night"
No Jacket Required
Atlantic Records, 1985

Phil Collins
"Don't Lose My Number"
No Jacket Required
Atlantic Records, 1985

John Cougar Mellencamp
"Authority Song"
Uh—Huh
Riva/Polygram Records, 1984

John Cougar Mellencamp
"ROCK In The USA"
Scarecrow
Riva/Polygram Records, 1986

VIDEOGRAPHY

John Cougar Mellencamp
"Lonely Ol' Night"
Scarecrow
Riva/Polygram Records, 1985

John Cougar Mellencamp
"Small Town"
Scarecrow
Riva/Polygram Records, 1985

John Cougar Mellencamp
"Hurts So Good"
American Fool
Riva/Polygram Records, 1982

John Cougar Mellencamp
"Rain on the Scarecrow"
Scarecrow
Riva/Polygram Records, 1986

Motley Crue
"Smokin' in the Boys' Room"
Theatre of Pain
Elektra Records, 1985

Motley Crue
"Home Sweet Home"
Theatre of Pain
Elektra Records, 1985

Dire Straits
"Money for Nothing"
Brothers in Arms
Warner Bros Records, 1985
Director: Steve Barron

Dire Straits
"So Far Away"
Brothers In Arms
Warner Bros Records, 1985

Dire Straits
"Walk of Life"
Brothers in Arms
Warner Bros Records, 1986

Dokken
"Alone Again"
Tooth and Nail
Elektra Records, 1985

The Dream Academy
"Life in a Northern Town"
The Dream Academy
Warner Bros Records, 1986

Duran Duran
"Reflex"
Seven and The Ragged Tiger
Capitol Records, 1983

Duran Duran
"Rio"
Rio
Capitol Records, 1983

Duran Duran
"A View to a Kill"
Original Motion Picture Soundtrack
Capitol Records, 1985

Duran Duran
"Wild Boys"
Arena
Capitol Records, 1985

ELO
"Calling America"
Balance of Power
CBS/Associated Records, 1985

Eurythmics
"Here Comes the Rain Again"
Be Yourself Tonight
RCA Records, 1984

Eurythmics
"Would I Lie to You?"
Be Yourself Tonight
RCA Records, 1985

Eurythmics
"There Must Be An Angel
(Playing With My Heart)"
Be Yourself Tonight
RCA Records, 1985

Eurythmics
"Sexcrime
1984 (For the Love of the Big Brother)
RCA Records, 1984

Eurythmics
"Missionary Man"
Revenge
RCA Records, 1986

Fabulous Thunderbirds
"Tuff Enuff"
Tuff Enuff
CBS Associated Records, 1986

Falco
"Rock Me Amadeus"
Falco 3
A & M Records, 1986

The Firm
"Radioactive"
The Firm
Atlantic Records, 1985

The Firm
"Live In Peace"
Mean Business
Atlantic Records, 1986

John Fogerty
"The Old Man Down The Road"
Centerfield
Warner Bros Records, 1984

John Fogerty
"Rock and Roll Girls"
Centerfield
Warner Bros Records, 1984

Foreigner
"I Want To Know What Love Is"
Agent Provocateur
Atlantic Records, 1984

Frankie Goes to Hollywood
"Relax"
Welcome To The Pleasure Dome
ZTT/Island Records, 1983

Frankie Goes to Hollywood
"Two Tribes"
Welcome To The Pleasure Dome
ZTT/Island Records, 1984

Frankie Goes to Hollywood
"Welcome to the Pleasure Dome"
Welcome To The Pleasure Dome
ZTT/Island Records, 1985

Aretha Franklin
"Freeway of Love"
Who's Zoomin' Who?
Arista Records, 1985

Aretha Franklin
"Another Night"
Who's Zoomin' Who?
Arista Records, 1986

Aretha Franklin and Annie Lennox
"Sisters Are Doin' It For
Themselves"
Be Yourself Tonight
RCA Records, 1986

Glen Frey
"Smuggler's Blues"
The Allnighter
MCA Records, 1985

Glen Frey
"You Belong to the City"
Miami Vice Soundtrack
MCA Records, 1986

Glen Frey
"The Heat Is On"
Beverly Hills Cop
Motion Picture Soundtrack
MCA Records, 1985

Peter Gabriel
"Shock the Monkey"
Peter Gabriel
Geffen Records, 1985

Peter Gabriel
"Sledgehammer"
So
Geffen Records, 1986

Genesis
"Invisible Touch"
Invisible Touch
Atlantic Records, 1986

VIDEOGRAPHY

Sammy Hagar
"VOA"
VOA
Geffen Records, 1985

Sammy Hagar
"I Can't Drive at 55"
VOA
Geffen Records, 1985

Van Halen
"Jump"
1984
Warner Bros Records, 1983

Van Halen
"Hot for Teacher"
1984
Warner Bros Records, 1984

Daryl Hall
"Dreamtime"
The Three In The Happy Machine
RCA Records, 1986

Daryl Hall and John Oats
"Out of Touch"
Big Bam Boom
RCA Records, 1984

Daryl Hall and John Oates (with
David Ruffin and Eddie Kendrick)
"Live At The Apollo"
RCA Records, 1985

Heart
"What About Love"
Heart
Capitol Records, 1985

Heart
"Nothin' At All"
Heart
Capitol Records, 1986
Director: Milton Lage

Heart
"These Dreams"
Heart
Capitol Records, 1986

Don Henley
"Boys of Summer"
Building the Perfect Beast
Geffen Records, 1984

Don Henley
"All She Wants to do is Dance"
Building the Perfect Beast
Geffen Records, 1985

Honeymoon Suite
"Feel It Again"
The Big Prize
(Used Digital Disk)
Warner Bros Records, 1986
Director: Danny Kleinman

Whitney Houston
"How Will I Know"
Whitney Houston
Arista Records, 1985

Whitney Houston
"Greatest Love of All"
Whitney Houston
Arista Records, 1986

Billy Idol
"Rebel Yell"
Rebel Yell
Chrysalis Records, 1983

Billy Idol
"White Wedding"
Billy Idol
Chrysalis Records, 1986

INXS
"What You Need"
Listen Like Thieves
Atlantic Records, 1986

Janet Jackson
"What Have You Done For Me
Lately"
Control
A & M Records, 1986

Jermaine Jackson
"I Think It's Love"
Precious Moment
Arista Records, 1986

Michael Jackson
"Thriller"
Thriller
Epic/CBS Records, 1983

Michael Jackson
"Beat It"
Thriller
Epic/CBS Records, 1984

Michael Jackson
"Billy Jean"
Thriller
Epic/CBS Records, 1984
Director: Steve Barron

The Rolling Stones
"She Was Hot"
Under Cover
CBS Records, 1983

Mick Jagger
"Harlem Shuffle"
Dirty Work
Rolling Stones Records, 1986

Mick Jagger and David Bowie
"Dancing In The Street"
EMI/America Records, 1985

Mick Jagger and Bette Midler
"Beast of Burden"
No Frills
Atlantic Records, 1984

Elton John
"That's Why They Call It The Blues"
Too Low for Zero
Geffen Records, 1984

Elton John
"Heartache All Over"
Leather Jackets
Geffen Records, 1986

Grace Jones
"Love Is The Drug"
Island Life
Island Records, 1986

Judas Priest
"Locked In"
Turbo
Columbia Records, 1986

Kiss
"The Tears Are Falling"
Asylum
Mercury/Polygram Records, 1986

Cyndi Lauper
"Time After Time"
She's So Unusual
Portrait Records, 1983

Cyndi Lauper
"Money Changes Everything"
She's So Unusual
Portrait Records, 1984

Cyndi Lauper
"Girls Just Want to Have Fun"
She's So Unusual
Portrait Records, 1983

Julian Lennon
"Stick Around"
The Secret Value of Daydreams
Atlantic Records, 1986

Annie Lennox and Aretha Franklin
"Sisters Are Doin' It For
Themselves"
Be Yourself Tonight
RCA Records, 1986

Madonna
"Lucky Star"
Madonna
Sire/Warner Bros Records, 1984

Madonna
"Borderline"
Madonna
Sire/Warner Bros Records, 1984

VIDEOGRAPHY

Madonna
"Like a Virgin"
Like a Virgin
Warner Bros Records, 1984

Madonna
"Getting Into The Groove"
Desperately Seeking Susan
Motion Picture Soundtrack
Orion Pictures, 1985
Producer: Stephen Ray

Madonna
"Material Girl"
Madonna
Sire/Warner Bros Records, 1985

Madonna
"Live To Tell"
At Close Range
Motion Picture Soundtrack
Hemdale Film/Orion Pictures, 1986

Madonna
"Papa Don't Preach"
True Blue
Sire/Warner Bros Records, 1986

Mama's Boys
"Mama, We're All Crazy Now"
Mama's Boys
Sire/Arista Records, 1984

Bette Midler and Mick Jagger
"Beast of Burden"
No Frills
Atlantic Records, 1984

Midnight Oil
"Best of Both Worlds"
Red Sails In The Sunset
Columbia/CBS Records, 1985

Ozzy Osbourne
"Shot in the Dark"
The Ultimate Sin
CBS Associated Records, 1986

Robert Palmer
"Addicted to Love"
Riptide
Island Records, 1985

Robert Palmer
"I Didn't Mean To Turn You On"
Riptide
Island Records, 1986

John Parr
"Naughty Naughty"
John Parr
Atlantic Records, 1984

Tom Petty and the Heartbreakers
"Don't Come Around Here No More"
Southern Accents
MCA Records, 1985

Pointer Sisters
"Neutron Dance"
Beverly Hills Cop
Motion Picture Soundtrack
Paramount Pictures/MCA Records, 1985

Police
"Synchronicity"
Synchronicity Concert
Home Video
A & M Home Video/IRS Video, 1985

The Powerstation
"Some Like It Hot"
Some Like It Hot
Capitol Records, 1985

Prince
"1999"
1999
Warner Bros Records, 1985

Prince
"Raspberry Beret"
Around the World in a Day
Paisley Park/Warner Bros Records, 1985

Prince
"Kiss"
Parade
Under the Cherry Moon

177

ROCKING AROUND THE CLOCK

Motion Picture Soundtrack
Paisley Park/Warner Bros
Records, 1986

Queen
"Radio Ga Ga"
The Works
Capitol Records, 1983

Queen
"Princes of the Universe"
The Highland Album
Capitol Records, 1986

Lionel Ritchie
"Hello"
Can't Slow Down
Motown Records, 1984

Lionel Ritchie
"Dancing on the Ceiling"
Dancing on the Ceiling
Motown Records, 1986

Romantics
"Talking in Your Sleep"
In Heat
Nemperor/CBS Records, 1983

David Lee Roth
"California Girls"
Crazy From The Heat
Warner Bros Records, 1985

David Lee Roth
"Just Like a Gigolo (I Ain't Got
Nobody)"
Crazy From the Heat
Warner Bros Records, 1985

David Lee Roth
"Yankie Rose"
Eat 'Em And Smile
Warner Bros Records, 1986

David Lee Roth
"Going Crazy
Eat 'Em And Smile
Warner Bros Records, 1986

Run—DMC
"Walk This Way"
Raising Hell
Profile Records, 1986

Scorpions
"Rock You Like a Hurrican"
Love At First Sting
Mercury/Polygram Records, 1984

Scorpions
"Big City Nights"
World Wide Live
Mercury/Polygram Records, 1985

Scorpions
"No One Like You"
World Wide Live
Mercury/Polygram Records, 1986

Bob Seger and The Silver Bullet
Band
"Old Time Rock and Roll"
Stranger In Town
From the Movie *Risky Business*
Capitol Records, 1983

Simple Minds
"Don't You Forget About Me"
The Breakfast Club
Motion Picture Soundtrack
A & M Records, 1985

Simple Minds (with Robin Clark)
"Alive and Kicking"
Once Upon A Time
A & M Records, 1985
Director: Zybigniew Rybczynski

Simple Minds (with Robin Clark)
"All The Things She Said"
Once Upon A Time
Digital Disk Video
A & M Records, 1986
Director: Zybigniew Rybczynski

Sly Fox
"Let's Go All The Way"
Sly Fox
Capitol Records, 1986

VIDEOGRAPHY

Bruce Springsteen
"Born in the USA"
Born in the USA
Columbia/CBS Records, 1984
Director: John Sayles

Bruce Springsteen
"Dancing in the Dark"
Born in The USA
Columbia/CBS Records, 1984

Bruce Springsteen
"I'm On Fire"
Born in The USA
Columbia/CBS Records, 1985

Bruce Springsteen
"Glory Days"
Born in the USA
Columbia/CBS Records, 1985

Rod Stewart
"Infatuation"
Camouflage
Warner Bros Records, 1984

Rod Stewart
"Baby Jane"
Body Wishes
Warner Bros Records, 1985

Sting
"Fortress Around Your Heart"
The Dream of the Blue Turtles
A & M Records, 1985

Sting
"If You Love Somebody, Set
Them Free"
The Dream of the Blue Turtles
A & M Records, 1985

Donna Summer
"She Works Hard for the Money"
She Works Hard For The Money
Mercury/Polygram Records, 1983

Talking Heads
"Burning Down The House"
Speaking In Tongues
Sire/Warner Bros Records, 1986

Talking Heads
"Road To Nowhere"
Speaking In Tongues
Sire/Warner Bros Records, 1986

Tears For Fears
"Shout"
The Hunting
Mercury/Polygram Records, 1985

Tears For Fears
"Mother's Talk"
Songs From The Big Chair
Mercury/Polygram Records, 1986

Tina Turner
"What's Love Got To Do With It?"
Private Dancer
Capitol Records, 1984

Tina Turner
"Private Dancer"
Private Dancer
Capitol Records, 1984

Tina Turner
"Typical Male"
Break Every Rule
Capitol Records, 1986

Twisted Sister
"Leader of the Pack"
Come Out And Play
Atlantic Records/Atlantic Video,
1985

USA For Africa
"We Are The World"
USA For Africa
Columbia/CBS Records, 1985

Gino Vannelli
"Black Cars"
Black Cars
HME/CBS Records, 1985

Weird Al
"Like A Surgeon"
Dare To Be Stupid
Rock—N—Roll/CBS Records, 1985

ROCKING AROUND THE CLOCK

Wham!
"Freedom"
Make It Big
Columbia/CBS Records, 1985

Wham!
"Bad Boys"
Make It Big
Columbia/CBS Records, 1984

Paul Young
"Everytime You Go Away"
The Secret of Association
Columbia/CBS Records, 1985

ZZ Top
"Legs Illuminator"
Illuminator
Warner Bros Records, 1984

ZZ Top
"Rough Boy"
Afterburner
Warner Bros Records, 1986
Director: Steve Barron

Y & T
"Summer Time Girl"
Open Fire
A & M Records, 1986

Bibliography

Althusser, Louis, "Ideology and ideological state apparatuses (notes towards an investigation)," in *Lenin and Philosophy and Other Essays*, trans. Ben Brewster (New York and London: Monthly Review Press, 1971), pp. 127–86.

Barthes, Roland, *Image–Music–Text*, trans. Stephen Heath (New York: Hill & Wang, 1977).

Barthes, Roland, "Upon leaving the movie theatre," in Theresa Hak Kyung Cha, ed., *Cinematic Apparatus: Selected Writings* (New York: Tanam Press, 1980), pp. 3–10.

Baudrillard, Jean, *Simulations*, trans. Paul Foss, Paul Patton, and Philip Beitchman (New York: Semiotext(e), 1983).

Baudrillard, Jean, *In the Shadow of the Silent Majorities . . . Or The End of the Social And Other Essays*, trans. Paul Foss, Paul Patton, and John Johnston (New York: Semiotext(e), 1983).

Baudrillard, Jean, "The ecstasy of communication," in Hal Foster, ed., *The Anti-Aesthetic: Essays in Postmodern Culture* (Port Townsend: Bay Press, 1983), pp. 125–36.

Bennett, Tony, "Texts in history: the determinations of readings and their texts," in Derek Attridge, Geoffrey Bennington, and Robert Young, eds, *Post-Structuralism and the Question of History* (Cambridge: Cambridge University Press, 1986).

Benveniste, Emile, *Problems of General Linguistics* (Miami, Fla: University of Miami Press, 1971).

Bordwell, David, Thompson, Kristin, and Staiger, Janet, *The Classical Hollywood Film* (New York: Columbia University Press, 1985).

Bowlby, Rachel, *Just Looking: Consumer Culture in Dreiser, Gissing and Zola* (London and New York: Methuen, 1985).

181

ROCKING AROUND THE CLOCK

Brown, Jane D., and Campbell, Kenneth C., "Race and gender in music videos: the same beat but a different drummer," *Journal of Communication*, vol. 36, no. 1 (Winter 1986), pp. 94–106.

Brunsdon, Charlotte, "Crossroads: Notes on Soap Opera", in E. Ann Kaplan, ed., *Regarding Television: Critical Approaches – An Anthology* (Los Angeles: American Film Institute, 1983), pp. 76–82.

Chen, Kuan-Hsing, "MTV: the (dis)appearance of postmodern semiosis, or the cultural politics of resistance," *Journal of Communication Inquiry*, vol. 10, no. 1 (Winter 1986), pp. 66–9.

Cohn, Nick, *Rock From the Beginning* (New York: Stein & Day, 1969).

De Lauretis, Teresa, "Oedipus interruptus," *Wide Angle*, vol. 7, nos 1–2 (1986), pp. 34–41. Cf. her extended discussion of similar issues in her *Alice Doesn't: Feminism, Cinema and Semiotics* (Bloomington, Indiana: Indiana University Press, 1984).

Doane, Mary Ann, "Woman's stake: filming the female body," *October*, no. 17 (1981), pp. 23–36.

Eisen, John, ed., *The Age of Rock: Sounds of the American Cultural Revolution* (New York: Random House, 1969).

Feuer, Jane, "The concept of live television: ontology as ideology," in E. Ann Kaplan, ed., *Regarding Television: Critical Approaches – An Anthology* (Los Angeles: American Film Institute, 1983), pp. 12–22.

Fiske, John, "MTV: post structural post modern," *Journal of Communication Inquiry*, vol. 10, no. 1 (Winter 1986), pp. 74–9.

Flitterman-Lewis, Sandy, "The *real* soap operas: TV commercials," in E. Ann Kaplan, ed., *Regarding Television: Critical Approaches – An Anthology* (Los Angeles: American Film Institute, 1983), pp. 84–96.

Flitterman-Lewis, Sandy, "Fascination in fragments: psychoanalysis in film and television," in Robert Allen, ed., *Channels of Discourse: Television and Contemporary Criticism* (Chapel Hill: University of North Carolina Press, 1987).

Foster, Hal, ed., *The Anti-Aesthetic: Essays in Postmodern Culture* (Port Townsend, Washington: Bay Press, 1983).

Foucault, Michel, *The Archaeology of Knowledge and The Discourse on Language*, trans. Alan Sheridan (New York: Pantheon, 1972).

Fraiberg, Selma, *Every Child's Birthright: In Defense of Mothering* (New York: Basic Books, 1977).

Frankovitz, André, ed., *Seduced and Abandoned: The Baudrillard Scene* (New York and Glebe, Australia: Semiotext(e) and Stonemoss Services, 1984).

Freud, Sigmund, *Beyond the Pleasure Principle*, Standard Edition, vol. XVIII, pp. 14–17.

Freud, Sigmund, "Female sexuality," in James Strachey, ed., *Collected Papers*, vol. 5 (New York: Basic Books, 1959), pp. 252–72.

Fricke, David, "Heavy metal," in John Swenson, ed., *The Year in Rock, 1981–82* (New York: Putnam, 1981), pp. 16ff.

Frith, Simon, *The Sociology of Rock* (London: Constable, 1978; revised and updated 1984).

BIBLIOGRAPHY

Frost, Deborah, "White noise: how heavy metal rules," *The Village Voice*, vol. XXX, no. 25 (18 June 1985), pp. 46–9.

Gledhill, Christine, "Recent developments in feminist film criticism," *Quarterly Review of Film Studies*, vol. 3, no. 4 (1978), pp. 35–46; revised and reprinted in Mary Ann Doane, Patricia Mellencamp, and Linda Williams, eds, *Re-Vision: Essays in Feminist Film Criticism* (Los Angeles: American Film Institute, 1983), pp. 18–48.

Grossberg, Lawrence, "The politics of youth culture: some observations on rock and roll in American culture," *Social Text* (Winter 1983–4), pp. 107–14.

Hall, Stuart, and Whannel, Paddy, *The Popular Arts* (New York: Pantheon 1965).

Heath, Stephen, *Questions of Cinema* (Bloomington, Ind.: Indiana University Press, 1981).

Hoberman, Jim, "Music video: the industry and its fringes," review of Museum of Modern Art exhibition, *The Village Voice*, 17 September 1985.

Holdstein, D., "Music video: messages and structures," *Jump Cut*, no. 29 (1984), pp. 1, 6.

Jahn, M., *From Elvis Presley to the Rolling Stones* (New York: Quadrangle, 1973).

Jameson, Fredric, "Postmodernism and consumer society," in Hal Foster, ed., *The Anti-Aesthetic: Essays in Postmodern Culture* (Port Townsend: Bay Press, 1983), pp. 111–25.

Jameson, Fredric, *The Political Unconscious* (Ithaca, NY: Cornell University Press, 1981).

Journal of Communication Inquiry, vol. 10, no. 1 (Winter 1986). Entire issue devoted to essays on MTV.

Journal of Communication vol. 36, no. 1 (Winter 1986). Cf. focus on essays about music television in this issue.

Kaplan, E. Ann, *Women and Film: Both Sides of the Camera* (London and New York: Methuen, 1983).

Kaplan, E. Ann, ed., *Regarding Television: Critical Approaches – An Anthology* (Los Angeles: American Film Institute, 1983).

Kaplan, E. Ann, "A postmodern play of the signifier? Advertising, pastiche and schizophrenia in music television," in Philip Drummond and Richard Paterson, eds, *Television in Transition* (London: British Film Institute, 1985), pp. 146–63.

Kaplan, E. Ann, "History, the historical spectator and gender address in music television," *Journal of Communication Inquiry*, vol. 10, no. 1 (Winter 1986), pp. 3–14.

Kaplan, E. Ann, "Sexual difference, visual pleasure and the construction of the spectator in music television," *The Oxford Literary Review*, vol. 8, nos 1–2 (1986), pp. 113–22.

Kaplan, E. Ann, "Feminist film criticism: current issues and problems," *Studies in the Literary Imagination*, vol. XIX, no. 1 (Spring 1986), pp. 7–20.

Kaplan, E. Ann, *Motherhood and Representation: The Maternal Discourse in Popular Literature and Film, 1830 to the Present* (London and New York: Methuen, forthcoming).

Kaplan, E. Ann, "Feminist criticism in television studies," in Robert Allen, ed., *Channels of Discourse: Television and Contemporary Criticism* Chapel Hill: University of North Carolina Press, 1986).

Kaplan, E. Ann, "Whose imaginary? Text, body and narrative in select rock videos," in Deidre Pribram, ed., *Cinematic Pleasure and the Female Spectator* (London: Verso, 1987).

Kaplan, E. Ann, and Phelan, Margaret, *The Fascination of Music Television: An Anthology.* (Forthcoming).

Kinder, Marsha, "Music video and the spectator: television, ideology and the dream," *Film Quarterly*, vol. 38, no. 1 (1985), pp. 1–15.

Lacan, Jacques, *Écrits: A Selection*, trans. Alan Sheridan (New York: Norton, 1979).

Laclau, Ernesto, "Populist rupture and discourse," *Screen Education*, no. 34 (Spring 1980).

Levaco, Ron, "Eikenbaum, inner speech and film stylistics," *Screen*, vol. 15, no. 4 (Winter 1974–5), pp. 47–58.

Levy, Stephen, "Ad nauseam – how MTV sells out rock and roll," *Rolling Stone*, 8 December 1983, pp. 36–9.

Marcus, Greil, *Mystery Train: Images of America in Rock 'n Roll Music* (New York: Dutton, 1975; rev. edn 1985).

Melville, Stephen, "Coda: the morning mail," paper delivered at the Lacan Conference, University of Amherst, Spring 1985. Much of the paper is included in "Psychoanalysis and the place of *jouissance*," *Critical Inquiry* (December 1986).

Metz, Christian, *Film Language: A Semiotics of the Cinema*, trans. Michael Taylor (New York: Oxford University Press, 1974).

Metz, Christian, "History/discourse: a note on two voyeurisms,"*Edinburgh Magazine*, no. 1 (1976), pp. 21–5.

Morley, David, *The "Nationwide" Audience: Structure and Decoding*, BFI Television Monographs, no. 11 (London: British Film Institute, 1980).

Morse, Margaret, "Postynchronising rock music and television," *Journal of Communication Inquiry*, vol. 10, no. 1 (Winter 1986), pp. 15–28.

Mulvey, Laura, "Visual pleasure and narrative cinema," *Screen*, vol. 16, no. 3 (Autumn 1975), pp. 6–18.

"Music directors' symposium," *Variety*, 14 March 1984, pp. 69–82.

Nowell-Smith, Geoffrey, "A note on history/discourse," *Edinburgh Magazine*, no. 1 (1976), pp. 26–32.

Orman, John, *The Politics of Rock Music* (Chicago: Nelson-Hall, 1984).

Peterson-Lewis, Sonja, and Chennault, Shirley A., "Black artists' music videos: three success strategies," *Journal of Communication*, vol. 36, no. 1 (Winter 1986), pp. 107–14.

Phelan, Margaret, "Panopticism and the uncanny: notes toward

BIBLIOGRAPHY

television's visual form," unpublished paper read at The Modern Language Association Convention, December 1986.

Phelan, Margaret, cf. Kaplan, E. Ann, and Phelan, Margaret, 1987.

Sobczak, Gene, "MTV, radio and unit sales," unpublished paper, Rutgers University, 1984.

Staiger, Janet, "Mass produced photoplays: economic and signifying practices in the first years of Hollywood," *Wide Angle*, vol. 4, no. 3 (1980), pp. 12–28.

Staiger, Janet, cf. Bordwell, David, Thompson, Kristen, and Staiger, Janet, 1985.

Stallybrass, Peter, and White, Allon, *The Politics and Poetics of Transgression* (London and New York: Methuen/Cornell, 1986).

Stam, Robert, "Television news," in E. Ann Kaplan, ed., *Regarding Television: Critical Approaches – An Anthology* (Los Angeles: American Film Institute, 1983), pp. 23–43.

Stern, Daniel N. "Mother and infant at play: the dyadic interaction involving facial, vocal and gaze behaviors," in Michael Lewis and L.A. Rosenblaum, eds, *The Origins of Behavior: vol. I The Effect of the Infant on the Caregiver* (New York: Wiley, 1974).

Swenson, John, ed., *The Year in Rock, 1981–82* (New York: Putnam, 1981).

Tetzlaff, Dave, "MTV and the politics of postmodern pop," *Journal of Communication Inquiry*, vol. 10, no. 1 (Winter 1986), pp. 80–91.

Thompson, David, cf. Bordwell, David, Thompson, Kristin, and Staiger, Janet, 1985.

Tribe, Keith, "History and the production of memories," *Screen*, vol. 18, no. 4 (Winter 1977/8), pp. 9–22.

White, Allon, cf. Stallybrass, Peter, and White, Allon, 1986.

Wright, Nick, "Pat Benatar," in John Swenson, ed., *The Year in Rock, 1981–82* (New York: Putnam, 1981).

Select glossary*

CINEMATIC VERSUS THE EXTRA-CINEMATIC Keeping this distinction clearly in mind prevents us from falling into the trap of sociological critics, and linking screen image and lived experience too simplistically. The CINEMATIC refers to all that goes on on the screen and to what happens between screen image and spectator (what results from the cinematic apparatus). The EXTRA-CINEMATIC refers to discussion about, for example: the lives of the director, stars, producers, etc.; the production of the film in Hollywood, as an institution; the politics of the period when a film was made; and the cultural assumptions at the time a film was made.

CLASSICAL CINEMA A controversial but convenient term referring to the feature-length narrative film made and distributed by the Hollywood studio system, roughly from 1925 through 1960. Central to the classical paradigm are conventions of film practice that are repeated from product to product (intentionally or not) and that the audience comes to rely upon and to expect. The characteristics of classical cinema can be determined on several levels: (1) in terms of *production*, the classical film can be categorized according to GENRE, stars, directors, producers (studios); (2) in terms of *narrative*, the classical film will have a tightly organized PLOT with clearly defined conflicts, ENIGMAS, cause–effect relationship, and a focus on individual characters; (3) in terms of *editing*, the classical film will adhere to the CONTINUITY system; and (4) in terms of *formal mechanisms*, the classical film will proceed by alternation and repetition (of its shots, camera set-ups, angles, signifying structures, such as editing patterns, reverse-angle, etc.)

*Courtesy of Rutgers Film Faculty, Sandy Flitterman-Lewis, and Miriam Hansen, who, along with E. Ann Kaplan, compiled the glossary from which these items are taken.

SELECT GLOSSARY

with a tendency toward balance, symmetry, and resolution such that the film appears to move inevitably from beginning to the point of closure. The latter two in particular are designed to produce a "reality effect," to create the illusion of reality for the spectator (cf. REALISM).

CLOSURE   A characteristic trait of classical narrative structure: we expect every element to be motivated, every event to have a cause (which will be explained in the course of the narrative), every conflict, ENIGMA and contradiction that the narrative sets up in the beginning to be resolved by the end.

CODE   A term used in SEMIOTICS (SEMIOLOGY) to describe a set of rules or conventions that structure a particular DISCOURSE. The cinema employs a complex system of codes pertaining to its heterogeneous levels of expression: codes of representation and editing, acting and narrative, codes of sound, be it music, speech or noise. Some of these codes are specific to the cinema (e.g. editing), some are shared with other forms of art and communication (e.g. codes of lighting and gesture with the theater, codes of narrative with the novel or short story).

CONNOTATION   The suggestive, associative, figurative sense of an expression (word, image, sign) that extends beyond its strict literal definition (DENOTATION), beyond what appears to be its "natural" meaning. In practice, denotative and connotative meanings cannot be that easily distinguished, especially when we are dealing with images.

CONTINUITY   A system of editing devised to bridge the gaps resulting from different camera setups, to stitch the spaces together in such a way that the spectator ignores the cuts ("invisible" editing); the continuity system subordinates space and time to the logic of narrative, action. Major conventions of continuity editing include: the 180 DEGREE RULE; the SHOT/REVERSE SHOT and POINT OF VIEW constructions, the latter depending on EYELINE MATCH; MATCH ON ACTION (or cutting movement); the 30 DEGREE RULE; an overall pattern of ESTABLISHING SHOT/breakdown/re-establishing shot.

DIEGESIS   (Greek for "recital of facts".) The denotative material of film narrative including the fictional space and time dimensions implied by the narrative; the fictive space and time into which the film works to absorb the spectator, the self-contained fictional world of the film.

DISCOURSE   Any social relation involving language or other sign systems as a form of exchange between participants, real or imaginary, particular or collective. Discursive exchange involves, as its points of reference, the conditions of expression, a source of articulation ("I") as well as an addressee ("you"), not necessarily explicit but always implied by the discursive structure. A discourse is shared by a socially constituted group of speakers; it defines the terms of what can or can't be said and extends beyond verbal language to a range of fields in which meaning is culturally organized (e.g. art, ideology).

FREUD AND THE OEDIPAL CRISIS   Before going on to discuss the mechanisms underlying pleasure in the cinema, it is necessary to outline

187

ROCKING AROUND THE CLOCK

Freud's notion of the Oedipus complex, which provided the cornerstone for his (at the time) revolutionary psychoanalytic theory and on which the other phenomena relevant to film theory depend.

Freud took the name Oedipus from classical mythology, particularly the story, dramatized by Sophocles, of how Oedipus unwittingly killed his father and married his mother, a deed for which he was severely punished. The myth represents for Freud the inevitable fantasy of the growing child: first bound in illusory unity with his mother, whom he does not recognize as Other, separate, or different, the child exists blissfully in a pre-Oedipal phase; as he moves into the phallic phase, the child becomes aware of his father. At the height of his positive Oedipal phase, he loves his mother and hates his father who takes mother for himself. Successful resolution of this Oedipal phase takes place on the boy's discovery that his mother lacks the penis, i.e. is castrated (he can only imagine that all people must originally have had penises). This bitter discovery propels him away from his mother, since he fears that by identifying with the one who lacks the penis, he will endanger his own organ. He now identifies with his father, whom he longs to be like, and he looks forward to "finding someone like his mother" to marry.

Freud did not pay much attention to the girl's Oedipal crisis, but post-Freudians have generally agreed that it is a much more complicated one. They argue that the girl turns away from her mother through penis envy and the belief that her mother is responsible for her lack of a penis. The girl tries to get from the father what the mother could not provide, now equating "child" with "penis," and looking to bear the child with a man like her father.

IDEOLOGY   While for Marx IDEOLOGY referred to the ideological components of all bourgeois institutions and modes of production, recent film critics have rather followed Althusser for whom IDEOLOGY is a series of representations and images, reflecting the conceptions of "reality" that any society assumes. IDEOLOGY thus no longer refers to beliefs people consciously hold but to the myths that a society lives by, as if these myths referred to some natural, unproblematic "reality."

LACAN'S IMAGINARY AND SYMBOLIC   Some aspects of Lacan have been useful in film theory because he combined Freudian psychoanalysis with semiology, thus offering a means for linking semiotic and psychoanalytic readings of films. Lacan's insight was to rephrase Freudian theory by using a linguistic model for the movement between different stages, as against the non-linguistic, essentially biological and developmental Freudian model. Lacan's concept of the imaginary corresponds (roughly) to Freud's pre-Oedipal phase, although the child is already a signifier, already inserted in a linguistic system. But the world of the imaginary is nevertheless *for the child* a prelinguistic moment, a moment of illusory unity with the mother, whom he does not know as Other. The Lacanian child is forced to move on from the world of the imaginary, not because of the literal threat of castration but because he acquires language,

188

which is based on the concept of "lack." He enters the world of the symbolic governed by the Law of the Father and revolving around the phallus as signifier. Here, in language, he discovers that he is an object in a realm of signifiers that circulate around the Father (= phallus). He learns discourse and the different "I" and "You" positions. The illusory unity with the Mother is broken partly by the mirror phase, with the child's recognition of the Mother as a separate image/entity, and of himself as an image (ego-ideal), creating the structure of the divided subject; and partly by introduction of the Father as a linguistic Third Term, breaking the mother—child dyad. Although the child now lives in the symbolic, he still longs for the world of the imaginary; it is this longing that the experience of the cinema partly satisfies, particularly in the sense of providing the more perfect selves (ego-ideals) evoked by the mirror phase and facilitating a regression to that phase.

METAPHOR   A figure of speech (a TROPE) consisting of two parts (traditionally called tenor and vehicle) expressing and creating a relation of comparison between two ordinarily unrelated elements, e.g. "the windmills of the mind."

MONTAGE   (French for "assembling" or "putting together".) Editing, usually referring to traditions outside the CONTINUITY system (e.g. Soviet cinema of the 1920s). In Hollywood films, montage sequences (sequences "telescoping" historical events, newspaper headlines, etc.) usually stand out by contrast to the dominant continuity style of editing.

180 DEGREE SYSTEM or RULE   Crucial to the CONTINUITY style in editing, this convention dictates that the camera remain on one side of an invisible line, the line of action or 180 degree line, thereby ensuring screen direction and general spatial orientation for the spectator. Movement of characters, objects or the camera automatically involves a re-establishing of the 180 degree space.

PLOT   The discursive organization of a NARRATIVE, i.e. the filmic actualization of narrative events. In contrast to the mental reconstruction of events which comprises a film's STORY, plot refers to the order and manner in which events are presented in the film itself. Story and plot *can* coincide, but they usually differ; the plot may alter the sequence (e.g. flashback), duration (e.g. a life time), and frequency (e.g. a repeated action) of events as they have presumably occurred in the story.

REALISM   (1) A summary term comprising literary and artistic conventions that have their origin in the first half of the nineteenth century; (2) in the cinema, an unspoken agreement between filmmaker and audience to accept certain modes of representation and narrative as "realistic," "faithful to reality," which implies a temporary belief in the "transparence" of the film, the three-dimensionality of the space projected on the screen, and in the "presence" of events unfolding, as if for the first time, before our eyes; (3) a style of filmmaking which attempts to approximate the look of reality (Bazin: "to recreate the world in its own image"), with emphasis on authentic locations and details, long shots and lengthy takes, eye-level placement of camera, a minimum of editing and special effects; often involving an effort to efface the traces of the film's construction, of the intervention on the part of the filmmaker.

REPRESENTATION   This concept indicates the "constructed" nature of the image, which Hollywood mechanisms strive to conceal. The dominant Hollywood style, realism (an apparent imitation of the social world we live in), hides the fact that a film is constructed, and perpetuates the illusion that spectators are being shown what is "natural." The half-aware "forgetting" that the spectator engages in allows the pleasurable mechanisms of voyeurism and fetishism to flow freely.

SEMIOLOGY, SEMIOTICS   (from the Greek root *sem-*, sign). A discipline devoted to the study of SIGNs, the basic unit of meaning in a process of SIGNIFICATION. Semiology or semiotics (depending on whether the particular approach is derived from the model of Structural Linguistics (Saussure) or from American Pragmatism (Peirce)) studies the systems of signs that enable human beings to communicate, to enter into discursive relations. All cultural utterances (in a broad sense, not just verbal utterances) are enabled as well as limited by systems or CODEs that are shared by all who make and understand them; semiology/semiotics attempts to describe the underlying patterns which structure those utterances.

SIGN, SIGNIFICATION   In SEMIOLOGY/SEMIOTICS, the sign is the basic unit in the process of signification, the process of articulating and conveying meaning. The sign has two aspects, the "signifier" (the material shape – sound, image – which carries meaning) and the "signified" (the concept signified, which in turn may refer to a potentially infinite number of "referents").

VOYEURISM   A psychoanalytic term referring to the erotic gratification of watching someone without being seen oneself; the activity of the Peeping Tom. As a clinical perversion, voyeurism is the active counterpart to EXHIBITIONISM, practiced primarily by men with the female body as the object of the gaze. Given the spatial and representational organization of CLASSICAL cinema, voyeurism is a crucial component of the pleasure offered to the spectator.

Index

advertising 1,2,11,12–21, 29, 41, 44, 46, 58, 106, 115, 143, 148, 152
aesthetic 40, 53, 144, 150, 153; "anti-aesthetic" 33, 53
A-ha 36, 133; "Take on Me" 36
Althusser, Louis 23, 49–50, 65, 150; see also Marxism
Anderson, Laurie 74, 75; "Language is a Virus" 74, 75
androgyny 17, 34, 61, 72, 93, 95, 106, 110, 157
Art of Noise 73, 74
avant-garde 2, 12, 23, 33, 36, 40, 48, 57, 73, 75, 123, 144

Bailey, Phil 16, 35; "Easy Lover" (made with Phil Collins) 16, 35
Bakhtin, Mikhail 68–9, 72, 93
Barnes, Jimmy 86; "Working Class Man" 86
Barron, Steve 36
Barthes, Roland 24–5, 43, 151
Baudrillard, Jean 44–5, 48, 50-2, 54, 57, 85–6, 91–2, 140, 145, 147, 149–53; see also simulacra
Beatles 2, 5, 6, 9, 10, 72, 155
Benatar, Pat 96, 116, 127, 130, 132–3, 137, 155; "Love Is A Battlefield" 116, 129 (illus.), 130; "Sex is A Weapon" 116
Bennett, Tony 26, 27, 153; see also reading formations
Benveniste, Emile 23, 40
black artists 2, 3, 9, 15, 115–16; collaborations with white artists 16, 138; see also racism, censorship
Bowie, David 13, 15, 36–7, 61, 102, 133, 155; "Dancing in the Street" 36; "D.J." 37, 61; "Blue Jean" 37
Boxer, Jo 67; "Just Got Lucky" 67
Boy George 102
British bands 5, 6, 10, 75
British youth 5, 6, 67–8, 72
Brown and Campbell 115
Brown, Julie 116, 137; "The Homecoming Queen's Got a Gun" 116, 137
Browne, Jackson 83, 84; "For America" 83
Brunsdon, Charlotte 29
Byrne, David 37, 74, 75

Cars 39–40, 46, 97, 113; "You Might Think" 39 (illus.), 40, 46; "Why Can't I Have You?" 97
censorship 15–17, 115; see also black

artists, racism
classical realist film 62, 125, 140,
148, 150; *see also* Hollywood film
classical realist texts and videos 127,
128, 135, 150
Cohn, Nick 9, 53; *Rock From the
Beginning* 9
Collins, Phil 35, 53, 58, 60, 85, 96,
97, 133; "Easy Lover" (made with
Phil Bailey) 16, 35; "One More
Night" 96–7
consumption 12, 20, 22, 29, 33, 44,
51, 52, 53, 54, 58, 65, 143, 147,
148, 155, 156, 157, 158;
commodity 17, 53, 54, 65, 147
Cougar, John *see* Mellencamp
Country and Western 9

de Lauretis, Teresa 27
de Palma, Brian 14, 37
Derrida/Derridean 147, 148
Devo 140; "Whip It" 140–2
Dire Straits 35, 36, 133; "Money For
Nothing" 35
Doane, Mary Ann 93
Duran Duran 37, 62, 102
Dylan, Bob 10

Eco, Umberto 24
"erotic" 58
Eurythmics 36, 96, 97, 102; "Here
Comes the Rain Again" 97;
"There Must Be an Angel" 96

Fabulous Thunderbirds 112; "Tuff
Enuff" 112
Farm Aid Event 84, 86, 151
feminism/feminist 26–7, 30, 127,
130, 138, 149–51; feminist
historians 24; feminist film
theorists/critics 61, 89, 90, 110;
see also postmodern feminist
fetishism 43, 61, 91, 92, 93
Feuer, Jane 29
film noir 60, 103, 108, 110
film theory 22–7, 40–1

filmic apparatus 28, 41, 44, 58, 120,
151
flow 3, 4, 12, 21, 31, 48, 52, 53, 65,
74, 90, 92, 115, 116, 126, 127,
137, 139, 140, 144, 156
Foreigner 96, 97; "I Want to Know
What Love Is" 96, 97
Foucault, Michel 4, 23, 24, 29, 71,
151
Fraiberg and Stern 95, 97
Franklin, Aretha 15, 16, 38, 116;
"Freeway of Love" 15; "Sisters
Are Doin' It For Themselves"
(video made with Annie Lennox)
16, 31, 38, 116, 137–9
Freud/Freudian 52, 57, 91, 149, 150,
186; *see also* Oedipal,
psychoanalysis

Gabriel, Peter 62, 73 (illus.), 74,
155; "Shock the Monkey" 62;
"Sledgehammer" 73 (illus.), 74,
155
gaze 27, 43, 48, 57, 58, 61, 80, 88,
89, 90, 91, 92, 93, 94, 95, 100,
101, 102, 106, 110, 111, 116, 119,
121, 122, 123, 126, 128, 139, 140,
149; camera's gaze 126, 139;
female 27, 139; Freud's
scopophilic gaze 94; male 27, 61,
89, 90, 91, 116, 119, 139, 149;
mirror gaze 94; mother–child gaze
94, 95; phallic 94, 101, 140;
voyeuristic gaze 102, 110
gender address 43, 48, 58, 60, 61,
89, 90, 97, 100, 101, 106, 107,
115, 137
Gentlemen Prefer Blondes 117, 117
(illus.), 118 (illus.), 119, 124, 125
German Expressionism 60, 103, 104
Grossberg, Lawrence 53, 60, 145,
147

Hagar, Sammy 68, 76, 81, 82; "I
Can't Drive at 55" 68; "V.O.A."
76, 81, 82

INDEX

Hall, Stewart 6
Hands Across America 86, 152
Heath, Stephen 25, 28
heavy metal video 93, 102, 106
Hendrix, Jimi 6, 10
Henley, Don 84; "All She Wants to do is Dance" 84
historical address 8, 10, 11, 22–31, 49, 50, 53, 54, 74
historicize 56; anti-history and anti-historical 27
history 8, 9, 10, 11, 22–31, 40, 47, 54, 144, 145, 146, 147, 148, 149, 153
Hitchcock 37, 46, 67; *Vertigo* 37
Hollywood film 23, 33–5, 46–7, 56–7, 61–2, 90–3, 102, 106, 110, 116, 119, 121, 123, 126, 140, 148
Houston, Whitney 15, 16
human face 48, 77, 95, 149

ideology 7, 50, 52, 54, 56, 58, 60, 65, 139, 187
Idol, Billy 102–7, 155, 156; "Rebel Yell" 103–6, 145
imaginary 5, 7, 25, 31, 42, 43, 51, 52, 58, 90, 92, 94, 133, 135, 188; *see* Lacan, symbolic

Jackson, Janet 16
Jackson, Michael 13, 15, 19, 34, 62, 86, 102, 133; "Billie Jean" 34; "Thriller" 13, 34, 62
Jagger, Mick 36, 98, 133; "Dancing in the Street" 36
Jahn 9, 53; *From Elvis Presley to the Rolling Stones* 9
Jameson, Fredric 45–7, 120, 145–7
jazz 52, 145
Jefferson Airplane 10
Joplin, Janis 6, 10

Lacan/Lacanism 33, 42, 43, 45, 49–50, 91, 93–5, 108, 143, 147, 150; mirror phase 42–3, 49–50, 91, 94, 95, 97, 119; *see also*

imaginary, symbolic
Laclau, Ernesto 153
Lauper, Cyndi 40, 58, 59, 96–7, 127, 130, 132; "Girls Just Wanna Have Fun" 40, 59, 127; "Money Changes Everything" 59; "Time After Time" 59, 96, 97, 127–8
Led Zeppelin 10
Lee Roth, David 35, 62, 111; "California Girls" 35, 62, 111; "Just Like a Gigolo (I Ain't Got Nobody)" 35, 62
Lennox, Annie 16, 31, 38, 102, 116, 137–9; "Sisters Are Doin' It For Themselves" (video made with Aretha Franklin) 16, 31, 38, 116, 137–9; *see also* Eurythmics
Levy, Stephen 17
Live Aid 84, 85, 86, 151

Madonna 19, 33, 115–27, 130, 131, 133, 155, 157; "Material Girl" 33, 116–27, 120–1 (illus.); "Like A Virgin" 115; "Papa Don't Preach" 130–3, 131 (illus.), 157; *Desperately Seeking Susan* 157; "Getting Into the Groove" 157; "Live to Tell" 157; "Open Your Hearts" 157
Marcus, Greil 8
Marx/Marxism 23, 24, 26, 27, 47, 50, 52, 149, 150; *see also* Althusser
masochism 61, 102
masquerade 93
Mellencamp, John Cougar 17, 31, 37, 62, 66, 67, 83–6, 90, 113–14, 155; "Jack and Diane" 37; "Small Town" 37; "Authority" 66 (illus.), 67; "Rain on the Scarecrow" 83; "Hurts So Good" 113–14 (illus.)
Metz, Christian 23, 24, 40
Midnight Oil 76, 79–80; "Best of Both Worlds" 76, 79
modernism 7, 12, 45, 65, 147

193

modernist 33, 46, 56, 65
Monkees 21
mother 42–3, 49–50, 67–8, 91, 94, 95, 97, 119
Motley Crue 63, 68–72, 93, 102, 155; "Smokin' in the Boys' Room" 68–70, 70 (illus.)
Mulvey, Laura 26
Music Television (MTV): as art form 123–4; film influences on 34, 38, 46, 60, 63, 64, 65, 67, 75, 77, 81, 103, 104, 108, 110, 127, 138, 145; Veejays 18, 19, 20, 41; video directors 14, 36, 37, 73; *see also* consumption, postmodernism, televisual apparatus

narcissism 51
narrative 27, 31, 33, 41, 44, 48, 56, 61, 63, 72, 89, 108, 123, 125, 128, 142, 149
Nazism 64, 71, 114
Nowell-Smith, Gregory 40

Oedipal 41, 42, 48, 51, 61, 91–5, 108–10, 140, 149–50, 153, 186; pre-Oedipal 91–5, 101, 128, 140; post-Oedipal 92; non-Oedipal 41, 106; *see also* Freud, psychoanalysis
Orman, John 82; *The Politics of Rock Music* 82
Osborne, John 67; *Look Back in Anger* 67

Palmer, Robert 111; "Addicted to Love" 111; "I Didn't Mean to Turn You On" 111
parody 33, 35, 46, 81, 120, 140–1, 145; *see also* pastiche, postmodernism
Parr, John 90, 110, 111; "Naughty, Naughty" 90, 110, 111
pastiche 33, 34, 37, 46, 56–7, 59, 63, 64, 90, 119–20, 140–1, 145; *see also* parody, postmodernism

performance videos 122–3; *see* nihilist videos
Phelan, Margaret 4
Pittman, Robert 1, 2, 3, 17
Pointer Sisters 15; "Jump" 15; "Neutron Dance" 15
popular culture 5–7, 33, 35, 47, 52, 106, 116; *see* postmodernism
post-holocaust 29, 30, 67, 68, 144, 145
postmodern feminism/feminist 116–17, 126–7, 130, 132, 137, 139, 140
postmodernism 1, 5, 7, 8, 10, 31, 33, 41, 44–6, 54, 56, 62, 63, 65, 68, 76, 89–90, 106, 114–15, 120, 126, 130, 139, 142, 144, 145, 147–53, 155, 158; *see also* parody, pastiche, consumption
postmodernist video 56, 64, 92, 140, 149; *see also* types of video
Presley, Elvis 9, 155
Prince 15, 17, 114, 155; "Raspberry Beret" 15; "Kiss" 15, 17; "Purple Rain" 15; "1999" 114
psychoanalysis 7, 22, 27, 41–3, 49–50, 90–7, 101, 106, 108, 133; "Freudian family romance" 41; *see also* Lacan, Freud, Oedipal, gaze, imaginary, symbolic

racism 2, 3, 15–17, 31, 115; *see also* censorship, black artists
reading formations 26, 30–2, 80, 81, 153; *see also* Tony Bennett
Ritchie, Lionel 58, 96; "Hello" 58, 96
rock music: history of 8–11, 53, 56, 144; acid rock 53; black pop 3, 54, 58, 96; heavy metal 3, 17, 34, 53, 56–7, 60, 81, 102, 107; new wave 3, 10, 53, 60, 83, 102, 144; punk 10, 53, 54, 60, 67, 83, 103, 148; rap 16
rock music, sexuality and violence in 6, 15, 16, 26, 31, 149;

INDEX

homosexuality 16, 26, 31; homoeroticism 61, 102; sadomasochism 31, 61, 102; sadism 114, 142; bisexuality 17, 31, 95, 96; transvestitism 31, 71; androgyny 17, 31, 61; *see also* censorship, subversive elements of rock

Rolling Stones 6, 9, 10, 18, 53, 62, 155

Romantics 111, 112; "Talking in Your Sleep" 111, 112

Rybczynski, Zbigniew 73

sadism 61

Sass, Louis 45

Sayles, John 14

schizophrenia 45, 147–8, 153

science-fiction film 30–1, 46, 62, 81, 145

Scorpion 107–9, 145; "Rock You Like a Hurricane" 107–9, 145

self-reflexivity in videos 34–6, 45, 57, 60

semiology 22–4

Sex Pistols 103

silent film 34, 138

simulacra 44, 52, 56–7, 74, 151; *see also* Baudrillard

soap operas 4, 12

social imaginary 49, 52, 115; *see also* imaginary, Lacan

Springsteen, Bruce 75–9, 76 (illus.), 78 (illus.), 82–4, 86–7, 155; "Born in the USA" 75–7, 79; participation in "Sun City" 76, 84, 87 (illus.)

Stallybrass, Peter 68

Stam, Robert 28

Stern and Fraiberg 95, 97

Stewart, Dave 138-9; see also Eurythmics

Stewart, Rod 62, 110; "Infatuation" 110

subject, the 22–6, 29, 44, 50, 91, 126; split-subject 42–3, 45, 49, 91, 94

subversive elements of rock 8, 31, 40, 45, 54, 56, 145, 152

subversive strategies/oppositional discourses 61, 62–74, 103–5, 148, 150, 152, 153

Summer, Donna 116, 127–8, 130, 132; "She Works Hard for the Money" 116, 128

symbolic, the 24, 42–3, 51, 74, 92, 94–6, 101, 115, 148, 188; pre-symbolic 95; *see also* Lacan, imaginary

Talking Heads 37, 74; *Stop Making Sense* 37; "Burning Down the House" 74

televisual apparatus 1, 3, 4, 7, 22–31, 32, 43, 44, 48, 50, 51, 57, 85, 89–91, 143, 145, 149, 151–3

Tom Petty and the Heartbreakers 141–2; "Don't Come Around Here No More" 141 (illus.), 142

Tribe, Keith 26–7, 29; *see also* anti-history

Turner Broadcasting 1–2

Turner, Tina 15, 116, 133, 135, 137, 139, 155; "Private Dancer" 116, 133–5, 134 (illus.); "What's Love Got to Do With It?" 135–7, 136 (illus.); "Typical Male" 137

Tyler, Bonnie 34; "Holding Out" 34

types of video on MTV 54–8, 55 (table), 149, 158; romantic 54–9, 92–3, 95, 101–2, 106, 127–8, 158; socially conscious 54–7, 64, 72–4, 86, 116, 127, 158; classical 54–8, 61–3, 90, 96, 101–2, 110; nihilist 54, 55, 57–61, 72, 82, 92–6, 101–3, 105–10, 145, 147, 158; postmodernist 54, 55, 57, 117, 140, 158

USA For Africa 76, 84, 86, 87, 151

195

Van Halen 103; "Jump" 103
voyeurism 37, 43, 61, 62, 90–3, 102,
    111, 114, 189
Westerns 34, 35, 46
Whannel, Paddy 6

White, Allon 68
Young, Paul 58, 95-101, 106,
    128; "Every Time You Go
    Away" 95-101, 128

ALSO BY BENJAMIN BLACK

A Death in Summer

Elegy for April

The Silver Swan

Christine Falls

VENGEANCE

VENGEANCE

A NOVEL

BENJAMIN BLACK

HENRY HOLT AND COMPANY • NEW YORK

Henry Holt and Company, LLC
Publishers since 1866
175 Fifth Avenue
New York, New York 10010
www.henryholt.com

Henry Holt® and ® are registered trademarks of
Henry Holt and Company, LLC.

Library of Congress Cataloging-in-Publication Data

Black, Benjamin, 1945–
    Vengeance : a novel / Benjamin Black. — 1st ed.
        p.   cm.

    1. Police—Ireland—Fiction.   2. Pathologists—Fiction.   I.   Title.
    PR6052.A57V46 2012
    823'.914—dc23   2012001842
    ISBN 978-1-250-02418-3
        Henry Holt books are available for special promotions and
        premiums. For details contact: Director, Special Markets.

First Edition 2012

Designed by Kelly S. Too

Printed in the United States of America

P1

VENGEANCE

ONE

1

DAVY CLANCY WAS NOT A GOOD SAILOR, IN FACT HE WAS
secretly afraid of the sea, yet here he was, on this fine summer
morning, about to set out on it in a boat that looked to him like
a large and complicated toy. It was, they all said, a perfect day
to be on the water. They did not say it was a perfect day to be
in a boat, or to be out sailing. No: *a perfect day to be on the
water,* as if it was their motto or something. And they were all
so jolly and brisk, smiling in a smug, self-satisfied way that set
his teeth on edge. Unlike him, they knew what they were doing,
the wind-burned men in yachting caps and khaki shorts and
shapeless sweaters playing at being old sea dogs, and their loud-
voiced, leathery wives—sea bitches, he thought, with a twinge
of bleak amusement. He did not belong here, among these sailing folk with their lazy expertise; he knew it, and they knew it,
too, which meant they had to behave twice as heartily towards

him, though he could see that look in their eyes, that gleam of merry contempt.

It was June, and although it had rained every day the first week of the holiday, this morning was sunny and warm with not a breath of wind. The tide was high and the water in the bay had a sluggish, swollen look, the surface oily with streaks of sapphire and pink and petrol blue. He tried not to think of what was below the surface, of the murk down there, the big-eyed fish nosing along, and things with claws scuttling around on the bottom, fighting in slow motion, devouring each other. Victor Delahaye had brought the jeep round to the front of the house that morning and they had rattled the ten miles over the mountain road to Slievemore Bay in silence. Going for a sail was the last thing Davy wanted to do, but it had not been possible to refuse. "You can crew for me," Delahaye had said the night before, in Sweeney's bar, and everyone had laughed, for some reason, everyone except Delahaye himself, and Delahaye's wife, who had looked at Davy narrow-eyed with that smile of hers and said nothing. And so here he was, about to venture out against his will on this frighteningly calm and innocent-seeming sea.

The Clancys and the Delahayes had been close for as long as anyone could remember. Samuel Delahaye and Philip Clancy had gone into partnership together at the turn of the century, running coal boats from Wales; later Samuel Delahaye had spotted the potential of the motorcar and the partners had opened one of the first big garages in the country, hiring in mechanics from England, France, Italy. The business had flourished. Although the founders were supposedly in equal partnership, everyone knew from the start that Samuel Delahaye was the boss and Phil Clancy merely his manager. Phil—poor Phil, as people were inclined to say—was not of an assertive disposition, and had quietly accepted his inferior role. Now Samuel's son, Victor, was in charge of the firm, and Phil Clancy's son, Jack, was supposedly his partner, but it was still as it had been in the old days, with Delahaye in charge and Clancy his second-in-command. Unlike his father before him, Jack Clancy resented his subordinate position—resented it deeply, though he tried hard, and mostly with success, not to let his dissatisfaction show.

But a Clancy could not say no to a Delahaye, that was understood, which was why Davy Clancy had only smiled and shrugged when in Sweeney's the previous night Victor Delahaye, on the way to getting drunk and with a soiled look in his eye, had leaned over the table and invited him to come out for a sail in the *Quicksilver.* Davy knew nothing about boats, but everyone had laughed, and someone had clapped him on the shoulder, and what could he do but say yes, thanks, sure, and bury his nose in his glass? "Right," Delahaye had said, smiling tightly and showing his teeth, "I'll pick you up at nine," and sauntered back to the bar. And that was when Delahaye's wife had looked over at Davy with that thin-lipped, mocking smile.

The two families spent their holidays together every summer; it was a tradition that went back to Phil and Samuel's time. Davy could not understand why his parents still carried it on. Old Phil was gaga now and in a nursing home, and Samuel Delahaye was in a wheelchair, and although Davy's father and Victor Delahaye kept up the pretense of friendship, it was an open secret how bad relations were between them, while Mona Delahaye, Victor's young wife—his second, the first wife having died—had barely a civil word to throw to Davy's down-trodden mother. Yet every summer the whole gang of them decamped for the month of June to Ashgrove, the Delahayes' big stone house halfway up the back slope of Slievemore. The place had ten or twelve bedrooms, more than enough to accommodate Victor Delahaye and his wife and their grown-up twin sons Jonas and James, as well as Victor's unmarried sister, Marguerite—Maggie—and the three Clancys. This year there was an extra guest, Jonas Delahaye's girlfriend, Tanya Somers. Tanya, a student at Trinity College, cut so provocative a figure in her one-piece black bathing suit that the men in the party, except her boyfriend and, of course, Jack Clancy, hardly dared allow themselves to look at her, a thing that added to the tension in an already tense household.

This morning the little harbor was crowded with boats, their owners' voices sounding sharp and clear across the lifeless surface of the sea amid the snap of ropes and the clink of brass fittings. Victor Delahaye was greeted warmly on all sides—he was commodore of Slievemore Sailing Club this season—but he hardly responded. He seemed preoccupied, and the flesh between his heavy black eyebrows was knotted in a fixed frown. Davy supposed he had a hangover. Delahaye wore sandals and tailored white trousers and a sailor's dark blue cotton shirt, and the rakish blue sailor's cap that he had brought back from a business trip to Greece. He had a tanned, craggy face that wore well its forty-something years. Walking dutifully behind him, Davy felt everyone must know him for the hopeless landlubber that he was.

The *Quicksilver* was moored at the end of the stone jetty, its sails furled. Seen close up, it did not look at all like a toy, but had the sleekly menacing lines of a giant white swordfish. Delahaye stepped nimbly down to the deck, but Davy hung back. He remembered being told once by a science teacher—Harkins it was, a Christian Brother, the one who had been sent away for interfering with the boys in the junior classes—that you could move a vessel as big as an oceangoing liner with just a push of one hand against the hull. He was supposed to be impressed, but the thought of such a huge thing being susceptible to the force of a boy's hand had filled him with dismay. Delahaye was already unwinding the mooring rope from the bollard. Sure enough, when Davy put his foot to the deck he felt the whole boat tilt a fraction, and his innards heaved. The contrast between the solid stone of the jetty underfoot and the boat's ponderous buoyancy made him giddy. He would probably be seasick, he thought gloomily, and saw himself hanging over the side, heaving and retching, while Delahaye stood above him with his fists on his hips, smiling in that cold fierce way, showing his teeth.

Davy had wondered how the boat would be made to go, since there was no wind, but now Delahaye went to the back—the stern—and started up the outboard engine there. That there was an engine seemed to Davy a kind of cheating, and the thought bucked him up a bit. But then the boat yawed out from the jetty and swept in a tight turn on the oily water and he had to grab for the rail to keep from being thrown off his feet. Delahaye stood at the wheel, with his cap over his eyes and his jaw squarely set, looking like Gregory Peck as Captain Ahab. Once again Davy pondered the question of why he was here, aboard this boat that had seemed so large, tethered to the jetty, and that now felt as if it were made of balsa wood, skimming towards the broad and desolate horizon. He thought he might know why, and hoped he was wrong.

The speed surprised him. In a few minutes they had cleared the headland and turned towards the open sea. Delahaye was all business now, shutting off the engine and unfurling the sails and pulling on cords and lashing ropes to those brass things on the deck. There was a good breeze out here, and the surface of the sea had begun pricking up everywhere in dancing white points. Davy sat on a bench at the back—the stern, the stern!—and tried to keep out of the way. He might as well not have been there, as far as Delahaye was concerned. A black bird with a long neck flew past in a straight swift line a foot above the surface of the sea—where was it going to, in such a hurry and so determinedly? The big sails shivered and rattled and then suddenly the wind filled them and at once the boat bounded forward, lifting its pointed front—the prow, he told himself, the prow was what it was called—as if it would take to the air. Davy closed his eyes, but that made him feel dizzy and he opened them again and fixed his gaze miserably on the swaying horizon. Everything was straining forward now, the mast and sails tensed like a cocked crossbow and the water slapping and sucking at the boards. He supposed they were not doing more than fifteen or twenty miles an hour—knots: are knots the same as miles?—but it felt as if they were going at an impossible speed, surging over the little waves and seeming barely to hold to the surface. His hands on either side were gripping the bench so hard his fingers had begun to ache. Delahaye, satisfied that everything was set just so, pushed past him, going towards the back of the boat, and Davy caught his smell: salt, sweat, aftershave, and something else, something sharp, sour, bitter. He sat down at the tiller and Davy turned on the seat to face him. The peak of Delahaye's cap still hid his eyes. What was he thinking? Davy was suddenly afraid of more than the sea.

What was the point of sailing? Davy did not know, and had never dared to inquire. Sailing, doing things in boats, was as natural as walking among the Delahayes. The Delahaye twins, Jonas and James, were champion yachtsmen, and had trophies to prove it; one year they had crewed on some millionaire's boat in the America's Cup. Even their Aunt Maggie was an expert sailor. Davy's father had tried to get Davy interested, and Davy had done his best, but it was no good; he could not overcome his aversion to that uncanny, treacherous realm, the main aim of which, as far as he was concerned, was to drag him under and drown him.

"You all right?" Delahaye growled, startling him. He nodded, trying to smile. He still could not see Delahaye's eyes under the peak of his cap but he knew he was watching him. What, *what* was he thinking?

Davy looked back; the land behind them now was a feature-less dark line. Where were they going? The horizon in front was empty. They were headed south, there would be no land now until—what?—Spain? Surely there would be a marker, a buoy or something, to tell them where they should turn around and start back. But on they went, and with every mile—every league?—they traveled the sea deepened under them; he thought of it, the coastal shelf falling away steadily into silence and utter dark. He shut his eyes again, and again felt dizzy.

Delahaye was saying something about Davy's mother. "Did you see her, this morning, before we left?"

Davy did not know how to reply. It sounded like a trick question, but what could the trick be? "Yes," he said warily, "yes, I saw her. She made breakfast for me." Queasily he conjured up again the rashers of bacon, the fried bread, the egg yolk leaking across the plate. His eyes closed this time of their own accord. His mind swam.

"Good," Delahaye said. "That's good."

Davy waited, but that seemed to be the end of the subject of his mother. He looked behind again at that thinning line of land. Should he suggest turning back? Should he say he had an arrangement to meet someone? It was half past ten. He could say he had an appointment, a date, at half eleven. But even as he heard himself say it in his head, it sounded wholly implausible. Yet they could not just keep going like this, towards that bare horizon—could they?

"Do you talk to your father?" Delahaye asked suddenly. "Do you and he . . . discuss things?"

Again Davy was baffled. What new line was this, and where was it headed? "We have a pint together, now and then," he said.

Delahaye made a dismissive grimace. "No, I mean, do you *talk*? Do you tell him about your life, what you're doing, what your plans are, that kind of thing?"

"Not really, no." Despite the cool breeze in his face, Davy realized he had begun to sweat, and he could feel the dampness at his wrists and between his shoulder blades. "My old man and I, we're not . . ." He did not know how to finish.

Delahaye pondered, nodding slowly. "No," he said, "fathers and sons, they don't really talk, do they. I don't talk to the boys, the twins, not much, anyway. I did when they were young, but now . . ." With the hand that was not holding the tiller he fumbled a packet of Churchman's from a pocket of his slacks and got one into his mouth but did not attempt to light it. Davy wished he could see his eyes; there was the glint of them there, under the cap's peak, but it was impossible to guess at their expression. "My father in his day didn't talk much to me," Delahaye went on. He chuckled grimly. "And these days, of course, we don't talk at all."

There were two white birds now, diving for fish; they would fly up steeply in a fluttering, corkscrew motion and then flip themselves over and draw back their wings and drop like blades, making hardly a splash as they entered the water.

Davy made a show of consulting his watch. "I wonder—" he began, but Delahaye was not listening and interrupted him.

"He was a great one for self-reliance, my father," he said. "Self-reliance and loyalty. *A man is not much if he can't depend on himself,* he used to say, *and nothing if others can't depend on him.*" He took the unlit cigarette from his mouth and rolled it between his fingers. "I remember one day he took me into town in the car. I was—oh, I don't know—six? seven? Young anyway. We were living in Rathfarnham then. He drove all the way across the city, out to Phibsborough, or Cabra, somewhere like that, and stopped at a corner shop and sent me in to buy an ice cream for myself. I don't think I'd ever been in a shop on my own before." He was leaning on the tiller now, relaxed, it seemed, and smiling thinly to himself, remembering. "Anyway, he gave me the money and I went in and bought a wafer of ice cream—you know, a penny wafer?—and when I came out he was gone. Just—gone. No father, no car, nothing."

He stopped, and there was silence save for the beating of the waves against the prow and the shrieking of the seabirds. Davy waited. "What did you do?"

Again Delahaye seemed not to be listening. He tossed the cigarette backwards over his shoulder and the churning wake swallowed it. "Funny feeling, I remember it, as if the bottom had fallen out of my stomach, my heart thumping. I must have stood there for a long time, outside the shop, rooted to the spot, because the next thing I was aware of was the ice cream dripping on the toe of my sandal. I can see it still, that corner, the curb painted in black and white segments and a hardware shop across the road. Strange thing is, I didn't cry. I went back into the shop and told the shopkeeper my daddy had gone away and left me. The shopkeeper went out to the back and fetched his wife, a big fat woman in an apron. They sat me up on the counter where they could get a good look at me, to see if I was fibbing, I suppose. The woman took what was left of the ice cream from me and wiped my hands with a damp cloth, and the shopkeeper gave me a barley-sugar sweet. I could see them looking at each other, not knowing what to do." He shook his head and chuckled again. "I can still taste it, that sweet."

When Davy tried to speak, his voice did not work the first time and he had to clear his throat and start again. "What happened?" he asked. "I mean—did he come back for you?"

Delahaye shrugged. "Of course. It seemed like hours to me but I suppose it was no more than ten or fifteen minutes."

"Where had he been?—where had he gone to?"

"Just round the corner. He took the shopkeeper aside and spoke to him, and gave him a pound. The woman looked as if she was going to spit on him, and marched back in behind the shop where she had come from and slammed the door. Then we went home. Here, take the tiller, will you?"

He stood up and they exchanged places. The arm of the tiller was damply warm where Delahaye had held it. Davy's palm was wet. He was still sweating, but he was cold, too, in his shirt, and wished he had brought a windbreaker. It struck him with renewed force how absurd a thing it was to be out here, skimming over God knew how many fathoms. And people sailed for fun and recreation!

Delahaye was gathering in the sails, first the smaller one at the front and then the bigger one. "Self-reliance, you see," he said, "a lesson in self-reliance. *You got a sweet out of it, didn't you?* was all my father said. *And I bet the woman was all over you. And you didn't cry.* That was the most important thing— that I didn't cry." He had folded the big sail expertly and was lashing it now to the horizontal part of the mast with salt-bleached cord. The boat faltered and seemed puzzled as it felt itself losing momentum, and dipped its nose and settled back with a sort of sigh, wallowing in the water, and for a second or two all sense of direction failed and the sea around them seemed to spin crazily on its axis. The sudden hush set up a buzz in Davy's ears. Delahaye, wiping his hands on his trousers, sat down on a big oak trunk set lengthways down the middle of the boat and leaned his back against the mast. He seemed weary suddenly, and lifted his cap to air his skull and then put it back on again, but not so low over his eyes as before. "What I couldn't help wondering, even at the time, was: where did loyalty figure in this lesson I had been taught?" He looked directly at Davy now with an odd, questioning candor. "What do you think?"

Davy's fingers tightened on the tiller. "About what?"

"Loyalty. You're a Clancy, you must know about loyalty—eh? Or the lack of it, at least." His eyes were of a curious glittering gray color, like chips of flint. Davy could not hold their steady gaze, and looked away. "Come on, Davy," Delahaye said softly, almost cajolingly. "Let's have your thoughts on this important topic."

"I don't know what to say," Davy said. "I don't know what you want me to say."

Delahaye was silent for a long moment, then nodded, as if something had been confirmed. He stood up from the wooden trunk and lifted the heavy lid and fished about inside and brought out something wrapped loosely in an oily rag. He stood in thought for a moment, hefting the thing in his hand. "Loyalty," he said, "it's not valued anymore, is it. Loyalty. Honor. What used to be called common decency. All gone, that kind of thing."

He began to unwind the rag, and as he did so Davy heard himself say something, exclaim something—*Whoa!* it sounded like—and he looked about wildly, as if, even out here, there might be a place to shelter behind. And yet at the same time he felt almost like laughing.

"Yes," Delahaye said, as if reading his mind and sharing in his desperate amusement, "it is an ugly bugger, isn't it. A Webley, Mark"—he brought the pistol close to his eyes and peered at the frame below the cylinder—"Mark Six. Pa got it off a fellow in the Civil War, I think it was." He glanced sideways at Davy with a sort of smile. "Oh, yes," he said, "it works. I tested it."

He sat down again, dangling the gun in both hands between his knees. It was an absurd-looking thing, all right, big and heavy and nearly a foot long, with a chamfered barrel and a hammer at the back like a silvery tongue sticking out. There was the faintest swell now, and the boat rocked gently from side to side, the small waves making a playful chattering sound against the hull. Davy tried to get his bearings from the sky, but the sky was empty. The boat seemed not to be moving at all, as if it were at anchor, but he supposed it must be drifting, at the mercy of tide and breeze, and that it only seemed motionless because there was nothing to measure movement against. He was amazed at how calm he felt, tranquil, almost. He might have been running in a race, a marathon that had been going on for so long he had forgotten he was running, and only now remembered, when everything had come to a sudden stop. Why was he not frightened? Why was he not terrified?

"I'd send you for an ice cream, if there were any shops," Delahaye said, and laughed, and turned the pistol about and put the barrel to his chest and pulled the trigger.

WHAT AMAZED DAVY WAS THAT THERE WAS SO MUCH BLOOD; that, and the vivid redness of it, which made him think of those spiders or insects or whatever they were, tiny scarlet specks, that used to fascinate him when he was a child, as they crawled among the rosebushes in his grandfather's garden. The blood had a faint smell, too, spicy and slightly sweet. The bullet hole in the left side of Delahaye's chest was black in the center with a ragged rim the color of crushed raspberries. The blood had quickly soaked the lower half of his blue cotton shirt and the lap of his white trousers, and had dripped out between his legs and made a puddle in the bottom of the boat with a single rivulet running out of it. Davy had managed to ease the packet of Churchman's out of the pocket of Delahaye's trousers—it had seemed important somehow that the cigarettes should not get blood on them. He checked his watch, as if it was important too to know what time it was.

The gunshot had sent Delahaye sprawling, with a look of astonishment on his face, and for the first seconds Davy had thought the boat would capsize, so violently did it yaw from side to side. He pictured the two of them sinking together feet-first through the water, down through the glinting light into the shadows, and then on into the blackness of the deep.

The awful thing was that Delahaye was not dead. He would be, eventually, that was certain—Davy had never seen anyone die, yet he knew Delahaye was a goner—but for now he was still breathing, making wheezing noises, like a child when it has finished crying and is trying to catch its breath. Once he moaned, and seemed to try to say something. His eyes stayed closed; there was that to be thankful for. He had slid off the trunk and was sitting at a crooked angle. He had dropped the pistol between his legs, and the handle was in the puddle of blood in the bottom.

Davy leaned forward, holding on with one hand to the what-was-it-called, the gunwale—he *hated* boats, *hated* them—and picked up the weapon by the barrel and flung it out of the boat as far as it would go; it landed in the water with a comical plop. He sat back, and realized at once that he should not have thrown the gun away. They would not think he had shot Delahaye, would they? But what if they did? He swore, over and over, punching himself on the knee with his fist.

He looked about, scanning the sea in all directions. There was no other vessel in sight. What was he to do? Down in the middle of the boat there was a pool of water—it was there that the single thin rivulet of blood was heading for—that swayed and shivered as the little waves nudged against the sides. It was not a lot of water, but what if it was not rainwater but seawater, coming from a leak? He remembered from films how leaks that sprang in the hulls of ships widened in a matter of seconds, until the sea was cascading in, washing sailors away and floating their bunks up to the ceilings. Maybe Delahaye had bored a little hole in the bottom, a little hole that would get bigger and bigger.

Davy looked at the dying man. His face was a bluish gray, like putty, and there was a film of moisture on his forehead and on his upper lip. His breathing was slower now. He looked at his watch and was surprised to find that not quite three minutes had passed since Delahaye had fired the gun—three minutes! It seemed to Davy that he was suspended high above the boat and looking down on all this, Delahaye slumped there, and the two puddles, one of blood and one of water, and himself, huddled in the stern, his two hands out and clutching to the sides in terror. For the first time it occurred to him that he too would die, lost out here in a sinking boat.

A plane appeared from the south, banking to the right, headed for Dublin. He jumped up and waved his arms frantically. The boat set up an angry rocking and at once he sat down again, feeling foolish and dizzy. The plane was too high, no one would see him, and even if someone did spot him he would probably look like some half-witted fisherman waving hello to the tourists as they flew in.

He examined the outboard motor. He had no idea how to start it. Should there be a key? He turned to Delahaye, and heard himself swallow. Did he have the stomach to search in those blood-soaked trousers again? He crept forward and ran his fingers over the outsides of Delahaye's pockets. He could feel no key. Maybe Delahaye had dropped it into the sea. *A lesson in self-reliance.* He sat back once more on the bench. The sun was high now, shining directly on the crown of his head, he could feel the beads of sweat crawling on his scalp like insects. He thought again of those blood-red mites in his Grandad Clancy's garden.

Delahaye opened dazed eyes and frowned at the sky. He gave a rattly groan and struggled forward as if trying to get to his feet, spoke a string of incomprehensible words in what seemed a tone of irritation, then slumped back into silence and died.

2

MARGUERITE DELAHAYE DID NOT LIKE HER BROTHER'S WIFE. She had tried to like her, had tried and tried over, but in vain. This troubled her, for Marguerite—or Maggie, as everyone called her, though she hated it—was a kindly soul and wished to think well of people. However, it was difficult to think well of Mona. Not that Mona seemed to care. There were not many things, it seemed, that Mona did care about. She was what Maggie's late mother would have called an awkward customer. Still, Maggie kept on trying. Mona was her sister-in-law, after all, and it was her duty to keep up the effort, even if in her heart she knew she would not succeed. In her heart too she suspected that Victor himself found it hard to like his wife. He loved her, that was certain—loved her too much, as Maggie knew to her chagrin—but she was sure it was perfectly possible to be in love with someone without liking the person. Disliking Mona meant that Maggie had to work all the harder at being nice to her. Mona took Maggie's tribute as she took all signs of kindness and regard: with indifference, or at best a sort of vacant amusement.

Mrs. Hartigan had put a crystal bowl of sweet peas on the table in the hall, and the lovely scent was everywhere in the house, even in the bedrooms and the big stone kitchen off at the end of the corridor behind the green baize door. Maggie, coming down from her room, stopped on the return to admire the flowers, arrayed there in soft sunlight falling in through the transom over the front door. The leads of the transom broke up the light and reassembled it into a bright, complicated shape, like a birdcage.

Maggie loved Ashgrove. She had been coming here with her family every year for as long as she could remember. The house had been old when she was young, yet she had the secret notion that it was somehow accompanying her through the years, keeping pace with her, its most favored visitor. For the rest of the year, when she was not here, she missed the old place, as she would miss a beloved dog, or a friend, even. A pity there had to be so many people in the house. She always made sure to arrive a day or two before the others, and to leave a day or two after they were gone. That was bliss, being on her own. She loved especially to lie awake early in the morning, the newly risen sun striping the counterpane and the house all around her stretching and creaking under the light of the new day. Solitude was her balm. She had never married. There had been offers, but she had wished to live her life in her own way, according to her own wishes and rules, without the interference of a husband.

She had spent most of the afternoon reading in her room, or

trying to read, sitting by the window in the faded green armchair, her favorite. The window looked down on a secluded corner of the garden, and now and then she would close her book—Agatha Christie; rather dull—marking her place with her thumb, and watch the blackbirds and the rabbits playing at the edge of the lawn. The rabbits, two or three of them, would venture out from the long grass under the trees, the birds would fly down quickly, and the rabbits would scamper back for shelter; this little game was repeated over and over. She supposed it was not really play, but she liked to think it was.

She had delayed for as long as she could before leaving the sanctuary of her room. Her father was in one of his moods and had deliberately said something to upset Mrs. Hartigan, and of course there were ructions that would go on at least till teatime. Her father had suffered a stroke three years previously and was confined to a wheelchair and therefore was bored and prone to rancorous ill temper, although even in his heyday he had not been exactly of a tranquil disposition. It pleased him to annoy people, to set them against each other. This afternoon it was Mrs. Hartigan's turn to suffer the edge of his tongue, and having started that particular fire he had then settled down contentedly to warm his hands before it. Mrs. Hartigan kept house for the weeks when the two families were here, and acted as caretaker for the remainder of the year. She was touchy, was Mrs. Hartigan—Maggie suspected she considered herself too good for such menial work—and took offense easily. And of course it always fell to Maggie to smooth her ruffled feathers. Standing in the hall now, still admiring the flowers, Maggie smiled to herself; ruffled feathers, yes—Mrs. Hartigan did look a bit like a plump excitable old hen.

Samuel Delahaye was in the lounge, which was what the main living room had always been called, listening to a program on the wireless. He had parked his wheelchair next to the sideboard on which the set stood, its green eye pulsing, and had his ear pressed up close to the mesh of the speaker; it was one of his amusements to pretend to be hard of hearing. He was a big man, broad-shouldered and barrel-chested, with a swept-back mane of silver hair; Maggie believed he modeled himself on William Butler Yeats—certainly he was as vain as the poet surely must have been. When she had entered the room and shut the door, and before she had spoken even a word, he flapped a hand irritably in her direction, as if she were making a commotion of some sort and interfering with his enjoyment of the program, which seemed to be about bees. He did not look at her.

She sighed. Her sister-in-law was seated on the long beige sofa in front of the fireplace, flipping through a glossy magazine. On a low table before her stood a tall glass of gin and tonic, with ice cubes and sliced lemon; the glass was misted down the sides. The French windows at the far end of the room were wide open onto the lawn, at the far side of which was the stand of ash trees that gave the house its name.

Maggie came forward, and Mona looked up from her magazine. "We thought you must have left and gone home," Mona said, in her languid way. "Where have you been hiding?"

Mona's abundant hair was the color of polished bronze, and her skin was porcelain pale. Her eyes were violet, and tapered at the outer corners. The only flaw in her beauty, Maggie considered, was her mouth, a thin scarlet slash that gave her something of the look of a mean and sulky child.

"Oh, you know, I was just pottering," Maggie said.

"For Christ's sake!" her father cried from across the room. "Can't you stop that racket and let me listen?"

Neither woman paid him any heed.

"Has Mrs. H. calmed down yet?" Maggie asked quietly of her sister-in-law. Mona shrugged; she was turning the pages of her magazine again, pausing only to examine the ads with a narrowed eye.

"How should I know?" she said. "The old bitch never speaks to me."

Maggie sat down at the other end of the sofa. "I do wish he wouldn't provoke her," she said. "If she were to leave, we'd be lost."

Mona gave a soft snort of laughter. "No fear of that," she said. "She has it too easy here."

"I think she works quite hard," Maggie said mildly, picking a speck of fluff from the hem of her skirt. "It's a very big house, and there's just herself and the girl she gets in at the weekends."

Mona did not reply to this, and leaned forward and took up her glass. Maggie watched her gazing before her vague-eyed as she drank. She really was an exquisite creature—to look at, at least. She was not yet thirty, which made her—what was it?—a good sixteen years younger than her husband. It always puzzled Maggie that Mona should have consented to marry Victor. Victor was handsome, of course, though she supposed his looks were faded a bit by now, and he was well-off, and generous, but he was not the kind of man Maggie would have thought Mona would *go for*, as she would say herself. The kind of man Mona would go for, Maggie would have thought, would be as careless and cruel as she was herself. Thinking this, Maggie immediately felt guilty, and even blushed a little, though it had only been a thought, with no one to hear.

The dance of the drones, the voice on the wireless was saying, *is thought to be a system by which returning bees direct their fellow workers to the richest sources of pollen in the vicinity of the hive. Bees will travel for distances of as much as—*

And then the telephone outside on the hall table began to ring.

A WEEK OF RAIN HAD LEFT THE GROUND IN A SOGGY STATE, BUT all the same Blue Lightning, the sprightly four-year-old from the late Dick Jewell's stables, that was supposed to like the going hard, romped home at seven to two, surprising everyone. Everyone except Jack Clancy. He collected his winnings from the bookie's in Slievemore and went round the corner to Walsh's and ordered drinks for everyone in the bar. The locals, he knew, would despise him for his largesse—*Who does your man think he is, playing the big fellow?*—but all the same they would drink his drink. Their contempt did not bother him. On the contrary, he was gratified to see the resentful looks they gave him, as they muttered behind their pints.

The publican's wife, a big redhead with green eyes—a splash of tinker blood there, surely—helped out behind the bar on race days. Jack sat in the alcove just inside the door and watched her as she worked. From here he had a view of the woman herself and also of her reflection in the fly-blown looking glass behind the bar. She was wearing a sleeveless summer frock and when she lifted her freckled arm to pull a pint he glimpsed a smear of sweat-damp coppery moss in the shad-owed hollow of her armpit. Her name was Sadie.

Watching the woman made him think of Jonas Delahaye's girlfriend. Not that Sadie resembled Tanya Somers even in the least degree. Just picturing Tanya in her black swimsuit gave him an ache at the root of his tongue. Not a hope there, of course. On the other hand, you could never tell. He was more than twice her age, but some young ones, he knew, had a taste for older men—look at Mona Delahaye. That would be some row, if he were to have a go at Jonas's stuck-up girlfriend and got found out. Jonas, that spoiled whelp. He knew Jonas and Tanya were sleeping together. They were in separate bedrooms, but that was only for the look of it, and not to scandalize old Ma Hartigan; every night after lights-out Jonas was in there like a shot, Jack knew it for sure. Victor Delahaye prided him-self on being broad-minded and modern, now that his father was ailing and he was no longer under the old man's thumb. Victor's sister was a different matter, though; when Tanya came sashaying through the house, Maggie's mouth got small and wrinkled, as if she were sucking on a sour sweet.

And what about Davy? Jack was uneasily aware that his son was of an age to be his rival when it came to the ladies. Davy was a handsome young fellow—Jack had seen the looks women gave him, even Mona Delahaye. What if Davy were to make a play for Tanya Somers? That was a possibility Jack did not care to contemplate. A row of that scale between the two families would be disastrous, especially now, when all his plans for the future of the firm were so delicately balanced.

• • •

HE THOUGHT, NOT FOR THE FIRST TIME, HOW STRANGE IT MUST be being a twin. The Delahaye brothers, tall, blond, blue-eyed, were like two peas in a pod. Imagine having someone around all the time who was your spitting image. Jonas and James did not seem to mind; in fact, they were always together. What, he wondered, did James make of Tanya Somers? Would he resent her, would he be envious—resentful of her for coming between him and his brother, and envious of his brother for having her? And Tanya: Was she able to tell the difference between the twins? What if Jonas and James were to swap places some night and James were to slip into bed with her— would she know it was him? Or what if the two of them got in with her, one on either side—would she be able to tell them apart? Those two big blond lads in bed with Tanya in the middle, that was a thought he had found himself entertaining on more than one occasion over these past weeks, with a mixture of excitement, envy, and sweet regret. He was forty-seven, himself, and hated it.

He signaled to Sadie for another Jamaica red rum. He handed over a ten-shilling note and when she brought the change she gave him a queer sort of smile, her lips pressed together and one eyebrow arched, and he did not know what to make of it. Either she was telling him she knew his type and he was not to bother trying, or the opposite, that she liked the look of him and would listen to any offer he might care to make. If it was the latter, it would be impossible, down here. He had made that mistake once before, years ago—a cattle dealer's wife over at Crosshaven, a redhead too, as it happened—and had got such a beating from the cattle dealer's three brutes of sons that there were bones in his shoulders and his back that still ached when the weather turned wet. But surely Sadie must come up to the city sometimes, to shop, or whatever. He would slip her his phone number before he left.

A fellow he knew from the sailing club came in and Jack stood him a drink and they talked boats for a while. Jack loved being in a pub at this time of a summer evening, loved the sound of slow talk and the rich reek of whiskey, loved the look of sunshine the color of brass coming in at the open doorway and lighting up the lazy swirls of cigarette smoke in the dusky air. Being here was not being at Ashgrove, a pleasure in itself. And then there was Sadie, and the possibilities she might represent.

The sailing club fellow's name was Grogan, a solicitor from Cork and, as Jack now belatedly remembered, a terrible bore. They had sailed together in the Slievemore regatta; Grogan in his *Mermaid* had taken the Commodore's Cup this year. He was saying something now about a boat with two men in it having been found adrift off Slievemore Bay—there had been a report about it on the wireless, on the six o'clock news. Jack was watching Sadie, admiring the way her frock tightened over her bust when she drew the handle of the beer tap back and down in a slow, effortful arc. Yes, he would definitely suggest a drink next time she was in Dublin. What had he to lose?

"One chap dead, it seems," Grogan said. "Sounds a funny business."

SYLVIA CLANCY STEERED THE BIG CAR ONTO THE CAUSEWAY below the village of Rosscarbery. She always liked to drive back from Cork along the coast road. Today, however, she had no eye for the scenery, for she was worried. This was not unusual.

Being worried was Sylvia's accustomed state of mind. How could it be otherwise? She was married to Jack Clancy and Davy Clancy was her son. Today, however, her specific concern was Mona Delahaye's party, to be held on the following Saturday night. Mona was what could be described as a party person. Three years ago she had thrown—surely the right word—the first Ashgrove Bash, as she called it, and since then it had become an annual event and the talk of the county, if not of half the country.

Most people who gave parties, Sylvia supposed, gave them in the hope that their guests would enjoy themselves and go home happy. Evidently Mona's intention was the opposite of this. She seemed to wish that everyone should have a good time, only she had a peculiar notion of what having a good time should involve. She did not want people standing about with drinks in their hands, chitchatting: arguments, insults, challenges, fights, even fistfights, these were the kinds of things Mona wished her parties to inspire. And if matters were not going her way—that is, if they were going peaceably and enjoyably—she was fully prepared to step in and set them awry. Mona had a genius for provocation. She stirred things up without seeming to, bestowing a smile here, a soft word there, inquiring, informing, advising. And as she progressed through the room there would spring up in her wake little conflagrations that were her doing but that yet appeared entirely unconnected with her. Then, reaching the far end of the room, she would turn and survey her handiwork with pleasure, her eyes narrowed and her thin mouth upturned at one corner.

Yet in her heart Sylvia felt sympathy for Mona. Mona was a child, really, with all a child's avidity and incurable mischievousness. Whatever was going on, Mona had to have it, and if she could not have it she would spoil it for others. It was simply her way. Sylvia suspected that Mona, like her, felt secretly that she had strayed into the wrong family. The Delahayes were a formidable clan, as were the Clancys in their different way, and to have married into them was to be devoured, or as good as. Could poor Mona be blamed for asserting herself in the only way she knew how? Mischief-making was her declaration of independence, which was why she and her father-in-law, old Samuel Delahaye, were fond of each other, if fond was a word that could be fitted to either of these willful, reckless, and malicious creatures.

Sylvia was driving the Delahayes' Mercedes—Jack was off at the races in their own old Humber—feeling nervous and at the same time faintly thrilled, for the big car frightened her, with its brutishly square front and that emblem on the bonnet that looked to her like the sight of a gun. Yet she had to admit it was exciting to be in control, however fearfully, of such a powerful machine. She had been to Cork to see a new osteopath—they were called bonesetters, down here—whom Mrs. Hartigan had recommended. Mrs. Hartigan swore by him and declared him a miracle worker, but Sylvia had consulted him only out of politeness to the housekeeper, a tiresome woman at the best of times. Sylvia had a bad back. No one had ever been able to discover why she should be suffering such awful, chronic pain, and this new man had been no wiser than the others, though he had talked a lot of mumbo jumbo about frozen joints, and fused discs, and plates—he was very hot on plates, whatever they were supposed to be. A foolish, ignorant man, Sylvia judged. However, the evening was so lovely, with the

sun flashing its burning arrows through the trees along the
roadside and the wheat and barley in the fields beyond swayed
and polished by the breeze, that her heart lifted, despite the
motorcar's slouching impatience and the ache in her lower
spine—which, if she was not mistaken, the bonesetter had only
made worse.

Sylvia was English. This seemed increasingly to be, for herself as well as for others, the most significant fact about her.
Yet by now she had spent more than half of her life in Ireland.
It did not matter. They would be conscious of her Englishness
until her dying day. Not that they expressed resentment or
showed prejudice towards her. Indeed, they seemed to admire
her pluck, to think her a good sport, for being undaunted
enough to make her life among them. The response in general
to the fact that she was English was a sort of amused fascination; people would look at her in that half-smiling, wondering
way and say, "And you're English, are you?" as if it were something outlandish, like being a racing driver, or a jungle explorer.
She was a permanent curiosity. She could not resent this. Probably they perceived in a dim way the inner life she continued to
live, which was mild, reasonable, tolerant, and self-mocking—
which was, in a word, English, or what she thought of as being
English, Englishness as she remembered it.

Just as Sylvia knew Mona should not have married Victor
Delahaye, so she knew that she should not have married Jack
Clancy. Oh, she loved Jack, whatever that meant now, after all
these years. At first, when they were young, certainly she had
adored him. She had never met—no, she had never conceived
of the possibility of there being a person such as Jack: charming, dangerous, darkly handsome, and given to a destructive

gaiety that she had found immediately irresistible. These things, the charm, the danger, the satanic good looks, that impish, corrosive humor above all, these, she understood now, were the very things that should have warned her off him.

She was taller than he was, taller by a good two or three inches. He had never seemed to mind this, and only made jokes about it. She, however, was acutely aware of the disparity, not for her own sake but for his, and in their first months together had devised a way of standing beside him with her chin lowered and her left leg drawn back a little way and her right knee surreptitiously flexed, which, if it did not reduce her height in any noticeable way, at least announced that she knew she was the one who must try to right the balance, and suffer the humiliation of not being able to do so. It was not that Jack was too short, but that she was too tall.

She slowed the car and turned in at the gate of Ashgrove.

Now her mind, going its own way as always, went back to the awful prospect of Mona's party. Last year Davy had got into a scuffle with the son of some local grandee and had bitten off part of his ear. She rather thought the other boy had deserved what he had got, for obviously he was a brat, but still, getting into fights and biting people was not the kind of behavior she would have expected of a son of hers. But then, many things in her life had turned out to be not as she had expected. Davy, she thought, was rather like this brute of a car, barely controllable, single-minded, and always eager to run ahead of himself. And now, all at once, a thought that had been lurking beneath her anxiety about the party came flashing to the surface of her mind and would not be pushed down again. It was the thought of that Somers girl. Tanya Somers had trouble written all over her. It always puzzled Sylvia that men could not see how calculating a girl like Tanya was, how all her effects were—not thought out, perhaps, but instinctive, measured, and sure. What if Davy tried to take her away from Jonas Delahaye? Yes, and what if—what if someone else were to attempt—? What if—?

She had stopped on the gravel in front of the house and was sitting behind the wheel, her appalled gaze fixed unseeing on the windscreen as she contemplated the possibilities for mayhem that Tanya Somers represented, when she heard what seemed to be the sound of someone crying in the house. She opened the door and stepped out onto the gravel and stood to listen. Yes, definitely, someone was crying, a woman: the sound was coming from one of the open upstairs windows, jagged sobs, and in between each sob a sort of labored mooing. Maggie. Maggie was weeping—those heaving gasps were the sounds she made when she was having an asthma attack. And why was the front door wide open like that? And what or whose was that black car, parked beside the laburnums?

Something had happened—something terrible, surely. Sylvia's first thought was: *Davy*. Her second was: *Jack*.

SUPERINTENDENT WALLACE HAD THOUGHT IT BEST THAT HE should come out himself to Ashgrove to break the news. Not that he had much time for these folk who descended on the house for a few weeks every summer and left the place standing empty and idle for the rest of the year. It was, he considered, a queer comedown for a grand mansion such as this, the seat of gentlemen and their ladies in centuries past, that it should be reduced to the status of a holiday villa for a gang of moneyed Dublin riffraff. The Superintendent was a mild man but, in secret, a great and unrelenting snob. Although his own origins were humble, and despite the fact that in most matters he tried to be accommodating and unjudgmental, he was implacably disapproving of the new Ireland, so called, which had grown up in the decade since the war, and of which the Clancys, and even the Delahayes, who might have been expected to live up to their venerable name, were, in his opinion, typical representatives.

He was not surprised by what had happened this afternoon—puzzled, certainly, but not surprised. The crust of civilization was very thin, and very brittle. In his youth he had lived through the War of Independence and the Civil War that had followed, and he had seen things done—young men slaughtered, great houses burned, the land laid waste—that flew in the face of what the priests taught and the former generations had believed in. Now there was peace in the country, yet on a sunny afternoon in the height of summer two men had gone out in a boat and one of them had been brought back dead, shot through the chest and wallowing in his own blood. It was a bad business.

Having delivered his dreadful message, he was uncertain how to proceed. Everyone had rushed off to other parts of the house and left him standing in the front hall with his cap in his hand. From upstairs he could hear Miss Delahaye crying—she was the best of the lot of them, a decent woman with a good heart—but somewhere nearby a tinny voice was delivering what seemed to be a lecture of some kind. Old man Delahaye, after a minute of slack-mouthed staring, had spun his wheelchair on the spot and bowled himself down the hall at a fast lick and disappeared into the back of the house. The dead man's wife—his widow, now—had also gone off somewhere and was not to be seen. It was as if, the Superintendent thought, he had brought the plague with him, which of course in a way he had.

There was a quick step behind him and he turned to see a tall woman hurriedly bearing down on him. She was a moving silhouette against the sunlight in the doorway and at first he could not see who it was. Then she spoke and he recognized the Clancy woman. "Tell me," she said urgently, almost whispering, her fingers clutching at the sleeve of his uniform. "*Tell me.*"

He told her. While he was speaking she watched him intently, nodding, her eyes fixed on his lips, as if to make out there the shape of the words she did not trust her ears to absorb. "A trawler out of Castletownbere spotted the boat adrift and brought it in," he said. "The poor man was long dead by then."

"And my son," she said, "where is he? How is he?"

"They have him in the Bon Secours in Cork," the Superintendent said. "He has a touch of sunstroke, they think. He'll be all right."

"My God—Cork," she said, shifting her stare to one side and fixing it on nothing. "I've just come from there." She seemed so incredulous of this small coincidence that for a moment he thought she was going to laugh. "I must go back," she muttered.

She made to turn away, patting the pockets of her loose cardigan in search of the car keys, but he caught her elbow and said it was all right, that her son would be brought down from Cork in an ambulance, that he was probably on his way already. She nodded. She was frowning now. "And Mr. Delahaye is dead, you say," she said, still unable to grasp it.

"Yes, ma'am," he said. "Shot."

She stared at him again in that almost hungry fashion. "But who shot him?"

"Well now," he said, "that's the question, ma'am."

He liked her voice, the softness of it, the gentility. He had never had anything against the English, himself, though the Black and Tans had murdered an uncle of his—he was only an uncle by marriage. She turned and walked slowly to the straight-backed chair beside the hall table and sat down, folding her hands in her lap. He had been noticing something odd and now he realized what it was: she had no handbag. He thought women never went anywhere without a handbag. Her hair was blond, or maybe more gray than blond, and gathered at the back in a bun that had already released a few stray straggles. That was as far as the disarray would go, he thought; this lady was not the kind to tear her hair out

Upstairs Miss Delahaye was still crying, but with less abandon now, her sobs become hiccups.

The Superintendent heard a whirring sound behind him, and turned to see old Delahaye reappear from the back of the house, wheeling himself along the black-and-white tiled hall with surprising speed and smoothness. He looked neither at the Superintendent nor at the woman sitting by the table, but wrenched the wheelchair to the left and put out a foot in front him and kicked open the door to the lounge and glided through. The door, sighing, swung slowly shut behind him. After a moment Sylvia Clancy stood up and followed him, and the Superintendent, not knowing what else to do, followed her.

Mona Delahaye was sitting on the beige sofa, facing the fireplace. She wore a frock of dark green silk. She was leaning forward, her clasped hands resting on her crossed knees. She held her head inclined a little to the side, as if she were listening for some faint, far-off sound. Samuel Delahaye in his wheelchair was at the open French windows, his chin sunk on his chest, glaring out at the garden. The crazy thought came to the Superintendent that perhaps these two people had not understood what he had told them, and that they were waiting for clarification, enlightenment; waiting for someone to explain it all to them again, more comprehensibly.

Sylvia Clancy went and sat down beside Mona on the sofa and tried to take her hand, but Mona kept her hands clasped, and did not look at her.

"I suppose," Mona said, mildly, thoughtfully, "we'll have to cancel the party, now."

Mrs. Clancy and the Superintendent decided not to hear this, and to act as if it had not been said. No doubt the young woman was suffering from shock. At the window, Samuel Delahaye made a snorting sound that might have been laughter.

Was that an ambulance siren, in the distance?

"I think, ma'am," the Superintendent said softly, addressing Sylvia Clancy over the back of the sofa, "I think I'll be on my way."

"Yes," the woman said, not looking at him.

Still he lingered. "There'll be people out, after me," he said. "To ask questions, and the like." He waited. No response came. He coughed delicately into his fist and turned away and walked as if on eggshells to the door. In the hall he brought out a handkerchief and took off his cap and gave the shiny peak a wipe. In the dimness at the back of the hall a white face appeared for a moment and was gone. The housekeeper—what was her name? Hennigan? No, Hartigan. He put on his cap again and went out to the car. The young Guard who had driven him down here—he could not remember his name, either—hopped out from behind the wheel and scurried round to the passenger side and opened the door for him and stood to attention. The leather seat was hot where the sun had been shining on it. "Right," the Superintendent said, with a grim sigh. "Let's go." The young Guard started up the engine, and did something to the gears that made the rear wheels spin in the gravel.

In the lounge, Samuel Delahaye wheeled himself away from the French windows and approached the two women seated on the sofa.

"That's a fine—" he began, glaring at Sylvia, and had to stop and cough harshly and start again. "That's a fine thing that cullion of a son of yours is after doing now."

3

INSPECTOR HACKETT THOUGHT WISTFULLY THAT HE WOULD HAVE enjoyed a jaunt to Cork. He was fond of the city, and the coast down there was lovely, especially at this time of year—he had spent a week in Skibbereen with the missus one summer and they had both loved it and vowed to return, though they never had. But Victor Delahaye's corpse had been brought up to Dublin earlier that morning, and the two families were on their way back to town, so there was no call for him to make the journey south. He spoke on the telephone to the Super down there, Wallace, that stuffed shirt, and Wallace told him that the forensics boys from Anglesea Street were examining the boat and when Wallace got the report he would send it up to him. No, no weapon had been found; the young fellow with Delahaye had said he had thrown the gun into the sea. It was not his gun, he said—he had no gun—but Delahaye's, that Delahaye had it on board already, wrapped in a rag and hidden in a chest. "Did you believe him?" the Inspector asked. He was leaning back in his chair with his boots on his desk, picking his teeth—his dentures, rather—with a matchstick. Wallace huffed and puffed and said yes, he did, he believed him. Hackett nodded into the mouthpiece. Wallace might be pompous and vain—and he was, he was surely—but he was not entirely a fool.

This, Hackett thought, dropping the sodden match into the ashtray on his desk, was going to be tricky. The Delahayes were a formidable clan, and would be bound to cause him heartache. First of all they would want the whole business hushed up. Their people would ring the newspapers, and the newspapers would ring him, and what would he say? If it was a suicide they would not want to know, since newspapers never reported suicides, and if it was not a suicide they would probably not want to know that, either, given who it was had been killed and who it had to have been that had done the killing. A high-society scandal would make juicy reading, but the Delahayes had clout in this town. He crossed one booted ankle on the other. What the hell had happened down there? It was not every day of the week a man took himself and the only son of his business partner off in a boat and once beyond sight of land brought out a gun and plugged himself. Or maybe the young fellow had done it, after all, despite John-Joe Wallace's best hunch? Which would be the bigger scandal?

He spent the next two hours on the telephone, talking to all the contacts he could think of and gathering from them every scrap of information that was to be had on Delahaye & Clancy, Ltd., its stock market value, its fiscal state, its standing in the business community. He was told many things that did not interest him and a few that did. There was something going on inside the company, some shift, some realignment. A management reorganization, a power struggle, a boardroom coup? No one knew the details, but more than one of his contacts insisted that something was definitely up. Was the company in trouble? No. Were its finances sound? Yes. What about Victor Delahaye's health? As far as anyone knew, he had not been sick. Hackett put down the phone and looked at the wall in front of him. A Clery's calendar from last year, a framed photo of de Valera in a top hat, a reddish smear where Hackett had swatted a bluebottle yesterday. He had a hum in his ear from being on the phone for so long. This was the part of police work he hated, the sense at the start of a case of being purblind, of stumbling in a fog, of nothing connecting with anything. He felt like a monkey with a coconut and no stone to crack it on.

He would go and talk to Dr. Quirke.

HE FOUND HIM IN MCGONAGLE'S. QUIRKE WAS PERCHED AT THE bar in his usual spot, with his back to a pillar that had a narrow mirror set into it, a glass of Jameson's at his elbow. "I see you're having your lunch," the Inspector said drily, sliding onto a high stool beside him. It was well past noon and coming up to the lunch hour and the hurried drinkers were getting in a last one before closing time. Quirke was looking about him with a thoughtful eye. "On how many occasions, would you say," he said, "have you and I been in this pub, Inspector?"

Hackett chuckled. "The two of us together, do you mean, or separately?" He took off his hat and set it on his knee. "Either road, too many times, I've no doubt."

Quirke was looking at the detective's hat. "I know a man," he said, "a civil servant, keeps two hats, one to wear and one to leave in the office. Anyone calls when he's out at the pub, the secretary says, *Oh, he must be in the building, his hat is on the hat stand.*"

"Civil servant, you say? That's what has the country the way it is."

"You're right. Skivers and skrimshankers. What are you drinking?"

"A glass of water."

"Oh, of course—you're on duty."

This time they both chuckled.

Hackett too looked about him now. He was interested in the lighting. His wife had been pestering him for months to put up new fixtures in the living room and he was on the look-out for ideas. Lights were awkward. A single bulb in the middle of the ceiling, no matter what sort of shade you put on it, gave the place the look of a prison cell—"Of course, that would suit you grand," May had said with heavy sarcasm—but standing lamps could be a curse; they had to be huddled under, like umbrellas, if they were to be of any use at all. Here the bulbs were set in two parallel rows close up to the ceiling; the dusty shades, of amber-colored glass with frilled edges, looked like little bonnets. Maybe that was the answer for the living room, half a dozen small bulbs installed at strategic points around the ceiling—over the table, above the shelf with the wireless set, and so on. Not the glass bonnets, though; he could imagine what May would say to the glass bonnets.

"Let me guess why you're here," Quirke said.

He was in his double-breasted black suit, as always—he must have, the Inspector thought, three or four of these suits, all identical. He was coming to look like an undertaker; it was an occupational hazard, perhaps, for a pathologist. He was putting on weight, too—the big shoulders that used to be all muscle were softening, you could see the flab compressed under the yoke of his jacket, and in the mirror behind him the back of his neck was squeezing over his shirt collar. Letting himself go; he needed a woman to smarten him up.

"Have you things to tell me?" the Inspector said.

Quirke drank off the last of the Jameson's and lifted his empty glass for the barman to see. "I take it you're referring to a certain illustrious corpse?" he said.

"Aye—one that came up this morning from Cork."

The barman, a big soft-faced man, brought Quirke's whiskey. "Drink up now, Doctor," he said softly. "We'll be closing up shortly."

"Thank you, Michael," Quirke said. "Oh, and the Inspector here will take a glass of water—do you think you could manage that?"

The barman gave him a droll look and went to the sink and filled a glass at the tap and brought it back and set it down in front of Hackett with a cardboard coaster underneath it. Quirke sipped his new whiskey. They were both gazing before them towards the ranked bottles behind the bar.

"So," Hackett said. "What did you find?"

"Pistol, heavy-duty," Quirke said. "Single shot. Bullet missed the heart and pierced the spleen—lot of blood—punctured the base of the left lung, causing a tension pneumothorax, leading to cardiorespiratory arrest, leading to you-know-what." He smiled bleakly and lifted his glass in a mock toast. "Farewell, cruel world."

"You'd say he did it to himself? I mean, is that the way it looks?"

Quirke pondered this. "I presume so. He was probably alive for five minutes or so after he was hit. There were just the two of them in the boat. Not a good thing to have to watch, a man lying in front of you shedding buckets of blood and the bullet hole in his chest sucking in air like a second mouth. If what's-his-name, the young fellow, did the shooting, I'd say he would have fired again, to finish him off—wouldn't you? The weapon wasn't found?"

"Clancy—the young fellow—says he threw it in the sea."

"It's the kind of thing you'd do."

"If it was you did the shooting. Why would he take it off the dying man and throw it away, if the man had shot himself?"

"Panic?"

The Inspector was rotating the base of his glass slowly on its coaster. "Do you ever wonder what causes it," he said, "that cloudiness in water? Is it the what-do-you-call-it, the chlorine, or just a whole lot of little bubbles, caused by coming through the tap?"

Quirke was smiling. "You have an inquiring mind, Inspector," he said.

The barman came and rapped the edge of a penny smartly on the bar in front of them. "Time, gents; time, please."

• • •

IN THE STREET THE AFTERNOON SUNLIGHT FELL IN ANGLED spikes and the air was grayed with exhaust smoke and drifts of summer dust. The two men walked together in companionable silence in the direction of the Bank of Ireland in College Green. There were smells of roasting coffee beans and horse manure—a Clydesdale that was tethered outside Switzers and harnessed to a green-sided Post Office dray had dropped a mound of steaming clods onto the road—and of scorched sugar from a candy-floss stall on the corner of Dame Street. It struck Quirke, not for the first time, that he and the detective had nothing to talk about beyond death and postmortems, crimes and criminals, murders and motives. What did they know of each other's lives? Next to nothing. Yet by now they had years of shared history behind them. This was, for some reason, a slightly dispiriting thought.

"Do you know them, at all," Hackett asked, "the Delahayes, the Clancys?"

The Inspector, Quirke knew, was of the belief that he enjoyed a wide circle of acquaintances and was intimate with important people at the highest levels of society, a notion that Quirke had long ago given up trying to disabuse him of. "I suppose I might have met Delahaye," he said.

"Has—had—a young wife. Number two."

"What happened to number one?"

"Died, four or five years ago. Two sons, twins, grown up now."

They had passed the bottom of Grafton Street, and Quirke ducked into Kapp & Peterson's to buy a packet of Senior Service. When he came out Hackett was waiting for him. Quirke offered him a cigarette and they lit up and walked on. The streets were crowded, this sunny summer day. "Mona Dela-haye," Hackett said, squinting across at the blue clockface above the gates of Trinity College. "That's the widow's name." He hummed distractedly.

Quirke sighed, then laughed. "All right," he said in a tone of weary resignation. "I'll come with you."

The Inspector turned to him in feigned surprise. "Would you do that?" It was another convention between them that Quirke had a silken tongue and could talk with ease to the gentry, while Hackett would be looked down on, laughed at, and lied to. "It might be handy, all right. Northumberland Road, big red-brick pile."

Quirke sighed again. "What time?"

"I said I'd be out there at five."

"And how do we account for my presence?"

Hackett gave a snuffly laugh. "I'll introduce you as Dr. Watson," he said.

"Very funny," Quirke said, turning away. "I'll see you at five."

IN THE EVENT, QUIRKE GOT THERE EARLY. HE HAD TAKEN A TAXI and was waiting on the pavement in the broad canopy of shade under a beech tree when Hackett arrived. Hackett had walked from his office in Pearse Street. He liked to walk, and nowadays, thanks to his seniority on the Force, he had the time and leisure to indulge in this simple pleasure as often as he cared to. He had come all the way up the canal along the towpath from Grand Canal Dock and turned left at Lower Mount Street onto Northumberland Road. This moneyed part of the city was spacious and handsome, but he was a countryman at heart and he missed the fields and the big skies of the Midlands of his childhood. He owned a bit of land in South Roscommon and intended to build a cottage on it to retire to. This plan he had kept to himself, so far; he would have to judge carefully when to put it to May, for May was fond of the city. All these renovations and improvements she had him making to the house were, he knew, aimed at tying the two of them inseparably to the place. He, though, would want to be rid of the city when the time came for him to retire; it had too many soiled associations for him. No, he would not spend his declining years in Dublin.

Quirke was leaning against the railing, his incongruously dainty feet crossed at the ankles and his black hat tipped over his left eye. The Inspector often wondered about Quirke's life, what he did in the evenings, what people he saw at the weekends. A strange and solitary man. There was that actress he used to go around with—what was her name? Galloway?—and then, of course, more recently, the Frenchwoman, who had run off to France and would not be coming back.

"The widow," Quirke said, "what did you say her name was?"

"Mona. Mrs. Mona Delahaye."

"Mrs. Number Two."

The red-brick house was large and plain, with tall, blank windows. They walked together along the graveled garden path and up the stone steps to the front door. A black crêpe bow was attached to the knocker. The story was in the evening papers—"DEATH OF PROMINENT BUSINESSMAN," "MYSTERY DEATH OF DELAHAYE"—and the Commissioner had been on the phone to Hackett already. Hackett had got the desk sergeant to say he was out and could not be contacted; he did not feel like talking to Commissioner Brannigan, and anyway he had nothing to tell him.

He pressed the bell.

The maid was a raw-faced girl with freckles and a mop of rust-colored curls. When Hackett identified himself she gave them both a jaunty grin that seemed to belie the black bow on the door, and went ahead of them along the hall, her uncorseted haunches joggling. The drawing room was at the rear of the house, with a tall window at the far end of it that looked into the garden. There was a bowl of roses on a sideboard, their musky fragrance mingling with the sharper tang of an expensive perfume.

Mona Delahaye was standing to one side of the window, facing into the sunlit garden—a deliberate pose, Quirke felt sure. She wore a green silk jacket over a calf-length black skirt. She delayed a beat before turning to them with a strained expression in her lustrous, Oriental eyes. Her rich dark hair, drawn back from her face, seemed to have lights like fireflies glinting in its depths. The two men stood a moment lost in contemplation of the vision of meticulously groomed and painted beauty that she was. Then the Inspector stirred, clearing his throat.

"Mrs. Delahaye," he said. "I'm sorry for your trouble. This is Dr. Quirke."

Hackett had taken off his hat and, not knowing what to do with it, was holding it behind his back, nervously rotating the brim. His inveterate blue suit, Quirke noticed, had a higher shine than ever at the elbows and the knees; he did not care to think what the seat of the trousers would look like.

Mrs. Delahaye came forward, barely glancing at the Inspector but looking Quirke up and down with her cool and candid

gaze. She gave him her limp pale hand to shake and let it lin-
ger in his for a moment longer than occasion required. "A doctor," she said, "I see," though it was not clear what she thought
she saw. She went to the sideboard and took a cigarette from a
mother-of-pearl box there and lit it with an ornate silver lighter
the size of a billiard ball. Trailing smoke, she walked to a sofa
opposite the window—Quirke watched her narrow shoulder
blades flexing like folded wings under the silk of her jacket—
and sat down, crossing one knee on the other and detaching a
flake of tobacco from her lower lip.

Did she ever do anything, he wondered, without having first
calculated the effect? She did not seem a woman lost in grief.
And yet he detected something in her which was not to do
with the death of her husband, something that would always
be there, something worried, tentative, watchful. Spoiled children had that look, of knowing deep down that all the petting
and the pampering might at any moment just stop, without the
slightest warning.

On the wall behind her there was a Mainie Jellett abstract
in a heavy gilt frame. She gazed up at the two men, widening
her violet eyes. "Have you found out what happened on that
boat?" she said. "I assume it was some kind of awful accident?"

They were conscious, Quirke and the Inspector, of looming
awkwardly before her; under her gaze Quirke felt like a less-
than-first-rate thoroughbred being assessed by an unconvinced
buyer.

"Well, Mrs. Delahaye," the Inspector said, still twirling the
hat brim behind his back, "that's what we wanted to talk to you
about." He fetched a chair and brought it forward, his boots
squeaking, and set it in front of the sofa and sat down, placing

his hat primly in his lap. "In fact," he said, putting on his gentlest, his most winning smile, "we were hoping you might be able to help us come to some conclusion about what exactly happened."

The woman looked past him to Quirke, still standing in the same spot, with one hand in a side pocket of his jacket and the other holding his hat. "*You're* not a policeman, though, are you?" she said, frowning.

"No," Quirke said. "I'm a pathologist."

"Yes," Mona said, putting on again the strained frown that was surely deliberate. "Is that like a coroner?"

Quirke smiled and shook his head. "No, not really. I did the—em—the postmortem, this morning, on your husband." She waited, wide-eyed but inexpectant—in fact, giving the impression that at any moment she might close her eyes and drift off into sleep, like a cat. "It seems he—well, it seems he shot himself," Quirke said. "I'm sorry."

"Oh," she said, "I know that—I mean, I know he was shot. They told me all that." She was looking about now for an ashtray. Quirke fetched one from the sideboard and she took it from him and set it on her knee and tipped an inch of ash into it. He stepped away from her and sat down, perching on the broad arm of the sofa. Although the room was large he felt disproportionate to everything in it, which gave him a giddy, toppling sensation. Mona Delahaye's loveliness seemed to pervade the room, heavy and sweet, like the smell of the roses.

Hackett tried another tack. "Tell me, Mrs. Delahaye," he said, "your husband's business—is everything all right in that regard?"

Mona Delahaye's eyes grew rounder still. "What do you mean?"

"I mean," the detective said, shifting on his chair, "there's not any—any financial problem, is there?"

Quirke looked from the woman to the detective and back again. She was leaning forward, gazing searchingly into Hackett's face. "I don't know," she said simply. "How would I know? Victor wouldn't have talked to me about things like that. You see"—she leaned still more intently forward—"Victor and I didn't really know each other, not in that way, not in a way that we would talk about his work or anything serious like that. He kept that kind of thing to himself." She paused, and glanced at the floor, then looked up again, and now switched her gaze to Quirke where he sat on the arm of the sofa, a large man in black, watching her. "When we got married, three years ago, Victor's wife, Lisa, his first wife, had died only a couple of years before, and I don't think he realized what he was doing— marrying me, I mean." She had the earnest air of a schoolgirl explaining that by some anomaly she had not been taught long division, or how to parse a sentence. Quirke thought he had never before encountered such a striking mixture of artlessness and calculation. "I've been thinking about all this since yesterday," she said, "since the news came. I suppose it sounds very strange, to say he didn't know what he was doing when we got married, but that's how he always seemed to me. Like a sleepwalker."

There was a pause. Far off in the house somewhere someone was whistling; that would be the redheaded maid, Quirke thought.

"Does that mean," the Inspector said, "that he might have been neglecting the business?"

Mona Delahaye stared at him and then shook her head and gave a little laugh. "Oh, no," she said. "He would never do that, he would never neglect the business. He was very good at what he did." She gestured with her cigarette at the surrounding room, with its plush upholstery, its pictures, its padded quiet. "He was rich, as you can see," she said. She might have been speaking of someone she had not known personally but had only heard of, the absent proprietor of all these polished possessions.

They heard voices in the hall. Mona Delahaye stubbed out her cigarette hastily, as if she were afraid to be caught smoking. The door opened and a young man with blond hair put in his head. "Oh, sorry," he said, seeing Quirke and the Inspector. He came in, followed by a young man who was his double. They were tall and slim, with long, slightly equine heads. Their hair was of a remarkable shade, almost silver, and very fine, and their eyes were blue. They had the look of a pair of fantastically realistic shop-window manikins. They were dressed in white, down to their white plimsolls, and brought with them a suggestion of sun-warmed grass and willow bats and scattered applause drifting across a trimmed, flat sward. "You must be the police," the young man said, and advanced on Quirke with a hand extended. "I'm Jonas Delahaye. This is my brother, James."

Quirke took the young man's hand and introduced himself. "He's a coroner," Mona Delahaye said. Both her stepsons ignored her.

"Pathologist," Quirke said to the twins. "This is Inspector Hackett."

Jonas Delahaye gave Hackett the merest glance, then turned back to Quirke and gazed at him with frank and faintly smiling interest. "Dr. Quirke," he said. "I think I know your daughter."

This put Quirke momentarily at a loss. "Oh," he said lamely, "Phoebe, yes." He had never heard his daughter mention Jonas Delahaye, or not that he could recall; but then, he was not much of a listener.

"At least, I know a friend of hers—your assistant, I believe. David Sinclair."

"Oh," Quirke said again, nodding. He felt acutely this young man's almost invasive presence. "Yes, David is my assistant," he said. "How do you know him?" Jonas ignored this question, as if he had not heard it, and went on gazing almost dreamily into Quirke's face. His brother had wandered to the table in the middle of the room, on which there was a pewter dish with apples. He took an apple and bit into it, making a crisp, cracking sound. He seemed dourly disaffected, compared to his smiling brother. Of the two, it was apparent that Jonas was the dominant twin. Neither one of them had given the slightest sign of acknowledgment of their stepmother, who had turned her face away and was gazing out into the sunlit garden.

"So," Jonas said, throwing himself down in an armchair and hooking one leg over the side of it, "what happened to my father?" He looked from Quirke to the Inspector and then at Quirke again.

"Your father died of a gunshot wound," Hackett said. "It seems he fired the shot himself."

Jonas pulled a dismissive face. "I don't believe it," he said. "Davy Clancy was with him on the boat. Have you spoken to him?" He was looking at Quirke. "He should be able to tell you what happened."

James Delahaye was watching them, leaning against the table and eating his apple. Mona Delahaye sighed, and leaned back on the sofa and closed her eyes. For a moment Quirke had a notion of the five of them, himself and the Inspector, the twins, the woman on the sofa, in a scene onstage, each one placed just so by the director, and all of them waiting for their cue.

Inspector Hackett swiveled about to look at Jonas Delahaye sprawled in the armchair. "Would you have any idea"—he glanced towards James—"either of you, why your father would kill himself?"

Jonas shrugged, lifting one shoulder and pulling down his mouth at the corners. His brother, crunching the last of the apple, looked towards his stepmother and laughed.

"I SUPPOSE," HACKETT SAID, "IF YOU WERE OF A CHARITABLE disposition, you could say they were obviously suffering the aftereffects of the great shock they've had."

He and Quirke were walking back along Northumberland Road towards the canal. The sun was still shining but the evening shadows were lengthening; twilight was gathering itself deep in the foliage of the beeches set at intervals along the pavement. They had been discussing the Delahaye twins, their remarkable attitude to their father's death, their cool insouciance. "Aye, they didn't seem exactly heartbroken," Hackett went on. "And neither did she." He glanced sidelong at Quirke. "What do you think?" But Quirke said nothing, only paced along in silence, frowning at his toecaps.

4

SYLVIA CLANCY WAS AFRAID OF BOTH HER HUSBAND AND HER son. She had tried for a long time to deny to herself that this was so, but it was. She did not feel menaced by them or believe they would do her physical harm. What she most feared was their potential to harm themselves, to damage their lives, and hers; to—the word shocked her but she had to admit it—to contaminate the little world the family shared together. They were not wicked, either of them, and probably they loved her, in their way, though it would not be the same as the way she loved them. She had them, as she always thought, in her care. They were her charges. She had to protect them, from the world but, much more, from themselves. She was aware of how outlandish this would sound if her husband were to hear her say it, and she was careful never to let slip the slightest hint of how she felt, how she thought. All the same, she wondered if they did know what she thought and felt, if they knew without knowing, in that way the Irish were so adept at doing.

She knew about her husband's infidelities. She was hurt, of course, each time she found out about a new one—and probably the ones she learned about represented only a fraction of the real number—but she had come to accept his affairs as a condition of her life, as unalterable as the pain she suffered constantly in her back. It was because of her back, she supposed, that Jack had strayed in the first place. It must have been hard on him, being married to a woman who flinched and drew in her breath every time he put his arms around her. She could hardly blame him for seeking comfort and release elsewhere. Yet she did blame him, she did—she accepted, but she blamed; she could not stop herself. He might have helped her reconcile herself to his waywardness, he might at least have tried. But he was too impatient for that.

Impatience, she thought, was what drove him, was what had always driven him; impatience and the awful resentment that went with it. She remembered the occasion, years, many years before, when she had seen these traits in him for the first time. That night, at the Delahayes' party, he had snatched the car key out of her hand and walked out into the rain with that look on his face, his mouth twisted all to one side and his eyes blazing. What was it she had said? Something about Victor and Lisa, about what a handsome couple they made, and how happy they seemed together. Had Jack been jealous of Victor? Had he wanted Lisa for himself? Perhaps he had got her—perhaps that was why he was so upset that night. Yes, perhaps Lisa and Jack had been lovers. It amazed her that she could admit this possibility with such dispassion.

Yet these speculations did weary her. Often she wished she could just walk away from everything, say nothing to anyone and just walk away. How much would they miss her, her husband and her son? She closed her eyes. If only she could empty her mind, dull her brain, kill her thoughts. That would be a kind of walking away.

How lovely the sunlight was this evening; how heartless.

She was climbing the stairs and had stopped on the landing a moment to look out of the high window there to Howth Head, far off on the other side of the bay. Below, in the garden, the blossoms of the peony roses were all falling over, dragged low by their own full-blown weight. She had tried to pin them up but they had drooped anyway, as if they wanted to hang their heads like that, as if that was how they saw themselves at their best. It was strange, she thought, to be thinking of flowers at such a time. But life, ordinary life, would not stop, even for a death.

The flowers were not the only things that needed attention. The big old house, in one of Dun Laoghaire's more stately terraces, was showing the signs of years of neglect. Jack was not interested in the house. Why would he be? He was rarely there. Jack had never got used to being married—*tied down* was what he would have said, she supposed—and could always find an excuse not to be at home. But that was Jack, take him or leave him.

She went on up the last flight. She had squeezed six big Outspan oranges and poured the juice into a jug, and was carrying the jug together with a glass on a wooden tray spread with a table napkin. Davy was in bed, suffering still from the effects of being out in that boat for hours with no protection from the sun. Who would have thought the sun would be so strong, even in June? When she came into his room she caught the warmish smell of his poor scorched flesh. He lay sprawled on the bed in his pajama bottoms, the sheet kicked aside. He was wearing the black sleep mask that she had not known the house possessed, and she could not tell if he was asleep or awake. She stood over him, listening to him breathe. The sun blisters on his arms had broken and the skin on the bridge of his nose was beginning to peel already. She felt a twinge of embarrassment, standing in his room like this, and thought of setting the jug of orange juice down on the bedside table and tiptoeing away. But then he woke, and pulled off the mask and struggled to sit up, blinking and coughing, and drew the sheet over his knees.

The tray, she realized, was the same one on which she used to bring up his good-night glass of milk when he was a child. How quickly the years had flown!

Davy was twenty-four but seemed younger, or seemed so to her, anyway. Maybe, she reflected, mothers always think their sons will never quite grow up. He was working for the summer as a storeman at the Delahaye & Clancy garage in Ringsend. He seemed to like the work and was diligent, Jack said, a thing that surprised Jack, and surprised her, too. She supposed he was trying to impress them. He had confided to her his plan to train to be a mechanic and get a permanent job, but not at Delahaye & Clancy. He had not told his father yet, and neither had she. Jack would make a fuss, but she knew there would be no point in arguing; Davy was as stubborn as his father, and would not be told, or cajoled, but would go his own sweet way.

She had asked him what he wanted to work at, if he was not going to continue at college, but he would not tell her.

"I brought you some orange juice," she said. She showed him the jug and the glass. "It's freshly squeezed." Looking exhausted, he sat slumped forward, with his head hanging and his arms draped over the mound of his knees. He was very fair—he had her coloring, which was why he had burned so badly under the sun. She looked down at him. A spur of hair stood up on the crown of his head, and she remembered how when he was little she used to have to wet the comb under the tap to get that same recalcitrant curl to lie flat. Was she wrong to dwell on the past like this? She should be treating him like an adult, not all the time harking back to how things were when he was still her little boy. "How do you feel?" she asked. He shrugged, still slumped over his knees. "Drink some of this juice," she said. "It will help to cool you down."

She poured the juice and tapped the glass gently against his shoulder, and with a shuddery sigh he took it from her and drank, and had to stop to cough again, and drank again. "That's good," he said. "Thanks."

She sat down on the side of the bed. Since she had come into the room he had not once met her eye. "How are you feeling?" she asked again.

"I can smell myself," he said. "I can actually smell my skin where it got burned. It's like fried pork."

She smiled, and he smiled too, ruefully, although he still would not look at her. He finished the juice and handed her back the glass. She asked if he would like more and he shook his head, and rubbed a finger rapidly back and forth under his

nose. It was no good trying not to see these little things—the
way he was sitting on the bed, the way he rubbed his nose,
that springy curl sticking up—that made her think of him as a
child again. The boy was still there, inside the young man's
body. It was the same with all of them, all the men she had
ever known, in her family or outside it; they reverted to childhood when they were hurt, or sad, or in trouble.

"A policeman telephoned," Sylvia said. "A detective. He wants
to talk to you. I said you weren't well, and that you were sleeping." Davy did not respond to this, only sat with his head hanging, his lower lip thrust out, and picked at a loose thread in the
seam of the sheet. "What will you tell him?" she asked. "I
mean, what will you say?" Oh, that look, she remembered that,
too, the brows drawn down and the lip thrust out and his neck
sunk between his shoulders. "Tell *me*, will you?" she said. "Tell
me what happened."

"I told you already," he said, with the hint of a whine in his
voice. *That sullenness,* she thought, *that resentment, just like his
father.* He tugged with miniature violence at the thread, drawing in his lip now and tightening his mouth. "There's nothing
more to say."

"Well," she said patiently, "why don't you tell me again. What
did—what did he say?"

"He said nothing."

"He must have said something."

A ship was leaving Dun Laoghaire Harbor, they heard the
sound of its siren shaking the stillness of the sunlit evening.
Once when they were crossing to Holyhead they had been on
deck when the horn went off like that, like the last trump, and

Davy, her Davy, who was four or five at the time, had been so
frightened by the terrible sound he had burst into tears and
clung to her legs and buried his face in her skirts. They had
been so close in those days, the two of them; so close.

"He told me a story," Davy said, "about when he was a child
and his old man took him out in the car one day and gave him
money to buy an ice cream and drove off when he was in the
shop."

"Drove off?"

"And left him there. To teach him self-sufficiency, self-
confidence, something like that—I can't remember."

Sylvia pursed her lips and nodded. "Yes, I'm afraid that would
be the kind of thing old Sam Delahaye would do, all right.
What else?"

"*What* what else?" That whining note again.

"Was that all Victor said? What happened then?"

"'What happened then,'" Davy said with heavy sarcasm,
mimicking her and waggling his head, "was that he produced
this pistol, a huge thing, like a cowboy's six-shooter, and stuck
the barrel up to his chest and fired."

Now it was she who began picking at the sheet. "Do you
think—do you think he meant to do it—"

"Jesus, Ma!"

"—that he didn't just mean it as a joke, or something, that
went wrong?"

Davy laughed grimly. "Some joke."

"He could be so—odd, at times. Unpredictable."

"He meant to do it, all right," Davy said. "There was no mistake about it."

"But *why?*" she almost wailed.

Her son closed his eyes and heaved a histrionic sigh of exasperation and annoyance. "I told you. *I—don't—know.*"

And why, she wanted to ask, *why did he take you for a witness—why you?* "Something must have been terribly wrong with him."

Davy snorted. "Well, yes, I'd say so. You don't put a bullet through your heart unless there's something fairly seriously the matter."

She did not mind the sarcasm or the mockery—she was used to it—but she wished he would look at her, look her straight in the eye, just once, and tell her again that he did not know why Victor Delahaye—Victor, of all people—should have taken him out to sea in a boat and make him watch while he killed himself. "What shall I tell that detective," she asked, "if he calls again? *When* he calls again."

He did not answer. He was looking about and frowning. "Give me my clothes," he said. "I want to get up."

JACK CLANCY WAS WALKING FAST ALONG THE FRONT AT SANDY-cove when he heard the sound of the ship's horn behind him. It made him think of his schooldays, long ago. Why was that? There had been a bell, not a bell but more like a hooter, that went off at the end of the lunch hour to summon the boys back to class. That sinking feeling around the diaphragm, he remembered that, and Donovan and—what was that other fellow's name?—waiting for him in the dark of the corridor where it went round by the cloakroom. They picked on him because he was small. They would pull his hair and pinch him. One day they yanked his trousers down and stood back, pointing and laughing. He had got his own back on Donovan, told on him for stealing hurley sticks from the storeroom and selling them. Funny: it was years since he had thought about those days—why now? Because, he supposed, there were so many other things that he could not allow himself to think about. He was in trouble, no doubt of that.

Dun Laoghaire, formerly Kingstown, is not a harbor but a port of asylum, so called because it was designed as a refuge for merchant ships that for centuries had been lashed by easterly gales and become embayed and were unable to enter the mouth of the Liffey because sailing vessels could not climb the wind and so—and so— His mind reeled, grasping after the old lore he used to have off by heart. His father loved the sea and had tried to teach him the history of the port, its facts and fables. But he had been a bad learner. *A good-for-nothing and a waster,* his father would say. *Wine, women and song, that's the limit of our bold Jack's ambitions.* Now the old bastard's wits were gone and all that useless knowledge with it. The old man had spent his life crawling to the Delahayes and where had it got him? First on his belly, groveling before that crowd, and now on his back, lost to himself and helpless and not even able to die.

Otranto Place—funny name. The evening was warm and there were bathers over at the cove still, on the sand and on the rocks, dozens of them, out from the city on the train, tenement families from Sean MacDermott Street and Summerhill, the women fat and the men lean, the kids skinny and white as grubs. Above the strand stood the Martello tower. It

had a comical look, he always thought, thick and squat, as if it
had once been tall but the top had been blown off by one of
Napoleon's cannonballs.

He turned up Sandycove Avenue. The house looked smaller
than in fact it was. One-storied, it too might have been cut off
at the top, with just the front door and a window on either
side and the roof sloping down. But at the back it extended a
long way out, and there were steps leading down to a garden
room, where the sun shone in all day in summer. He knew
these things because it was he who had found the house, and
had even made a down payment on it, though that had been
conveniently forgotten. Women tended to take things like
that for granted.

Jack rapped softly with his knuckles on the door, *rat-a-tat-
tat-tat, tat tat,* the old signal. She might be out. Her name was
Bella. That was what she called herself; her real name was—
what? Anne? Angela? He could not remember. She was an artist: blue skies over poppy fields and bare-breasted hoydens
lolling in the grass with flowers wreathed in their hair.

He knocked again and waited.

Dun Laoghaire, formerly called Kingstown.

Otranto Place.

Trouble.

The door opened. "Well well," she said, one hand on the
door frame and the other on her hip. "Hello, stranger." She was
wearing ski pants and sandals, and a white woolen shawl, one
corner of it flung over her shoulder and pinned there somehow,
like a Roman senator's robe. Her dyed-blond hair was piled
on top of her head and stuck through with what looked to
him like two wooden knitting needles. He noted a pair of

spectacles—he had not seen them before—resting on the slope of her bosom and attached to a string that went around her neck. There was a fan of fine wrinkles at the outer corner of each eye. Yes, it had been a long time.

"Hello, Bella," he said.

She was giving him an appraising eye, her head cocked. Had she heard what had happened in Cork?

"Come in," she said. "I was just about to take a bath."

WHEN HACKETT ARRIVED AT NELSON TERRACE, MRS. CLANCY herself let him in. She took his hat and hung it on the hat stand and walked with him through the house to the kitchen at the back. Young Clancy was there, sitting at the table with a mug of tea in front of him. He was not small, exactly, Hackett thought, that was not the word, but compact, with a rugby player's shoulders and a neat, squarish head, his reddish hair cut short and standing upright in a flat mat of bristles, in the style of the day—Hackett could imagine some girl running the palm of her hand over that ticklish crest and wriggling inside her dress. He seemed hardly more than a boy. He certainly did not look like a killer.

Mrs. Clancy offered tea; the detective declined out of politeness, then regretted it. The woman was tall and stood in a curiously stiff way, as if someone had just said something offensive and she had drawn herself up and back in indignation.

"This is a shocking business, Inspector," she said.

English accent, but English to look at, too, somehow—with that bony face and the hair tied neatly behind, and the friendly yet remote expression.

"Indeed, ma'am," he said. "Shocking."

Together they turned to look at the young man sitting by the table. He did not lift his eyes. A mother's boy, Hackett thought, but with something of a boxer about him, too.

"How are you getting on?" the Inspector asked him. "You've been in the wars."

Davy Clancy sighed impatiently. "I'm all right," he said. "I got a bit of sunburn."

"A bit!" his mother exclaimed, and seemed startled herself at the sudden vehemence of her tone. "You should see his arms, Inspector."

Davy plucked instinctively at the cuffs of his white shirt, as if he thought his mother might take hold of him and roll up his sleeves herself and show off his blisters.

"The sun can be a terror, all right," Hackett said, nodding. "Especially on the water—I believe the reflected sunlight is worse than anything." He put his hand on the back of a chair and lifted an eyebrow in Mrs. Clancy's direction.

"Of course," she said, "of course, please, sit."

He sat. The chair gave a little cry, as if in protest at the weight of him. He leaned forward, setting his clasped hands on the table. For some moments he said nothing, not for effect but simply because he could not think how to start, yet he felt the atmosphere in the room tightening. A person's feeling of guilt was a hard thing to measure. He had known entirely blameless people to start babbling explanations and excuses before the first question had been asked, while the hard cases, the ones who five minutes previously had been sluicing blood off their hands, could be as cool as you like, and not bat an eyelid or offer a word unless provoked to it.

"I don't suppose," he said, looking at the whorl of hair on the crown of the young man's bent head, "you've any idea why Mr. Delahaye did what he did?" Davy Clancy shook his head without lifting it. "No," Hackett said, with a little sigh, "I didn't think you would."

Mrs. Clancy, behind him, spoke. "Tell him," she said, sounding anxious and as if aggrieved, "tell him what you told me." Davy, looking up at last, frowned at her, as if not knowing what she meant. "The story he told you," his mother said, "about old Mr. Delahaye taking him out in the car and abandoning him."

Davy scowled. "It wasn't anything," he said.

"Tell it anyway," his mother said quickly, suddenly sharp and commanding. "The Inspector will want to know everything there is to know."

Davy shrugged and, forced into this wearisome duty, recounted in jaded tones the story of Victor Delahaye's father and young Victor and the ice cream. Hackett listened, nodding, a pink lower lip protruding. "And did he say," he asked, when Davy had finished, "what the point of the story was?" He smiled, showing his tarnished dentures. "Was there a moral in the tale?"

Davy was peering into his mug. "He said his father said it was to teach him to be self-reliant. And as he was putting the gun to his chest he said it again: *a lesson in self-reliance.*"

"I see." Hackett leaned close to the table. "And what do you think he meant by that?"

Davy rolled his shoulders. "I don't know. Maybe he thought he was doing to me what his father had done to him."

"And why would he do such a thing, do you think?"

"I told you—I don't know."

The detective nodded again. "And that was it? That was all he said? Nothing else?"

Davy, still looking into the mug, shook his head; he had, Hackett thought, the air of a schoolboy hauled on the carpet by his headmaster. He muttered something, and Hackett had to ask him to repeat it. "What more would he have said?" the young man almost snarled, lifting his head suddenly, with a look of fury in his eyes. "What was there to say?"

A moment of silence passed. "How did Mr. Delahaye seem?" Hackett asked. "Was he agitated?"

"I don't know what he was. He didn't say much. He never talked much to me anyway."

Hackett thought the boy—he kept thinking of him as a boy—was lying, if only by omission. It was clear from his evasive manner that he knew more than he was prepared to say. What exactly had happened on that boat, out on the sunlit sea? Hackett tried to picture it: the furled sails, the sudden quiet, the lapping of the water on the keel and the cries of the seabirds, the man speaking and then the shot, not loud, a sound like that of a piece of wood being snapped in two.

"My son is very upset, Inspector," Mrs. Clancy said. "He's had a terrifying experience."

The boy—the young man—looked at her with another flash of anger, his mouth twisting. "Maybe he was agitated, I don't know," he said to Hackett. "He must have been—he was going to shoot himself, wasn't he?"

Davy pushed the mug away and stood up and walked to the window with his hands thrust into the back pockets of his trousers and looked out at the garden.

"Would you hazard a guess," Hackett inquired, in a conversational tone, "as to why it was you he chose to bring with him?"

"I keep telling you," Davy said without turning, "I don't know why he did any of this—why he went out in the boat, why he brought me, why he shot himself. *I don't know.*"

Hackett turned on the chair to look at Sylvia Clancy. She held his gaze for a moment, then gave a faint shrug, of distress and helplessness, and turned away.

IN THE GARDEN THE LAST OF THE EVENING SUNLIGHT WAS THE rich soft color of old gold. "Isn't it wonderful," Bella murmured, "how long the day lasts at this time of year?" They were lying on a chaise longue in the garden room, she nestling in the crook of Jack's arm and Jack asprawl with a hand behind his head. Bella had pulled her white shawl over them; the rest of her clothes she had dropped in disarray on the floor, mixed up with his. He craved a cigarette, but he did not want to move, did not want to interrupt this little interval of longed-for rest. He felt as if they were balancing something between them, he and the naked woman, some delicate structure spun out of air and light that would collapse if he made the slightest stir. He was trying to remember where he had first met Bella. Was it at the party in Pembroke Street that night at the solicitor's flat— what was his name?—when the two fellows who worked for the Customs and Excise had brought a crate of confiscated hooch and they had all got wildly drunk and gone out and danced in the street? He remembered Bella leaning her back

against a wall with her hands behind her, swaying her front at
him and smiling with those smoky eyes of hers. Or was that
someone else, some other girl out for a good time?

"A penny for them," she said now, running her fingers through
the grizzled hairs on his chest.

"I was thinking of the first time I met you," he said.

"Oh, yes—that opening in the Ritchie Hendriks Gallery.
You told me I had nice earlobes." She pinched his right nipple.
"Always the sweet talker, pretending to appreciate things no
one else would bother to notice. Earlobes, indeed—it wasn't
earlobes you were after."

Whose opening had it been? He had no memory of it—he
was not even sure he had ever been in the Ritchie Hendriks
Gallery. Maybe she too was thinking of someone else. He felt
a sudden sweet pang for the lost past, all those possibilities
now gone, never to be offered again. He kneaded the plump
flesh of her flank just below her ribs and she twisted away
from him and laughed and told him to stop, that he knew how
ticklish she was. He released her and stood up, then bent to
find his jacket on the floor and the cigarettes in the pocket.
Lighting one, he walked to the big picture window and stood
there naked, smoking, squinting out at the sunlight.

"Let me guess why you're here," she said.

He glanced over his shoulder. She was lolling on her back
on the chaise, the shawl covering her lap. He saw how her
breasts, slacker than he remembered them, were slewed sideways, the nipples as if looking at him, endearingly cock-eyed.
She was a handsome woman still, and he was sad to see the
signs of how she was aging.

"Guess away," he said. "Why am I here?"

"Because of what's-his-name, your partner, Delahaye."

"Oh. You heard."

She laughed. "It was all over the papers!" She turned over onto her stomach, and the shawl slithered to the floor. She wriggled her behind. "What happened? The papers said it was an accident. Was it?"

He turned back to the window and the overgrown garden. Those tangled roses looked sinister, he thought, like briars in a fairy tale. "You have convolvulus," he said.

"I have *what*?"

"Bindweed. That creeper, with the white flower. It'll strangle everything if you don't get it dug out."

"Jack Clancy, nurseryman," she said, and laughed again, throatily. She rose and came and stood beside him, picking up the shawl and hitching it round her waist for a makeshift skirt. He caught her familiar smell: perfume, sweat, warmed flesh. She took the cigarette from his fingers, drew on it, and gave it back, blowing smoke in the direction of the ceiling. "Do you not want to talk about it?" she said.

"Talk about what?" He was still eyeing the convolvulus.

"All right, sulk." She went to the pile of clothes and pulled on her knickers, her shirt, the tight black trousers. "He killed himself, didn't he," she said.

"How do you know?"

"When it's a suicide, the papers have a certain way of reporting it. You can always tell. What was it? Was he sick?"

"Not that I know of."

"Business in trouble?"

"On the contrary. Business"—he gave a brief laugh—"is booming."

She stood a moment studying his back; he still had a nice bum, she thought, though it was scrawnier now than she remembered. "You don't seem exactly heartbroken," she said.

He turned. "Don't I?"

She went on looking at him, slowly arranging the shawl about her shoulders and pinning it up again at one corner. "You know why he did it, don't you," she said; it was not a question. "You know, but you're not saying." She came to him and touched a fingertip to his face. He looked back at her blankly, his eyes gone dead. "You're in trouble, aren't you," she said softly. "Aren't you? You can tell me, you know. I'm the wild horses' despair, I am."

He turned from her to the garden again. "You should get that convolvulus seen to," he said. "It's a killer, if you let it get established."

She went up the steps, and he heard her in the kitchen up there, opening drawers and cupboard doors. He got dressed; he felt as if he were putting on not his clothes but his troubles, the ones that had fallen from him earlier when Bella had wound her arms round him and whispered hotly in his ear. How long was it since he had been here last? Two years? Three? Bella had always been an easygoing girl. You turned up, she opened wide her arms, you lay down together, then you got up again and left. Never once, in all the times he had walked out of here, had she asked if he would be coming back. Maybe she was the kind of woman he should have married.

She came down the steps again, carrying a straw-covered bottle of Chianti and two wine glasses. She held the bottle aloft in a Statue of Liberty pose. "Have a drink," she said, "before you go."

They took to the chaise again, sitting side by side this time, facing the big window. The sunlight had gone from the garden but a bronze glow lingered, polishing the rosebushes and lending an amber tint to the white convolvulus flowers. Jack lit another cigarette. The wine tasted bitter in his mouth. He had a cavernous sensation behind his breastbone, as if his chest had been hollowed out and emptied of every organ. It was not exactly fear he felt but a heavy, dull dread. Something was coming that would not be avoided.

"And how," Bella asked, "is the Lady Sylvia?" She put on a prissy accent. "Spiffing form as usual, I suppose, what?"

He drank his wine and said nothing. He did not mind her mocking his wife. He supposed he should. He felt protective towards Sylvia, most of the time. She had done her best with him, for him, and he was grateful to her, in his way. Thinking this, he imagined her turning aside from him with that deliberately abstracted expression, frowning, as if she had lost something and was trying to remember what it was. *Grateful, dear? I must say, you have a funny way of showing it.* It was true. He owed her a debt, he knew that, but he knew too that he had no intention of settling it, not yet, anyway, not while he still had this fire in him; not while he still had Bella, and the others like her, discreet, easy, indulgent. He closed his eyes briefly. He knew in his heart that it was all over, that old, carefree life. There would be no more simple fun; from now on, everything would be complicated, knotted, insoluble. Half an hour ago, lying here in Bella's arms, he had relaxed and felt like weeping.

"I suppose you'll be the boss now?" Bella said.

"Do you think so?" He cast a crooked smile at her and she saw that flash of mischief she remembered from the old days, that look of a boy who has got his first kiss and means to have more.

"Isn't it what you always wanted?" she said, smiling in her turn.

Her warm haunch was pressed against his leg, and there was a look of slightly unfocused merriment in her eye—she never could hold her drink; it was something that had always amused him. In a minute she would be swarming all over him again. He made to stand up, but she put a hand in the crook of his elbow and held him back. "Don't go," she said.

"Got to," he said. "I'm expected."

Yet he lingered. He did not want to go home, did not want to face Sylvia, did not want to meet that look she would give him, anxious, soulful, searching. How much did she know, how much did she guess? All this past year he had been sure she knew he was up to something. She did not trust him, never had; he could hardly have expected that she would. He did not trust himself, anymore.

"How is the widow?" Bella asked. "What's her name—Monica?"

"Mona."

"He was about twice her age, wasn't he?"

"She's young, yes."

He felt a sort of ripple in her thigh, and she sat forward and swiveled about to look closely into his face. "Oh, Jack," she said softly, "I hope you haven't been a naughty boy, have you? Haven't been putting in your thumb there and pulling out a plum, as you always do?"

"Oh, for God's sake," he said.

She wagged her head at him, making a tut-tutting sound
with her tongue. "Oh, Jackie-boy. I see now the reason for your
sudden appearance on my doorstep. It wouldn't be the first
time you came running to Bella for shelter when the Hound of
Heaven was at your heels. Or just a husband on the warpath."

He sighed. "Shut up, Bella," he said wearily. "You have a one-
track mind."

"Yes," she said, and made a grab at the crotch of his trousers, "and you haven't, I suppose."

He batted her hand aside and held out his glass. She groped
for the bottle on the floor and poured another go of wine.

"I hope you're not intending to make a lamp out of that, are
you?" he said, indicating with his chin the bulbous bottle in its
straw jacket.

"Is that what you think of me?"

"Oh, yes, I forgot—you're an artist." He had not meant it to
sound so sour.

"Dear me," she said, "we are on edge today." She put the
bottle on the floor again and sat back, holding her glass in both
hands and nursing it against her breast. "Were you that fond of
your late partner?"

He did not respond, only drank his wine and gazed before
him, frowning. "David was on the boat with him," he said.

"Who?"

"My son, Davy."

She stared. "My God. Why?"

"He asked him to go with him—Victor, that is, asked Davy.
The night before, when we were all in the pub, he invited him
to come out. Davy hates the sea, but he went, all the same."

"My God," Bella said again, more softly this time, more won-
deringly. "Did he—did he see him do it? Did he see him shoot
himself?"

Jack watched one last, anxious-seeming bubble crowding at
the brim of his glass. "Yes," he said, "he saw it."

"But—but why?"

"Why did he take Davy with him? I don't know. Maybe to
get back at me."

"For what?"

The wine bubble burst.

"I don't know."

She was watching him, staring at his profile. "I think you do
know," she said, in a voice that made her suddenly sound sober.
"I think you're lying."

He put a hand over his eyes and massaged his temples at
either side with a finger and a thumb. "There was a—there was
a problem, in work. In the business."

"What sort of problem?"

He took the hand away from his face and turned towards
the window. She saw the pulse working in his jaw. He was still
good-looking, with that small neat head, that strong nose, those
broad lips that had a twist to them at once humorous and sly.
There used to be something about him, something weak and
furtively vulnerable. Now that was gone, that youthful defense-
lessness, but what had come in its place was not strength, only
hardness. She put her glass on the floor beside the wine bottle.
She should not drink so early in the evening; it always went
straight to her head. It was not an occasion to be tipsy; a girl
had to watch herself around Jack Clancy.

"He could never let go of anything," he said, with a distant look now, talking to himself. "He could never relent. Always had to be top dog, and have everyone around him acknowledge it. Got that from his father, of course, Old Ironsides himself. A pair of them in it—overbearing and ruthless yet still expecting the rest of us to treat them like proper gentlemen of the old school. And all the time they'd cut your heart out for a farthing."

He stopped. She had an urge to put her finger to that pulse in his jaw to stop it twitching. "Did you know?" she asked.

"What?"

"Did you know he was going to do it?"

"No. How could I? If I had, do you think I'd have let Davy go out with him? Do you think I'd have let my own son's life be put at risk?"

She picked up her glass again from the floor—what good would staying sober do? "Tell me what was going on in the business," she said. "Were you fiddling the books?"

He said nothing for a moment, then laughed harshly. "Fiddling the books? For Christ's sake, Bella."

"Then what was this 'problem' that you're so concerned about?"

He shrugged, and looked away from her again. "Nothing," he said. "Forget I mentioned it."

"Had he found out about it, your partner, Delahaye—had he found out what you were up to, whatever it was?"

He shook his head as if amused. "What I was 'up to'—as if I was an office boy, stealing the tea money." He lay back against the sofa, suddenly weary-seeming. "You don't know what it's like, having something going round and round in your head, round and round. I don't sleep, I just lie there, thinking."

She waited, but he had lapsed into silence. His eyes were

closed. She could hear him breathing; he might have been in a
fever, or asleep and having a bad dream. She felt sorry for him,
but she was apprehensive, too. She realized that she did not
want to know what it was that was going round and round in
his head. Some things it was better not to know, especially
when they were things that Jack Clancy knew. It had been a
long time since they had seen each other but it might have
been yesterday, so familiar was the sense she had of his resentment and pent-up anger. He was a dangerous person. Not violent, not menacing, even, yet in some way dangerous, all the
same. That was why she had let him go, before; he had been
too much for her. She stood up, not looking at him. She wanted
him to leave. Something had come into the house with him,
the presence of which she felt only now; it was as if some animal had loped in silently behind him and hidden itself and now
was getting ready to spring out at her. She felt suddenly vulnerable. It was catching, whatever it was that was tormenting him.

"I have to change," she said. "I'm going out."

"Where?"

"Just out."

"A date."

"Yes. A date."

It was a lie, but it did not matter, he was not listening.
A dense shadowy glow had come into the window now, as
it always did at this time of day. She felt like shivering. That
strange light was on Jack's face, a phosphorescent sheen. *What
did you do, Jack? What did you do that made your partner shoot
himself?*

5

QUIRKE HAD NO BIRTHDAY. HE HAD BEEN AN ORPHAN—HE WAS an orphan still, he supposed, though it was odd to think so—and his records, if there had been any, were lost. Not knowing his date of birth, and therefore having no particular day on which to celebrate the annual crossing over as others did, was not something that troubled him. He knew his age, more or less accurately, though he did not know how he knew it. Some-one, at some time, long ago, when he was a child, must have told him, and the figure must have impressed itself on his mind, though he could not remember being told, or having been told. It was just there, an accumulating number, as meaningless as any other, and as lacking in significance for him. Each New Year's Day he took down mentally another used-up calendar from his inner wall, and lifted a glass in a sardonic toast to him-self. It amused him, especially when he was in his cups, to picture his gravestone and the lopsided legend on it: a blank, a dash, and then a date. Of course, they could count back, his relics, and put in a notional year of birth, but it would not be certain they were right: whoever it was who had told him how old he was might have lied, or might have been mistaken.

Phoebe, of course, insisted he should have a birthday, and would pick a date each year and surprise him with it. This year she chose a random day in June, just because it was summer and the sun was shining. She and David Sinclair, Quirke's assistant and her boyfriend, took him to dinner at the Shelbourne Hotel. She had reserved his favorite table, in the corner by the window to the left that looked across the street to the trees in St. Stephen's Green. The evening was overcast and muggily warm, but Quirke nevertheless was in his black suit, the jacket fastened tightly and his white shirt cuffs on show. Phoebe wished he would let her take him over and smarten him up a bit, get him fitted for a good three-piece tweed suit in Brown Thomas and buy him a shirt or two of some shade other than white. It was not that he did not spend money on his clothes—that suit was Italian, his shoes were handmade—but he always managed to look *dusty,* somehow. Not dirty, or unlaundered, or shabby, even, but as if he had been standing for too long in some spot where a very fine silt had settled on him, out of the air, without his noticing. Her present to him this year was a tie of shimmering green silk. She apologized for being so unimaginative, but he said no, it was very handsome—he took it out of its cellophane wrapper and held it up to the light from the window and turned it this way and that, an emerald snake, and thought of Mona Delahaye—

and besides, he said, he had been in need of a tie for ages, most of the ones he had being old and greasy by now. Sinclair had bought him a book, Yeats's *Autobiographies* in the handsome new Macmillan edition in its smart cream jacket. Quirke, to hide how touched he was, pored over it for so long, with his head bent, that Phoebe in the end had to take it away from him.

They had ordered Dover sole and a Sancerre that when it came was interesting enough though almost colorless. Quirke was fussy about his wine. Tonight he was making himself drink slowly, his daughter saw, and she wanted to tell him she appreciated it—Quirke with drink taken could be difficult, especially on occasions such as birthdays or other supposed celebrations—but she said nothing, only filled his water glass to the brim and passed him the plate of bread rolls. She felt sorry for him. He seemed slightly lost, in the awkwardness of the moment, suffering smilingly the enforced gaiety that none of the three of them could quite carry off. She supposed he found it difficult to make the adjustment between work and here, and probably David's presence made it more difficult still. But then, David too was being required to adjust. How strange it must be for both of them, dealing with the dead all day and now being here with her, marking an invented day of birth, with the elegantly crisp wine and the fragrance of the food and the glint and shimmer of that suddenly sinister-seeming tie.

"I met someone yesterday who knows you," Quirke said to Sinclair, looking at him over the rim of his glass.

Sinclair's expression turned wary. "Oh, yes?" he said.

"Young chap, name of Delahaye. Jonas Delahaye."

For a moment Sinclair looked as if he would deny knowing

any such person, thinking himself the victim of one of Quirke's odd jokes; Quirke had an unpredictable sense of humor. But then he nodded. "Oh, yes," he said again, more flatly this time.

Phoebe was looking from one of them to the other with lively interest. She enjoyed watching them together, though in a slightly guilty way. They made her think of two highly strung but excessively well-behaved prize dogs, Quirke a black boxer, say—were there black boxers?—and David one of those pure-bred terriers, aloof and watchful and not averse to showing a fang when the occasion required. David's attitude to Quirke was always circumspect, and Phoebe wondered how they managed to work together. But then, the Saddle Room in the Shelbourne was bound to be a far cry from the pathology department of the Hospital of the Holy Family. Or so she supposed, looking doubtfully at the half-eaten fish on her plate.

"Delahaye," she said. "Why do I know that name?"

"The father . . . died," Quirke said.

Phoebe frowned. "Yes, of course, it was in the papers. What happened?"

"Shot himself."

She flinched. "The papers didn't say that."

Quirke shrugged. "Well, no. Our fearless purveyors of the truth in the news don't report suicides."

Sinclair with his fork was picking over the bones of his fish with fastidious thoroughness. "How was Jonas?" he asked.

"Very calm," Quirke said drily. "And the brother, the two of them—very calm and collected." He turned to Phoebe. "They're twins, Jonas and—what's the other one called? James? Have you met them? Replicas of each other." He turned back to Sinclair. "You know both of them?"

"Hard not to—they're never apart. I see them in Trinity now and then—they play cricket. Tennis, too, championship standard. I had a match against Jonas once." He shook his head ruefully. "Never again."

"Yes," Phoebe said, "I remember that. He did trounce you." Sinclair looked at her dourly and she smiled and touched the back of his hand.

"They work—worked—for their father, yes?" Quirke said.

Sinclair turned to him. "I believe so. One is in the shipping end, the other in road freight, I think. Don't ask me which does which—they probably swap around and no one notices. I doubt they actually *work*. It wouldn't be quite their style."

Quirke was looking out the window at the trees across the road. Their tops were touched with the last copper glints of evening sunlight. Since he had met them, the Delahaye twins had been on his mind. Their manner, especially Jonas's—cool, amused, faintly insolent—had fascinated him, and unnerved him, too, a little. Theirs was not the demeanor of sons suffering from the shock of their father's sudden death, as Hackett had charitably suggested might be the case. Quirke knew about shock. In his work over the years he had dealt with many people in various distraught states. In some cases, it was true, the bereaved, especially sons, behaved in what might have seemed a callous or uncaring fashion in the immediate aftermath of a death, but that was the result of bravado mixed with helplessness. For sorrow does baffle, especially the young. The Delahaye twins, as far as he could see, were not baffled, they were not helpless.

"Is it known," Phoebe asked, "why their father killed himself?" She had been watching Quirke. She knew that look, of concentration and faint vexedness, as if he were trying to scratch an inner itch and failing. "Or do you think," she said, "that it wasn't suicide?"

He stirred, and turned to her. "Why do you ask?"

Sinclair held up the wine bottle, but Phoebe covered her glass and shook her head. He was lacking one of the fingers of his left hand, the result of his involvement last year with one of Quirke's more calamitous attempts to scratch an itch.

"I ask," she said to Quirke, "because I can see there's something in this business that interests you. What is it?"

He put down his knife and fork and leaned back in his chair and smiled. "Ah, you know me too well," he said. Their history together had been fraught—for most of her life he had denied she was his daughter and had let her be brought up by his adoptive brother and his wife—and only lately had Phoebe allowed them to come to some kind of laying down of arms. She loved him, she supposed, for all his shortcomings, all his sins. She took it that he in turn loved her, in his hesitant and fumbling fashion. She would assume it to be so. It was the best she could hope for, the best she could do. Quirke was not lavish with his emotions. "I can see you're half involved already," she said.

He looked away, and busied himself with his food. "I don't like to leave questions unanswered," he said.

"It's you who ask them in the first place," his daughter replied sharply.

David Sinclair leaned between them tactfully, like an umpire, pouring the wine. This time Phoebe did not cover her glass, and when she lifted it she realized her hand was trembling slightly. It rather appalled her, the almost instantaneous way in which she and her father could come to the edge of a fight. "I'd have thought," she said, "your friend Inspector Hackett is the one who should be asking the questions and doing the investigating."

Quirke said nothing to that, only went on mopping up the last of his peas and mashed potatoes. He cast a glance from under his brows at David Sinclair. Odd fellow, Sinclair, he thought. They had been working together for—what was it, five, six years?—but Quirke knew not much more about the young man now than he had at the start. He switched his glance to Phoebe. What were they to each other, he wondered, she and Sinclair? They had been going out together for more than a twelvemonth now, but what, these days, constituted going out? He looked at his daughter's long pale hands, her dark head bent over her plate, her neat little jacket, like a toreador's, the cameo brooch, the bit of white lace she always wore at her throat. There was something irredeemably old-fashioned about her, which he liked, but which he imagined might irk a boyfriend. Not that Sinclair was exactly a rake. Perhaps they were better suited to each other than it might seem. If so, how serious was it between them? Were they—he shrank mentally from the thought—sleeping together?

He did not know what young people expected of each other nowadays. In his time the rules had been rigid—a hand inside the blouse but outside the bra, a caress of the bare skin above the stocking tops but no farther, a French kiss on only the most special of occasions. What must it have been like for girls, to be constantly under siege? Had they found it flattering, funny, annoying? Had they found it humiliating? He glanced at Phoebe covertly again with a spasm of helpless affection. His feelings for her were an unpickable knot of confusion, doubt, bafflement.

"I suppose," he said, "he must have been in some kind of trouble." Both of them looked at him blankly. "Delahaye."

Phoebe turned her gaze now to a spark of light glinting in the bottom of her wine glass. "Yes, he must have been, surely. People don't kill themselves for nothing."

"Sometimes they do," Sinclair said. "Sometimes there's no apparent reason. They just do it, on a whim. I had a cousin, when I was young, hanged himself in the stairwell one morning when my aunt was out shopping. He'd just got a place in college, was going to study medicine."

"His poor mother," Phoebe murmured.

"Yes," Sinclair said, "it was her that found him, when she came home from the shops. My Aunt Lotte. It nearly killed her."

A heavy silence fell. Quirke watched as his daughter touched Sinclair's maimed hand again in a quick gesture of sympathy.

"I don't think," Quirke said, "Victor Delahaye was the kind of man to do anything on a whim."

They finished dinner soon after that. There was a wrangle over the bill, until Phoebe plucked it out of Quirke's hand and passed it to Sinclair. He produced his wallet while she delved in her purse. "Don't worry," she said to Quirke, "we're going halves."

For a second Quirke saw himself and Phoebe's mother, at this very table, a long time ago, bickering over something—what was it? He looked out at the trees, trying to remember.

When they were leaving the hotel, and Phoebe and Sinclair had gone through the revolving door, Quirke stood back to let someone come in. It was Isabel Galloway. She wore a slim blue suit and a pillbox hat pinned at a jaunty angle to the side of her head. They both halted, staring. "My God," Isabel breathed, then quickly recovered herself. "Quirke!" she said brightly, and pressed her elbows into her sides as if to shore herself up. "You're looking well."

Quirke smiled queasily. "Isabel," he said. "How are you? You look . . ." He fumbled after words but could not find them.

Isabel's smile glittered. "Silver-tongued as ever," she said, then frowned, annoyed with herself it seemed, and dropped her eyes and moved past him quickly and strode on into the lobby. He let her go, and stepped between the turning panels of the door, hearing behind him the familiar sharp clicking of her high heels on the marble floor.

Phoebe and Sinclair were waiting for him on the pavement. The last of the daylight was a greenish, crepuscular glow above the trees.

"Wasn't that—?" Phoebe began, but stopped, seeing Quirke's look.

Quirke realized he had left the Yeats book behind him, on the windowsill beside the table where they had sat. He turned back, muttering, and pushed his way through the heavy paneled door again.

ROSE GRIFFIN MAINTAINED A STOIC VIEW OF LIFE AND THE MIS-fortunes that life piles upon what, in her best southern-belle drawl, she would describe as *us poor lost creatures of the Lord*. Not that she believed in the Lord, or disbelieved in Him, either. She rarely let her thoughts dwell on things beyond this world, this world being, as she felt, enough of a conundrum.

She was intolerant of complainers, since, as she said, there was little to be gained from complaining, unless a body considered the pity of others a thing worth having. She felt pity for no one, on inclination as much as on principle. To pity people was to cheapen them, in her opinion. She realized this could make her seem hard-hearted, but she did not care. She *was* hard—what was wrong with that? Too much softness about, too much floppy, warm emotion. She had pointed it out once to Quirke, what they had in common: a cold heart and a hot soul.

She was shocked to discover that her friend Marguerite Delahaye was a blubberer. She would not have thought it of Maggie, whom she had always taken to be, underneath her spinster's genteel veneer, as tough as she was herself. It was midafternoon and the two women were taking tea together in the drawing room of Rose's large gaunt house on Ailesbury Road. It was a splendid day and they were seated in a splash of sunlight at a little table in the deep bay of a window that overlooked the front garden and the quiet street. To distract herself from Maggie's sniffles, Rose was admiring the undulating spiral of steam rising from the spout of the teapot, and the pink roses painted on the dainty china cups, and the rich gleam of the antique silver cutlery. She could never understand why people seemed to pay so little regard to the small but, to her, essential pleasures of life—this knife, for instance, a fine old piece of Georgian silver, the blade worn thin from use and the handle solid and weighty as an ingot in the hand. She thought of all the people who had used it over the years, all of them gone now, while she was here.

"I'm sorry," Maggie said, dabbing at her red-rimmed nose with an absurdly dainty handkerchief with a lace edging. "It's

just that I can't believe that Victor is . . . I can't *believe* he's
gone!"

"Yes, dear," Rose said soothingly, "I understand." Did she?
She did sympathize, more or less—she had suffered her own
losses—but she was not sure she understood. Maggie was
behaving as if she had lost not a brother but a husband, or even
a lover. Rose had siblings herself, but she rarely thought of
them, and for long periods forgot about them altogether. Had
she ever cared enough for her brothers that the loss of one of
them would have reduced her to the kind of extravagant grief
her friend was displaying? She thought it very unlikely. "Yes,
I'm sure a sudden death like that is hard to accept," she said.
She paused. "They're certain it was—I mean, they're satisfied
he was the one that pulled the trigger, yes?"

Maggie nodded, and a fresh spasm of sobbing made her
shoulders shake.

When she had heard of Victor Delahaye's death, Rose had
first been surprised, and then not. Killing himself was just the
sort of damn-fool thing that man would do, and the way he
had done it—the boat, the deserted sea, the pistol, and young
Clancy for a witness—was, of course, typically melodramatic
and self-serving. He had entertained large notions of himself,
had Victor. She had not known him well, had only met him a
few times, on social occasions, but she had taken the measure
of him straight off. Vain, pompous, humorless. Victor Delahaye had seen himself, preposterously, as a Renaissance figure, one of the great merchant princes, say, heir to a dynasty
and father in turn to twin princelings who would carry on and
embellish the grand family traditions. But inside every self-
proclaimed great man there crouched in hiding a shivering boy

terrified of being discovered and hauled out by the ear, wriggling and whimpering. Rose knew about these things: her first husband, the late Josh Crawford, had been one such great man.

Still, it was a puzzle. What had happened that had led Victor Delahaye to knock himself off his own pedestal? Something must have hit him where it hurt most, in his pride, or in his pocket, or maybe in both. No, his pride; he would not have killed himself over money. Something had damaged his estimate of himself. She pictured Mona Delahaye smiling, that thin scarlet mouth of hers turned up at the corner.

Maggie was talking again, between sniffs, about her brother, saying what a wonderful man he had been—a faithful husband, diligent father, loving sibling. An all-round saint, in fact. Rose suppressed an impatient sigh. The dead get so much more than their share of praise, she thought, and all just for being dead. "Come now, Maggie dear," she said, "don't upset yourself so—think of your asthma."

She wondered what would happen now to Delahaye's business. She doubted his partner, what's-his-name, would be taking over. The company might be called Delahaye & Clancy, but everyone knew who it was that ran it. Nor did she think the Delahaye twins would be picking up the reins, at least not right away, while they were still busy planting their wild oats all over town. Those boys had a reputation, oh, they certainly did.

The Delahayes were Protestant, of course, while the Clancys were Catholics. That distinction, she knew, meant everything here. She had spent a deal of time in this country, over the years; Josh Crawford had been more Irish than American, and now she was married to a man who was one hundred percent a native son. All the same, there was an awful lot she still did not understand about life here, and probably never would understand, try though she might. The people's fear of the priests, for instance, never failed to surprise her; also—and, you might say, on the other hand—their reverence for the Protestants. The Protestants were a tiny number, yet the Catholics had only to hear one of them speak, in that drawling, cut-glass accent, to start doffing their caps and tugging their forelocks and all the rest of such nonsense. This fascinated her, and pleased her, too, in a silly sort of way. It was as if, living here, she had gone back to an olden time, to a civilization that was both developed and primitive—Byzantium, somewhere like that?—where the mass of the people were held in thrall and ruled over by a secret, aristocratic caste whose power was so pervasive the members of it did not even have to reveal themselves except now and then, by certain offhand yet subtle signs. Yes, that was it: she felt like an anthropologist who had been magically transported through time to an archaic world of mysteries and strange laws, strange rituals and taboos.

She heard the front door opening and, after a moment, softly closing again. That would be Malachy; her husband's quietness and diffidence of manner could be sensed even through walls. She called out to him—too shrilly, making Maggie jump—and he put his head in at the door, smiling in that vague and vaguely troubled way of his. He was tall, with a narrow head. He wore tweeds and a bow tie. His eyes behind the dully gleaming lenses of his spectacles were pale and slightly watery.

"Oh, don't just dither there!" Rose called to him with humorous exasperation. "Come and sit down with us and have some of this good tea—it's that kind you like, Lapsang Souchong, that smells of old Cathay." Mal entered and closed the door

behind him and came forward creakingly, his smile congealing
into a slight queasiness. Rose supposed he could not remember
exactly who her guest was; new people always worried him.
"You remember Marguerite Delahaye," she said, loudly, "my
friend Maggie."

"Ah, yes," Mal said, relieved, his smile clearing. "Miss Delahaye. How are you?"

He drew up a chair and sat down. Only now did he notice
Maggie's red-rimmed eyes and the shine on her nose, and faint
alarm spread over his face again, and he touched self-consciously
the flesh-pink bulb of the hearing aid in his left ear.

"Maggie has had a bereavement," Rose said, pronouncing
each word distinctly, so that she could not help sounding overbearing and even a little cross. "Her brother—"

"Lord, yes, of course!" Mal said quickly, half rising from the
chair but keeping his back and his long legs bent in a sitting
position; what an endearingly absurd man he was, Rose thought,
not by any means for the first time. "Of course," he said.
"Your—Mr. Delahaye—your brother." Slowly he subsided onto
the chair. "I'm very sorry for your trouble."

It was not convention, he did seem genuinely sympathetic,
and this set Maggie off again. Rose threw her eyes to the ceiling. "It's very sad," she said, somewhat shortly, "very tragic, of
course."

Mal was pouring himself a cup of tea. The tea smelled of
straw and smoke. Rose watched him, his elaborately slow and
deliberate movements, still feeling that exasperated fondness
she always felt before the spectacle of Mal's mole-like ways.
Mal had been an obstetrician at the Hospital of the Holy Family but was retired now. She often wondered what he did all

day. He would leave the house in the morning, quite early sometimes, and come back in the afternoon looking, she always thought, ever so slightly shamefaced. In their early days together she used to ask him straight out what he had been up to, just for the sake of conversation, but he would take on a look of mousy alarm and say quickly that he had gone for a walk, or that he had met someone he knew. Somehow she never believed him. She had an image of him stalled on some street corner, and just standing there haplessly for hours, gazing at nothing, noticing no one and not being noticed, the passersby stepping around him as if he were a fire hydrant, or a tree that had somehow grown up on the spot overnight. It still surprised her that she had married him. Not that she regretted it, or was unhappy; only they were, as even she could see, a most unlikely couple, whiling away together the autumn of their lives.

He was asking Maggie if she would take another cup of tea, but she said no, and sat up on her chair and straightened her shoulders, and put the sodden hankie away in her bag and fastened the clasp with a decisive snap. She had a remarkably long neck, and now she extended it in a swanlike fashion, elevating her head and thrusting out her nose and her sharp little chin. Her already graying hair was untended, and had the look of a clump of steel wool, or an abandoned bird's nest.

"I want to ask, Dr. Griffin," she said, "I want to ask—" She stopped, and looked at her fingers fixed on the rim of the handbag in her lap. She tried again: "Do you think that he— do you think my brother—would he have suffered?"

Malachy frowned. Medical questions were the one thing that were sure to concentrate his attention. Yet Rose could see how torn he felt now, eager to discuss the likely details of

Victor Delahaye's suicide yet hesitant in the presence of the dead man's close relative.

"It depends," he said, "on where he—on where the bullet entered." He clasped his hands, moving forward to the edge of his chair. "If the shot penetrates the heart, the person will experience first what we call a prodromal period, very short in duration, which is like the sensation before fainting, with lightheadedness and nausea, and after that there'll be a neurocardiogenic syncope. Sorry—big words, I know. Most people's blood pressure on fainting is restored by lying flat, but here, you see, this is impossible, as the pumping mechanism is destroyed. The person would have only moments after being shot before they fell over and exsanguinated—bled to death, that is. Some victims of attack say they didn't even notice they had been stabbed or shot until they saw the blood. And then—"

"What he means," Rose said heavily, "is that your brother would have died instantly." She turned to her husband, signaling with her eyes. "Isn't that the case, Malachy?"

Mal sat back on the chair and issued a soft, sighing sound, like that of a very small balloon very quietly deflating. "Yes," he said meekly, "of course, that's what I mean, that he would have died instantly," then added, faintly, "or almost."

Maggie gazed at him unhappily, trying to believe him, Rose saw, yet not succeeding. "It's what I keep thinking of, you see," she said, with a tremor in her voice. "I keep imagining him in agony, regretting what he'd done but knowing it was too late." She was clutching the bag in her lap so tightly now the blood had drained from the joints of her fingers. "I suppose people don't think, when they're going to do something like that, of how it will feel, of what the pain will be like. I suppose they're so desperate they just—" She shut her eyes and two fat shiny tears squeezed out between the lids and rolled down swiftly on either side of her nose. Malachy in alarm looked at his wife, and Rose reached out and covered Maggie's clasped hands with one of her own.

"Oh, my dear, don't," she said. "You're just tormenting yourself."

"I know," Maggie said, nodding like a child, with her chin tucked in and her eyes clamped shut and more tears squeezing out between the lids. "But I can't help it—I can't stop thinking of him out there in that boat, putting the gun to his chest, and—" She sobbed, her swollen lower lip shaking and the tears flowing down her face. Her breathing was becoming increasingly hoarse, and Rose hoped she was not going to suffer an asthmatic attack. Her first husband had died of emphysema, and she remembered that awful gasping and hooting he used to do at the end.

"Malachy," she said, "why don't you go and see if you can find something to give to Maggie." He threw her another wild look, and she smiled patiently. "Some *brandy*, maybe? Brandy, or something like that?"

"Oh, no!" Maggie said hastily, like a child again, threatened this time with a dose of castor oil. "I'm all right, really."

Mal rose silently and left the room, shutting the door so softly behind himself the catch did not even click.

"When will the funeral be held?" Rose asked. She was bored now, and wished her friend would drink up her tea and go.

"Tomorrow," Maggie said. "I don't know how I'm going to get through it."

"Oh, you'll manage," Rose answered brusquely, and smiled to soften the harshness of her tone.

There was a pause, and, as if to mark it, the shadow of a cloud swept across the garden outside, and in the room the daylight dimmed for a moment as though a switch had been pressed. Rose was trying to recall when it was she had last seen Victor Delahaye. Was it at that reception at the embassy last year, to do with some yacht race or other—the America's Cup?—that somehow she and Malachy had been lured to, although Rose had never been to sea on anything much smaller than the *Queen Mary*. Quirke had been at the reception too, she recalled—what had *he* been doing there, other than soaking up the Ambassador's bourbon?

Rose had found herself at one point standing by a window in a small circle of people that included Victor Delahaye and his baby-doll wife. Delahaye had been pronouncing on some point of nautical etiquette. What a donkey he had seemed to Rose, in his navy blue blazer and gray slacks and his slip-on shoes gleaming like mahogany, standing there pontificating about tides and currents and knots and God knows what all. Good-looking, though, in a somehow artificial sort of way, with that craggy profile and his tastefully graying hair swept back from his temples. His wife, standing beside him, had looked as bored as Rose had felt. Rose guessed she must be a good fifteen years younger than her husband, maybe twenty, even. What was her name? Mona. Mona Delahaye. The name suited her. Cat eyes, a mean mouth. Was it she who had caused Delahaye to load up his pistol and take himself out to sea, never to return? Rose had known finer and more sensible men than Victor Delahaye who had been ruined by their women. Used to happen a lot, that kind of thing, where she came from; the noble code of the Southland.

"I'm sorry, I seem to have driven Malachy away," Maggie said, managing to sound aggrieved. Rose gave her a look. She had not realized how tedious her friend could be. How was it they had become friendly in the first place? Rose did not make friends easily, or without due consideration. The two women had met through one of the charities Rose's late husband had supported, the Glentalbot Trust, which had its headquarters in a drafty old house in the Wicklow Mountains. Rose was on the board of the Trust, and so was Marguerite Delahaye, who had taken over the seat once occupied by Victor Delahaye's first wife, now deceased. Rose had paid scant attention to Maggie, the token Protestant on the board, until that now infamous emergency meeting at which Rose had demanded the resignation of the director of Glentalbot House, a drunken incompetent. Maggie, to everyone's surprise, had supported her, and between them the two women had won the day and routed the director's party. After the meeting Rose had sent her car and driver back to town and had taken a lift in Maggie's rattly old Morris Oxford. On the way in they had stopped at a hotel in Enniskerry and drunk a bottle of wine together to celebrate their victory. That day Rose had seemed to see, piercing through Maggie's prim and proper manner, a hard cold gleam of steel. Looking at her now, sitting before her sunk in a puddle of sorrow and self-pity, Rose wondered if she had been mistaken, if what she had seen in Maggie was simply something she had wanted to see, a reflection only of her own glinting toughness.

As if she had sensed Rose's disenchanted musings, Maggie now stood up, saying she should go. She went to the mirror over the fireplace and looked at herself with a faint cry of dismay, and took a compact from her bag and dabbed powder on her cheeks and on the sides of her inflamed nose, with not much effect. Rose turned on her chair to regard her, and before she knew she was going to say it said, "And you really don't know why he did it?"

Maggie stopped and stood very still, facing the mirror, the powder puff suspended. "Oh, Rose," she said, "there are things I can't allow myself to think about, not yet."

Rose looked at her friend's haggard face reflected in the mirror. There was something about Maggie, something faintly but definitely strange. It was as if she had an emotional squint. You felt when she looked at you that she was not seeing you straight. She had odd ways, odd tics. She was given to sudden pauses, sudden halts in the midst of things, when she would stand for five or ten seconds gazing before her with a stricken expression, as if she were seeing horrors. Then she would blink, and give herself a shake, and be quite normal again, or as near to normal as she ever got. Poor Maggie. She should have married. But then, who would have married her?

Malachy came back, bearing a dusty bottle with an inch of cherry brandy in the bottom. "Sorry," he said, "this was all I could find."

The two women looked at him.

JACK CLANCY STOOD AT THE BOTTOM OF BOW STREET SMELLING the warm, rancid stink of fermenting barley from behind the beetling walls of Jameson's distillery. He always thought it funny that old Samuel Delahaye, a teetotaler and a zealous promoter of the temperance movement, should have chosen this place, so close to the distillery, as the site for the offices of Delahaye & Clancy. Nor could he have welcomed the proximity of the Capuchin friary round the corner in Church Street. Samuel was an old-style Unionist whose people had originated in the black hills of Antrim, and he did not take kindly to Catholics, even though he had brought in one of them, Jack's father, to be his business partner. To Jack all that seemed immensely far off now, as if it had happened hundreds of years past, and not just a generation ago.

He set off walking slowly, over the cobbles. This street was strange, always had been, so hushed and secretive, with a silence all of its own, flat yet echoing. It was because of the height of the walls on either side, he supposed, and the narrowness between them; the cobbles, too, probably acted on sounds in some deadening way. As a child he had always been frightened when his father brought him here, to the office, and they walked along where he was walking now, hearing their own footsteps. Yet when had his father brought him here, and why? He would not have wanted him about the office, under his feet, and anyway he would have been afraid of what Samuel Delahaye would say, for old Samuel, the senior boss, certainly was not fond of children. Yet Jack saw in his mind the two of them walking along here, hand in hand, the stooping man, only in his thirties and in failing health already, and himself in short trousers and a peaked cap with a button in the crown. Was he remembering or imagining?

He stopped at the squarish brick mansion opposite Duck Lane. It was of modest size, somewhat squat, with two windows to either side of the front door and five more above, on the second floor. The bricks were pale brown with flecks of yellow, as if butter had been mixed into them. The afternoon sun shone kindly on them. The front door too was squat, with a heavy black knocker and a glass fanlight above it where the name of the firm was painted in discreet, gilt lettering:

DELAHAYE & CLANCY LTD.
IMPORT EXPORT

He realized, with a curious shock, how fond he was of this house, solid and foursquare as it was. It seemed to him suddenly an old friend he had neglected for a long time but who now had stepped forward diffidently to offer him—to offer him what? Reassurance? Forgiveness? Shelter? He thought of the people inside. A few days ago he had been one of them, a man in an office, quietly working. Now it seemed to him something he had dreamed, another life, commonplace yet fantastical.

He did not suppose the twins would be at their desks. They rarely were. They dropped in once in a while, nonchalantly, to sign a few letters and collect their expenses. Such behavior would not have been tolerated in old Samuel's day. Maverley, the head bookkeeper, had tried once or twice to discipline them but they had laughed at him. Maverley was the one Jack had always worried about, the one he knew would find him out, if anyone would, and now he had. He should have got Maverley on his side, should have brought him in on the plan, should have involved him in the grand and secret strategy he had been working on for years. But Jack had been afraid to show his hand to anyone, and that, he saw now, had been his weakness.

For what he had been doing could not be done successfully by one man alone. He should have taken a partner.

Maverley would have been the obvious choice, but Jack had not considered it for a moment, and that had been his downfall. Maverley was a weasel, but weasels have sharp teeth. The bookkeeper, it turned out, had been watching him for months, watching his every move. Jack had secretly set up dummy companies, in Belfast, in Jersey, on the Isle of Man, to buy shares in Delahaye & Clancy—a daring and damn clever thing, even if he said so himself—and he had been on the brink of becoming the major shareholder when Maverley struck. Maverley had not been man enough to confront Jack directly, but had gone instead to Samuel Delahaye and told him everything. And the old bastard, of course, had told Victor.

Jack knew that Victor had never understood him, had taken him for granted. Victor treated him as he treated his twin sons, with a kind of easy, tolerant contempt. At board meetings Jack somehow always found himself at the far end of the table, with ten feet of gleaming mahogany between him and Victor up at the top, sitting in what used to be his father's chair, directing the order of business with a lordly ease. Occasionally, for the look of the thing, Victor would ask for Jack's opinion, and while Jack spoke he would sit back, with an index finger to his cheek, suppressing a smirk, or so it seemed to Jack, while the rest of the board members drummed their fingers and waited impatiently for him to finish. Victor made little jokes at Jack's expense, delivered little digs. "Oh," he would drawl, when some trivial topic was mentioned, "that would be Jack's territory, not mine—isn't that right, Jack?" And Jack would have to smile and squirm and take the mockery, as if he were an office boy brought in to be consulted on something too vulgar for Victor Delahaye to know anything about.

He looked up at the frontage of the house, at the glowing, buttery tiles, the rippled windowpanes, the tastefully painted sign over the door. He would never again cross the threshold here, all at once he knew it, and he turned aside quickly and walked away.

Jack wished he could forget his last meeting with Victor, but it kept returning to his mind, each time as vivid as if it were taking place all over again. Victor had called him into the boardroom. When Jack entered, Victor was standing at the window with his back turned, looking out at the brick chimneys of the distillery. Fury, accusations, recriminations—all that Jack could have coped with. But Victor had not shouted or threatened. He had seemed more tired than angry. His shoulders were sloped and his back looked crooked somehow, like Sylvia's, as if he were in pain, like her. "My father spoke to me," he said. Those were his words, *My father spoke to me*. It had sounded to Jack like something out of the Bible. *Depart from me, ye cursed . . .*

Had he caused Victor to do what he had done? Would Victor have killed himself because he had learned his partner had been plotting to take control of the business? Would he? If so, it had been Victor's ultimate dismissal of him, his final gesture of disdain for Jack and his secret plans. And now it was all gone. All the months of scheming, of planning, of putting the pieces into place, of hiding and watching, of waiting, of making himself wait—all gone. The twins, that pair of wastrels, would inherit the lot—them, and Victor's bitch of a wife. They would have it, and he would have nothing—Maverley would make sure of that.

He turned into Smithfield. A rag-and-bone man on his cart went past, his nag's hoofs clomping and the iron bands on the cartwheels harshing against the cobbles.

What now, Jack? he asked himself. *What now?*

He went out to the river and hailed a passing taxi. The driver wore a cap and did not try to make conversation, sitting in front of him sunk in his seat, his shoulders up and his big red ears sticking out. What would it be like, Jack wondered, to be him, rattling around all day in this old motor, picking up strangers and never saying a word to them? It might not be bad at all. It would require so little, just to exist. In the past Jack had rarely thought about other people's lives. Now he seemed to be on the outside of his own life, suddenly; one minute he had been safely indoors, in the thick of things, the next he had been seized on roughly and hustled out and dumped on the pavement, like a character in a cartoon, with his shirt collar standing up and stars flying in a circle round his head.

Why had Victor done it? *Why?* Was it really his fault, Jack thought, was he really to blame?

He told the driver to stop at Kenilworth Road and got out and set off walking towards the square. It was a habit he had fallen into; even when he drove himself he would stop short and park and go the rest of the way to the nursing home on foot. By that means he got an extra few minutes' delay, an interval in which something might happen, in which some accident might occur, some sudden summons be delivered, so that he could turn back and cancel that day's visit. Ridiculous, of course; nothing ever happened, and he would have to go on, at an increasingly leaden-footed pace, until despite everything he arrived at the front door and the four granite steps leading up, which might have been the steps to the gallows.

The front hall as always smelled of stewed tea and soiled mattresses. His father's room—or cell, as Jack thought of it— was on the first floor. Up here the spacious Georgian rooms had been divided by means of partition walls into smaller units that were narrow and cramped but had absurdly lofty ceilings with cut-off plaster-cast borders at an angle to each other on two sides. There was a bed, a chair, a bedside locker. A copper beech tree outside loomed in the high sash window, darkening the room within and giving it an underwater look. Jack's father inhabited this cisternlike space with the indolent furtiveness of an elongated, big-eyed, emaciated carp. Over time he had taken on protective coloring, so that always when Jack entered the room it took him a moment to make out the old man's fig- ure against the background of drab wallpaper and the brown blanket on the bed and the rusty light in the window.

"Hello, Dad," he said, trying to appear cheerful but sound- ing, as always, alarmed and querulous.

His father, standing by the window, peered upwards, frown- ing, and put his head to one side, as if he had heard his son's voice as a faint cry or call coming from a long way off. Jack sighed. What added to the torment of these visits was the eerie feeling he had that there was no one else here, that he was alone and talking to himself. His father seemed to feel the same thing, that he was alone yet being talked to, somehow. And so they would blunder through a painful half hour, the son shouting himself hoarse in an effort to penetrate the fog of his father's senility, while his father grew increasingly agitated, thinking probably that spirit voices were speaking to him loudly but unintelligibly out of the ether.

As a young man Philip Clancy had been tall and thin and now he was stooped and gaunt. He had a small head with a domed forehead and a curiously pitted skull on which a few last stray hairs sprouted like strands of cobweb. His nose was huge and hooked, a primitive axe head, and his mouth, since he had given up wearing his dentures, was thin-lipped and sunken. The Delahayes had treated him negligently all his working life, and now that he was worn out there was not one of them who would come to visit him, here where he was held in captivity, vague and lost to himself and the world.

Jack walked to the window and stood with his hands in his pockets, looking out. Why would they not cut down that bloody tree, or prune it back, at least, and let in a bit of light? He had asked them often enough to do something about it and they had promised they would, but of course they never had. The fellow who ran the place was an oily type, ferret-eyed behind a fawning manner, while his washed-out wife had the dazed look of someone trying in vain to understand how she had ended up like this, running a home for the old and the sick and the mad.

Jack's father was watching him with a wary surmise, running his eye all over him as if in search of a clue as to his identity. Somewhere in the house an electric alarm bell was ringing, an insistent buzzing that seemed to loop on itself slowly, over and over.

"I'm in trouble, Dad," Jack said, still gazing out of the window. "I tried to take over the business and I failed. Or I was beaten. Suicide you can't win against." He paused, shaking his head slowly from side to side in bitter and angry regret. "I did it partly for you, you know," he said. "To get back at them for the way they used you, all those years." He stopped again. Was it true? It sounded fake, yet he so much wanted it to be true. He wanted to believe that there was, if not a nobler, then a higher motive for what he had done, what he had tried to do. He did not care to think it had all been for himself, to satisfy his own resentment and jealousy.

His father, standing there peering at him, made a sound, a sort of questioning click at the back of his throat. What went on in his head, Jack wondered, what shards and tail ends of thought were floating about in there, the splintered wreckage of a life? "Ah, Dad," Jack said, feeling suddenly worn out. Something was happening in his throat, his sinuses, behind his eyes. He put a hand to his face, and all at once the tears came, and he opened his mouth and released a sound that was half a sob and half a wail. Still covering his eyes, he reached out his other hand blindly before him and, finding his father's cold and bony arm, held on to it, and wept.

6

THE NIGHT WAS TOO HOT FOR SLEEPING BUT THEY WOULD PROB-
ably not have slept anyway. Quirke sat on the side of the bed,
smoking a cigarette. He was naked, yet still he was sweating.
It was strange, being here again in the little house in Portobello,
in this low-ceilinged bedroom with the narrow bed and the
Fragonard reproduction on the wall and that little square
window looking out onto the canal.

The hour was past midnight but there was still a faint glow
in the sky above the rooftops. He did not like this time of year,
with its slow lethargic days and eerily short nights. In summer
he always felt slightly unwell, with headaches and pains in his
joints and a constant faint sensation of nausea. He thought he
must have an allergy, that there must be some kind of pollen
or dust in the air that his system could not cope with. He should

have a test. He closed his eyes briefly. There were many things he should do.

"I suppose you'll be off now," Isabel Galloway said, "having got what you came for."

She was sitting up in the bed, propped against pillows, wrapped in the silk teagown he remembered, with red and yellow flowers printed on it. She was smoking too, with an ashtray in her lap. Although his back was turned to her, he could feel her angry eye fixed on him.

"Do you want me to go?" he asked.

"Oho no," she said, with a bitter laugh, "don't try that old trick—I'm not going to make it easy for you."

He was squinting through the window out into the undark night. The streetlamp at the corner was casting a sulfurous sheen on the still surface of the canal. He thought of being out there, even saw himself, walking along the towpath in the calm mild air, moving between pools of lamplight, his long shadow shortening at his back and rising up swiftly and then the next moment falling out in front of him. To be alone, to be alone.

"I'm sorry," he said.

"Yes, of course you are." Isabel spoke behind him, in a tone of angry sarcasm. "You're always sorry, aren't you."

"I shouldn't have come here."

"No, you shouldn't. And will you please turn around? I want to make sure you're not smirking." He half turned towards her, showing his face to her, his expression of weary melancholy. Their lovemaking had felt to him more like a surgical procedure. Isabel had thrust herself angrily against him, all elbows, ribs, and bared teeth. Now she sat there furious in her painted gown like an Oriental empress about to order his beheading. "You hurt me, Quirke," she said, with a tremor in her voice that she could not suppress. "You broke my heart. I tried to kill myself over you." She shook her head in rueful wonder. "What a fool."

He tapped his cigarette on the edge of the ashtray. "I should have telephoned," he said. "I should have kept in contact. That was unforgivable."

Her eyes blazed, glittering with unshed angry tears. "But of course you're asking to be forgiven, aren't you."

He looked down. Somewhere nearby a church bell tolled once, marking the half hour. The chime hung for a second or two in the upper air, a trembling pearl of sound. "I thought," he said, speaking very slowly, "I thought we might try again, you and I."

Isabel stared at him steadily for a long moment, then flung herself from the bed and swept out of the room, her bare feet slapping on the polished wood floor. The bathroom door down the corridor slammed shut. He listened to the faint distant tinkle of her peeing. He put out a hand and felt the warm spot in the bed where she had sat. He saw clearly, like a forking path, the two possibilities that lay before him: either stay or get up now and hurry into his clothes and leave before she returned. He did not move.

They went downstairs, Quirke barefoot and in shirt and trousers. He sat on the sofa in the living room while she fetched glasses and a bottle from the kitchen. "I only have gin," she said, holding up the bottle. She smiled wryly. "I am an actress, after all. And there's no ice, as usual. The fridge is still not working." This was how it had been the first night he had come here, the warm gin and the flat tonic in this airless, cramped little room.

Isabel sat down sideways to face him at the opposite end of the sofa. "Well," she said, putting on a brisk and brittle tone, "shall we make small talk? You go first."

He smiled, shrugged. "I don't know what to tell you. Nothing notable ever happens to me."

"Aren't you at your sleuthing? You always enjoy that—murder and mayhem, all of it happening to other people."

He had left his cigarettes upstairs. Isabel pointed to a silver box on the mantelpiece, one that he remembered, and he stood up and fetched it and offered her a cigarette and took one himself. Passing Cloud—Phoebe used to smoke them; did she still? He did not know. He thought perhaps she had given up. He settled himself on the sofa again. The warm gin tasted like perfume, cloying and slightly viscous. "Ever come across Victor Delahaye?" he asked.

She frowned, and shook her head. "No. Should I?"

"He died. It was in the papers. He—" He stopped.

"He what?" Isabel asked.

"Killed himself."

"Did he, now." She watched him narrowly, with amusement. "I do believe you're blushing, Quirke."

"Sorry."

"You don't need to be." Her smile was as bright as steel. "I've got used to thinking of myself as a failed suicide, so there's no reason to be embarrassed and avoid the subject. Tell me about this man—what did you say his name was?"

Quirke took a long swallow of his drink, and winced again at the glutinous texture. "Delahaye," he said. "Victor Delahaye.

Business family—Delahaye and Clancy, shipping, coal, timber, garages, I don't know what else."

"And why did he kill himself?" She gave her mouth a twist. "Not for love, I imagine."

"No one seems to know. Or no one is saying, anyway."

"Aha—and your little gray cells are working overtime, are they?" She sipped her drink, watching him over the edge of her glass. "You really are a strange person, Quirke. Tell me, why did you decide to be a pathologist?"

Why? He could not recall, now. "I don't know that I decided," he said. "I think I just drifted, as everyone does."

"Your morbid streak led you on, did it?"

"That's it. My morbid streak."

For a reason that neither of them could understand this little exchange lightened the atmosphere between them, and Isabel extended a foot and caressed his bare ankle with her toes. "Poor Quirke," she said fondly, "you're such a mess." He was about to reply when she sat up straight suddenly. "I know what's the matter with me," she said. "I'm hungry. And do you know what I want? Chips! I want a bag of chips and one of those disgusting rissoles they make out of mashed-up seagull." She stood up, extending her hand. "Come on, get your shoes on, we're going out." She hurried ahead of him up the narrow stairs, singing.

Despite himself, he was glad he had stayed.

THEY HAD TO GO ALL THE WAY TO RINGSEND TO FIND A CHIP shop that was still open. Isabel had a little car now, a Fiat, bright red and glossy, like a ladybird. Quirke was touched to see how

proud of it she was. He had briefly owned an Alvis, and was
secretly relieved to be rid of it. They drove down by the canal,
under the dark and motionless trees. The roads were empty
at this hour. There was a childish excitement in the car, as if,
Quirke thought, the two of them had slipped out together in
the dark, hand in hand, bent on adventure.

Isabel, crouched over the steering wheel, kept shooting him
sidelong glances with her eyebrows lifted and her lips mischie-
vously pursed. "Oh, God, Quirke," she said with a laughing
groan, "I have to admit it, I'm glad you're back."

And he? Was he glad, really? He made himself smile at her.
He felt as if he had been sheltering under a stone and now the
stone had been lifted, exposing him to the sudden glare of
the sun. He did not deserve such kindness, if kindness it was.
He had let nearly a year go past without ringing Isabel even
once, if only to ask how she was faring. Was he to be forgiven
this easily? It seemed to him almost a scandal.

The chip shop was a box of harsh white light behind a big
square plate-glass window. The metal counter was chest-high—
why were chip shop counters always high like that? Quirke
wondered—and the owner, a dour fellow with a paunch and
a lazy eye, had the look of a former boxer. His wife, thin as a
whippet, kept to the background, tending the cauldrons of
seething fat. Quirke and Isabel were the only customers. They
stood at the counter waiting for their order to be prepared.
Despite the late hour and the dinginess of the surroundings
there was for some reason a sense of comedy in the situation,
and Isabel kept giving off waves of muffled hilarity, so that
Quirke, conscious of the shopman's drooping and suspicious
eye, had to work hard at maintaining an expression of stern

solemnity. When the food was ready they took it to eat in the car, and sat with all four windows wound fully down to let out the fatty fumes. "My God," Isabel said happily, "this rissole really is revolting, isn't it?" She grinned at him. There was a smear of grease on her chin. "You see, Quirke?" she said. "Being happy for the odd moment now and then isn't so difficult."

Having eaten their food, they drove out to Sandymount and walked along the front to calm their queasy stomachs. The night air was still, and a vast and slightly crazy-looking moon hung at what seemed a crooked angle above the horizon, laying a thick trail of gold across the water. "Look at that," Isabel said, "like a road you could walk on." Quirke was thinking of her in her hospital bed a year ago, with her face turned to the wall, and him standing helpless in the room, not knowing what to say. "Don't brood," she said, as if she had read his thoughts. She linked her arm in his and pressed herself against him and shivered.

"It's chilly," she said. "Let's go home. I mean, let's go back."

When they got to the house Isabel sent Quirke to sit on the sofa while she was in the kitchen preparing tea. The rissole, a glistening lozenge of grayish meat mixed with grain, had left a coating of slime on the roof of his mouth that would not be dislodged. He smoked a cigarette but even that would not take away the taste. There was what sounded like a party going on somewhere nearby—he could hear talk and laughter and the tinny wail of a record player.

"Tell me about what's-his-name," Isabel called from the kitchen. "Delahaye."

He rose and went to the kitchen doorway and stood with his hands in his pockets. He had taken off his shoes again and the floor was pleasantly cool under his stockinged feet. Isabel, who had changed into her silk gown, was measuring spoonfuls of tea into a willow-pattern pot. "What do you want me to tell you?" he asked.

"Tell me why you think there's something funny going on— because you do, I know you do. I know that look."

He pondered, gazing at the floor. "Well, from what I know of Victor Delahaye, he wasn't the kind of person to kill himself."

"Is there that kind of person?"

She carried the teapot past him and set it on a cork mat on the little table in front of the sofa. He watched her, admiring the glimmer of a pale breast in the opening of her gown, the full curve of her thigh pressing against the silk. She was a handsome woman, russet-haired, long-limbed, and slim. He wished . . . He did not know what he wished.

"He took his partner's son with him, in the boat," he said.

He went and sat on the sofa again. Isabel handed him his tea and offered the milk jug. "What age is he—the son?" she asked, settling herself beside him.

"I don't know. A young twenty-five?"

"Were they close, him and Delahaye?"

"I doubt it."

"Then why did he choose him to take with him?"

"That's what everyone wants to know." He sipped his tea. It seemed only to add another coating of scum to his mouth. "I suppose he wanted a witness."

Isabel was gazing before herself with narrowed eyes, holding the cup and saucer close under her chin. "People usually don't want other people watching at a time like that," she said quietly. She gave a faint laugh. "A private moment, if ever there was one."

Quirke thought it best to let this pass. He waited for a beat, watching the curl of steam above his cup. "Delahaye was a vain man," he said.

"And yet he shot himself. In front of his partner's son."

"So it seems."

They sat in silence. From where the party was there came a woman's screams of laughter, and a new song started up.

"There *is* something fishy, isn't there," Isabel said. "Even I can sense it."

Quirke was lighting a cigarette. "Yes," he said, "there is."

"Did the young man do it?"

"I don't think so."

"Then he did kill himself."

"Yes. But what I want to know is why. He was vain and pompous and full of his own importance. He had to have been driven to it."

Down the street, the record twanged and wailed.

She took the cigarette from his fingers, drew on it, gave it back, slightly stained with lipstick. "Sorry," she said. "I'm trying to give up. They're saying now they cause cancer."

"Life causes cancer."

She refilled his cup and her own and leaned back on the sofa, balancing the saucer against her bosom. She studied him, smiling a little. "Well, Dr. Quirke," she said. "What's next, for us?"

He shook his head. "I don't know." It was the truth.

"What about your French *amour*? Is she gone for good?"

Françoise d'Aubigny. He said the name to himself and felt a click of pain, as if a tiny bone in his breast had snapped. He had loved Françoise, despite all she had done, despite all that she had turned out to be. "Gone, yes," he said, tonelessly. "Gone for good."

"And you're back."

She was still smiling but the smile had a flaw in it, like a crack across a mirror.

"Yes," he said. "I'm back."

What else could he say?

7

INSPECTOR HACKETT SPOTTED QUIRKE BEFORE QUIRKE SPOT-
ted him. They were among the crowd outside St. John's, milling on the gravel in the sunshine in front of the church doors.
Smell of warm dust, of hot metal from the parked cars, of the
women's face powder and the men's cigarettes. Faint smell of
death, too, of clay and lilies and the varnished wood of the
coffin. Hackett was thinking what curious occasions they
were, funerals, or this bit of them, anyway, the interval after
the church service and before the burial, when no one seemed
to know exactly what to do or how to behave, trying to keep a
solemn demeanor yet feeling guiltily relieved, and almost light-
hearted. They talked about all kinds of things, politics, the
weather, who was going to win the match, but no one at this
stage of the proceedings ever spoke of the person who was dead;
it was as though a dispensation had been given for these few

minutes, and everyone had been let off mentioning the one and only reason they were gathered here.

Hackett had arrived a minute or two before the service ended, having wanted to avoid going inside the church. When he was a lad the priests used to say that any Catholic who went into a Protestant church was committing a sin, and although he no longer believed in such things he still instinctively obeyed. Anyhow, it was not as if he was one of the family, or even a family friend.

He took himself off to the side and lit a cigarette and eyed the crowd, in their dark suits and black frocks and black hats with veils—a regular fashion show, it looked like—picking out the ones whose faces he knew and watching how they behaved. There were the Delahaye twins, uncannily alike. Which was which? That must be James, the one staying silent, while the other one, Jonas, talked and smiled. The dead man's widow was with someone he did not recognize, a tall sleek man with ash-colored hair brushed back like an eagle's plume—her brother, maybe, or was he too old? She wore a dark blue two-piece costume the skirt of which was very tight and emphasized the curve of her behind. Hackett looked at the seams of her stockings, and looked away.

The Clancys, parents and son, were in the crowd and yet seemed apart from it, surrounded as it were by an invisible enclosure. Jack Clancy was dragging on a cigarette as if he was suffocating and it was a little tube of oxygen. His son, looking more than ever like a bantamweight contender, was frowning at the sky, as if wistfully expecting something to swoop down out of it and carry him off to somewhere less grim than this balefully sunlit churchyard. Mrs. Clancy—what was her name?

Celia? Sylvia?—held herself in that peculiar way that she did—
standing on her dignity, Hackett thought—with her handbag on
her wrist and her gaze turned elsewhere. The three of them
looked as if whatever it was that was holding them together
might loose its grip at any moment and send them flying
asunder.

And then there was the sister, Miss Delahaye—Margaret,
was it?—raw and red-eyed and coughing steadily like a motorcar with a faulty spark plug.

Trouble on all sides, Hackett told himself, and sighed.

It cheered him, seeing Quirke, skulking as it seemed beside
the church door, also lighting up a furtive cigarette, glancing
swiftly about as if expecting someone to be challenged, his
black hat pulled down over his left eye. Quirke was probably
the only one among all these people today who had not needed
to change into a funeral suit.

"There you are," Hackett said. He lowered his voice. "Grand
day for a planting."

Quirke did his crooked smile.

The mourners were drifting towards the graveyard, led by
the vicar in his surplice and stole and walking behind the coffin carried on the shoulders of James and Jonas Delahaye and
four of what must be their friends, curt-looking young men in
expensive suits. The women in their high heels stepped over
the grass carefully, like wading birds, while the men, conceal-
ing their half-smoked cigarettes inside their palms, took a last
few surreptitious drags. Quirke and the Inspector joined the
stragglers.

"There's a sign somewhere in Glasnevin Cemetery," Quirke
said quietly. "'Planting in this area restricted to dwarves,' it

says." The Inspector's shoulders shook. Quirke did not look at him. "I think," he said mildly, "it's trees that are meant."

They went on, pacing slowly in the wake of the mourners.

"By God, Doctor," Hackett said, catching his breath, "you've the graveyard humor, all right."

The burial was quickly over with. The vicar droned, his eye fixed dreamily on a corner of the sky above the yew trees, a hymn was raggedly sung, someone—Delahaye's sister, probably—let fall a sob that sounded like a fox's bark, the coffin was lowered, the clay was scattered. The vicar draped a silken marker over the page of his black book and shut it, and with his hands clasped at his breast led the solemn retreat from the graveside. Hackett had been admiring the two grave-diggers' shapely spades—he was always interested in the tools of any trade—and now they stepped forward smartly and set to their work. Mona Delahaye, passing him by, smiled at Quirke and bit her lip. Quirke doffed his hat. Hackett watched the young woman, not looking at her nylon seams this time. "Mourning becomes her, eh?" he said, and cocked an eyebrow.

The cars were starting up and one or two were already creeping towards the gate. "Have you transport, yourself?" the Inspector asked. Quirke shook his head. "Fine, so," Hackett said. "It's a grand day for a walk into town."

Hackett heard a step behind them on the gravel and turned to meet a pale, middle-aged man with a dry, grayish jaw and oiled black hair brushed slickly back.

"Are you the detective?" the man asked.

"I am," Hackett said. "Detective Inspector Hackett."

The man nodded. He had a curious way of blinking very slowly and comprehensively, like a bird of prey. He wore a starched, high collar—who wore collars like that, anymore? His teeth were bad, and Hackett caught a whiff of his breath.

"Might I have a word?" the man said. He slid a glance in Quirke's direction.

"This is Dr. Quirke," Hackett said. "We—we operate together."

Quirke shot him a glance but the policeman's bland expression did not alter. Hackett did not often make a joke.

"Ah, yes," the man said. "Garret Quirke. I've heard of you."

"Not Garret," Quirke said. Why had people lately started calling him by that name?

"Sorry," the man said, though he did not seem to be. "Maverley—Duncan Maverley. I work—worked—for Mr. Delahaye." He glanced over his shoulder at the dispersing crowd and gestured towards the gate. "Shall we—?"

The three men went out at the gate and turned right and walked slowly along the pavement in the shade of the plane trees. The Delahayes' car passed them by and Hackett fancied he glimpsed a flash of Mona Delahaye's eye, trained in Quirke's direction. The bold doctor, he thought to himself, had better go carefully, where that brand-new widow is concerned.

"I'm the head bookkeeper with Delahaye and Clancy," Maverley said.

He was walking between the other two. He wore a drab black suit slightly rusty at the collar and the cuffs, and there were speckles of dandruff on his shoulders. He was, Quirke thought, every inch what a head bookkeeper should look like.

"A very sad thing," Hackett said, "Mr. Delahaye going the way he did."

"Yes," Maverley said, somewhat absently; his mind seemed

elsewhere. "I wanted to talk to you, Inspector," he said, "about certain—certain anomalies that I've encountered, in the affairs of Delahaye and Clancy."

"Anomalies," Hackett said, as if he were unfamiliar with the word.

"Yes. In the accounts. Certain movements, certain transfers, of fundings and shares. It's a complex matter, not easily grasped by the layman."

Quirke and Hackett, the two laymen, exchanged a glance past Maverley's head. Maverley, caught up in his thoughts, appeared not to notice.

"Can you give us an idea," Hackett said, "an outline, of what the effect is of these—these anomalies?"

They had gone on some way before Maverley spoke again, in a voice that seemed hushed before the enormity of the matter that was being contemplated. "The effect," he said, "in essence, is that Mr. Delahaye—young Mr. Delahaye—Mr. Victor—was being—" He hesitated. "What shall I say? His position was being undercut, steadily, systematically, and, I may say, very skillfully, so that in effect he is—was—no longer in the position at the head of the firm that he believed he occupied."

"You mean he was being edged out," Quirke said, "without his knowing?"

"Not *being* edged out, Dr. Quirke; he *was* out. Or perhaps that is too strong." They had come to a corner and there they stopped. To the right, at the end of a short stretch of the road, the sea was suddenly visible, a sunlit blue surprise. Maverley inserted an index finger under the starched collar of his shirt and gave it an agitated tug. He cleared his throat. "Let me put it this way," he said. "The balance of power within the firm has shifted—has *been* shifted, so that Mr. Delahaye, Mr. Victor, who was the leading partner in the firm, has become, *had* become, very much the lesser. And all this without his knowing, until I"—a soft cough—"apprised him of it."

A silence fell. Inspector Hackett was squinting down the road towards the sea; he took off his hat and ran his hand around the sweat-dampened inner band. Quirke watched him. There were occasions, not momentous or even especially significant, when it came to him how scant was his knowledge of this man, how little he knew of how his mind worked or what his deepest thoughts might be. The two of them, he reflected, could not have been less alike. Yet here they were, wading together into yet another morass of human cupidity and deceit.

"And who might it be," the Inspector said, turning his gaze towards Maverley again, "that's behind this bit of clever maneuvering?"

Maverley pursed his pale lips. "Well now, Inspector," he said slowly, "I don't believe I'm in a position to say."

Hackett pounced. "You mean you don't know or you're not saying?"

"I mean," Maverley repeated, in a chill thin voice, "that I am not in a position to say." He brought out a handkerchief from the sleeve of his jacket and mopped a brow that to the other two seemed as dry as the handkerchief itself. "I simply felt that in the circumstances, in these tragic circumstances, I should bring this matter to the attention of the authorities. I've now done so, and I have nothing more to add. Good day to you."

He began to turn away but Hackett laid a hand, as if lackadaisically, on his arm. Maverley looked at the policeman's hand,

and then at Quirke, as if calling him silently to witness this act of constraint.

"The thing is, Mr. Maverley, I'm wondering what it is you expect me to do with this information you've passed on to me in such a public-spirited way." He released his hold on Maverley but then, to Maverley's obvious consternation, slipped his arm through the bookkeeper's and turned with him down the road towards the sea. Quirke followed, and Maverley looked back over his shoulder at him with an expression of outraged beseeching, as if urging him to remonstrate with the policeman. Quirke only smiled. He knew of old the Inspector's playful methods of coercion.

"You see," Hackett was saying, "what I'm trying to discover is why you've told me this stuff in the first place, especially in the light of the fact that you're only prepared to tell me so much of it, and no more. Such as, for instance, the identity of the person who has been chicaning away at the heart of the firm of Delahaye and Clancy." He chuckled, and waggled the arm that was still entwined with Maverley's. "Would it be, Mr. Maverley, that you expect me to guess the identity of the certain party you're unwilling to name?"

Hackett had quickened his pace, and Maverley hung back, so that it seemed the detective was dragging him along against his will. Maverley glanced back at Quirke again, with a deeper look of desperation. "Dr. Quirke—" he said, his voice squeaking, but Hackett was unrelenting. "Because," the detective said, "I think I can guess who this gentleman is. Unless I'm greatly mistaken, in which case I'd be expecting you to put me right."

At last Maverley, by a sudden violent maneuver, succeeded in freeing his arm from Hackett's, and stopped short on the pavement like a balking horse, indignantly hitching up the lapels of his suit jacket and smoothing down his mourner's narrow black tie. Hackett, whose momentum had sent him on a pace, stopped too, and turned and strolled back, smiling easily. Quirke took a step back, but Hackett flapped a lazy hand at him to draw him again into the little circle of the three of them. But Maverley would have no more of it. "I'm sorry, Inspector," he said, lifting a hand and holding it up flat against the two men before him. "I've said all I have to say. And now, if you don't mind, I have work to go to."

He turned on his heel and strode away. Hackett, a hand in his pocket and his head on one side, stood with his lazy grin and watched him go. "Do you know what it is, Dr. Quirke," he said, "but that fellow is the spitting likeness of a tax inspector that used to come and harass my father on the bit of a farm he had when I was a child. *Mr. Hackett,* he used to say, *it is my duty to inform you that if you do not fill up the forms and pay your taxes I will be compelled to set the Guards on you.* Oh, I can see him still, and hear him, that pinched voice of his." He turned to Quirke. "Would you say no to a drink, Doctor?"

Quirke laughed. "I would not, Inspector."

They went to a pub on the corner of Sandymount Green. They ordered wilted cheese sandwiches—"Isn't the sliced bread a curse," the Inspector sadly observed—and a glass of Guinness each. Strong sunlight slanted in at the doorway and down from the clear top of the painted-over front window. Down the bar from them a very old man was perched on a high stool, drowsing over a copy of the *Independent,* his eyelids drooping and his head lolling. They tackled their sandwiches. "Give me over that mustard there," Hackett said, "for I declare to God this yoke tastes like two wedges of cardboard with a slab of mildewed lino stuck in between."

Quirke sipped his stout and was sorry he had not asked for whiskey. He had been careful with his drinking in recent months, and felt quietly proud of himself for it. "So what," he asked, "did you make of Bartleby the Scrivener and what he had to say?"

"Maverley, you mean?" The Inspector was munching bread and cheese with an expression of sour disgust. "I kept thinking I was my father and that I should run the bugger off the property." He took a deep draught of his drink, and wiped away a cream mustache with the back of his hand. "It must be the partner, Clancy, that he's talking about. Who else would there be?"

"Delahaye's sons—the twins?"

"Arragh," the Inspector said, flapping his lips disdainfully, like a horse, "they wouldn't have the wit, those two."

"Are you sure?"

The Inspector glanced at him askance. "Are we ever sure of anything, in this vale of tears?"

Quirke pushed his quarter-eaten sandwich away and brought out a packet of Senior Service and offered it to the policeman with the flap lifted and the cigarettes ranged like a set of miniature organ pipes. "What if it is Clancy that's on the fiddle?" he asked.

Hackett shrugged. "Aye—what if? Am I supposed to think what he's up to is against the law and not just the usual skulduggery that goes on in offices and boardrooms every day of the week?"

"It must be serious, for Maverley to buttonhole you like that and tell you about it."

"Yes," the Inspector said. "It must be serious." He took another judicious drink of his stout. When he set the glass back on the counter the yellow suds ran down inside and joined what remained of the head. It was strange, Quirke reflected, but in fact he did not much like drink and its attributes, the soapy reek of beer, the scald of whiskey. Even gin, which he considered hardly a drink at all, had a metallic clatter in the mouth that made him want to shiver. And yet the glow, that inward glow, that was a thing he did not wish to live without, whatever the state of his liver or his brain.

He thought of Isabel last night, the warm gin and tonic, the scummy chips and putrid rissole—he would remember that rissole for a long time—then the ritual of the tea, the faint taste of her lipstick on his cigarette, and the stronger taste when she kissed him. He thought of lying in the faint glow of her bedroom, and of her sleeping, her heavy head cradled in the crook of his arm. Was it a mistake to take up with her again? Probably. And yet in a sequestered corner of what he called his heart the fact of her glowed like an ember he had thought was ash but that the mere sight of her had quickened again into warm life. What everyone told him was true: he was too much among the dead. But who was going to venture down into the underworld and fetch him up into the light? Isabel? Well, why not? Why not she, as good as any other? If it was not too late.

"I suppose," the Inspector said thoughtfully, leaning his elbows on the bar, "we might go and have a word with him, the same Mr. Clancy."

"'We'?"

Hackett looked at him in surprise and feigned dismay. "Ah, now, Doctor, you wouldn't think of abandoning me at this stage of the proceedings, would you? I'm not up to these fancy folk, you know that. You're the one that speaks their lingo."

Quirke toyed with his glass, revolving the bulbous knob at the base between his fingers. "You know, Inspector," he said, "you really have some peculiar ideas about me."

NOW THAT THE FUNERAL WAS OVER, MAGGIE DELAHAYE WON-dered if she might return to Ashgrove and finish her holiday. It shocked her a little that she should entertain such a notion, with her brother hardly cold in his grave, and yet why should she not go back to Cork? In fact, since Victor's death it had crossed her mind more than once that really there was nothing to stop her from moving permanently to Ashgrove.

When she looked at the thing dispassionately she had to ask what was keeping her here. When Victor's first wife had died, Maggie had sold her own little house in Foxrock and moved into the red-brick barn on Northumberland Road to look after her brother. She supposed now it had been a mistake. She had grown up in that house, and should have known she could not go back there without encountering ghosts. But her father, after his stroke, was becoming increasingly difficult, and the twins were still in college and were running wild, as young people often did after the loss of their mother. Victor simply would not have been able to cope on his own. But then, after only a couple of years, Victor out of the blue had announced his intention to remarry.

Nothing had been the same after Mona's arrival in the household. Victor was besotted with her, to an extent that to Maggie seemed, she had to admit, to border on the indecent. He had adored Lisa, and now he adored her successor even more. That could not be right. It was not that Maggie would have expected Victor to spend the rest of his days pining for his lost wife, but there was such a thing as moderation.

She did not hold Victor responsible for this state of affairs. Victor was only a man, after all, and Mona, though a vixen, was beautiful and probably—Maggie had to search delicately for the word—probably very passionate, and that was important for a man like Victor, well into his forties yet vigorous still. For Victor was just as childish as his wife, though in a different way, of course. Mona was greedy and grasping, and had a child's instinctive cleverness when it came to getting her own way; poor Victor, on the other hand, was like one of those schoolboy heroes in the books he used to read when he was young, full of high ideals and silly romantic notions of what other people were like. He was entirely taken in by Mona's little-girl act, and could not see how she was manipulating him, making him hop to her every command and laughing at him behind his back. Oh, yes, Maggie had the measure of Mona. Her brother, her lovely, brave, silly brother, was wasted on that woman.

And yet for all Victor's besottedness, Maggie was still convinced that deep down he had recognized something unpleasant in his wife, something cheap and ugly and in some way—yes, in some way *soiled*. She wondered if that was part of the attraction for him. Some men liked that kind of thing, liked to think of women being dirty and depraved. Maggie knew how possessive Victor had been of Mona, and how jealously he had watched over her. He had tried to hide his vulnerability behind the famously sophisticated façade he maintained, but he could not deceive his sister. They had always been close, she and Victor. They had grown up together as allies against their father's bullying and their mother's neglectfulness. One day, in their hiding place among the trees at Ashgrove, they had made a solemn vow that when they grew up they would marry each other, no matter what anyone said. And, in a way, Maggie had always felt that they *were* married, if only in spirit.

It had been hard for her when Victor actually did marry, and harder still when he married a second time, but she had said nothing, on either occasion—what could she have said?—yet it had pained her to watch him throwing himself away on those two women who were worth so much less than he was. Lisa at least had been harmless, a timid, rather gawky girl always anxious to please, who when she fell ill had surprised everyone by putting up a brave, uncomplaining, but in the end useless fight for survival. Mona, however, was not timid; Mona was not harmless.

Maggie had been as baffled as anyone by her brother's death. She could not accept that he had taken his own life. People had assured it was the case, but still she could not accept it. She had tried at first to convince herself that Davy Clancy must have done it—why had he thrown away the gun?—but it was no good; she knew that Davy was weak and incapable surely of killing anyone, least of all a Delahaye. But why had Victor taken him out in the boat—why him? It had been Victor's way of sending a message, of leaving a signal as to why he had done what he had done. But what message was it, and to whom did he think he was directing it?

No: if Davy Clancy had not been the cause of Victor's death, then Maggie was convinced that Mona must have been involved, in some way that she could not explain or account for. She would have to get away from this house, the horrible, oppressive atmosphere, the awful sense of there being some secret in the air, hidden from her but known to others. Yes, she would go back to Ashgrove. She would have peace there.

She put her book away—pages of it had gone by without her registering a word—and went and sat in front of the mirror of her dressing table and took up a tortoiseshell brush and applied it fiercely to her hair. Brushing her hair was usually a thing that soothed her, but today she went at it almost violently, with hard long strokes that drew the skin of her forehead tight and made her eyes widen, so that in the glass she looked a little mad. But then, she thought, perhaps she was a little mad. There was a streak of insanity in the family, on her mother's side, and neither had her father's people been the sanest, with their Bible-thumping and their furious hatred and fear of Catholics. They had never forgiven her father for moving south and going into business with a Taig, which was what they would have called Phil Clancy—a dirty Taig.

She put down the hairbrush and stared at her reflection, her eyes still wide. Maybe that was what had happened to Victor, maybe it had been an attack of temporary insanity. But no, Victor had not been mad. Passionate, yes, and fanciful, with all kinds of wild notions about himself and the people around him, but not mad. Something or someone had driven him to take himself and Davy Clancy in that boat out of Slievemore Bay that day with a gun in his pocket and despair in his heart.

· · ·

WHEN SHE CAME DOWNSTAIRS SHE FOUND HER FATHER IN THE drawing room, slumped in his wheelchair at the window above the garden. She thought at first he was asleep but when she approached him she saw that was not so. She saw too that his eyes were damp. This startled her. She did not think she had ever seen her father in tears before—he had not wept even at the funeral of his only son. "Are you all right, Daddy?" she asked, but it was not until she put a hand lightly on his shoulder that he responded, jerking himself away from her touch and glaring up at her, first in surprise and then in fury. He had been away somewhere in his thoughts.

He did not speak, and she could not think what else to say to him. She felt compassion for him, but in a detached way; it was as she would feel for someone whose misfortune she had been told about, or had read about in the papers. She had never been close to her father. He had not welcomed closeness, in fact had discouraged it, by his remoteness, his wounding sarcasm, his sudden rages. Yet, for all that, she admired him. He was tough, self-sufficient, unforgiving, which were qualities she held in high regard. As for love, well, love did not come into it.

Tea arrived, wheeled in on a trolley by Sarah the red-haired maid. The taking of afternoon tea was something Victor's first wife had instituted—poor Lisa, she had been so thrilled to find herself married into the grand and mighty Delahayes. Sarah maneuvered the trolley into the bay of the big window. Maggie said that she would take over, and the maid smirked—a brazen girl, with scant respect for anything, but a good worker—and sauntered away, humming. Maggie poured a cup of tea for her father, adding milk and two spoonfuls of sugar as she knew he liked, and brought it to him. He waved it away with a violent sweep of his arm. "Don't want tea," he growled. "I'm sick of drinking tea."

Maggie sighed. "Have you taken your pill?"

"No I have not!"

"You know what the doctor said about—"

"Ach, to blazes with that. What do the doctors know? Look at the state they've left me in"—he had got himself convinced somehow that his stroke was due to medical incompetence— "stuck in this blasted contraption and wheeled around like an infant."

Maggie might have laughed at that—the idea of her father letting anyone wheel him anywhere! She waited patiently, standing back a little, then proffered the cup again. "Take your tea," she said.

He let her put the cup and saucer into his hands. She was afraid he would spill the tea, scald himself perhaps, but one of the things the doctors had told her was that he must be allowed to fend for himself as much as possible. He set the saucer in his lap, the cup clattering. He did not drink; he was glaring into the garden.

"Are you sure you didn't take your pill?" Maggie said.

He turned his head and looked at her with furious contempt. "What was the good Lord thinking," he said, "to take my only son from me and leave me *you*?"

He watched her, almost smiling, eager to see the barb strike home. Maggie was thinking how remarkable it was that his accent had never softened, though he had lived down here in the Republic for half a century. It was another of the things he clung to, unrelenting, that Northern growl. "Drink your tea," she said again, mildly.

She brought a chair and sat down by the trolley and poured a cup of tea for herself. They both turned their eyes now to the garden. How strange to see everything in bloom and the sun shining so gloriously. But then, why was it strange? Death did not come only in times of dark and cold. It must have been beautiful, out in the bay, when Victor turned the gun against himself and fired. What would have been going through his mind, what terrors, what memories? She felt tears welling in her eyes but held them back by force of will. Her father was furious that he had let her see him weeping; she would not allow him to have redress by weeping herself, now.

"I was watching the birds," the old man said. "Thrushes, blackbirds. There's a robin, too, that comes and goes. Fierce creature, the robin—did you know that? Courage a hundred times his size. Aye, he holds on, that bird, doesn't weaken and let go." He made a fist of his left hand and brought it down with a thump on the arm of the wheelchair, making the cup in his lap joggle and slopping the tea.

It occurred to Maggie that what pained her father most about his son's death was the shame of it, the disgrace. Or was she being unfair? He was as capable of grief as she was. She speculated as to whether he might know what had driven Victor to do what he had done. Should she ask him? Surely a time such as this should permit them to speak as otherwise they never would? She glanced at her father, his carved profile, his poet's shock of silver hair. She knew nothing about him, next to nothing. He had never bothered with her; a daughter was nothing to him. And now he had no son. How would he not be furious? And heartbroken, perhaps; perhaps that, too.

Jonas came in. Automatically she looked to the door to see James entering behind him, as always. But Jonas was alone. This was so unusual that she gave him a questioning look, which he ignored. "Any tea in that pot?" he asked.

Maggie laid her hand against the teapot's cheek. "It's gone cold. Sarah can bring a fresh pot."

Jonas shrugged. "Doesn't matter. It's too hot to drink tea anyway." He threw himself down in an armchair. He had changed out of the black suit he had put on for the funeral, and wore dark slacks and a white silk shirt and loafers with no socks. His slender ankles were tanned. He had not wept at the graveside either. The suspicion came to Maggie sometimes that she allowed herself to feel things far too deeply. Her brother's death had set going in her a rushing underground river of grief that would in time slow down but that would be there always, running under everything. There were other streams from the past that were still flowing. Billy Thompson, a boy she had been sweet on when she was young—he had died, and she mourned him yet, all these years later. She looked at Jonas draped there in the armchair, a dazzling creature, so seemingly at ease. Surely he too was grieving for his father, in his own, subterranean fashion.

"How are you feeling, Grandad?" he asked.

The old man lifted a hand and let it fall again limply in a gesture of weary dismissal. "I'm no better than the rest of us," he said, still eyeing the garden, his jaw working.

Jonas turned to Maggie. "And what about you, Auntie?" he inquired, jaunty and ironical. He addressed his aunt always in a tone of half-fond raillery. He seemed, she thought without rancor, to find her something of a joke. But then, she supposed she was a joke—the spinster sister living in the home she had always lived in, despised by her father, mocked by her nephews, abandoned now by her beloved brother; even Sarah the maid paid her no regard. Yes, she should retire to Ashgrove, live there alone, keep cats, and become the local eccentric. "By the way," Jonas said, in an undertone, "you and I need to have a talk."

"Yes? What about?"

He frowned, and glanced in the direction of his grandfather. "I'll tell you later."

MONA TOO HAD CHANGED OUT OF BLACK, INTO A SILK DRESS OF dark sapphire that set off her milky pallor and the rich bronze textures of her hair. When she entered the drawing room she paused in the doorway, seeing the three of them—Maggie, her father-in-law, one of the twins—in their separate places at the far end of the big bright room, posed there like actors awaiting the entrance of the leading lady.

She came forward, stopping at the sideboard to take a cigarette from the box and light it with the fat heavy lighter. She was conscious of the three of them watching her. She was accustomed to being the center of attention, but this was different. Becoming a widow had given her a new role. It was a curiously pleasant, light-headed feeling. A widow, at her age! It seemed absurd, like something in a stage musical. The merry widow. She was still herself, of course, and yet she was someone else at the same time, the Mona Vanderweert she had always been and now Mrs. Victor Delahaye, whose husband was dead. It made her feel—well, it made her feel grown-up, in a way she had not felt before.

"Oh," she said, "am I late for tea?"

It was not tea she wanted, anyway, but a drink, though she supposed she had better not ask for one. It had been a trying day and did not seem set to get any easier. Everything felt flat. She would have liked the mourners to come back to the house after the funeral but her father-in-law had not wanted it. It would have been interesting to stand here being sad but brave among all those people.

Maggie had risen from her chair by the tea trolley. "How are you, my dear?" she asked. *As if she cared,* Mona thought.

"I'm fine, thank you. I seem to be a bit—dizzy." Her sister-in-law stood before her with her hands clasped under her bosom, what there was of it, gazing at her with a forlorn expression. All at once she had a vision of time stretching before her like a tunnel, or no, like an avenue in a cemetery, lined with dark trees, and a person standing mournfully under each tree, looking at her in just this way. A silent scream formed inside her. Boredom was one of her acutest fears. "Really," she said, turning away, "I'm fine."

None of them liked her. She had taken their precious Victor away from them, which was bad enough, but now they seemed to think she was somehow responsible for his death. They would not say so, of course, but she could feel them thinking it. She looked at the twin—was it James? for she was never quite sure which of them was which, even after all this time—and wondered what he knew. Both twins had been very cold towards her at the funeral, not that they were ever exactly warm where she was concerned. She would have to be careful. She supposed she had been foolish, had taken a foolish risk. Had Victor done it just because . . . ? No: she would not let herself think that, she would not, it was too absurd.

She turned to the young man in the armchair. "Where's Jonas?" she asked.

He sighed, and his mouth tightened. "I'm Jonas." He held up his left hand and showed her the ring on his little finger. "Jonas is the one who wears this, remember?"

She laughed, and put a hand to her mouth. "Oh, sorry, yes, I didn't look." His angry sarcasm amused her. Did they really expect her to check their little fingers every time she met them? It was not her fault that he and his brother were a pair of freaks. "Sorry," she said again, and looked around for an ashtray.

Samuel Delahaye sat slumped in the wheelchair with his chin sunk on his breast, glowering out into the garden. Mona went and stood beside him. He was the only one of them she had any time for. She had tried to get him to like her, and believed she had been successful, though of course he would never let on. He was such a grouch, shouting at everyone, insulting everyone. Often, when he was in one of his rages, she had an awful urge to laugh, but knew that if she did he would probably come rearing up out of that chair and slap her face. It would be interesting, to be hit like that. Old Sam was still handsome, and rather cruel-looking, like his grandsons only not weak like them; when he smiled, if what he did could be called a smile, he bared his lower teeth, just as Victor used to do.

Suddenly, at the thought of Victor, she felt sad. It was hard to grasp that he was actually gone, that he was in that wooden box, in the ground, already beginning to rot. She shivered. She had liked Victor. He had been handsome too, more handsome than his father, in fact, but in a different way: *softer around the edges,* she thought. Yes, that was it, softer around the edges.

He had known nothing about her, she knew that. She had preferred it that way. Being married to Victor had been like living inside a fine, sound, well-appointed house, a house that was not hers but that gave her shelter and protected her and yet left her free to come and go as she pleased, a little gold key safe in her palm. She recalled his smell, of tobacco and pomade and that special soap he used to wash his hands with—the skin of his hands was sensitive and chapped easily. She tried now to see those hands in her mind, and was slightly shocked to realize that she could not. Had she ever really looked at them? Had she ever paid genuine attention to her husband? These were not questions that troubled her, but it was odd to find herself asking them. She was always careful how she positioned herself in front of things, looking, and being looked at. Sometimes she thought of herself as a separate object, a figure outside herself that she could regard from a distance, appraising, approving, admiring.

Victor had thought she loved him. It would have been unfair to let him think otherwise.

"Look," her father-in-law said suddenly, dragging himself up in the wheelchair and pointing beyond the window to the garden with a trembling finger. "Robin Redbreast! Aha, the wee warrior."

· · ·

IT WAS NEARLY MIDNIGHT WHEN HE LEFT BELLA'S HOUSE, AFTER
his second visit. It was not two weeks since Victor had died,
but it seemed far longer ago than that. Bella stood in the doorway watching him go. When he was turning the corner at the
bottom of the road and glanced behind him she was still there,
he could see her figure silhouetted in black against the light
from the hall. He stopped, and stood looking back at her, hearing himself breathe. Why was she still there? The night was
calm and mild, and the soft feel of the air made him think of
summer nights in the past, and of himself walking away from
some other girl's door, smelling the dew on the privet and the
salt reek of the sea and hearing the birds far out in the bay
calling and crying. He had an urge suddenly to hurry back,
before Bella closed the door, and make her take him inside
again, and lie down with him and hold him in her arms. He did
not want to be out here, alone.

He went on, and turned the corner.

There was a big moon shining above the bay, it seemed to
him a huge gold eye watching him askew. He hoped Sylvia
would be asleep, but probably she would not be. She knew he
was in trouble, and that the trouble was connected with Victor
Delahaye's death. She had not challenged him, of course, had
not made even the mildest inquiry. That was his wife's way, ever
careful, ever discreet.

He knew he should have told her what was going on, what
he was up to, surely he had owed her that. Instead he had kept
it all to himself. It was not that he did not trust her, only how
could he have told her, what would he have said—how would
he have phrased it? *Well, you see, dear, the thing is, over the past
couple of years I've been positioning myself to elbow Victor aside*

and take over the jolly old firm—what do you think of that? He
knew what she would think of it. He knew very well. Would
she leave him? She was English, and the English had a funny
sense of what was right and proper and what was not. He
could say to her it was just business—and what was it except
business?—but she would throw that back in his face. Yet
what did she expect? Did she think he should be content to
spend the rest of his working life with his neck under Victor
Delahaye's boot—no, under the heel of his John Lobb penny
loafer with the hand-stitched seams and scalloped tongue?

Victor Delahaye was what Sylvia would have called an ass:
stupid, smug, conceited, and lazy. All his life Victor had coasted
in the shelter of the business that both their fathers, Samuel
Delahaye and his partner, Phil Clancy, had built up through
hard work, shrewdness, and unremitting ruthlessness. Had Victor been in sole control, the thing would have done no more
than drift and, who knows, might have foundered, if Jack had
not been there to keep a firm grip on the tiller.

How many dangers had Jack steered them past? There had
been that strike the dockers went on after the war, the strike
old Samuel thought he could break and that Jack had been left
to fix, by paying off the union bosses and cracking the heads
of a few hard chaws who would not be brought on board. And
what about the time Clem Morrissy and his brothers had
tried to set up that rival chain of garages and once again Jack
had been called on to send in the muscle and keep the monopoly safe for Delahaye & Clancy? Always it was Jack who had
done the dirty work, while Victor preened and boasted and
played the gentleman. And then—

And then. Who would have thought Victor would have it in

him to go out that way? Who would have thought it would affect him so disastrously, to discover himself sidelined? Who would have thought. There must have been something else; something else must have driven him to put a bullet through his heart, Jack was convinced of it. But what? If he could find out, maybe all was not lost, maybe something of all he had been working for could be saved.

Should he make one last try? Did he have it in him? He had always been a fighter, unlike Victor, who had everything handed to him on a silver platter. Yes, he would keep on, he would not be done down by that bastard Maverley and Victor's wastrel sons. That was what would keep him going, the thought of the twins and Maverley using Victor's death to defeat him. For they would get shot of him entirely if they could—oh, yes, they would. Already Maverley was putting the machinery in place that would grind him up and spit him out on the street. Did he imagine Jack had not seen him, after the funeral, sloping off for a quiet word with that detective, the one with the cow shit still on his boots, and his sidekick in the black suit? Jack could imagine the bookkeeper, with his gray jaw and his brown breath, counting out the insinuations like so many pounds, shillings, and pence, blackening the name of Jack Clancy, accusing him by innuendo and trying to undo by stealth all that he had put in place with such care, such finesse, such inventiveness.

The front was deserted, and yet, as he walked along, it seemed to him somehow that he was not alone. More than once he stopped, and turned, and peered back along the path beside the sea. Was it a shadow that had slipped behind that bush? He stood, his nerves tingling, and strained to see into the gloom, listening past the washing of small waves against the seafront wall. There was nothing to be seen, nothing to be heard.

The grass was silver in the moonlight. He walked on, wanting to hasten his steps yet dreading the thought of reaching home. He pictured himself at the front door, easing the key into the lock and wincing at the crunch it made, and then standing in the shadows in the hallway, taking the measure of the house, trying to guess if Sylvia was asleep or if Davy was in, and feeling, too, the lingering damp warmth in his groin. The guilt that he felt was part of the thrill, always had been, although being thrilled by his guilt made him feel guiltier still. Such a tangle his life had always been. But who was it that had made it tangled? Who was there to blame, but himself?

He came to the house and stopped, and stood with his hands on the coolly clammy top bar of the gate, looking up at his own bedroom window, where a faint light glowed. Sylvia would be awake, propped up in bed, with her spectacles on the end of her nose, reading, or at her sewing. Since Victor's death she had been sleeping badly—well, who had not? She would know, of course, or guess what he had been up to tonight. She would not know the details—she was not aware of Bella's existence, he was confident of that—but she would not need to. He sometimes thought she was glad to be rid of him for so much of the time. She had her own life. He was not a prime requirement in it.

He lit a cigarette, turning away in case the match flame might be visible from that far window, and then walked aimlessly on, musing on his wife, of whom, if truth were told, he knew so little. He had loved her, once, this cool pale slender

distant woman. He had wanted her because she was so different from the women he had known before he knew her, and
whom he continued to know, despite being married. And she
had loved him—loved him still, probably. Despite everything.

He passed by the bandstand. It looked eerie, a filigreed iron
gazebo standing in the moonlight, silent and brooding.

Stop. Listen. There was definitely someone behind him.

He was suddenly hot with fear, and the skin on the back of
his neck crawled. He dared not turn, but then he did turn.
Still there was no one to be seen, yet he knew there was someone, the same someone who had started up after him when he
left Bella's house. "Who's there?" he called out softly, feeling
foolish, his voice unsteady. "Who is it? Show yourself!"

Silence, with the sense in it of stifled, jeering laughter. He
slipped into the bandstand and stood in the webbed shadows
there under the wrought-iron canopy. The concrete floor gave
off a mingled smell of piss and fag ends. He thought with desperate yearning of how it would have been here earlier, when
the mail boat was getting ready to set out, the passengers hurry-
ing and people shouting farewells, the porters bumping luggage
up the gangplank and the ship sounding its grave, portentous
note. He could have lost himself in all that bustle, could have
slipped away, and been safe.

A woman was approaching along the pavement. He shrank
back into the shadows. Why had he come in here? The bandstand offered no protection, it was open on all sides. He turned
his head this way and that. The woman's footsteps were closer
now. He seemed to hear his name spoken, very softly, but
thought he must have imagined it. He was looking all around,
trying to see in all directions. He almost laughed to think of

himself, like a wooden doll, his head spinning and his eyes
starting in fright. Always, behind everything, there was a part
of him that stood back skeptically. Now he told himself he was
being ridiculous, that there was no one after him, that all this
fear and foreboding was the product of a fevered and guilty
mind.

The woman had drawn level with the bandstand. He stepped
forward, lifting a hand, ready to speak to her. He knew her!
What was she doing here, at this hour? He began to say her
name. The blow landed behind his right ear. He felt it distinctly, a dull shock without pain, and thought of a felled tree
crashing to the ground. As he pitched forward he saw the moon
slide sideways down the sky and disappear in darkness.

8

IT TURNED OUT THE DELAHAYE TWINS WERE AT THE PARTY.
Phoebe and Sinclair met one of them coming down the stairs
just after they arrived. He was with his girlfriend—Phoebe
recognized her but did not remember her name—and they
stopped to talk, although they could hardly hear themselves
above the din. The house was on a cobbled back street in the
North Strand with an iron railway bridge running over it. It was
a funny little tumbledown place, with everything on a miniature scale, the tiny windows, the low front door, the narrow
staircase leading up to two cramped bedrooms and a bathroom hardly bigger than a cupboard. Whenever a train went
past the entire place wobbled and shook like a jelly out of its
mold. Breen, the fellow whose house it was, had been at college with Sinclair, and fitted well with the place, being short
and stout, with a shock of black curls and rimless glasses that

kept sliding down the glistening, concave bridge of his snub nose.

Neither Phoebe nor Sinclair cared much for parties, and they had come to this one only because they had worried no one else would, since poor Breen was not exactly known as a social magnet. To their surprise they found the house throbbing with people and noise. Breen came bustling to meet them, sweaty and shiny and snuffling with happy laughter. He took the bottle of Bordeaux they had brought and glanced appreciatively at the label and said there was wine open in the kitchen. He gestured with pride at the heaving mass of people around them. "The joint," he said, "is jumping." He wore plimsolls and checked tweed trousers hoist at half-mast by a pair of bright red braces and a shirt of emerald green with a floppy collar. He used to profess a desire to be a painter, Sinclair recalled. He worked in the Coombe hospital, delivering babies, "by the yard, like sausages," as he said.

Now he plunged off, with their bottle of claret under his arm, and the last they saw of him was his tweed-clad, Bunteresque backside disappearing into the crowd. They looked at each other, smiling in dismay. Phoebe took Sinclair's hand and they set off upstairs, where it might be less crowded, and met the Delahaye twin and his girlfriend coming down. "Don't bother," Delahaye said, or yelled, rather, "it's bedlam up there!"

They went together, the four of them, down the short hall to the back of the house. Phoebe plucked at Sinclair's sleeve and put her mouth close to his ear. *"Which one of them is it?"* she asked, but Sinclair only lifted his hands helplessly and shook his head.

In the crowded kitchen they found paper cups and sloshed

them full of Mooney's Spanish Burgundy and went on out to the
garden, where the soft night air was a sudden balm. The garden
was really no more than a walled yard, smelling of drains and
dustbins, with a square of weed-choked clay and in one corner a
privy with a broken door. There was a crowd of people out here,
too, smoking and drinking. A couple were kissing in the shadow
of the privy. Beyond the back wall the moon was perched on a
distant chimney pot.

"This is Tanya Somers, by the way," the young Delahaye
said. He wore a black blazer and white sailing trousers with a
Trinity tie for a belt. "And I'm Jonas, in case you're wondering."
Phoebe and Sinclair smiled and shrugged as if to say that of
course they had known which twin he was. "People are never
sure, I know," Jonas said. "James is here somewhere," he added.

Tanya Somers had lazy good looks and a jaded manner. She
wore her hair long, in a smooth, gleaming black swath that
she kept pushing from her shoulders with negligent sweeps of
the hand. She made no attempt to hide the fact that she did
not know who Phoebe and Sinclair were, and that she was not
much interested in finding out. When she spoke, Phoebe recognized the Rathgar accent. "This wine is filthy," she said.
With a deft flick she emptied the contents of her cup into the
weeds. "I'm going to see if there's any beer." She went off at an
insolent slouch, tossing her hair back.

"I'm sorry about your father," Phoebe said to Jonas.

He shrugged. "Yes—I think people were a bit shocked to
see me—us—here, considering it only happened so recently. I
suppose they expected us to go into mourning for a year and a
day, like in the old song."

"Oh, I'm sure they'd understand," Phoebe said, too quickly.

Jonas Delahaye looked at her, the corners of his mouth twitching with amusement, and she felt herself flush and was glad of the darkness. "I mean," she went on, "it's not like the old days, when everybody used to go into mourning for months, it seemed." She felt Sinclair's elbow nudge her gently in the side. "Anyway, that's what I think," she finished lamely.

"Yes, well, I daresay you're right," Jonas said, doing his patrician drawl. He looked into the paper cup and frowned. "Tanny is right—this stuff is awful." And he too threw the wine into the weeds and, giving them both a quick little smile, stepped past them and went into the kitchen.

"Oh, God," Phoebe wailed softly.

"I don't really think he was offended," Sinclair said drily.

"And you, just standing there—you could have said something!"

He laughed. "Such as what? You were doing perfectly well yourself, digging the hole deeper and deeper." He cupped a hand fondly against her cheek. "Anyway," he said, "you're getting as bad as your father."

"What do you mean!"

"You know very well what I mean—poking your nose into other people's business, asking questions and looking for clues." Again he laughed, and this time pinched her cheek. "Our own Nancy Drew, female investigator."

She took a step backwards. "You—!" He reached out and took her in his arms. She beat her fists softly against his chest, and now she too was laughing. "Pig," she said.

"That's a nice thing to call a Jew."

She kissed him. "*My* Jew," she said softly, her breath mingling with his.

They went inside and for several minutes wandered about in the party, going in single file, Sinclair ahead and leading Phoebe by the hand, the two of them pressing themselves sideways through the dense, hot-smelling crowd. There was a gramophone somewhere, and now a new record began—Elvis Presley, of course, whining about his blue suede shoes. Phoebe had no ear for pop music.

They encountered the second Delahaye twin standing in the doorway of one of the bedrooms, talking to a dark-haired girl with a fringe. He had backed her against the doorjamb, and she was looking up at him out of large, luminous eyes as he leaned over her, one hand on the jamb and the other against the wall, enclosing her in an almost embrace, as if he would menace and at the same time caress her. He had a paper cup of wine in one hand and a smoldering cigarette in the other. A bright red handkerchief drooped from the breast pocket of his pale linen jacket. Sinclair tapped him on the shoulder. "Hello, James."

Delahaye turned his head. There was a bleared look in his eye. "Oh, hello, Sinclair," he said, slurring a little. "You here too? God, what a scrum, eh? This is"—he turned back to the girl— "what did you say your name was?"

"I didn't," the girl said, and smirked.

"Anyway, you're a smasher." He turned again and this time addressed Phoebe. "Isn't she a smasher?"

Phoebe gave him a cool bland smile and moved on, but not before she had linked a finger around Sinclair's thumb and tugged at it.

"Take care, James," Sinclair said. He smiled at the girl. "You too."

They found a corner of the bedroom that was inexplicably

free of people and immediately took possession of it. Breen's bed was heaped with discarded jackets and cardigans, and in the midst of the heap a couple lay on their sides facing each other, glued mouth to mouth. The boy's hand kept moving up the girl's stockinged leg, trying to get under the hem of her skirt, and she kept batting it away, with an almost lazy gesture. Phoebe and Sinclair tried to ignore them.

"You must admit," Phoebe said, "it's very strange, the way that man died."

"Which man?" Sinclair asked innocently. She smacked his hand.

"Don't tease, you," she said. "The twins' father, I mean, as you very well know."

"Funny," Sinclair said, "calling them twins. You never think of grown-ups being twins—but they certainly are. You never see one but you see the other."

Phoebe gave a little shudder. "I'd hate to be a twin—wouldn't you?"

He offered her a cigarette, but she shook her head, and he lit one for himself, thinking. "I don't know," he said. "I haven't even got a sibling."

"Well, neither have I."

They were silent briefly. The subject of Phoebe's past and parentage was a delicate one, not to be lightly alluded to. Quirke had not been a good father.

"I must say," Sinclair said, "they don't seem very—well, they don't seem very upset. Would you do it? Go out to a party?"

"I don't know."

The girl on the bed moaned softly. The boy had succeeded in

getting his hand under her skirt and was rummaging urgently in her lap. Phoebe turned away. Sinclair was half sitting against the sill of the little square window, and she had an urge to sit on his knee, but did not.

There was a square of moonlight in the window with two bars of shadow making an out-of-kilter cross. She realized that she had never before considered the possibility of her father dying, of his being dead. For the first nineteen years of her life she had thought Quirke was her uncle, and even still she was wrestling with the fact of what he really was to her. *Father* was not a word that sat easily in her mind, but father he was, and very much living. How would she feel if he were dead? She did not know, and this surprised her, and faintly appalled her.

"Of course, I know what you think," Sinclair said, mock-innocently again. "I heard you telling Jonas Delahaye—you're all for casting aside those old fuddy-duddy notions about mourning and all the rest of it."

"Oh, stop," she said distractedly. She was still puzzling over the prospect of Quirke's projected demise. Would she be sad? Of course she would. Would she suffer, would she grieve? That was an altogether different question.

The girl on the bed wriggled out of the boy's embrace and struggled up and sat there among the crumpled clothes, blinking, a hand plunged in her hair. The boy sat up too, more slowly, and pawed at her shoulder entreatingly. The girl wriggled again, and disconsolately he let fall his hand. The two of them seemed unaware that anyone else was in the room, although there were people milling at the foot of the bed and in the doorway.

In the moonlight at the window Sinclair, still seated awkwardly, put an arm around Phoebe's hips and drew her close to him. "I'm sorry," he said.

"Why?" She touched him under the chin and made him look up at her. "What are you sorry for?"

He glanced aside. "Oh, you know. Fathers. Death. All that."

"Yes," she said distantly, as if not to him but to someone else. "All that."

HE WOKE, IF IT COULD BE CALLED WAKING, INTO LIQUID DARKness. Everything was moving under him with a slewing, sideways roll that was familiar. He thought of his student days, when he was starting to drink, and after half a dozen beers he would wake in the middle of the night with a parched mouth and a thudding headache, while the bed on which he lay revolved slowly around him like a broken carousel. Also, he was wet. He was lying on his side with his legs drawn up to his chest and half his head submerged in water. It was seawater, he knew from the texture of it. A boat, then, but a boat that had something wrong with it. There was none of the sense of a boat's trim lightness; this vessel felt stodgy, like the barely floating hollowed-out stump of a tree.

He tried to sit up, and indeed saw himself doing it, as in a piece of trick photography, a wraith rising up out of himself while his body lay there lumpy and inert. The pain in the back of his head seemed a kind of noise, a dully pulsing roar that made the bones of his skull vibrate. He turned his head and peered up at the stars. They too seemed to be vibrating, zigzagging about, like fireflies. The last thing he had seen was the moon sliding down the sky—where was it now?

At last, with a groan, he got himself up to a sitting position. He had been wedged into the space between the two thwarts. His clothes were sopping. He put a hand cautiously to the back of his head and winced when he felt the pulpy knot under his ear. What had he been hit with? Something wooden. He looked about. Ahead there was only the darkly gleaming sea to the horizon, behind him were the lights of Dun Laoghaire, a long way off. And what was that? A boat, gliding away from him landwards, silent, white-sailed, a light glimmering at the tip of its mast. He tried to shout but his voice would not work. He was shivering now, sitting there in the slopping, warmish, deepening water. He looked to the mast. There was no sail: it had been taken away.

Deepening. The water was deepening.

He pressed forward onto his hands and knees and felt about, under the puddle of water. Sound workmanship, clinker-built. It was—could it be?—yes, it was the *Rascal,* his own twelve-footer. His questing hands, scrabbling and splashing, found what they had been looking for, what he had known they would find. Someone had taken a crowbar to the bottom of the boat and opened a crack between the boards six inches long and a good half inch wide; he could feel the current of colder water coming up through it, a silken flow. He had been scuttled. A strange calm came over him. *She's sinking,* he thought, *and I'm going to drown.*

It seemed almost a joke, a prank someone had played on him. Then panic surged up like bile and he plunged both his hands over the rent in the boards, as if that way he could stop the water coming in. But water was a thing that would not be stopped. He groaned and cursed. This was wrong, this was all wrong—he could not drown, it was impossible. He looked over his shoulder towards the other boat, but all he could see of it now was the mast light, swaying and winking. He tried again to cry out—*Help! Wait!*—but the paltry words stuck in his swollen throat. He began to weep helplessly. The bruise on the back of his head, as if angered by his tears, set up a violent hammering that drove him down on all fours again, with his head hanging.

The water was coming in faster now. He tried to stand but the blood rushed from his head and he fell over, making a great splash. The boat tipped heavily sideways and then righted itself, the water sloshing around his knees. He was very cold now, shivering in rhythmic spasms, and his teeth chattered. His mind raced, skittering this way and that, like a rat in a trap.

He stood up again, and this time managed to stay upright. He gazed at the far dark shore with its swaying lights. He thought of the people there, sleeping, dreaming, and of the ones who were awake, doing ordinary things, making love, drinking, fighting—alive, all of them. Would Sylvia be asleep? Maybe she was lying awake in the dark, wondering where he was. Or maybe she had got up: maybe she was standing at the window in the living room, looking out anxiously into the night, watching for him.

The water was up to the gunwales now, and lapping round his knees. Terror had tightened his throat and he could not swallow. The mast light of the other boat was no longer to be seen. He held his cold face in his hands.

No, he would not go this way, he would not let the boat take him with her. He sucked in a deep breath, the air rasping in his throat, then closed his eyes and clambered over the side.

How black the water was, wrapping him round like swaths of icy satin. He was a good swimmer, always had been. He should have taken off his clothes.

Mother! Oh, Jesus. Oh, God.

The pain pounded in his head. His arms were tired already, his muscles beginning to lock.

The lights of shore seemed farther off than ever.

He stopped flailing.

No good, no good.

Convolvulus.

TWO

9

ANOTHER FUNERAL, WITH THE SAME MOURNERS AS BEFORE, save the one who was in the coffin. Yet to Quirke the atmosphere this time was different, even though he could not at first say what the difference was. Perhaps it was just the weather. On the day of Victor Delahaye's funeral the sun had shone as if for a festival, but today there was rain, a fine warm mist that drifted down absently yet still managed to soak its way rapidly into everyone's clothes, so that the inside of the church smelled like a sheep pen.

He stood at the back as the priest, up at the altar, droned his way through the funeral Mass. He looked over the heads of the congregation, trying to identify individuals from behind. That was surely Mona Delahaye in the big floppy black hat, while the tall upright woman with the graying blond hair must be Jack Clancy's widow; and that would be her son beside her.

There was no mistaking the Delahaye twins, of course, with their long, straw-pale heads. Hackett was there too, in an aisle seat halfway up. Hackett without his hat, shiny-haired, with a bald patch, always seemed to Quirke somehow incomplete, a novice monk, perhaps, tonsured and prematurely aged.

There was another blond woman, younger than Mrs. Clancy, and nearer the back. She wore not a hat but a navy blue beret, jauntily tipped to the side, and a purple silk shawl over a dress of scarlet corduroy. In this flaunted outfit she had the look of a passionflower stuck in among a funeral wreath.

Two days after Jack Clancy's disappearance, his sunken boat, lodged on a sandbank five miles off the Muglins, had got tangled in a trawler's net and was dragged up. The trawler's skipper saw at once where the boards in the bottom had been pried apart and called the Guards. Another two days had elapsed before Clancy's body was washed into a stony cove at the back of Howth Head. Quirke had left the postmortem to Sinclair. Death by drowning, but there was the question of a bruise behind the ear. The old conundrum: Did he jump, or was he pushed? Did he sail out into the bay and make the hole in the bottom of the boat himself, or did someone bang him on the head and load him unconscious into the *Rascal* and force those boards apart?

It had been all over the papers. "SECOND TRAGEDY STRIKES CITY FIRM." "DEAD MAN'S BUSINESS PARTNER DROWNS." "By the Lord Harry," Inspector Hackett had said, lifting his hat and scratching his head with his little finger, "they're certainly doing an awful lot of dying, these folk."

When the Mass ended the undertaker's men carried the coffin to the waiting hearse, and the churchyard became a

mass of blossoming black umbrellas. The woman in the blue
beret was alone, and seemed to Quirke lost. He made his way
to her, a little surprised at himself, and offered her a cigarette.
She too was surprised, and gave him a questioning look.

"The name is Quirke," he said.

"Are you—?" She hesitated. "Are you a friend of the family?"
He shook his head, offering her his lighter. She gave a tight,
small laugh. "No, neither am I." She leaned down to the lighter's flame, then lifted her head back and blew smoke into the
air. "Bella Wintour. With an oh-you." He looked baffled, and
she laughed again, and spelled the name in full.

"Ah," he said, "I see." They were both aware of getting wet.
Out of the corner of his eye Quirke saw Hackett making his
way towards them. He touched a finger to Bella Wintour's
elbow. "I'm not going to the cemetery, are you? No? Cup of tea,
then?"

As they moved towards the gate they passed by Mona Delahaye, standing beside her father-in-law in his wheelchair, holding an umbrella over them both. She smiled at Quirke in her
deliberately sultry way, and he tipped his hat to her, and cleared
his throat.

"My my," Bella Wintour murmured as they went on, "widows
everywhere you turn."

THEY WENT TO THE ROYAL MARINE HOTEL AND SAT IN ARM-
chairs in the lounge. Bella's beret and the shoulders of Quirke's
suit were grayly furred from the fine rain. When the waitress
came Bella said that what she needed was not tea but a vodka
and tonic. "It is noon," she said. "Sun and yardarm and all that."

Quirke asked for whiskey, and the waitress sniffed and went away. "What is a yardarm, anyway?" Bella asked. "I've always wondered."

"No idea," Quirke said, producing his cigarettes again. "Not a sailing man, myself."

"No," she said, looking him up and down with a faint, sardonic glint, "I wouldn't have thought so."

She glanced about. He could see her sensing him watching her. The rainlight gave to the air in the room a quicksilver, melancholy sheen. Her wandering gaze came to rest on him again, a slightly strained amusement in her gray eyes. "I was Jack Clancy's girlfriend," she said. "One of them, at any rate." She twirled her cigarette in the ashtray and made a glowing pencil point of the tip. "Are you shocked?"

"Not shocked, no," Quirke said. "Curious."

"What's there to be curious about? If you knew anything about Jack, you'd know he was fond of the ladies."

"I don't know much about him at all."

"That's obvious." She leaned back against the dingy plush of the chair. "Are you"—she smiled in the surprise of hearing herself ask it—"are you a policeman?"

He shook his head. "Pathologist."

"I see. You must be dedicated to your job, if you attend the funerals of your—what do you call the people you pathologize? Not patients, surely."

"I don't think there is a word. Corpse. Cadaver."

"No longer people, then, just things."

He did not answer that.

The waitress came with their drinks. As the girl was setting

them out, Bella continued to examine Quirke with a quizzical
eye. Quirke paid and the waitress went off with another disapproving sniff. "Cheers," Bella said, lifting her glass. "Here's to
life, eh?"

They drank in silence for a time, both looking off in different directions now, aware of a constraint. They were strangers,
after all.

"So you knew Jack Clancy," Quirke said.

She was looking towards the windows still, towards the pools
of silvery light congregated there. "Yes, I knew him. On and
off—you know. He used to call in, now and then." She glanced
at him, and shrugged, and gave her mouth a sadly grim little
twist. Then she looked away again. When she lifted her glass
it cast a metallic uplight on her throat. Quirke tried to guess
her age. Forty? More? A woman on her own, beginning to
wonder if independence was all it was cracked up to be. "In
fact," she said, "he called in that night, the night that he—the
night that he died."

"Did he," Quirke said, keeping all emphasis out of his voice.

Bella nodded, sucking in her underlip. "I keep going over it,"
she said, "over and over, what he said, how he seemed, the way
he looked."

"And?"

She shrugged again. "And nothing." She stubbed her cigarette
into the ashtray. The butt kept burning, sending up a skein of
acrid smoke. "There was something on his mind, all right," she
said. "It was his second visit to me in the space of days, though
I hadn't seen him in—oh, I don't know. Years."

"And what did he say?"

She gave him a sharp look. "What did he say about what?"

He opened his hands in front of her, showing his palms. "I don't know. You said there was something on his mind."

"And so there was. But he didn't *say* anything." She seemed angry suddenly. "He wasn't the kind of person to *say* things. Or maybe"—she sighed, and shook her head—"maybe he was but he just didn't say them to me. We weren't what you'd call close, at least not in that way."

Quirke was aware of a faint but burgeoning inner warmth, as if a pilot light in his breast had flickered into life. He recognized the sensation. He savored slightly illicit occasions such as this, a rainy lunchtime in a shabby hotel bar, with the fumes of strong drink in his nostrils and sitting opposite him a blonde of a certain age, circumspect and feisty, whose game eye seemed to offer possibilities that, if followed up in the right way, might lend a larger glow to the long afternoon stretching before them. He was supposed to be at the hospital, but Sinclair would cover for him. He thought of Isabel Galloway. She was rehearsing something by Chekhov that was coming to the Gate.

"Shall we have another?" he said to Bella Wintour.

HE LIKED HER LITTLE LIGHT-FILLED HOUSE. SHE MADE COFFEE for them, and they sat side by side on the sofa in the garden room, facing the big window. She told him this was where she had last sat with Jack Clancy. At such a moment another woman would have shed a tear, or produced a sorrowful sniff, but not this one. The rain had stopped and a watery sun was struggling to shine, and the garden sparkled, and a virtuoso thrush was doing its liquid whistling. Quirke would have preferred a drink but sipped his coffee with as much good grace as he could muster.

Bella had kicked off her shoes and sat sideways on the sofa with her bare, pink-soled feet drawn up. She was smoking one of his cigarettes. She had set a big glass ashtray on the sofa between them. Quirke was eyeing the chipped crimson polish on her toenails. He found women's feet at once endearing and slightly repellent. He made himself look into the garden. "What's that flower?" he asked. "The one with the white blossoms shaped like the end of a trumpet."

"It's a weed," Bella said. "I can't remember the name."

"There's a lot of it."

"Yes. It'll choke everything else, apparently, if I don't do something about it." She shifted the position of her legs, grunting, and refolded them under her. "Tell me what your interest is," she said.

"What?"

"In Jack Clancy. In his death."

He said nothing for a moment, tapping his cigarette on the edge of the ashtray, his eyes hooded. "Why do you think," he said, "he would have committed suicide?"

She widened her eyes. "Is that what they're saying, that he killed himself? The papers only said he drowned."

"He was an expert sailor—he had trophies to prove it."

"Even experts make mistakes."

He nodded, still with his gaze downcast. "There was some bruising, to the head."

"Bruising? What sort of bruising?"

"To the back, just here." He lifted a hand to his own head to show her. "A bad one. The blow would have knocked him unconscious."

"He had a fall, then?"

"Maybe. There was no sail on the boat."

"What happened to it?"

He shrugged. "Currents tore it off, maybe."

"Is that possible?"

"I don't know. *I'm* certainly no expert when it comes to boats."

She sat very still, hardly breathing, looking into his eyes. "You think he was killed, don't you," she said.

"I don't know. Someone might have hit him on the head and put him in the boat and taken the sail away so that if he woke up he wouldn't be able to hoist it and get back to land."

"Someone?"

He stubbed out his cigarette and rose and walked to the window and stood with his back to the room, looking out. "You remind me of Jack," Bella said behind him, "standing there. Only you're bigger."

Quirke made no comment. "You're sure he didn't tell you, that night, what was on his mind?" he asked.

"I told you," she said, "Jack and I weren't like that, we weren't—intimate."

He glanced at her over his shoulder. "You weren't?"

"I *told* you—not that way. And for God's sake don't keep standing there like that, will you?"

He came back to the sofa, but did not sit. "I think I should go," he said. He found he was as much surprised by this as she was.

She looked up at him, tightening her lips and moving her teeth as if she were nibbling on a small hard seed. "Why did you come here?" she asked.

"Because you invited me."

She was still watching him, her eyes narrowed. "You came to see what you could find out about Jack, didn't you."

"Yes."

At the front door, as he was putting on his hat, she asked if he would come to see her again. He chose to misunderstand, and said that if there was anything she wanted to tell him, or to ask him, she could call him at the hospital. She smiled coldly. "That wasn't what I meant," she said. "But it doesn't matter."

Before he reached the garden gate she had shut the door.

INSPECTOR HACKETT FELT PUT OUT. HE HAD CAUGHT QUIRKE pretending not to see him in the churchyard, before he went off with the woman in the beret. He tried not to mind, but he did. Of course, he knew about Quirke and women; but all the same.

Who was the blonde, anyway? he wondered. Somehow he did not think she was a relative of the dead man. He had spent his working life studying people, how they looked, the stances they took, the way they moved, and he had seen at once that this woman did not belong among the Clancys or the Delahayes. He guessed she must be one of Jack Clancy's old flames— Jack was rumored to have had quite a few. And Quirke would have spotted her straightaway for who she was, being something of an expert himself in that particular field. The blonde, he thought, would be well able for Quirke. He chuckled. Poor old Quirke, always getting himself in the soup.

Once out of the church gate he walked down to the seafront and turned right along Queen's Road. A pleasant way, with the trees in heavy leaf and the fine houses standing back in seclusion behind them. A feeble rain was falling; he disregarded it. He liked the smell of rain on grass and leaves; it reminded him of his boyhood and his grandfather's farm. Happy times, long gone.

This was a peculiar business. First Delahaye had done away with himself and now Jack Clancy is drowned. What the connection was between the two deaths he did not know; not yet. But there had to be a connection. Quirke was convinced Clancy had been murdered, because of the knock to the head. This seemed fanciful to Hackett, but he trusted Quirke's instincts in these matters. Quirke knew the dead the way he himself knew the living. He chuckled again.

It was only a bit after noon but he realized he was hungry. He retraced his steps, leaving the seafront behind and climbing the hill towards the town. Halfway up he stopped at a pub—Clancy's; now there was a coincidence—and sat on a stool at the bar and ordered a ham sandwich and a glass of red lemonade. The barman, a pustular fellow with a missing front tooth, lent him a copy of the *Press* to read. "MINISTER URGES HIGHER TURF PRODUCTION." Emigration was up, burglaries were down—the one, no doubt, the consequence of the other. "ANIMAL GANG MEMBER SENTENCED." He sipped his lemonade, the syrupy sweet taste another echo of boyhood days. As his eye skimmed the columns of print his mind kept drifting back to the question of Jack Clancy's death, touching it lightly here and there, as if it were the man's corpse itself. Clancy's son had been on the boat when Delahaye had shot himself—his presence there a thing for which no explanation had yet presented itself—and then Clancy himself goes down in a boat that either he or some other or others had scuttled. An eye for an eye, a tooth for a tooth? That had to be it. Vengeance. But who was the avenger, and what was the cause?

There was a flurry of movement and a young man with red hair perched himself on the stool next to his. Hackett sighed. The bloody pub was empty, yet this fellow had to choose to sit right here beside him. He concentrated on the paper, frowning irritably. *Productivity, the Minister said, was the key to solving the country's economic and social problems.*

"Hello, Inspector," the young man beside him said. He turned. Widow's peak, narrow face, freckles. Who—? Reporter, yes. Jimmy somebody. The *Mail*? The young man seemed mildly offended not to have been recognized straightaway. "Minor," he said. "Jimmy Minor."

"Ah, yes," Hackett put on a large, slow smile. "One of our representatives from the fourth estate, if I'm not greatly mistaken."

Jimmy Minor took out a packet of Gold Flake, lit one, put the packet away. "Thanks, no, I won't," the Inspector said with soft sarcasm. Minor took no notice. Hackett took a bite of his sandwich.

"You were at the funeral," Jimmy Minor said.

"Were you there?" the Inspector said, chewing. "I didn't see you."

"We blend into the crowd, us fourth estaters."

Hackett was fascinated by the way the young man smoked,

almost violently, twisting up his mouth and sucking at the cigarette as if he were performing an unpleasant task that had been imposed on him and that he was condemned to keep carrying out, over and over. He had ordered a glass of stout and a sandwich, and now the barman brought them.

"Were you there for the paper?" the Inspector asked.

"No."

"Ah." Minor had lifted a corner of the sandwich and was examining doubtfully the slice of bright orange cheese underneath and the thin smear of butter. "Just curiosity, then?" Hackett said. It came to him that Minor was a friend of Quirke's daughter, Phoebe. A sort of friend, anyhow—friendship, he surmised, was not likely to be a thing that Minor would give much energy to. The barman, idling behind a skittle row of beer taps, was fingering an angry red crater on his chin. Hackett watched him, regretting the sandwich he had just eaten, which those fingers had probably assembled.

"Well," Minor said, with the air of a man getting down to business, wiping a thin line of creamy beer froth from his upper lip, "what do you think?"

Hackett could not take his appalled eye off the barman and those probing fingernails. "What do I think of what?" he asked distractedly.

Minor snickered. "This business with Clancy and Delahaye, the two of them gone within less than a fortnight of each other."

"A remarkable coincidence, all right," the Inspector said mildly, and took a sip of his lemonade.

Minor turned to him with an exaggerated stare of incredulity. "A coincidence?" he said. "Do you think I came down in the last shower, or what?"

Hackett brought out a packet of Player's and with pointed courtesy offered Minor a cigarette, which Minor was about to take when he realized he already had a Gold Flake going.

"So tell me," the Inspector said, "what do you think these two misfortunate deaths were due to, if not coincidence?"

"There's no such thing as coincidence." Minor was waggling his empty glass, trying to catch the attention of the dreamy barman. "I think," he said, "there's something distinctly—another glass here!—something distinctly queer about the whole thing. I hear, for instance, that Clancy had half his head knocked off before the boat went down. He hardly did that to himself."

Hackett sighed. This, he reflected, was how things got about, to muddy the water and darken the air. "Half his head, you say? I hadn't heard that."

It was clear that Minor did not believe him.

"And furthermore," Minor said, as the barman slid a second glass of Guinness across the counter to him, "I hear there's something going on behind the stout high walls of Delahaye and Clancy, Limited." He waggled his fingers. "Hands in tills, that kind of thing."

Inspector Hackett, taking a slow draw of his cigarette, leaned back on the stool and squinted at the ceiling. "Is that so?" he said, eyeing the light fixtures. "I must say, Mr. Minor, you seem to hear an awful lot of things, in the course of your day." Two forty-watt bulbs in flowerpot-shaped lampshades made of that tallow-colored stuff that looked like stretched human skin. Mrs. Hackett, he thought, would not be impressed. "And do you hear," he asked, "whose hand it was that got slammed in the till?"

Minor drank his Guinness, giving himself another mustache of lather. "I'm guessing the late Mr. Clancy was involved."

"Ah, yes," Hackett said, "that would be a reason for the poor man to put an end to himself, if he had been found out."

Minor stared at him sideways. "You think it was suicide?" he said incredulously.

Hackett waved a hand in mild dismissal. "I don't think anything," he said. "You're the one that's doing all the thinking."

Minor was silent for a moment, watching the policeman out of a narrowed eye. "Look, Inspector," he said, lowering his voice, "you and I could help each other in this."

"Could we?" Hackett asked, in a tone of large surprise. "How would that be, now?"

Minor would have none of the policeman's feigned innocence, and shook his head impatiently. "I hear things, you know things," he said. "What's wrong with a fair trade?"

The Inspector smiled almost indulgently. "Ah, Jimmy my lad, I don't think it works that way." He took his hat from the bar and stepped down off the stool. "I don't think it works that way at all."

He nodded, and put on his hat, and sauntered away, whistling softly.

IT RAINED AT FIRST, A NASTY DRIZZLE THAT CLUNG LIKE GREASE to the windscreen, but once Maggie had got past Carlow the clouds broke and the sun struggled through. Drifts of cottony white mist clung to the tops of the mountains off to the left— hills, really, she could not remember what they were called— and everything shimmered and glowed, the trees and the wet

green fields and the tarmac of the road before her. It would be
so lovely at Ashgrove, the countryside there always looked so
dramatic in weather like this. The only blemish on the day was
the guilty niggle that she could not free herself of. Was she
running away? But even if she was, what of it? They had hardly
noticed her going, the twins and Mona, of course, but even
her father, too. They were probably glad to be rid of her, the lot
of them. After all, was she not, in her heart, glad to be rid of
them?

She tried to think of things to distract herself from these
troubling matters. Her name, for instance. Marguerite Delahaye. It was a nice name, she thought. She should never have
allowed herself to be called Maggie: it sounded so common.
Miss Marguerite Delahaye, late of Dublin and now of Ashgrove House in the County of Cork.

Everything felt strange. It was strange the way time went
on, calmly as ever; it seemed shameful, somehow. Surely there
should be another pace for things to move at, after all that had
happened. Death had stepped so suddenly into her life, like a
thief, no, like a robber, brutal and violent. She had wept for
Victor so much and for so long that she felt dried up now. Arid,
that was the word; she felt arid. The bitterness had not abated.
She suspected it never would abate. She imagined it, a sort of
knot inside her. She had thought it would shift after Jack
Clancy died, but it had not, it was still there, a hard dry chan-
cre of bitterness lodged under her heart. And yet she felt lightened, too, lightened in spirit. It was as if a burden had been set
on her shoulders but she had managed to shrug it off. She was
free. The road unwound before her as if it would never end.
All that hate and horror was behind her. Yes, she was free.

She closed her eyes for a second and when she opened them there was a child on a bicycle in the road in front of her. She pressed hard on the brake pedal and wrenched the wheel first to the right and then to the left, and the car bounced onto the grass verge and the engine gave a great roar, as if enraged, and abruptly cut out. There was a smell of exhaust smoke and hot rubber. She looked in the rearview mirror. The child had stopped too, a girl of eight or nine, with dirty curls and a dirtier face. It was an adult's bike she had, much too big for her, so that she had to reach up to grasp the handlebars. Where had she come from, as if out of nowhere? Maggie in her mind saw with awful clarity what so easily might have been, the mangled bike on its side, its front wheel spinning, and beside it the motionless form lying on the road like a little pile of bloodstained rags. *It's following me,* she thought. *Death is following me.*

She stopped in the next town—she did not notice its name—and found a hotel, a dingy place smelling of boiled cabbage, and sat in a corner of the bar and drank a glass of brandy. It made her cough at first, for she was not used to spirits. A man came in and sat at the next table. He was a big florid fellow, with thick lips and starting eyes. He wore a tweed jacket and a yellow waistcoat, and gaiters—she had not seen anyone wearing gaiters since she was a child. He went to the bar and ordered whiskey—*a ball of malt,* she heard him say—and came swaggering back to the table, grinning at her as he went past.

She tried to ignore him but there was something grossly fascinating about him. He sat at the table with his legs opened wide, showing off the big round bulge in the crotch of his trousers. Each time he took a sip of his drink he would let the whiskey flow back into the glass, mixed with spit that sank to the bottom of the glass, stringy and white. He spoke to her, remarking what a grand day it was, thank God, now that the rain had cleared. She did not answer, only gave a quick cool smile, nodding. He asked if she was staying in the hotel. No, she said; she was on her way to West Cork. "Cork!" he said. "Sure, I'm from Bandon, myself." She nodded again. She had gone hot, and could feel a flush rising up from her throat. The man asked if she would care for another drink—"A bird never flew on one wing!"—but she thanked him and said no, that she would have to be on her way. He grinned again, and wished her a safe journey, and asked her, with a laugh, to say hello to Bandon for him, if she happened to be going in that direction.

She gathered her things, her handbag, the car keys, her chiffon scarf, and stood up. She was afraid that he would reach out and touch her as she went past, would catch hold of her cardigan or try to grab her hand. But then she noticed that he was looking at her strangely; his expression had changed and he seemed surprised, even shocked. She must have said something to him, though she had no idea what. She often did that nowadays, blurted things out without thinking. Sometimes she even spoke without knowing she had done so, and she wouldn't realize it until she saw people backing away from her, looking offended or frightened. Her father had threatened more than once to have her put away; especially now, she would have to be careful and guard her tongue.

In the car she had to sit quite still for a minute to calm herself, but then it occurred to her that the man in the gaiters might come out and try to accost her again, and she started up the engine and drove away quickly.

She could not wait to get to Ashgrove.

10

MONA DELAHAYE TELEPHONED HIM AT THE HOSPITAL. THE GIRL
on the switchboard got the name wrong, and said there was
a Mrs. Delaney wishing to speak to him. He knew no Mrs.
Delaney, but asked for her to be put through anyway. When
he heard Mona's voice he felt a sudden tightness under his
shirt collar that surprised him. As she spoke he pictured her
thin wide crimson mouth, curved in a smile of malicious
enjoyment—he had told her of the mix-up in the names, and
she had laughed delightedly—and he could almost feel her hot
breath coming to him all the way down the line. He asked
what he could do for her and she suggested he might come to
the house, as there were things she wanted to speak to him
about. "No one will tell me anything," she said, with a pout in
her voice. He did not know what she meant by this. What

were the things she was not being told, he wondered, and who were the people who were not telling them to her?

He put his head in at the door of the dissecting room. Sinclair was there, getting ready to operate on the corpse of a tinker girl who had drowned herself in the sea off Connemara. "Have to go out," Quirke said. "You'll hold the fort?" Sinclair looked at him. Sinclair was used to holding the fort. "Mrs. Victor Delahaye wants to see me," Quirke added, thinking an explanation was required. Sinclair had the gift of making him feel guilty.

Sinclair considered the scalpel in his hand. "Maybe she's going to confess to killing Jack Clancy," he said.

"Oh, I'm sure," Quirke said. "I'll be back in an hour."

On Northumberland Road the recently rained-on pavements were steaming in the sun, and the humid perfume of sodden flowers and wet loam hung heavy on the air. The maid with the rusty curls opened the door to him. With her grin and her green eyes she reminded him of a young woman he had encountered years before, in a convent. Maisie, she was called. He wondered what had become of her. Nothing good, he suspected. He had not even known her surname.

He was shown into the drawing room, where he stood in front of the sofa with his hands in his pockets, looking idly at the Mainie Jellett abstract and rocking back and forth on his heels. The window and the sunlit garden beyond were reflected in the glass, so that he had to move his head this way and that to see the picture properly. He did not think much of it but supposed he must be missing something. Around him the house was drowsily silent. It still did not feel like a house in mourning.

Mona Delahaye entered. She shut the door and stood leaning against it with her hands behind her back, her head lowered, smiling up at him. Today she wore black slacks and a
green silk blouse and gold-painted sandals. Her toenail polish
matched her scarlet lipstick. "Thanks for coming," she said.
"Like a drink?" She went to the big rosewood sideboard, where
bottles were set out in ranks on a silver charger. "Gin?" she
said. "Or are you a whiskey man?"

"Jameson, if you have it."

"Oh, we have everything." She glanced over her shoulder,
doing her cat smile. "I'll join you."

She came to him bearing two glasses and handed one to him.

"Thanks," he said.

"Chin chin." She drank, and grimaced. "God," she said
hoarsely, "I don't know how you drink this stuff—liquid fire."

She stood very close to him, half a head shorter, her civet
scent stinging his nostrils. The top three buttons of her blouse
were open, and he looked down between her small pale breasts
and saw the sprinkling of freckles there. "There was something you wanted to speak to me about?" he said.

"Did I?"

"That's what you said on the phone."

"Oh, yes." She was gazing vaguely at his tie. "It's just that no
one tells me anything." She lifted her eyes to his. "Your friend
the detective—what's his name?"

"Hackett. Inspector Hackett."

"That's it. He has a way of talking without saying anything.
Have you noticed?"

"Yes," Quirke said, "I've noticed that. What would you like
him to say?"

She was looking into her glass now. "I think I've had enough of this, thank you," she said. She returned to the sideboard and put down the undrunk whiskey and took another glass and poured into it an inch of gin and a generous splash of tonic. She lifted the lid of a silver bucket and swore under her breath. "No ice, again," she said.

There were certain women, Quirke was thinking, who seemed doubly present in a room. It was as if there was the woman herself and along with her a more vivid version of her, an invisible other self that emanated from her and surrounded her like an aura. It came to him that he very much wanted to see Mona Delahaye without her clothes on. His grip tightened on the whiskey glass. Her husband was hardly cold in his grave.

"The thing is," she said, turning with her glass and moving towards the white sofa, "people think I'm stupid." She glanced back at him. "You, for instance—you think I'm completely brainless, don't you." He could see no way of replying to this. She sat down on the sofa with a not unhappy little sigh. "That's why you'd like to go to bed with me." She smiled and drank at the same time, looking up at him merrily. "Come," she said softly, patting the place beside her, "come and sit down." He hesitated. It was the playful lightness of her tone that made the moment seem all the more dangerous. "Oh, come on," she said, "I won't bite you."

He went to the sideboard and poured another whiskey, trying not to let the neck of the bottle rattle against the glass. He could feel her watching him, smiling. He went and perched on the arm of the sofa, at the opposite end from where she sat, as he had done the first time he was here, with Hackett. "What is

it you want to know?" he asked. "The reason why your husband killed himself?"

"Oh, no," she said, "I know that, more or less." She crossed
her legs and draped one arm along the back of the sofa. She
lifted her glass to her lips, but did not drink, and wrinkled her
nose instead. "Gin without ice is sort of disgusting, isn't it."
Quirke thought of another woman, sitting on another sofa, with
a glass of warm gin in her hand. Mona Delahaye was watching
him, reading his mind. "Are you married, Dr. Quirke?" she
asked.

"No."

"You have a sort of married look about you."

"I was married, a long time ago. My wife died."

Mona nodded. "That's sad," she said, with calm indifference.
She went on scanning his face, her thin mouth lifted at the
corners. "So you're a gay bachelor, then."

"More or less." He swirled the whiskey in his glass. "Why
did your husband kill himself?"

She took her arm from the back of the sofa and leaned forward. "Oh, I didn't mean that I *know*," she said dismissively. "I
sort of do." She paused, looking at the narrow gold band on the
third finger of her left hand. "He was terribly—well, terribly
jealous, in a ridiculous sort of way. He used to worry that I had
a lover"—she smiled—"or lovers, even."

"And did you?"

She ignored the question. "He was forever going on about
it," she said, "until I got bored, and then of course I'd start
to tease him. Awful of me, I know, but I couldn't resist it." She
looked at him again, frowning. "Did you know my husband?"

"I met him at a reception once, I can't remember where."

"Was I there?"

"I believe you were."

"That's odd. Surely I would have remembered meeting you." She smiled slyly, then frowned again, and let her eyes slide away from his until she was gazing at nothing. "He had no sense of humor, that was the trouble—none at all. And that really is very boring, you know, if you're married to the person." She finished her drink and rolled the empty glass between her palms. The shadow of a cloud darkened the window for a second and then the brightness flooded back. "Honestly," Mona said, glancing towards the window, "you'd think it was April, wouldn't you." She looked at him again. "He left a note, did I mention that?"

"No," Quirke said, "you didn't mention that."

"Well, he did. But look"—she shook her head at him with pretended displeasure—"I wish you wouldn't sit there like that, all tensed up like a corkscrew. Sit here, beside me—come on."

"Mrs. Delahaye," Quirke said, "I'm really not sure why you asked me here today."

"No," she said brightly, "neither am I. But it would be nice if you came and sat down." She smiled. "We could discuss the matter," she said, in a husky tone of mock solemnity. "You like discussing things, don't you?"

He got to his feet and stood irresolute. His glass was empty again. He felt dizzy. What was he to do? The woman on the sofa sat at her ease, looking up at him, with what might have been a warmly sympathetic smile, as if she understood his dilemma. She held up her glass. "Get us both another drink," she said. "I'd like one, and I think you need one."

He took his time at the sideboard, pouring the drinks. When he carried them to the sofa Mona tasted hers and shook her head. "No," she said, "I can't drink another one without ice. Would you be a dear—? The kitchen is at the end of the hall." She indicated with her thumb. "Sarah will be there, she'll show you."

He took the ice bucket and walked with it down the hall, into the dim recesses of the house. Sarah the maid was not to be found; he had once been in love with a woman named Sarah, who was dead, now. The kitchen was large and impersonal, and smelled faintly of gas. The squat refrigerator stood in a corner murmuring to itself, like a white-clad figure kneeling in rapt prayer. He extracted the crackling ice tray from its compartment and took it to the sink and struggled with it, the pads of his fingers sticking to the plump cubes sunk in their metal chambers. At last he thought of turning the tray over and running the tap on it, and then of course the cubes all fell out at once with a clatter and he had to chase them round the bottom of the sink with fingers that by now were turning numb.

At last he got the cubes into the bucket and set off back through the house. In the hallway he heard voices, and as he was passing by a door it opened suddenly and one of the Delahaye twins, coming out, stopped on the threshold and looked at him in surprise. He was dressed in white, as usual—white sports shirt, duck trousers, plimsolls—and carried a wooden tray with glasses on it. Quirke glanced past the young man's shoulder into the room. There was a billiard table, and a darkly pretty girl was sitting on it, with her left foot on the floor and her right leg raised, her hands clasped around her knee. The other twin stood in front of her, with a hand resting on her hip. Impassive, they returned his stare. No one spoke. In a second or two the little tableau—Quirke in the hall, the twin in the doorway, and the couple at the table—was over, and Quirke passed on. He had a strange feeling of lightness, as if he were passing through a dream.

Mona Delahaye was reclining now against the back of the sofa. She uncrossed her legs slowly and leaned forward, holding up her glass, into which he dropped a handful of ice from the bucket. "You're such a pet," she said, watching the cubes jostle amid the tonic bubbles.

Quirke retrieved his whiskey glass and sat down again on the arm of the sofa. "You say your husband left a note," he said.

"Yes." She frowned, as if petulantly. "I threw it away. Burned it, actually. Or did I flush it down the you-know-what?" She twinkled at him. "You see? I'm such a scatterbrain."

"May I ask what he said—what he wrote?"

"Oh, silly stuff. How much he loved me and how jealous he was—all that, the usual." She sipped her drink thoughtfully. "There's really nothing you can do for people who are jealous, is there. And they make such a—such a *spectacle* of themselves. It's always too pitiful." She looked at him. "Don't you think?"

He drank his whiskey, then brought out his cigarettes and offered her one, and took one himself. Leaning down with his lighter he looked again into the front of her blouse. Her skin was so pale there, and would be so soft to touch. "Was he jealous of Jack Clancy?" he asked.

She gave a little silvery laugh. "Oh, he was jealous of everyone," she said. She pushed out her lower lip and directed a thin stream of smoke upwards past his face.

"Is that why he tried to kill his son?"

She frowned in puzzlement. "What?"

"Because he was jealous, is that why he abandoned young Clancy in the boat miles offshore and left him to fry in the sun? To get back at his father?"

She gave him an odd look, tight-lipped and wide-eyed, as if he had said something richly funny at which she must not allow herself to laugh. "I hadn't thought of that," she said, blinking slowly, trying to show him how impressed she was by his perceptiveness. "I'm sure you're right. In fact, I'm sure he intended to kill Davy, but lost his nerve at the last minute and shot himself instead. It would be just the kind of thing Victor would do. He really wasn't very—he wasn't very *competent*, you know. He had this reputation as a ruthless businessman"—she broke off for a second to laugh again, almost in delight—"but it was all nonsense. He hadn't an idea. It was his father who kept the business going, even after he was supposed to have retired. Then when poor old Sam had his stroke that creep Maverley stepped in and took charge. And there was Jack, of course— Jack knew the business inside out." She darted her cigarette in the direction of the ashtray that she had set on the floor beside her foot. "Victor's trouble was his mother. You wouldn't have known her—a real monster, hiding behind a mask of niceness. She ruined him, gave him ridiculous ideas of how clever and important he was, at the same time working away to undermine his confidence. *Oh, Victor, don't try to be like your father,* she'd say, *you couldn't possibly be like him.* And she'd smile, very sweetly, and pat his hand. It's her he should have killed, though conveniently she died."

Forgetting himself, he slid down from his place on the sofa arm until he was sitting beside her. She smiled, and it seemed for a moment she might move sideways and lean her head on his shoulder, or nestle against his chest. "Will you tell me what was in the note—the suicide note?" he asked.

She stared at him, again with that look of almost laughing. "I didn't say it was a *suicide* note," she said. "Just a note. He often wrote things down that he couldn't bring himself to say."

"And what was it he wrote that last time—what was it he couldn't say?"

"I told you—about being jealous."

"Of Jack Clancy?"

"Um." She dipped a finger into her glass and stirred the gin and what was left of the ice cubes, then put the tip of the finger into her mouth and sucked it, looking at him sidelong. He held her gaze. He was acutely aware of the presence of others in the house, of Sarah the maid, of the twins, and that dark-haired girl. What had the three of them been up to in the billiard room? Nothing good, he was sure of that.

"Did you know what he was going to do?" he asked. She shook her head, still with her finger in her mouth. "But you weren't surprised," he said softly.

She took his glass from his hand and rose and walked to the sideboard and poured them each yet another drink. "What do you know about me?" she asked, busy with bottles, glasses, ice.

"Know about you?"

"Yes. Where I'm from, for instance. Can you tell from my accent?" He had not noticed an accent. "Maybe I've lost it," she said.

She brought their drinks and gave him his and sat down again beside him.

"We'll both be drunk," Quirke said.

She folded one leg under herself with balletic grace. "Yes," she said gaily, "that's my aim." She clinked her glass against his. "Bottoms up."

The whiskey this time burned his throat. He needed to eat something. He was beginning to hear himself breathe, and that was always a bad sign. Drink seemed not to affect Mona Delahaye, except to lend her expression a brightly impish gleam.

"So," he said, "where are you from?"

"You really can't tell? I don't know whether to be glad or not—I mean about having lost my accent. I'm from South Africa. My name, my"—she giggled—"my maiden name, used to be Vanderweert." Quirke nodded. He could not imagine this woman ever having been a maiden. "I was born in Cape Town," she said. "Ever been there? Very beautiful."

"You're a long way from home, then."

Her look became pensive. "Yes, I suppose so. Though it's hardly home, anymore." She glanced at him, smiling. "I suppose you're thinking of diamond mines, and kaffirs being flogged, and so on, while I loll on the verandah in the cool of evening drinking something tall with ice in it and admiring the sun setting behind Table Mountain. Not like that, I'm afraid, not like that at all. My father was—is—a civil servant, third class, as they say. I grew up in a bungalow in Parow."

"Where's that?"

"Suburb of Cape Town. Not the loveliest spot on earth."

"How did you meet your husband?"

"Victor?" she said, as if she had forgotten that she had once had a husband. "He was visiting Cape Town, pretending to be on business—he loved to travel about the world, being the high-powered executive—and I was working as a typist in the office of one of the firms he called in to. He took me to dinner, we danced, the moon rose, and by morning the deal was clinched." She was watching him, ironical and amused. "The way things really happen is always grubby, isn't it. I could have lied to you, you realize that. I could have said I was a De Beers heiress, and that Victor had to plead for my hand with my father the plutocrat, and you wouldn't have known any better. But I thought you'd prefer the truth. I thought you *deserved* the truth, dull as it is." She chuckled. "Victor would be furious—he liked to pretend I was the daughter of some grand colonial family. Poor Victor."

She looked convincingly sad for a moment. Quirke had an urge to take her hand; he must not drink any more, he must not. "I'm sorry," he said, "I never properly offered you my condolences."

She brightened. "Oh, how sweet!" she said. "But really, it's all right. In fact, at times like this you need someone absolutely heartless around, to buck you up." She turned her head and peered at him, looking deep into his eyes. "You do want to go to bed with me, don't you?" she said. "I wasn't wrong about that, was I?"

He did not know how to reply. The feline candor of her gaze both unnerved and excited him. He was sweating a little. He was glad of the commonplace things around them, the room, the sunlight in the garden, the presence of other people in the house. Surely she was teasing him, being scandalous to see how he would take it.

"Tell me what you think about Jack Clancy," he said, to be saying something.

"What I think about him?" she said. The light in her eye was more erratic now, and when she frowned it was as if she had lost the thread of something and was having trouble finding it again. The gin having its effect at last; he was faintly relieved.

"About what happened to him, in the boat," he said.

"Don't you know? I thought you knew everything, you and your detective friend."

He leaned forward and put his glass carefully on the floor and clasped his hands before him. He could clearly hear the air rushing in his nostrils, in his chest, and knew he was drunk. Not seriously drunk, not drunk drunk, but drunk, all the same.

"Jack Clancy drowned," he said, "but before he did, someone or something hit him on the head."

"Oh, yes?" she said absently. He was not sure she had been listening. She leaned down to pick up his glass from where it stood on the carpet between his feet. He moved to stop her. "Come on," she said, "just one more, and then we can go and see if there's anything to eat for lunch."

He would not let her have his glass, but took hers and walked with both to the sideboard. He had intended to leave them firmly there, yet found himself refilling them. Just one more, as she had said; a last one. The skin of his forehead had tightened alarmingly, and there seemed a very faint mist in front of his eyes that would not clear no matter how often he blinked. He carried the glasses back to the sofa. Something was scratching at the back of his mind, insistently, but he ignored it. Just this one, and then he would leave.

He realized he was leaning over her, she seated and he

standing, grinning, and swaying a little. A great wash of happiness, childish and vacant, swept through him like a thrilling gust of wind. *Quirke,* he told himself, *you are a damned fool.*

HE WOKE WITH A START AND DID NOT KNOW WHERE HE WAS. The light in the room was shadowed, but there was a rich warm tint to it of old gold. High ceiling, a plaster cornice on four sides, the walls painted apple green. Two windows, lofty, the curtains of heavy yellow silk, drawn, with sunlight in them. Wardrobe, dressing table, a hinged screen, silk again, swooping birds painted on it. He lay amid tangled sheets, under a satin eiderdown, much too hot. There was sweat on his upper lip and in the hollow above his clavicle. His tongue burned, whiskey-raw. He remembered, of course. *Oh, Lord.*

She lay at his side, her back turned to him, her hair splashed like a rich dark stain on the pillow. She was snoring softly. He eased himself out of the bed, sliding his legs sideways under the eiderdown and setting his feet cautiously on the floor, and crossed the room at a crouch, looking for his clothes.

"Going already?" she said behind him. He straightened, turned, his heart sinking. She was lying on her back now, with an arm under her head, looking at him along the lumpy length of the eiderdown. "Give us a fag before you go," she said.

When he bent to pick up his clothes from where he had discarded them on the floor something began beating angrily in his head. He pulled on his trousers. His jacket was draped over the back of a little gilt chair in front of the dressing table. He found his cigarettes and his lighter and returned with them to the bed. Mona still lay with her head resting on her arm. One pale small breast was exposed.

"Sorry," he said.

"For what?"

"I should be at the hospital."

"Oh, of course you should. Busy busy busy." She pulled herself up in the bed, leaning on her elbows. He put a cigarette between her lips and held the lighter for her. "Anyway," she said, "I'm used to men creeping out of my bed." She laughed, a subdued little hoot. "That sounds awful, doesn't it. What a slut I must seem." She peered more closely at him in the curtained gloom. "You are a big fellow, aren't you," she said. "All muscle and fur. Come back to bed—come on."

He brought an ashtray from the dressing table and put it on the bed where she could reach it. Her breasts, palely pendent, made him think of a small soft big-eyed animal—a lemur, was it? He sat down and the mattress springs gave a faint, distant jangle of protest. She had scrambled higher still in the bed and was lying back against a mound of pillows, watching him—no, *surveying* him, he thought—as if she were measuring him against a model in her head and finding him sadly though perhaps not hopelessly wanting. The ashtray bore the legend HÔTEL MÉTROPOLE MONTE CARLO. She saw him looking. "Stolen," Mona said. "By me. I like to steal things. Nothing valuable, just things that take my fancy. People's husbands, for instance."

"I told you," Quirke said, "I'm not married."

"Yes. Pity." She squirmed a little, making a face. "Ach— I'm leaking." She saw him flinch, and smiled. "Why are you so afraid of women?" she asked, with no hint of accusation or disapproval, but seeming curious only. "I suppose your mother is to blame."

"I have no mother," Quirke said. "*Had* no."

"She died?"

He shrugged. "I never knew her. Or my father."

"Dear dear," she said, with an odd, harsh edge to her voice, "a poor little orphan boy, then. Let me picture it. There was the workhouse, and the beatings, and the bowls of gruel, and you a little lad scrambling up chimneys for tuppence and a rub of soap, yes?"

He did not smile. "Something like that, yes."

"So how did you get from there to here?"

"That's a long story—"

"I like long bedtime stories."

"—and a boring one."

She drew on her cigarette. "I suppose we shouldn't risk another drink? No, no, you're right, goodness knows what we'd be driven to do." She leaned forward, draping her bare arms over her knees. "So," she said. "No mummy, and afraid of women ever since."

"Why do you think I'm afraid of women?"

She shook her head mock-ruefully. "A girl can always tell things like that. It's not so bad, you know, being nervous. Quite appealing, in its way." She ran a fingertip over the back of his hand where it rested on the sheet. "Quite attractive, sometimes."

The sweat had dried on his skin and he felt chilled suddenly. He went and found his shirt and pulled it on, then returned to the bed. "Tell me what's going on," he said.

She stared. "How do you mean? What's going on where?"

"Here. All this. Your husband killing himself, then Jack Clancy dying too. The business. Davy Clancy. Your sister-in-law—"

"My *sister-in-law*?" She was staring at him incredulously. "You mean Maggie?"

"Your husband's sister, yes."

"What about her?"

"What about any of you? There's something behind all this. It's tangled up together, somehow."

"Well, of course it is. How would it not be? Two families, in business together and living in each other's ears. How would it not be *tangled*?"

Of the many things this young woman might be, he reflected, brainless was not one of them.

Suddenly she leaned forward and kissed him on the lips, hard, almost violently, almost in anger, it seemed. Her mouth tasted of cigarette smoke and, faintly, of gin. So many things that were happening had happened before, in identical circumstances, with another woman, other women. He felt the tremulous coolness of her breasts against his skin. She drew back a little way and stared at him. Her eyes seemed huge at such close range. "What a fool you are," she said, as if fondly. "What a hopeless, foolish man."

HE WENT ON TIPTOE ALONG THE HALLWAY TOWARDS THE FRONT door with his hat in his hand. There were indistinct voices behind him in the house. He hoped he would not have to encounter again the twins or the girl. They were so cool, that trio, so seemingly detached, looking at him in that amused, measured way, tossing their secret knowledge from one to another, like a tensely springy, soft-furred tennis ball. He would find out what it was, that secret, the secret they were all playing with.

As he drew open the front door—still no sign of Sarah the maid, thank God—he saw himself as a kind of clown, in outsize trousers and long, bulbous shoes, staggering this way and that between two laughing teams of white-clad players, jumping clumsily, vainly, for the ball they kept lobbing over his head with negligent, mocking ease. Yes, he would find out.

11

PHOEBE COULD NOT GET THE DELAHAYE TWINS OUT OF HER
thoughts. She had not really wanted to go to the party that night
in Breen's tiny gingerbread house under the railway bridge. She
did not like parties, they always left her feeling unsettled and
giddy for days afterwards, but she had felt she had to go, since
that was what girlfriends did with their boyfriends.

Girlfriend. Boyfriend. The words brought her up short, and
almost made her blush, not for shyness or bashful pleasure,
but out of an embarrassment she could not quite account for.

What was it about the Delahaye brothers that made them
so striking? Of course, twins were always a little bit uncanny,
but with the Delahayes it was not only that. A fascinating aura
surrounded them, fascinating, alarming, worrying. There was
their coloring, so blond, with that dead-white skin, waxy and

almost translucent, and their strange silvery blue eyes, transparent almost, like the eyes of a seagull. But mostly what drew her to them was their manner, remote, and with such stillness, as if they were always posing for their portraits, as if—

Drew her to them. Once again she was struck. Was that what she had meant to think? Was she drawn to them?

Gulls, yes, that was what they were like, those two, standing always at a remove, pale-eyed, watchful, disdaining.

She was thinking about them the day she met Inspector Hackett. It was lunchtime and she came out of the shop she worked in, on Grafton Street, the Maison des Chapeaux, and there was the detective, strolling along in his shiny blue suit with his hands in his pockets and his little potbelly sticking out, his braces on show and his battered old hat pushed to the back of his head. It seemed that every time she encountered Hackett he was out and about like this, at his ease, without a care. Today he was obviously enjoying the sunshine, and he greeted her warmly, with his elaborate, old-fashioned courtesy.

"Is it yourself, Miss Griffin!" he exclaimed, throwing back his head and puffing out his cheeks for pleasure. She believed he really was fond of her, but she could never understand why. She seemed to remember he had no children; maybe she made him think of the daughter he might have wished for.

"Hello, Inspector," she said. "Isn't it a lovely day."

"It is that, indeed," Hackett said, squinting at the sky and seeming at the same time to wink at her. She liked the way he exaggerated his quaintness for her amusement, playing the countryman come to town and exaggerating his thickest Midlands drawl. She knew very well how clever he was, how cunning. It occurred to her that she would not wish to be a

miscreant upon whom Inspector Hackett had fixed his mild-
seeming eye.

They went into Bewley's. It was crowded, as it always was
at lunchtime, and there were the mingled smells of coffee and
fried sausages and sugary pastry. They sat at a tiny marble table
at the back of the big scarlet-and-black dining room.

Hackett, with his hat in his lap, asked the waitress for a
ham roll and "a sup of tea"—he was really putting on the clod-
hopper act today—and then turned back to beam at Phoebe,
and inquired after her father. She was aware that of late the
detective and Quirke had been seeing each other regularly
again because of the Delahaye and Clancy business, so Hackett must know how her father was; nevertheless she said that
Quirke was very well, very well indeed. This was a coded way
of saying that Quirke was not drinking, or at least not drinking
as he sometimes did, ruinously. Hackett nodded. He had a
way of pursing his lips and letting his eyelids droop that always
made her think of a fat old Roman bishop, a Vatican insider,
worldly-wise, calculating, sly.

"Wasn't it awful," she said, "about that poor man, Clancy,
who drowned. Such a terrible accident, and so soon after his
partner had died."

She watched him. Her breathless schoolgirl tone—he was
not the only one who could put on an act—had not fooled him,
of course. He nodded, his chin falling on his chest. "Oh, aye,
terrible," he said, and gave her a quick sharp glance from under
those hooded lids.

"Do they know what happened to him?" she asked. She was
not to be put off.

"They?" he asked, all puzzlement and mild innocence.

"The family," she said. "The authorities." She smiled. "You."

The waitress brought their orders. Phoebe had asked for a cup of coffee and a slice of toast. Hackett eyed her plate dubiously. "You won't grow fat on that, my girl," he said.

She nodded. "That's the point."

Hackett slopped milk into his tea and added three heaped spoonfuls of sugar. The rim of his hat had etched a line across his forehead and the skin above it was as pink and tender-looking as a baby's. His oily black hair was plastered flat against his skull—she wondered if he ever washed it. What did she know about him? Not much. He was married, she knew that, and he lived somewhere in the suburbs. Beyond these scant facts, nothing.

He reminded her of a dog she had once owned, when she was a little girl. Ruff was his name. He was a mongrel, with black-and-white markings and half an ear missing. He loved to play, and would fetch sticks she had thrown for him, and would drop them at her feet for her to throw again, sitting back on his haunches and grinning up at her, his impossibly long pink tongue hanging out. One day, when she was staying in Rosslare on a holiday, she had seen Ruff out on the Burrow, the strip of grass and sand between the hotel and the beach. He had caught something in the grass, a young hare, she thought it was, a leveret, and she had stood watching in horror as he tore the poor creature to pieces. Ruff had not seen her and, unsupervised, had reverted to being a wild creature, all fang and claw. At last she had called out his name, and he had glanced at her guiltily and then run off, with what was left of the baby hare in his mouth. Later, when he came back, he was once again the Ruff she knew, grinning and happy, with that ragged half ear flapping. No doubt he expected her to have forgotten the scene on the Burrow, the torn fur and the gleaming dark blood and the white, rending teeth. But she had not forgotten; she never would forget.

She did not know whether it was she or Hackett who had brought up the subject of the Delahaye twins. To be talking about them was like an extension of her thoughts, and she realized how much indeed they must be on her mind. She told of seeing them at the party at Breen's house, and how surprised she had been that they were there, at a party, so recently after their father's death.

"When was that, exactly?" the Inspector asked, stirring a spoon round and round in his tea.

"Saturday," she said. "Saturday night."

"Ah."

She waited, but he seemed to have no more to say on the subject. Then she remembered. Saturday night was the night Jack Clancy had died, out in a boat too, on the lonely sea, like his partner.

She saw Jimmy Minor come in. He had stopped in the entrance to the dining room and was lighting a cigarette. Quickly, on instinct, she turned her face aside so that he might not see her. This surprised her, but then, she often found herself surprised by things she did. Yet why had she wanted to avoid Jimmy? He was supposed to be her friend.

Feeling guilty, she half rose from her chair and waved, so that he could not miss seeing her. He waved in return, and began to make his way through the crowded room, weaving between the tables and trailing smoke from his cigarette. She could not imagine Jimmy without a cigarette. He reminded her of a boat of some kind, a tramp steamer, perhaps, with his red hair like a flag and that plume of smoke always billowing behind him.

When he caught sight of Inspector Hackett he raised his eyebrows and hesitated, but Phoebe waved again and he came up. "Hello, Pheebs," he said. "In the embrace of the long arm of the law, I see."

Inspector Hackett nodded amiably. "Mr. Minor," he said. "We meet again. Will you join us?"

Jimmy gave Phoebe another twitch of his eyebrows, and borrowed a chair from the next table, and sat down. He wore a ragged tweed jacket, a white shirt, or a shirt that had been white some days ago, and a narrow green tie with a crooked knot. His bright red hair was trimmed close to his skull and came to a point in the center of his pale, freckled forehead. His hands had a chain smoker's tremor. Inspector Hackett was watching him, was *inspecting* him, with a sardonic expression. There was something between the detective and the reporter, that was clear: they had the air of two wrestlers circling each other, on the lookout for an opening.

The waitress came and Jimmy ordered a cup of black coffee. "No food?" the waitress said. She was a delicate girl with the face of a Madonna. Jimmy shook his head and she went off. Jimmy, it seemed, rarely noticed girls.

"Tell me, Mr. Minor," Hackett said, "have you been hearing anything interesting since last we met?"

Jimmy Minor shot him a look. "A thing or two," he said. "A thing or two."

"Any one of which you might care to share?"

"Well now, Inspector, I doubt I'd have anything to tell you that you don't know already."

"You could try me with something."

Jimmy winked at Phoebe. He was rolling the tip of his cigarette along the edge of the ashtray, shedding ash neatly into the cup. It occurred to Phoebe that if you smoked as much as Jimmy did you would always have something to do. Perhaps that was why he did it.

Years before, when she was little, her father, her supposed father, Malachy Griffin, had smoked a pipe for a while. She had envied all the things he had to play with, the tobacco pouch of wonderfully soft leather with a buttoned flap, and the little knife with the tamper on the end of it, and paper packets of woolly white pipe cleaners, and those special imported matches—Swan Vestas, they were called—that could only be got from Fox's on College Green. She had liked the smell of the tobacco he smoked, one that he had made up specially, also at Fox's, a blend of Cavendish and Perique—how was it she could remember so many of these names from the past?—and more than once when he had set down his pipe and gone off to do something she had pretended to take a puff from it, not minding the sour wet feel of the stem in her mouth. How warmly the bowl sat in her palm, how smooth it felt. The silver ring where the stem was fitted into the bowl had a tiny hallmark on the underside; it was like the silver band Malachy wore on his little finger, that had once belonged to his father—

She frowned, staring at her empty cup. Something had snagged in her mind, like a ragged fingernail catching in silk. Something to do, again, with the Delahaye twins—what was it? She remembered one of them, James, she thought it was, leaning over the girl in the doorway upstairs at Breen's house, his head turned to look at her, at Phoebe, his arm lifted and his hand pressed against the doorjamb.

What? What was it? No: gone.

Jimmy was saying something about the firm of Delahaye & Clancy. A clerk there had told him—what had he told him? She had missed the beginning of it. "—a whole trail of transfers," he was saying, "thousands of shares shifted between one place and another, and nobody knowing what was going on."

Inspector Hackett, listening, nodded slowly, in an absentminded way, once more stirring the spoon in his tea, which by now must have gone quite cold. "Tell me," he said, "are you doing a story about this?"

Jimmy gave a scoffing laugh. "Are you joking?" he said. "Do you think my rag would print anything that might suggest something peculiar was going on at the highly respected firm of Delahaye and Clancy?"

"I don't know," the Inspector said, playing the innocent again. "Would it not?"

Jimmy turned to Phoebe. "You know who we're talking about?"

"Oh, she does," the Inspector said. "She knows the family, in fact. Don't you, Miss Griffin?"

An eager light had come into Jimmy's eye. "Do you?" he asked.

"I've met the twins, Jonas and James, and Jonas's girlfriend, Tanya Somers. And Rose Griffin knows their aunt."

Jimmy whistled, shaking his head. "The small, tight world

of the gentry," he said. He turned back to Hackett. "Big fleas have little fleas, eh, Inspector? And so ad infinitum."

Phoebe felt her forehead go red. Jimmy had a nasty side to him that he really should not let be seen. "That's not a very nice image," she said sharply, "me as a flea, hopping on people's backs."

Jimmy only grinned at her, the sharp tip of his dark red tongue appearing briefly and then quickly withdrawing. Phoebe thought of a lizard on a rock.

"As a matter of fact," Hackett said blandly, as if he had registered nothing of this sharp exchange, "Miss Griffin was at a party with the Delahaye lads the night their father's partner died."

Jimmy looked at her with a speculative light. Yes, she thought, Jimmy really could be ugly when he was after a story. She realized she was blushing again, not because of Jimmy's nastiness this time, but at the mention of the Delahayes. She felt a twinge of annoyance. What was the matter with her? "It was at Andy Breen's place," she said to Jimmy. "I'm surprised you weren't there."

"Down the country," Jimmy said offhandedly. "Following a lead."

Phoebe smiled to herself. Jimmy had seen too many movies with hard-bitten newsmen in them—he even had a trace of a Hollywood accent sometimes. She pictured him in a trench coat and a fedora with a PRESS sign stuck in the band. The image amused her, and she felt the blood subsiding from her face.

Inspector Hackett was watching her, amused in turn by her amusement. "And was it a good party?" he asked.

Phoebe looked at him. The more innocent the detective's questions sounded, the more pointed they seemed to be. She shrugged. "Not particularly. But then, I don't much like parties."

"Is that so?" the Inspector said. Suddenly he stood up, and fished in his trouser pocket and brought out a florin and put it on the table. "I'll say good day to you," he said. "Miss Griffin. Mr. Minor." And carrying his hat, he turned and sauntered away.

Jimmy sat back on his chair and watched him go. "He's a cute hoor, that one," he said, almost admiringly.

Sunlight through the stained-glass window above them gave the big room a churchly aspect, and the people at the tables roundabout might have been a congregation. Smoke as of incense drifted on the heavy air. Jimmy drank off the dregs of his coffee and then he too stood up. "Go for a stroll?" he said.

Phoebe smiled up at him thinly. "Haven't you things to do?" she asked sweetly. "Leads to follow, that kind of thing?"

Jimmy's pale brow turned paler; other people flushed when they were angry, but Jimmy turned chalk white. He was a tiny person, almost a miniature, with dainty little hands and feet, and he was easily offended.

Phoebe rose briskly and took his arm. "Yes," she said, "come on, let's go for a stroll." From her purse she took a shilling and added it to Hackett's florin. That's threepence for a tip, she thought, and for some reason wanted to laugh.

They went up to Stephen's Green and walked in the cool inky shadows under the trees. They could hear the voices of children at play out on the grass. Somewhere above them an airplane was circling, making an insect drone.

It was almost time for Phoebe to be back at work. She looked up into the sea-green light under the dense canopy of leaves. At moments such as this, rare and precious, the possibility of happiness came to her with all the breathtaking force of something suddenly remembered from the past. Would she always be ahead of her own life, looking backwards?

"What are they like," Jimmy said, "the Delahayes?"

"Why do you ask?"

He had paused to light yet another cigarette. For a moment he had the look of a greedy baby, leaning over the match with the cigarette clamped in his pouted lips like a soother. He never seemed to have a girlfriend. She wondered, not for the first time, if he might be—that way inclined. It would explain the bitter brittleness of his manner, behind which she could always sense a tentativeness, a yearning, almost. She felt a sudden rush of compassion for him, this fearsome, discontent, babyish little man. She linked her arm in his.

"There's a story in this business," he said, staring hard ahead, "if only I could tease it out." He glanced at her. "What does your father think?"

"You mean, does he think there's a story in it for you?"

Jimmy frowned at the tip of his cigarette. "You know, Pheebs," he said, "humor really isn't your strong suit."

"Well," Phoebe said cheerfully, "at least I try, not like some I could name."

They went on, Jimmy scowling and Phoebe smiling at her shoes. Were there any men, anywhere, she wondered, who were really grown up?

"You know Jack Clancy was murdered," Jimmy said. It seemed not quite a question.

A black-stockinged nanny went past, wheeling a black pram with enormous wheels and high, humped springs.

"Do I?" Did she? It shocked her a little to realize that she did not care about Jack Clancy and how he had died. Did any of them care? What was it to them, to her father, to Jimmy Minor, to Inspector Hackett even—what was it to them, in the long run, whether the poor man had drowned himself or had been pushed under by someone else? They pretended, all of them, to be after the facts, truth, justice, but what they desired in the end was really just to satisfy their curiosity. At least Jimmy was honest about it. "Do you know it for a fact that it was murder?" she asked.

"I have a feeling in my gut," Jimmy said. "It all seems wrong, somehow. They're covering up."

"Who's covering up? My father? That detective?"

"I don't know." He gave a sharp little laugh. "When I was a kid, I used to read detective stories, couldn't get enough of them. Arthur Conan Doyle, Dorothy L. Sayers, John Dickson Carr and Carter Dickson—those two were the same guy, in fact—Josephine Tey, Ngaio Marsh, whose name I never knew how to pronounce and didn't know whether it was a man or a woman. All those—I loved them. They made everything so squared off and neat, like a brown-paper parcel tied up with twine and sealing wax and an address label written out in copperplate. There was a body, there were clues, there were suspects, then the detective came along and put it all together into a story, a true story, the story of the truth—the story of what happened."

He laughed again, more softly this time. "I used to get such a warm feeling when I reached the end and everything was explained, the killer identified and taken away by the police, and everybody else going back to their lives as if none of it mattered, as if nothing serious had taken place. I wanted to be Sherlock Holmes and Poirot and Lord Peter Wimsey, all rolled into one. I knew I could be. I knew I'd get all the clues and work out who had done it and at the end would get to point my finger at the culprit and say, *You, Miss Murgatroyd—it was you who waited behind the curtains in the library with the stiletto in your hand . . .* And Miss Murgatroyd would be led away, cursing me, and everyone would gather round and congratulate me, and Major Bull-Trumpington's niece, the pretty one, would hang on my arm and tell me how wonderful I was." He stopped, and laughed again, shortly. "And then I grew up."

It was odd, Phoebe thought, how they could walk along arm in arm like this, when a while ago, in the café, she had been so angry with him. But no, she corrected herself—they were not arm in arm. She had her arm linked in his, but he had his hand in his pocket, and was as stiff as he always was, stiff and vexed and simmering with resentment. Resentment at what, at whom? At her? She kicked a leaf. In this latitude there were fallen leaves all year round. The leaf—sycamore, was it?—looked like a hand, crook'd and clutching at the ground. She thought of those two men, out on the sea, in their separate boats, facing their separate deaths. Such a waste; all such a waste.

"But isn't that what you're doing still," she said, "trying to find out the story? You said so a minute ago. You're still trying to put it all together so everything will be explained."

"Everything doesn't get explained," he said. He sounded weary now, weary and almost old. "You find a few pieces of the jigsaw puzzle, some of them fit together, some of them you just leave lying on the board, by themselves. That was the point of those detective stories I used to read—there was nothing that didn't mean something, nothing that wasn't a clue. It's not like that in real life."

"What about red herrings? Didn't the people who wrote the stories put in things purposely to throw the reader off the scent?"

It came to her, so suddenly that it almost made her laugh. Two rings, on two little fingers. Or one, on two. "Listen," she said quickly, letting go of his arm, "I have to go back to work, I'm late already." She brushed her fingertips against his cheek. "Cheer up," she said. "I'm sure you'll get your story."

As she set off along the path under the trees, Jimmy turned to watch her go, a flickering figure moving through dappled shadow. He heard the children's voices again. That plane was still there too, buzzing at some edge of the sky. He lit another cigarette, and walked on.

INSPECTOR HACKETT AMBLED TOWARDS PEARSE STREET AND his office. At the junction where D'Olier Street met up with College Green there was a concrete triangle with grass in it, too small and mean to be called a traffic island. The spot always annoyed him, he was not sure why. It was not the patch of grass itself, dry and brittle now from the summer heat, that he found provoking, but just the simple fact of its being there, for no reason. Why grass? It could all have been of concrete; that would have done as well, and would have been better suited to the location. As it was, the little triangle was no use to anyone, except for dogs to do their business on.

Yes, he supposed that was it: he felt sorry for the grass, and angry with those who had been so thoughtless in putting it there. Some damn fool official in the Board of Works, he supposed, poring over papers on a wet Monday morning, licking his indelible pencil and putting a tick beside a line: *to wit, one triangle, with grass, junction of . . .* And look at the result: dry straw, baked clay, dog shit, fag ends, a chewing gum wrapper. Nobody cared enough about anything, and so everything was let go to hell. He was coming more and more to hate this city, its crowds, its dirt, its smells—the river was particularly foul today—its incurable dinginess. There were days when he longed for the fields and streams of childhood, as a man lost in the desert would thirst for water.

He tramped up the uncarpeted wooden stairs to his office, and at the return on the second landing he was assailed by another reminder of childhood. The hot sunlight coming in at the big window there made a fragrance in the dry dusty air that brought him back instantly, as if the years were nothing, to the little two-room schoolhouse on the Grange Road outside Tulsk where Miss McLaverty had taught him his lessons when he was a little fellow. He had loved Miss McLaverty dearly. She used to look very stern, with her long tweed skirt and her rimless glasses and her hair tied back in a tight bun with a net over it. But she had a soft spot for him, and often she would let him sit on her knee at breaktime when all the senior infants had goody to eat—that was another smell he remembered, of the bread with the sugar on it soaked in hot milk—and helped him, too, when he could not add up his sums or got stuck on a hard word during reading lessons. She too had a smell, very different from his mother's smell, delicate and cool, like the scent of wet lilac. She would lean over him and point at the figures or the letters in his copybook with a wonderfully clean and polished fingernail. Such tears he had wept when the time came for him to be taken out of Miss McLaverty's care and sent to the Christian Brothers' school in Roscommon town.

He sighed, putting his knee to the office door, which was warped in its frame and always stuck. Old fool, he thought, maundering over the lost past. And look at that desk! There were files on it that had been sitting there for months, untouched, gathering dust. He took off his hat and with a flick of his wrist sent it sailing in the direction of the hat stand, but it missed, of course, and he had to bend down, groaning, and retrieve it from where it had got wedged under the radiator and dust it off with his elbow and hang it on the hook, where it waggled from side to side as if mocking him. He sighed again, and slumped down in the swivel chair behind his desk and scrabbled crossly in his pockets for his cigarettes.

He knew what the matter was, of course. This moment came in every case, when his thoughts, beginning at last to concentrate and yet not wanting to, would skitter off and fix on anything other than the business in hand. It was, he believed, what the mind doctors called *transference*. There was something all wrong about the deaths of Victor Delahaye and Jack Clancy. He could, if he wished, accept the thing for what it seemed: one had taken his own life for reasons only to be guessed at; the other, distracted by being caught out in a scheme to cheat his partner, had made a mistake at sea and fallen and hit his head and tumbled overboard and drowned. But he knew it was not that simple, it could not be. The course of events was unpredictable, sometimes chaotic, often farcical, but there was always a thread of logic to be grasped. This entire business felt wrong; a fume of heat came off it, like the steam off a dunghill on a winter morning.

He turned about in his chair. Through the grimed window behind his desk the sunlight on the chimney pots outside seemed unreal, a matte, honey-colored glaze.

If the story had involved just Victor Delahaye and Jack Clancy, it might well have been as simple as it seemed, the grotesque coincidence of Delahaye's suicide followed by Clancy's fatal accident. Yes, it was not the dead that troubled him but the living. He thought of them, set them out in his mind one by one, like the pieces on a chessboard.

There were the Clancys, mother and son. What was he to make of Sylvia Clancy, tall, straight, stately as a heron, with her hoity-toity accent and her shield of impenetrable politeness? Was she too good to be true? And the young fellow, Davy Clancy, the spoiled boy-child, his father's son, furtive, sly, too good-looking by far—what did he know that he was not telling?

Then there was Delahaye's widow, a shrewd and avid calculator whose trick it was to lie in wait behind the mask of an empty-headed minx—he had seen the way she looked at Quirke that day in the churchyard, with her husband not yet cold in the ground. That poor fool Delahaye would have been no match for her. Old Samuel, Delahaye's father, now, he would have had the measure of her, and indeed would probably have preferred her for a daughter to the daughter he did have. What was her name? Margaret? No—Marguerite. An odd party, that one. Keeper of secrets, storer of grudges, an aging embittered woman disguised as the long-suffering spinster daughter whose only care is for her family and ailing father, in her father's house. Oh, yes, he knew the type, hard done by and sad but liable suddenly to turn and bite, and bite deep.

And there were the other Delahayes, the twins. A rich man's sons, too satisfied, too sure of themselves, dismissive, careless, and uncaring. He thought again of the traffic island with its scorched grass.

He turned and pressed an electric bell on the corner of his desk, and presently heard heavy, dull footsteps on the stairs. There was a pause, then a brief knock on the door, and his assistant, young Jenkins, clattered in. Jenkins—pin head on a long stalk of neck, cowlick of hair across a narrow forehead, blue serge, boots, an ever-eager eye—was of a type that Headquarters seemed to think Hackett deserved; certainly at least they kept sending them to him, raw recruits fresh out of the Garda training college at Tullamore with less of an idea than the man in the moon of what a real policeman is and does.

"Yes, boss?" Jenkins said.

"Couple of lads I want you to round up," Hackett said. He wrote out the Northumberland Road address—it was always best to write things down for Jenkins—and handed over the slip of paper. Jenkins frowned at the address as if it were a line of hieroglyphics.

"Am I to arrest them?" he asked, his face brightening with eagerness. Hackett put a hand to his forehead.

"No, no," he said quietly, "no. Just bring them in. Tell them we believe they might be able to help us with our inquiries."

"Right." The young man started to go.

"Oh, and Jenkins—"

He put his head around the door again. "Yes, boss?"

"Go easy, right? This is the quality we're dealing with here."

The young man nodded. "Right-oh, boss." His head, at the end of that neck, resembled nothing so much as an oversized Indian club.

MAGGIE DELAHAYE WAS BLISSFULLY HAPPY—BLISSFUL, YES, IT was the only word. Mrs. Hartigan had got everything ready for her before she arrived, had opened all the windows to air the house, had put fresh flowers on the hall table and made up her bed. She had even, Maggie saw with amusement, brought up a chamber pot from the back-stairs lavatory, for there was the china handle of it peeping out discreetly from under the frill of the old lace bedspread that had belonged to Maggie's grand-mother.

She stood at the window in the sun, looking down at the lawn. No rabbits this afternoon; they would be out in the morning, at first light, hopping around on the grass in that funny, hesitating way they did, like faulty clockwork toys. How peaceful it was, how quiet! She gazed out over the sweltering fields to the far, gray-blue mountains outlined against a hazy sky. This, this was where she belonged. Here she would rest, and let the great world pass over her, like a wave.

She deserved a little peace, a little contentment, at last. True, she felt guilty for having left her father. But he would manage. Her father always managed.

On the kitchen table she found that Mrs. Hartigan had left

a plate of salad and sliced ham for her, covered with a tea
towel. There were wedges of soda bread, too, on another plate—
Mrs. Hartigan's soda bread was famous throughout the parish—
and fresh milk in a glass jug with a little lace doily on it to keep
the flies out. She realized that she was hungry, and sat down
to eat. How pleasant it was to hear nothing but the clinking of
knife and fork—she always liked to be silent at mealtimes, and
wished others would follow her example. She poured some
milk into a glass, but it was warm and tasted as if it might be
on the turn, although perhaps it was just that she was not used
to milk so fresh, straight from the dairy, heavy with cream.
She pushed it aside, feeling slightly queasy, and went to the
dresser and took another glass and brought it to the sink and
held it under the tap, but paused, and did not fill it.

A faint savor remained of the brandy she had drunk in that
hotel—was it the village of Horse and Jockey she had stopped
in?—and now it occurred to her that a glass of wine might
settle her stomach. Also she should mark her arrival, her *homecoming,* as she thought of it, with a toast to herself—why not?
There used to be bottles of wine at the back of the old stable—
her father jokingly called it his cellar—and they were probably
still there, if Jack Clancy had not guzzled them all. Why her
father had ever let the Clancys come here to share the house
each summer she did not know. Who were the Clancys, what
were they to the Delahayes? In her heart she had always thought
Jack Clancy common, for all his pretense of being a gentleman,
with his swagger and his jokes and his genteel English wife.

She went out by the back door, leaving it on the latch, and
made her way to the stables. There was a smell of horses still,
after all these years! She thought of Tinsel, her pony that had

died under her one day coming back from a ride—the poor thing's heart had given out, just like that. What age was she then? Eleven, twelve? Happy times. She had never got another horse, for she could not bear to think of replacing Tinsel.

The wine was there, in a long rack against the back wall, the bottles dusty, their labels tattered and faded. She took one out at random, and brushed off the grime. Château Montrose, 1934. Goodness! To think of all that had happened since then, in the world, and in the family—her mother's death, then Victor's wife Lisa dying and Victor remarrying in such a rush, and then her father's stroke. The twins had not even been born in 1934. And now Victor, too, was gone. She lifted the bottle and held its cool flanks between her palms. She would not weep, no, she would not start weeping again. She had come here to be happy, to forget and be happy. But how could she forget? The daytime was all right, but the nights, ah, the nights. A shiver ran along her spine, or not a shiver but a sort of flinching sensation. Someone walking over her grave, as the old people used to say. Someone walking over her grave.

She was on the way back to the house, with the wine bottle cradled like a baby in the crook of one arm, when the idea came to her of clearing all of the Clancy things out of the house. They would not be coming here anymore, surely, now that Jack was dead. Sylvia would not want to come, she was certain of that. By the time she got to the kitchen the plan had seized hold of her imagination, and in her excitement she almost overturned the bottle when she was trying to get the corkscrew into the cork. Yes, she would empty out all the bedrooms on the west side, the Clancys' side, so called, and put the things, the clothes and bed linens and all the rest of it, into boxes and crates and ship them off to Dublin. Sylvia would find room for it all in that big house in Nelson Terrace, and what she did not need or want she could give to the St. Vincent de Paul.

Carefully she poured out a glass of wine, holding the bottle in one hand and supporting the neck on the fingers of the other. At the first taste the wine seemed musty and dry as ink, but she took another sip, and another, and suddenly it blossomed in her mouth like a flower, so soft and velvety. It came to her that it was the past she was drinking, the past itself, that mysterious other place where sometimes it seemed to her she lived more immediately, more vividly, than she did in the present. She sat down and ate some of the salad and a thin sliver of ham. The wine had taken the edge off her hunger. She looked again at the mildewed label: 1934! A whole world away.

Who was it she had hit, that time, with the bottle? Some girl Victor had brought home. She almost laughed to think of it. What age was she then? Old enough to know better. They were at dinner here, the whole family and the Clancys, and the girl had said something to Victor, teasing him. She was a big, stupid girl with an enormous bosom, like two footballs under her blouse, Maggie could not take her eyes off it. When the girl laughed Maggie could see the food in her mouth, half chewed. Then, a moment later, the girl had been crying and holding her head and there was blood where her ear was cut. Someone had jumped up and taken the bottle out of Maggie's hand, she remembered—Jack Clancy, it was. Wine had spilled all down the front of her dress. It seemed she had hit the girl, had grabbed the bottle by the neck and swung it round and bashed her with it on the side of the head. She had no recollection of having done it, but she was not sorry that she had. It would teach Miss Big-bust not to laugh at her brother. Strange, how she could do things and forget having done them.

There was the question, of course, of what to do with the bedrooms once she had cleared the Clancys' things out of them. She knew a furniture dealer in Cork who would come and advise her. Anything she bought to replace the Clancys' things would have to be not only good but authentic; it would have to fit in. She had no intention of doing anything that would damage or compromise the delicate fabric of Ashgrove. She poured herself a little more of the wine. It would be a great house again, with all traces of the Clancys gone from it. And she would be the lady of the house.

She smiled, her lips curving on the rim of the glass. She would have visiting cards printed, with *Miss Marguerite Delahaye, of Ashgrove House, in the County of Cork* written in italic lettering. Why was there no word to go after a woman's name, like *Esquire* for a man? She could call herself *The Honorable Miss Marguerite Delahaye*—who was there that would challenge her right to a title? Anyway, she *was* honorable. Where honor was concerned, men did not have a monopoly. She had done the honorable thing.

THE TWO YOUNG MEN ARRIVED AT PEARSE STREET WITH AN AIR of polite but jaded interest, as if they were on a visit to a third-rate tourist site. Dressed alike in elegantly crumpled cream-colored linen suits and open-necked white shirts, they glanced with indifference at the bare floorboards and the institution-green walls, the crowded notice board, the duty desk with its wooden flap and the duty sergeant presiding over his big black ledger, like Saint Peter, as Hackett often thought. The two avoided meeting each other's eyes, seeming afraid they would burst into laughter.

At a sign from young Jenkins, the duty sergeant lifted the flap to let them through, and Jenkins led the way down a set of narrow wooden stairs to the basement. The atmosphere was close and dank and there was a smell of old cigarette smoke, sweat, and stale urine, and the sunlit day outside suddenly seemed a distant memory. Inspector Hackett had directed that the twins be put in separate interrogation rooms, where they were to be locked in and left alone with only their thoughts for company. He had not told Jenkins what it was they were to be questioned about, exactly, but Jenkins trusted his boss, and went out to the yard at the back, where the Black Marias were parked, to smoke a cigarette and dream of the promotion he had been dropping hints about to the boss for weeks.

In fact, Hackett himself was not sure what line of questioning to adopt with this pair, in their silk shirts and their expensive suits. He had gone out to the top of the stairs in time to glimpse Jenkins conducting them down to the basement. They were certainly not your usual suspects, who in Hackett's mind came in two varieties, the cringers and the swaggerers. The Delahayes would certainly not cringe but they did not swagger, either. They looked as if they had strolled in from a picnic and were confident that they would be returning to it presently. Hackett wondered what it would be like to be so self-assured. And how was he to shake that self-assurance?

He went back to his office and sat with his feet on the desk and brooded, looking vacantly out of the grimy window and picking his teeth with a matchstick. He had never played chess, did not even know the rules, but he imagined that for grand masters of the game the moves they made on the board would be only a clumsy manifestation of altogether more subtle configurations in their minds. It was something like that with him, too. The people involved in this case, the Delahayes on one side and the Clancys the other, shifted and glided in his thoughts like so many black and white pieces executing immensely intricate maneuvers in a luminous mist.

Somewhere there was a pattern, if only he could find it. Jack Clancy's death had been the direct result somehow of Victor Delahaye's suicide, he was convinced of that. He was convinced too that Clancy had been murdered. Was it the twins who had murdered him? If so, why? Had Clancy driven their father to kill himself? Had they wreaked vengeance on him? There was also the question of the alibi. Quirke's daughter had told him she had seen the twins at a party on the night Clancy died. How then could they have taken Clancy out in his own boat in Dublin Bay and drowned him? But somehow they had. He knew it was they who had done it, a lifetime of experience told him so.

He rose wearily, hitching up his trousers. The room was unbearably stuffy, for the single window behind the desk had been stuck fast for years. He sighed heavily; nothing for it but to go down and deal with those two buckos.

Jenkins, of course, did not know which one he had put in which room. "They're the spitting image of each other, boss," he said defensively, with the hint of a whine that never failed to set Hackett's teeth on edge.

"Yes," Hackett said drily, pushing past the junior policeman, "that's because they're twins." Jenkins blushed. He was very susceptible to blushing, was young Jenkins.

They went down the wooden stairs, Hackett in the lead with his assistant clattering at his heels. The first door they came to had a brass number 7 nailed to it; no one knew how or why the room had come to be numbered so, since it was the first one in the corridor. Hackett thrust open the door and swept inside—it was always best to start off with noise and bustle. Young Delahaye, whichever one it might be, was sitting at his ease before the little square wooden table with the rickety legs. He was leaning back on the straight-backed chair with an ankle crossed on a knee. He looked over his shoulder and smiled at the two men as they entered, and for a second it seemed he might leap to his feet and welcome them warmly, as if he were in his own house and the unfurnished and windowless cell were a grandly appointed reception room.

"Good day to you," Hackett said brusquely, coming forward and offering his hand. "Which one are you?"

The young man cast a skeptical look at the hand being offered, then took it, and uncrossed his legs and rose slowly to his feet, seeming to unwind his long slender frame as if it had been twined around the chair, all the while shaking Hackett's hand with a show of solemn courtesy. He was some inches taller than the detective. "I'm Jonas Delahaye," he said. "Where's my brother?"

Hackett did not reply. He had given Jenkins a bulging cardboard file to carry, and Jenkins came forward now and dropped it on the table with a thump, and retreated and stood with his back against the door, his arms folded. There was nothing in the cardboard file but a bundle of out-of-date documents that had nothing to do with the deaths of Victor Delahaye or Jack Clancy, but a file always looked impressive, and some people were unnerved by its bulky presence on the table. Not Jonas Delahaye, however, who hardly gave the thing a glance. Hackett walked around the table and sat down on the second of the two chairs, which, along with the table, were the sole items of furniture in the room. The walls were a somber shade of bile green and bore a shiny gray film of damp, as if they were sweating. Directly above the table a sixty-watt bare bulb dangled from a double-stranded flex. Below the bulb a trio of flies were circling slowly in a sort of dreamy waltz.

"Now then," Hackett said briskly. He opened the file and riffled through the grubby documents and shut it again. "Can you tell me where you were on Saturday night last?"

The young man opposite him, leaning forward with his elbows on the table and his fingers clasped, beamed, as if he had made a bet with himself as to what the first question would be and was pleased to find he had won. "Let me see," he said, frowning and putting on an effortful show of remembering. "That would be the night that Mr. Clancy died, yes?" Hackett nodded. "Then I was at a party. Stoney Road, North Strand. Home of a chap I know, a doctor, Breen is his name, Andy Breen. Why?"

Hackett leaned back and said nothing. In the silence Jenkins's stomach rumbled like a roll of distant thunder, and he coughed and shuffled his feet. Jonas Delahaye was still smiling, holding the detective's scrutinizing gaze. From outside came the sound of an approaching siren, a plaintive keening muffled by the thickness of the walls.

"A bit strange, wouldn't you think," Hackett said, "going out to a party so soon after the death of your father?"

The young man paused a moment, and frowned again, to show that he was giving the question judicious consideration. "Ye-es," he said, "I suppose it might seem like that. I didn't think of it at the time, but I see what you mean."

Hackett waited, but the young man merely sat, bright and attentive, with his hands still clasped before him, waiting for the next question. Long ago, at school, Hackett had known a fellow that this one reminded him of. What was his name? Geoffrey something. Tall, pale, with a shock of yellow hair and uncannily pale gray eyes. Geoffrey, never Geoff. His people had a big house out on the Longford Road. Well-off Catholics with a Protestant name—what was it? Geoffrey was a delicate youth, and used to get two days off school at the start of every month to be brought up to Dublin for some special medical treatment that he never spoke about. There was something about him, an air of separateness, of detachment, and a sense too that he knew some amusing thing that no one else did. —Pettit! That was his name. Geoffrey Pettit. What had become of him? At the end of the summer holidays one year he had not turned up, and no one had heard any more of him. But Hackett remembered him well, and surely others did, for he was the kind of person people would remember. He leaned back on his chair. If he was not mistaken, Geoffrey Pettit too had worn a signet ring, on his little finger, just like this blandly smiling, sinister young man sitting opposite him now.

This was for Hackett the pivotal moment in every investigation, the moment when he sat down face to face with a person he believed had killed another human being. There was always the problem of plausibility. Killers never looked like killers, for what would a killer look like? Of the handful of proven murderers he had come across, the only thing seemingly out of the ordinary he had detected in them was a certain quality of self-absorption, of being somehow removed, turned inward and lost in awe before the breathtaking enormity of the deed they had committed. It was there in all of them, even the most careful and crafty, this sense of hushed wonderment. Did he detect it in Jonas Delahaye? He was not sure there was anything detectable in him, behind that hard smooth bright exterior. The detective felt a faint shimmer along his backbone. It occurred to him that he might be in the presence of a refined and intricate madness.

"So you went to a party," he said, "you and your brother. Was your girlfriend there—what's her name?"

"Tanya. Tanya Somers." The young man nodded. "Yes, she was there."

"Good party, was it?"

Jonas smiled; his teeth were wonderfully white. "Middling. The usual, you know. Brown-paper bags of stout, charred bangers and sliced bread to eat, the girls tipsy and half the fellows looking for a fight. We didn't stay long."

"Oh? What time did you leave, would you say?"

"Midnight? One o'clock? Something like that." His smile turned mischievous. "If it was the pictures, this would be the moment for me to ask, *Just what are you driving at, Inspector?* Wouldn't it."

Jenkins, at the door, made a sound in his throat suspiciously like laughter quickly stifled; Hackett decided to ignore it. He brought out a packet of Player's and pushed it across the table, sliding it open with his thumb as he did so. Jonas shook his head. "You don't smoke?" Hackett said.

"I do," the young man answered pleasantly. He was still smiling.

Hackett stood up and began to pace back and forth at his side of the table, smoking his cigarette, a fist pressed to the small of his back. He was wondering idly for how many hours of the day in this place did he have his behind planted on a chair. What would life be like elsewhere? He thought again of Geoffrey Pettit, and of the Pettits' home, a square white mansion set on the side of a green hill above the Shannon looking south towards Lough Ree. The Pettits and the Delahayes of this world had it soft.

"So let's refresh our memories here," he said. "Your father dies, and a bit over a week afterwards you and your brother and your girlfriend are at a party in your friend's house in North Strand, the very night, as it happens, that your father's business partner is drowned out in Dublin Bay. Would that be right? Is that the right sequence?"

The young man again made a show of considering the question, then nodded. "Yes," he said calmly, "that's right."

"Did your mother know you were intending to go to a party that night?"

For the first time something like a shadow passed over the young man's features. "My mother?"

"Your stepmother."

"Oh. Mona." He gave a faint snicker. "Who can say what Mona knows or doesn't know. Things go in"—he pointed to one ear—"and then"—pointing to the other—"out again, usually without pausing on the way."

"You're not fond of your stepmother?"

The young man pursed his lips and shrugged. "Are people ever fond of their stepmothers? Isn't that what they're for, to be feared and disliked?"

Hackett paused in his pacing. "Feared?" he said softly.

"Oh, you know what I mean," Jonas snapped, with an impatient gesture. "Snow White, the poisoned apple, all that. Mona is not the wicked witch, she's just Mona. We pay her no attention."

Hackett sat down again. "But she'll inherit the business, and so on?"

The young man placed his hands flat on the table before him and leaned back with a large, slow smile. "These are very personal questions, Inspector," he said calmly. "Impertinent, I'd almost say."

Hackett was wondering where this young man had gone to school; somewhere in England, surely, chosen probably by his Unionist grandfather. He too smiled broadly. "Sure, aren't we in a police barracks," he said jovially, "where all kinds of liberties are allowed?"

The young man, though maintaining his smile, was watching him with a certain narrowness now. "I've seen my father's will," he said. "It's quite clear. Mona will be well provided for. The business stays with my brother and me."

"Ah," Hackett said, nodding. "I see. That sounds right and fair."

"Yes. My father had his weak points, but he was always fair." He widened his smile again. "It's a family tradition."

"And the Clancys?" Hackett asked quietly.

The corner of Jonas's mouth twitched in faint amusement.

"There'll be some money for Mrs. Clancy. He—Jack—was a partner more in name than anything else. Did you know he'd been buying up shares in the business on the quiet? We've made sure to get them back, of course. Chap of ours, Duncan Maverley, handled that—what'll we call it?—that readjustment."

Hackett stubbed out his cigarette in the tin ashtray on the table and offered the packet to the young man again—"You're sure you won't join me?"—then lit a fresh one for himself. He sat back, rubbing a hand vigorously along the side of his jaw, making a sandpapery sound. "There'd be plenty of people would have seen you at the party," he said, "that would remember you being there, yes?"

"Of course. In fact, your friend Quirke, the pathologist, his daughter was there, with her boyfriend, who's Dr. Quirke's assistant, as it happens."

"Ah. Miss Griffin, and young Dr. Sinclair. I see. And you spoke to them?"

"I met them as they were arriving."

"And did you see them later on?"

"I'm sure I did. I must have—it's a tiny house, built for gnomes."

"And your brother, he spoke to them?"

The young man bit his lip to stop himself smirking. "You'll have to ask him that yourself," he said, "won't you, Inspector."

Over at the door, young Jenkins's stomach was rumbling again.

• • •

EACH MORNING WHEN SHE WOKE, SYLVIA CLANCY HAD TO
adjust herself anew to a transformed world. Shock, bewilder-
ment, grief, these were the things she would naturally have
expected after the death of her husband, and when they came
she found she could cope with them more easily than she had
ever thought she would. But this sense of everything having
suddenly become unfamiliar left her feeling helpless and lost.
Things looked skewed, tilted off balance; even the daylight
had a sort of acid tinge that had not been there before.

She did not know how or why Jack had died. He was a master yachtsman, easily the best sailor in his class, here and in
Cork, though Victor, of course, had imagined he was the more
experienced and skilled of the two. What was Jack doing out
on the bay that night, so late, and alone? Why had he not told
her he was going out? Jack had his secrets, but he was considerate and always let her know when he was going to be away,
or out sailing, even though she knew that "sailing" was often a
cover for other activities. She had been careful not to give him
any sense that she was keeping tabs on him. He had his freedom, and knew it; that had been how it was between them
from the start. Had she been wrong? Should she have insisted
on rules, limits, demarcations? She did not know; she was not
sure of anything, anymore.

That night, the night of his death, she had sat in bed reading until quite late; it had been close to midnight when she put
her book aside and turned out the bedside lamp and opened
the curtains. She always slept with the curtains open, for she
loved to see the lights of the harbor shining in the darkness
like jewels, white, emerald, ruby red, laid out on a velvet cloth,

and to hear the mast ropes clinking in the wind. Had she been awake while Jack was drowning? She had felt no intimation of it, no start of dread, no inexplicable shiver, no sigh or whisper on the air. She could not bear to think of him dying out there alone and helpless, with no hand to hold, no one to cling to, no one to bid him farewell on his final voyage, into the dark and silent depths. He had loved her in his way, as best he could, she knew that. What did she care, now, about his girlfriends, his flings, his "bits on the side," as the wags in the club would say, smirking behind their hands?

It tormented her to think that she would never know the true circumstances of his death. Had it been an accident? That seemed impossible—though he was impulsive in many ways, when it came to boats he had never been one to take risks, to cut a corner. Perhaps he had been tipsy, and had stumbled somehow and fallen overboard and hit his head as he was falling. He was a strong swimmer, and would surely have survived if he had been conscious when he fell into the sea. It had been a summer night, the cold would not have hampered him and made his limbs cramp up. But what other possibility was there? She did not like to think about other possibilities, yet she was aware of them, thronging just beyond the borders of her mind, clamoring to be let in.

Despite everything she knew to be the case, she could not believe that Jack was gone. She knew he was dead, of course, yet she could not accept it. She kept thinking that he was being held up somewhere and prevented from coming back, and that if she did certain things, performed certain as yet unknown rites, and waited long enough, he would return. At moments in the day she would stop whatever she was doing and stand very still, listening, as if to hear his step in the hall, as if the door would open and he would come walking in, whistling, with the paper under his arm. At night especially she listened for him, for the small distant sound of his key in the front door lock, for the creak of the loose board on the first step of the stairs, for the bathroom tap to run, for the lavatory to flush, for the light switch to click off. It was all nonsense, she knew, this breathless waiting for the impossible to happen, yet she could not stop herself. It comforted her, imagining that he would come back.

She was glad of Davy's presence in the house, infrequent though it was. He stayed out as much as he could, but when he was there he was some kind of company. They did not talk about his father, or the circumstances of his death. Death, she had discovered, causes an awkwardness, a kind of embarrassment, among the bereaved. The thing was too big to be dwelled on. It was as if some huge thing had been thrust into their midst, as if a great stone ball had come crashing through the roof and sat now immovable between them, so that they had to negotiate their way round it and at the same time pretend it was not there.

Davy shied from her, and would hardly meet her eye. He had been like that before his father died, throughout the week after Victor Delahaye's death. She was reminded of when he was a boy and she had walked into his room one day without knocking—she could not believe she had been so careless—and found him lying on the bed with his trousers open and doing that thing to himself that men did. For weeks afterwards he would not look at her and blushed furiously if she came near him. Now it was like that again, only worse. Did he hold her responsible in some way for Jack's death? She had read somewhere that when children lose a parent they sometimes blame the one who has survived, and Davy in so many respects was still a kind of child. But what about Victor's death? How could he think she had any responsibility for that? It was Davy himself whom Victor had taken with him on that last terrible trip out to sea.

Did Davy know more than he was saying, about both deaths? Not that he said much. These days he was like an animal in hiding, folded into himself, showing nothing but sharp spines.

She tried her best to bring him out of himself, to make him talk to her, to tell her whatever things it was he knew and was keeping secret. She had him drive her to visit Jack's grave every day. They ate lunch together, in the kitchen, in silence. She cooked dinner for him, too, but as often as not he stayed out until long after dinnertime, and she would make up a plate and leave it for him on top of the stove. It was an eerie sensation to come down in the morning and find the food eaten, the plate washed and put away. Her son was more of a ghost for her than Jack was. Unlike Davy, however, Jack was not a presence but a vast absence. She might wait in constant expectation for him to come back, but he would not come back, not ever again.

On Davy's twenty-fifth birthday she took him for a treat to lunch at the Hibernian Hotel. She could see he did not want to go, but she insisted he should put on a suit and tie, while she wore a dark blue suit that she did not think looked too much like widow's weeds—the occasion was supposed to be a celebration, after all—and together they took a taxi in from Dun Laoghaire. They were late, but they still managed to get a good table, by the window, looking out on Dawson Street. She had fish while Davy ate a steak. She persuaded him to drink a glass of wine, although usually he drank only beer, and not much of that.

She watched him across the table as he ate, and a lump came to her throat to see how much like his father he was becoming, with the same deftness, the same attentiveness to the smallest things. He was a good boy, she thought—and was glad he was not able to hear her refer to him as a boy—even if he could be difficult at times. She knew so little about him, what he did, where he went, who his friends were. Did he mean to be secretive, to keep things from her, or was that just the way all grown-up sons were with their mothers? Lonely though her own life would be from now on, she must not attempt to pry into his affairs, or make him think she expected him to share things with her. After all, he was not a boy, he was a man, and his own man, at that. Just like his father.

Glancing about, she caught sight of someone at a table on the other side of the dining room whose face she knew although for a moment she could not put a name to it. He was large, and wore a double-breasted black suit. There was a woman with him, who was also somewhat familiar, though Sylvia was sure she had never met her. When the couple had finished their lunch they passed close by on their way out, and the man stopped, and a second before he spoke she remembered who he was.

"Mrs. Clancy," he said, "how are you? My name is Quirke. I'm a—I'm an associate of Detective Inspector Hackett's. I was at your husband's funeral. I'm very sorry for your loss."

She thanked him, and introduced Davy, who gave him an

openly hostile stare and turned away and glared out the window into the sunlit street. Quirke's lady friend had gone on a
few paces, and stopped now and looked back with a polite vague
smile. She was that actress; Sylvia suddenly recognized her—
what was her name? Galligan? Galloway? She was good-looking,
in an actressy sort of way.

Quirke was still standing there, beside the table, as if he
expected her to say something more, to do something more.
She was keenly aware of his dark bulk, which seemed to lean
over her a little, and suddenly something gave way inside her,
and she thought she might be about to weep. What was the
matter with her? She did not know this man, had only glimpsed
him once before, in the churchyard, and now here she was,
ready to clasp his hand and bury her face in his sleeve and
shed hot tears. She tried to speak. "I—I wonder if—" She
snatched up her handbag from the floor where she had left it
leaning against the leg of her chair and opened it and rum-
maged in it for a handkerchief. She must not cry, not here, in
front of these people, this man, this stranger!

He had started to move on. She twisted about on the chair,
looking up at him urgently. What did she want of him? He
paused, seeing the silent appeal in her look. He frowned and
smiled, seeming to understand. But to understand what? She
did not herself understand what was happening, why she
wanted him not to go but to stay here beside her. "I'll come
back," he said. "Just a minute." He stepped away, and touched a
finger to the actress's elbow, and they went on, moving between
the tables, and a moment later Sylvia saw them outside on the
pavement, Quirke speaking and the actress looking at him

with a quizzical smile and then shrugging and turning to walk away. Quirke, feeling himself watched, glanced back and caught Sylvia's eye through the window, and they continued gazing at each other for a long moment.

THEY SAT IN ARMCHAIRS IN THE LOBBY WITH A LITTLE TABLE between them on which a waitress had set out a pot of coffee and cups and saucers and plates of biscuits and thin square sandwiches. When Quirke had come back into the dining room, Davy had put down his napkin and gone off, angrily, it seemed to his mother. What was there for him to be angry about? Surely she could speak to whomever she liked.

She no longer felt like crying, and anyway the tears that had threatened would have been tears not of sorrow but relief. Yes, relief. There was something about this man sitting before her that she felt she could trust. It was not that he seemed particularly warm or sympathetic. Quite the opposite, in fact. She felt he was the kind of man she could speak to precisely because of a certain coolness, a certain stoniness, she detected in him. She could tell him her secrets and he would keep them, not out of discretion or consideration for her, but out of—what? Disinterest? Indifference? Well, that would be fine. Indifference would be fine.

"Tell me, Mr.—what did you say your name was?"

"Quirke."

"Tell me, Mr. Quirke, why did you come to the funeral? You didn't know my husband, did you?"

"No, I didn't."

She waited, but obviously nothing more was coming. She poured herself a cup of coffee. "Do I remember seeing you at Victor Delahaye's funeral, too?"

"Yes, I was there." He had ordered a glass of whiskey with his coffee. She could smell the sharp hot fragrance of the liquor. "A tragic business," he said. "First Mr. Delahaye, and then your husband. You must be very shocked." His hands were quite delicate, she noticed, pale and soft-looking. His feet were small too, for such a large man.

"Yes, we're all shocked, of course," she said with a flicker of impatience; she had no time for small talk now.

He drank his whiskey. She could see him watching her without seeming to. She did not know what she wanted to say to him, what secrets they were she thought she might trust him with. Yet something was pressing inside her, like some small trapped thing pressing to be released.

"Your husband was an experienced sailor, I think," he said.

"Yes, he was. Very experienced, very expert. He had won trophies—" She broke off; how fatuous that sounded. "He had," she said levelly, "a great love and knowledge of the sea. I think—" She stopped again. What on earth was it that was coming? "I think my husband was killed." She swallowed, making a gulping noise. "I don't think he died by accident. I think he was murdered."

She was not sure what she would have expected him to do, but whatever it might have been, he did not do it. He merely sat there, with his elbows on his knees and the whiskey glass in one hand, gazing at her without the slightest expression that she could see. She thought what a peculiar man he was. "Why do you think he was murdered?" he asked.

She almost laughed. "Do you mean why was he murdered, or why do I think he was?"

He shrugged. "Both, I suppose."

"I have no idea!" It was almost a cry, the way she said it. She could hardly believe that she was uttering these things aloud, to this bizarre man, in a hotel lobby, on what was otherwise a perfectly ordinary afternoon in summer. *Did* she believe Jack had been murdered? As far as she was aware, the possibility had not entered her head before she'd blurted it out just now. Was this what had been inside her all along, struggling to get out, without her knowing what it was? She felt as if she were standing on the very brink of a dizzyingly deep abyss. What things were down there, at the bottom, writhing and struggling? "I'm sure I'm being fanciful," she said. "You must forgive me." Her coffee cup rattled in the saucer when she set it down. "It's probably hysteria—certainly that must be what you're thinking. I'm sorry."

Quirke nodded; she had the impression his mind was elsewhere.

"Mrs. Clancy," he said, "I wonder if you're aware that I'm a doctor, and that a postmortem was carried out on your husband?"

She gazed at him, appalled, yet fascinated, too. She must not look at his hands again, she must not; to think what they had done to Jack. "I knew a postmortem had been carried out, of course," she said, controlling herself.

He nodded again. "And there'll be an inquest. I'll be giving evidence to it."

"Oh, yes?" She felt a thrill of dread. "And what will it be, your evidence?"

"That your husband died by drowning."

She waited; talking to this man was like making a long-distance telephone call on a faulty line. "Nothing else?" she said.

He took the last sip of his whiskey and set the empty glass down on the table. For such a large man his gestures were curiously precise, even finical. "There was a bruise on the back of his head, on the right side, just behind his ear." He touched a finger to his own head to show her the place.

"Yes," she said, "someone told me that." She was breathless, as if with excitement. What did this man know? What things had he found out?

"The blow he suffered," he said, "was the kind of blow it would have been difficult for him to inflict on himself, I mean by falling and hitting his head on some part of the boat, say."

"Maybe the sail, I mean the mast, the what-do-you-call-it, the boom, maybe it swung somehow and hit him on the head."

He made a show of considering this, and gave her a squinting look. "Do you sail, Mrs. Clancy?"

"No, no. Jack took me out sometimes, but I had no feel for it. To be honest, I've always been a little afraid of the sea." Her mouth twitched in a faint smile. "I must have had a premonition."

Quirke smiled too, lifting his shoulders. "I don't know much about boats either," he said. "But I know that the night your husband died there was hardly a breath of wind. I think there would have to have been a gale for the boom to swing hard enough to make such a traumatic bruise."

There was a silence. She gazed at him as if hypnotized, her eyes very wide. "Are you saying, Dr. Quirke, that you agree with me? That you think my husband was killed?"

"I don't know. I'm not a detective."

This amused her. "A person could be forgiven for thinking otherwise."

He inclined his head in a small bow of ironical acknowledgment. "I have a great curiosity," he said. "If I were a cat, I'd have been dead long ago."

The sunlight was gone from the street outside, and when she looked past Quirke to the glass front door she saw that a summer shower had started up. She imagined being out there, in the damp coolness, with the soft rain falling on her face, her hands. She closed her eyes for a moment. She tried to picture Jack as he was the last time she had seen him and could not; poor dear foolish Jack, who was dead.

"Tell me why you think your husband was murdered," Quirke said.

She opened her eyes. "You asked me that already."

"I'm asking again."

The rain was heavier now, and she fancied she could hear faintly the hiss and drum of it as it beat down on the city. When she was a little girl she used to love to watch the rain. She saw herself at the window of her Granny Morgan's house in Colwyn Bay, leaning on the sill with her chin on her hands, smelling the dusty cretonne of the curtains. What a dreamer she was in those days. Every July the family came up from London to stay for a week with her grandmother. Wales was nice. Such friendly people, with that lovely lilting accent. Granny Morgan's house was at the top of a steep street, and when the rain was heavy the drops would hit the road and hop up again, and she would imagine a vast corps of tiny silver ballerinas pirouetting down the hill.

"I think he was having an affair," she said.

Once again she had startled herself. The man opposite her cleared his throat and shifted heavily in the armchair. She looked down and saw his preposterously dainty feet, crossed at the ankles, and again she felt she might laugh in delight. It was a very long time since she had spoken like this to anyone, let alone a man she hardly knew. Or had she spoken like this before, ever?

"I'm sorry," Quirke said. "This is no business of mine."

"Would it be, if you were a real policeman?" The tone of her own voice, teasing and playful, shocked her. Was she *flirting* with this man? One is never too old or too distressed, she reflected, to make a bloody fool of oneself. "Forgive me," she said, with a faint laugh. "I don't know why I'm being so—so giddy." Quirke, his eyes downcast, was lighting a cigarette, and she could not make out his expression. A sudden crimson flash of pain struck along her spine and made her catch her breath. She forced herself to sit up straight and stay very still. Her pain was like a child she was carrying inside her, she had to nurse it, to lull it, so that it would not wake fully and set to clawing at her with its tiny sharp nails.

Quirke picked up the empty whiskey glass and turned it in his fingers. She gazed at him. "I'm sorry," she said, "I shouldn't have blurted that out about Jack and—and my suspicions. If he was having an affair, it wasn't the first time." She looked at him almost pleadingly. "I suppose that detective has found out about my husband's reputation. Unlike many men, Jack genuinely liked women. He found them"—she gave a rueful laugh—"interesting. To talk to, I mean. That makes a man very attractive, if women feel he's interested, and will listen to them. And he could be funny, too. That's another attraction. So, all in all, there was nothing for me to do but grin and bear it. He always came back to me in the end—"

She broke off and laughed again, more sadly this time. "That's what every woman in my position says, isn't it. Pathetic." She took a sip from her cup; the coffee had gone cold, and had a bitter taste. "It's a thing you discover, how hackneyed it all is. You hear yourself saying things that you'd laugh at if you read them in a magazine story. It makes it all the harder."

Quirke lifted his hand and signaled to the waitress, and when she came he ordered another whiskey, then turned and asked if she would like something else. "More coffee, perhaps?"

"No, thank you." The girl began to move away. "Or wait, yes, I will have something." She thought. "I'll have a sherry, please. Dry." When the girl had gone she smiled at Quirke a little shamefacedly. "I shouldn't, really—I had a glass of wine at lunch. Alcohol goes straight to my head, I'm afraid. I'll get tipsy and you'll think me a complete idiot."

Quirke leaned back in the chair, watching her, the smoke from his cigarette curling up past his jaw, so that he had to half close one eye, which gave him the look of a screen villain, and she had to bite her lip to keep from smiling.

"If your husband was—involved with someone," Quirke asked, "do you think it's connected with the way he died?"

"I don't *know*," she cried. "Maybe some irate husband went after him—maybe there was a fight."

"Is there anyone you can think of that might have been angry with him?"

She shook her head. "Jack never talked about the people he saw, for obvious reasons. And I never asked, for the same reasons." She made a fist and struck it into the palm of her other hand. "My God, why does it all have to be so banal, so— so grubby."

Their drinks came. She tasted the sherry; it was sweet, of course. She did not have the heart to send it back. In the street the rain had stopped, and suddenly the sun came out, as if a curtain had been drawn swiftly aside, and the tarmac shone and car roofs threw off big floppy flashes of light, like huge bubbles forming and bursting. Quirke's face had retreated into shadow, but she could see his eyes, fixed on her speculatively.

"Did your husband talk about work, at all?" he asked.

"Work?" she said. "You mean the office and all that? Hardly." She laughed. "I don't think the affairs of Delahaye and Clancy were ever uppermost in his mind."

"So he didn't ever say anything to you about there being— disputes, that kind of thing?"

"What do you mean, disputes? With the office staff? Strikes?"

"No, no." He hesitated. "It seems there was something going on inside the company. Shares were being manipulated, moved around."

"Shares," she said blankly. "Company shares, you mean?" She stopped, then began slowly again. "Are you saying—are you saying my husband was—I don't know—embezzling money from the business?"

"No, not embezzling."

"What, then?" Under the sleeves of her suit she had a crawling sensation along the inner sides of her arms.

"Do you know a person called Maverley?" he asked.

"Duncan Maverley?" Her mouth took on a sour twist. "Of course. What about him?"

"At the funeral—the funeral of Mr. Delahaye—this man Maverley spoke to Inspector Hackett and me. He wasn't very clear—I mean, he wasn't very forthcoming—but what he seemed to be intimating was that your husband was planning, was in fact carrying out, a wholesale takeover of the business, to put himself in Victor Delahaye's position as head of the firm."

She reached out gropingly and grasped the sherry glass and took a gulp of the oily sweet drink. She had hoped the alcohol would steady her nerves but it was only making her feel more shaky still. This was madness, all madness. That dreadful little man Maverley, what kind of mischief was he attempting? "I don't know what to say, it seems an insane accusation. Jack didn't have that kind of ambition. He was content to be the junior boss—you know that's how everyone referred to him, and how he often referred to himself—and sail his boat and see his friends at the yacht club and—" She stopped. *And play at love with his girls* was what she might have said, too.

And yet. Who knows what goes on inside the minds of other people? She had been married to Jack Clancy for more than a quarter of a century, but could she put her hand on her heart and swear that she had known him? What had he been like when he was with one of his "bits on the side," for instance? If she had seen him cavorting with some trollop—and, thank God, she never had—would she have recognized him? He had despised and resented Victor Delahaye, she knew that, but surely he had long ago reconciled himself to a secondary position in the house of Delahaye & Clancy? But then, what if he had not? What if these accusations the poisonous Duncan Maverley had made were true? She felt pity, suddenly. Poor

Jack, scheming and plotting like a little boy, planning, for years probably, to do down the Delahayes and make himself the senior boss, without ever a word of it to anyone, not even to her. Had his life been nothing but shame and humiliation, as he chafed under the disdainful patronage of a man for whom he felt nothing but contempt? Was that why he had chased after girls, in order to have a little success in some aspect of his life? Had they given him the admiration and sympathy that everyone else had withheld from him? Everyone else, including her. Yes, surely that was it. How had she not seen it? If she had seen it before now, she might have been able to help him, might have done something to assuage his shame and frustration, his rage against himself and the world.

But no, she told herself, no—she *had* known, of course she had. She had known and had chosen not to know. It was exactly what she had always secretly despised in the Irish, that capacity for self-delusion, that two-faced way of dealing with the world. She was just as dishonest, as hypocritical, as anyone else, and might as well admit it.

She stood up suddenly, clutching her handbag and looking about herself wildly. Her lower lip was trembling. She needed the lavatory urgently. Quirke, too, rose to his feet, and she reared back almost in fright—she had almost forgotten that he was there. He was saying something, but she was not listening. She shook her head and stepped back. "I must go," she said, in a choked voice. "I'm sorry, I have to—" And she turned and fled.

12

THE FIRST THING THAT STRUCK PHOEBE WAS THE FACT THAT they had known where to find her. But how had they known? She had been in the habit of stopping at the coffee shop two or three evenings a week on her way home from work. It was a place where she could be on her own—she had not even told David Sinclair about it. The owner of the shop, Mr. Baldini, an Italian man of middle age with wonderfully soft eyes and a melancholy smile, knew her well by now, and would greet her when she came in, and would show her to her favorite table by the window, as if she were a regular at some grand restaurant and he the maître d'. She would sit at the plastic-topped table in a wedge of evening sunlight and read the paper, and drink a cup of milky coffee and eat one of the dismayingly sweet little cakes that the owner's wife baked in the kitchen at the back, from where there wafted warm smells of vanilla and chocolate

and roasted coffee beans. She prized these intervals of solitude, and was shocked this evening when the Delahaye twins
came in and without being invited sat down at her table.

She could not get used to the uncanny likeness between
them. Looking at them sitting there smilingly side by side,
she had the unnerving sensation, as she always had in their
presence, that a fiendish and immensely complicated trick was
being played on her, by means of mirrors and revolving chairs
and walls that only looked like walls. They were dressed alike,
in brown corduroy slacks and short-sleeved gray woolen shirts,
and each had a cricket sweater slung over his back with the
sleeves loosely knotted in front. She would not have been surprised if they had begun to speak to her in unison, like a pair
of characters out of the Alice books.

"Hello," she said, keeping her voice steady and her tone light.
"I thought I was the only one who knew about this place."

"Ah," the one on the left said, "but you see, we're good at
nosing out secrets." He pressed his smiling face forward across
the table, making snuffling noises, like a pig after a truffle.
Then he lifted a hand and showed her the signet ring on his
little finger. "I'm Jonas, by the way, to save you having to ask."

The other one, James, laughed. She looked at him. She had
noted before how strange his eyes were, hazed over somehow
and yet alight with eagerness, as if he lived in constant expectation of some grand and hilariously violent event that he was
convinced would begin to unfold at any moment. She wondered uneasily if his mind was quite right. "Where's your boyfriend this evening?" he asked, with a sort of playful truculence.

"Yes, where is he?" Jonas said. "We thought one of you was
never seen without the other, like James and me."

James at this gave a snort of laughter, as if it were richly funny.

"He's at work, I think," Phoebe said. These days he always seemed to be at work, whatever the time of day. That was why she was here now, trying to fill in some of the long night that was ahead of her.

"Mit ze cadavers, ja?" Jonas said, putting on a comic accent and making a broad slicing gesture, as with a scalpel. "Professor Frankenstein in his laboratory."

She did not know what to reply. She pushed her coffee cup aside and gathered up her purse and her *Irish Times* and made to rise, but Jonas reached across and pressed an index finger to the back of her hand, quite hard, and she sat down again, slowly. "Don't go," he said pleasantly. "We've only just arrived."

Mr. Baldini came to take the twins' order. He was from a hill town in Tuscany, he had told her. She often wondered how he had ended up here, but did not like to ask. The twins said they would have coffee and a cake, like her. Mr. Baldini nodded, unsmiling. His soft brown eyes slid sideways and met hers, as if to send a warning signal. Had the twins been here before? Did he know something about them that she did not? "For you, signorina?" he said. "Something else, perhaps?" She shook her head and he turned to go, as if reluctantly, and gave her again that odd, cautioning look.

"Enjoy the party?" Jonas said.

"The one at Breen's house?"

"Where we saw you, yes."

"It was all right. A bit too noisy for me."

Jonas played a brief tattoo on the edge of the table with his fingers. "Good old Breen, eh?" he said. "Good old Breen." He was looking at her with what seemed a dreamily calculating air. She wondered what he was thinking, but decided it was probably better not to know.

"Breen is a brick," James said, more loudly than was necessary. "A real brick."

"James is fond of rhyming slang," Jonas said, and grinned, and winked.

Mr. Baldini brought the coffee and the cakes. "Two and eightpence," he said.

Jonas glanced up at him, and the Italian stared back stonily. For a moment there was the sense of something teetering in the air, dipping first this way and then that. Then Jonas shrugged. "Pay the man, Jamesy," he said quietly, smiling at Phoebe, and began to hum under his breath the tune of "O Sole Mio." James handed over a ten-shilling note, and Mr. Baldini went off again.

Jonas, pushing aside the coffee and the plate with the cake on it, extended his arms straight out in front of him across the table, almost touching Phoebe's face, and turned his hands backwards and linked his fingers and pressed them against each other, making his knuckles crack. Then he gave himself a shivery shake and blew loudly through slack lips like a horse. "Seeing your chap later, are you?" he asked. Phoebe nodded. "Jolly good," Jonas said, giving her again that narrow speculative stare. "In the meantime," he said, "why not come along with us?"

She stared back. "Come along where?"

"We're off to the ancestral pile. Have a glass of something, bite to eat, listen to the wind-up gramophone. Typical relaxed evening chez Delahaye. What do you say? The stepmater is home, I'm sure she'd love to meet you. She's a bit of a party girl herself, though you mightn't think it to see her in her widow's weeds."

She looked at the two of them, Jonas lazily smiling and James with that avid light in his eye. It would be foolish to go with them, she knew, and yet, to her surprise, a small sharp voice in her head immediately spoke up, urging her to accept.

"All right," she heard herself say, with an insouciance she did not really feel, "but just for an hour."

"That's settled, then!" Jonas exclaimed, and smacked both his palms flat on the table and stood up. He was wearing a Trinity tie for a belt. *"Avanti!"*

He went first, with Phoebe after him and James following. Phoebe could feel the twin's eye on her, and a tiny tremor made her shoulder blades twitch. At the door she glanced back and saw Mr. Baldini standing by the big silver espresso machine, looking after her with a grave and melancholy gaze.

The evening was smoky and hot. They walked along by the railings of St. Stephen's Green, the two young men sauntering with their hands in their pockets and Phoebe in the middle, to where Jonas's car, a low-slung, two-door red Jaguar, was parked under the trees. "See that shop?" Jonas said, pointing across the road to Smyth's. "I once bought a jar of honey there with bumblebees drowned in it. And a box of chocolate-covered ants."

"Why did you do that?" Phoebe asked.

Jonas was unlocking the door on the driver's side. "Wedding presents," he said, "for our new mummy, when Daddy bethought himself to marry again."

Phoebe was not sure if she was meant to laugh. "And did she like them, your stepmother?"

"Scoffed the lot. You should have heard her crack those ants between her little pearly teeth."

James climbed into the narrow back seat while Jonas took

the wheel, with Phoebe beside him. They roared off in a cloud
of tire smoke. Phoebe was aware of her heart madly beating.
What was she thinking of, how had she dared?

In Northumberland Road the tree-lined pavements were dappled with late gold, and midges in clouds bobbed and rose like
bubbles in a champagne glass. Jonas slewed the car in at the
gate almost without slowing, making the gravel fly, and drew to
a bucking stop beside the front steps.

As they walked up to the door, James lagged behind again, to
have another look at her, Phoebe felt sure. A phrase came
to her, *drawing up the rear,* and she smiled somewhat bleakly
to herself. Would she tell David about this exploit she had
allowed herself to be taken on? She thought not. She could
imagine the look he would give her, out of those liquid brown
eyes of his, with his head skeptically tilted and his chin
tucked in.

The hall was cool. A seething patch of sunlight from the
open doorway settled briefly on the parquet. "Welcome to the
House of Usher," Jonas said gaily, and James did another of his
snorting laughs. Phoebe, despite herself, rather liked the idea
of being the menaced innocent in a gothic tale. A red-haired
maid, young, with thick ankles, appeared at the other end of
the hall and, seeing Phoebe with the twins, gave a sardonic
half grin and withdrew to wherever she had come from. "The
staff, as you see," Jonas said, "lack a certain polish." He made
a deep bow, with an arm extended. "This way to the funhouse,
ladies and gents!"

The drawing room glowed with greenish light from the garden. Phoebe noted the vast white sofa, the Mainie Jellett on
the wall behind it, the sideboard with bottles, cut-glass decant-

ers, a soda siphon. There was a big bunch of red and yellow roses in a china bowl on the table.

"A drink," Jonas said, making for the sideboard. "My dear, what will you take?"

Phoebe hesitated. Should she drink? Probably not. "Gin," she said firmly. "I'd like a gin and tonic."

"That's my girl! James, be a dear and fetch some ice from the kitchen. And see if there's a lime, will you?" He grinned at Phoebe. "Lemons are so *common,* don't you think?"

Phoebe walked to the window and stood looking into the garden. She was conscious of herself as a figure there, as if she were posing for her portrait. *Young Woman by a Window.* She had grown up in a house like this, not so large or luxuriously appointed, but with the same hushed air, the same high ceilings, the same fragrance of roses and floor polish. Here, though, there was something else. What was it? The faintest hint of something sickly, as in a room where lately an invalid had lived, that even the musky scent of the roses could not mask.

James came back with the ice, lobbing a lime high into the air and catching it expertly in his palm with a small sharp smack.

"By the way," Jonas said, plopping ice cubes into Phoebe's glass and handing it to her, "we were questioned by the rozzers— did you know?"

She thought at first he was making a joke, but decided he was not. "No," she said carefully. "What did they want to ask you about?"

"Yes," he said, ignoring her question, "the good old third degree. Shall we sit?"

They took to the sofa, with Phoebe perched in the middle, Jonas lounging to her right, and James sitting a little too close to her on the left. Now that she was seeing them properly and had a chance to study them, she realized that far from being identical they were in fact entirely distinct. The circumstance of looking so alike might be no more than an ingenious piece of mimicry, the putting on of a kind of camouflage behind which they could hide in order to spy on the world. Jonas was the brighter of the two. He was clever and quick, and funny in a brittle sort of way, while James, with that laugh and that air of avid anticipation, was distinctly alarming. Yet if she were to be afraid of them, she knew, it was Jonas who would frighten her the most.

"It was just like in the movies," Jonas was saying now. "They took us downstairs, to the basement, and put us in separate cells, so we wouldn't be able to coordinate our stories, and asked us all kinds of things." He nodded at her glass. "Need some more ice?"

She shook her head. "What kinds of things did they ask?"

"Oh, silly stuff. It was that pal of your dad's, Inspector—what's it?"

"Hackett?" she said, surprised.

At the name, for some reason James, on her other side, laughed. She thought of the monkey house at the zoo.

"Yes, that's it," Jonas said. "Hackett. Good name for a detective. Bit of a rough diamond. Country cute, I'll grant you, but not what you'd call bright. *Can you tell me now, young lad,*" he said, doing an uncannily close imitation of Hackett's tone and accent, "*where you were on the night of the full moon, and can you produce a witness to prove it?"* He smiled at her, and his voice sank to a purr. "That would be you, my dear. Our witness."

"Me?"

"Yes. At Breen's place, the night of the party. I told you already."

"Why did he want to know where you were? Why that night?"

The brothers glanced at each other. Jonas laughed. "Because, my dear, that was the night Jack Clancy fell out of his boat and drowned."

She looked away. Yes; yes, of course.

Abruptly Jonas sprang up from the sofa. "Music," he said. "Let's have some music."

At the other end of the room there was a radiogram, a great mahogany brute standing on four little braced peglike legs. Jonas opened wide the cabinet doors and leaned down to read the spines of the record sleeves. "Eeny meeny miney mo," he murmured, and extracted an album, "catch old Frankie by the toe!" He turned, showing the record cover with its stylized portrait of the singer—the hat, the cigarette—standing in a melancholy mood on a street corner at night. "Frankie-boy," he said, "every bobby-soxer's damp dream. Here we go." He took out the disc and put it on the turntable. There was a faint hiss and then came the first plinking notes of the tune picked out against a soupy orchestral background. Jonas struck a pose, head back, nostrils flared, his arms encircling an invisible partner, then danced a sweeping step or two, singing along with the record. Phoebe could feel James beside her laughing without sound. Still singing, Jonas now supplied his own lyrics.

"Where were you, lad, on that fatal evening?
Can you prooooove your whe-ere-abouts?
If I ask Miss Griffin if she saw you
Will she back up your cast-iron al-i-biiieee?"

He danced now in the direction of the sofa, and as he swept past he grabbed Phoebe's wrist and drew her stumbling to her feet and took her in his arms and waltzed her off around the room at such a pace she felt her feet were hardly touching the floor. His brother, meanwhile, threw himself back on the sofa, clapping his hands and raucously whinnying.

Phoebe, her heart hammering in its cage, saw the room spinning around her. She was dizzy already. She could smell the man who was holding her, his odor a mingling of sweat, cologne, and something else, sharp and sour, a faint acid reek. On the second turn around the room she glimpsed over Jonas's shoulder the door opening, and someone, a woman, coming in. For a second the woman's face, slender and pale, was a point of stillness in the general whirl; then Jonas swept on, whirling Phoebe with him. They passed by James, asprawl with his arms stretched out at either side along the back of the sofa, watching her with huge enjoyment. Then in rapid succession came the window, the sideboard, the sofa and James seated, the Jellett abstract, and then the woman again, in the doorway.

Jonas too had seen her, and veered towards her now, and letting go of Phoebe's left hand he caught the woman by the wrist and pulled her into the dance with them. On they dashed, three of them now, whirling and whirling. The woman seemed quite calm, and merely amused, as if she were used to this kind of thing. Smiling, she kept her eye fixed on Phoebe. Abruptly Jonas let go of both of them and flung himself down with a great laughing gasp to sprawl beside his brother. Phoebe stumbled, and would have fallen if the woman had not put an arm round her waist and held her firmly. They waltzed on together, the woman keeping no better time to the music than Jonas had. She was wearing a green silk blouse and a black skirt with petticoats underneath it.

"I'm Mona," she said. "Mona Delahaye. And you're Phoebe, yes? I know your father, a little."

The song ended and they stopped, and Phoebe stood panting, and smiled back at the smiling woman, and thought how little like a widow she seemed. Both twins now regarded them with keen interest. Mona ignored them, and walked to the rosewood sideboard and poured herself a gin, and added a splash of tonic. "You two," she said accusingly, addressing the twins over her shoulder, "you've used all the ice again!"

Jonas looked sideways at his brother, and James put his hands on his knees and heaved himself to his feet with a histrionic sigh. "Oh, all right," he said, "I'll go."

When he had left Mona went and sat where he had been sitting, pressing down her skirt and ballooning petticoats with a careless gesture, and smiled at Phoebe again and patted the place beside her. "Come," she said, "come and sit." She turned her head and spoke to Jonas. "Move over, you."

Phoebe did as she was invited and came and sat down beside Mona. She felt exhilarated, but dizzy, too, more than dizzy—how much gin had she drunk?—and her tongue felt thick and she had difficulty focusing her eyes. Mona had grabbed Jonas's glass and with her fingers fished out what remained of the ice cubes in it and dropped them into her own drink.

"Hey!" Jonas said, laughing as he attempted to take back his glass. "You are a cow."

"And you're a pig," Mona answered complacently.

They were like a pair of spoiled siblings fighting over a toy, Phoebe thought. This observation seemed to her at once profound and funny. She blinked—could she be tipsy already?

Mona turned to her. Mona had the most extraordinary violet eyes that tapered at their outer edges and turned up into points. Her scarlet lipstick made her face seem all the more pale. She was very lovely, though her lips were a little thin. Phoebe wondered what it would feel like to be a man kissing that mouth. At that moment, as if Mona had read Phoebe's thoughts, she parted her lips and Phoebe glimpsed between them the fire-pink sharp little tip of her tongue. That was what she would do if she were being kissed, she would open her mouth like that, just barely parting the lips, and the tip of her tongue would dart out.

"You look quite wild," Mona said. "What have these two brutes been doing to you?"

"Oh, just—dancing," Phoebe said. Her head felt terribly heavy all of a sudden, and she leaned back against the sofa, letting her shoulders droop.

"She's a very good dancer." Jonas spoke in a soberly judicious tone.

"Yes, she is," Mona said.

She was still smiling and gazing searchingly at Phoebe.

"She has wings on her heels." Jonas, too, was looking at Phoebe, leaning forward to see past Mona.

"Have you?" Mona said, still gazing at Phoebe. "Have you wings at your heels?"

With both those pairs of eyes fixed on her, Phoebe felt as if she were an exotic creature perched in a cage and being stared at. What a narrow face Jonas had, a narrow face and a wide mouth, which gave him a faintly cruel look.

James came back with the ice and Jonas insisted that they all have another gin and tonic. Phoebe protested feebly that she did not want anything more to drink, but was ignored. She was still sitting with her head leaning against the back on the sofa and her hands resting limply in her lap. Mona, beside her, touched her hair, peering more deeply still into her eyes. "Jonas," she said, "you haven't given her anything, have you?"

Jonas, at the sideboard again pouring drinks, threw her a look of exaggerated outrage. "As if I would!" He brought them their glasses. Phoebe had difficulty holding hers, though it felt wonderfully cool. She lifted it before her face in both hands and watched with fascination a drop of condensed moisture making its way in a gleaming zigzag down the misted side. It seemed to her magical, a thing never witnessed before now. She wanted to tell the others about it but did not think she would be able to find the words.

"Come along," Jonas said briskly, extending a hand to each of them and taking Phoebe's glass. "Let's us face the music, my dears, and dance!"

The two women stood up. Phoebe's knees wobbled, and she reached out before her for support, and Mona took her hand and put an arm round her waist again, and slowly they began to dance. James and Jonas too were dancing together now. Round and round the floor they went, the two couples, in opposite directions. Each time they passed each other Jonas would make an elaborate, eighteenth-century bow, and James would laugh his laugh.

Phoebe, her head spinning, felt herself gliding off into a sort of trance. Her feet seemed very far away, and glancing down she saw with surprise that they were moving as if by themselves, to their own rhythm, pacing out the measure of the dance. Once her arm brushed against the side of Mona's breast, but Mona seemed not to notice. The scarab-green silk of Mona's blouse felt as if there were electricity running through it.

On the record, Sinatra's voice had a sad little sob in it.

Someone kicked the door from outside and it flew open and an old man in a wheelchair, with a mane of gray hair, propelled himself over the threshold. He glared at the dancing couples and his face darkened with fury, and there was a sort of rumbling sound in his chest as the words gathered there, and he made a fist of his right hand and smashed it down on the arm of the wheelchair. *"This is a house of mourning!"* he bellowed, in the thundering tones of a hellfire preacher.

The dancers halted. Phoebe swayed on her feet. Mona's arm was still encircling her waist. She seemed to be laughing, very softly.

"Hello, Grandad," Jonas said brightly. "Care for a snorter?"

The man in the wheelchair looked at him, his head trembling and his eyes blazing. "You young whelp!" he said, half choking on the words.

Everything in front of Phoebe had begun to swim. Her head felt so heavy, so heavy. She took a step forward and leaned her forehead on Mona's shoulder. "I think," she said, and her voice was so thick now she could hardly make it out herself, "I think I'm going to . . ."

ISABEL WAS LATE, AS SO OFTEN. QUIRKE DID NOT MIND. HE WAS in McGonagle's, in the back snug, known for some reason as the Casbah, where only the most regular of regulars were allowed to enter. He had the *Evening Mail* before him on the table, quarter-folded, which was the way he liked to read a newspaper, and a large whiskey at his elbow. The Casbah, cramped and cozy, struck a faintly nautical note. It might have been the cabin of a trawler. There was a lot of dark brown wood that somehow was always faintly and stickily damp to the touch, and the head-high wooden partition that separated it from the rest of the pub had a row of small low-set frosted-glass windows that were reminiscent of portholes. The air was shadowed and smoky, but a chink of evening sunlight from somewhere had set a glowing jewel in the bottom of the whiskey glass.

He was reading a story about a case of criminal conversation, in which a man had sued his business partner for having an affair with his wife. "Criminal conversation." Who thought up these terms? Maybe it was a direct translation from the Latin. The case was a nasty one, with evidence not only from the three people involved but also from hotel clerks and chambermaids and even from one of the conductors on the Howth tram. What must the woman feel? Perhaps he might ask Isabel.

He knew very well he should not be drinking whiskey so early in the evening. In fact, he should not be drinking spirits at all. He had promised Phoebe he would keep to wine only, and that even wine he would take in moderation, yet here he was, breaking that promise. It was a familiar sensation, this slight buzz of shame at the back of his mind.

There were certain conditions, most of them bad, that had become ingrained in him over the years, so that now he could not imagine his life without them. First and foremost of these conditions was dislike of himself, a mild but irresolvable distaste for what he did and what he was. In his better moments, his rare self-absolving moments, he regarded this permanent state of self-deprecation as, paradoxically, a sign of some virtue. For if he disapproved of himself, must there not be a finer side to him, however firmly it was turned away, that was doing the disapproving? Surely the truly wicked ones thought nothing of their wickedness, were not even aware of it, or if they were they gloried in it, like Iago or Milton's Satan. Of course, by maintaining a low regard for himself he was giving himself the excuse to carry on as he wished to, with no thought for anyone else. Being bad, as he was, and as he acknowledged he was, lifted a weight of responsibility from his soul. *I do as I do and can do no other.* That was a motto a man could live with.

Isabel arrived at last, a vision of summer itself in a loose white linen dress and red slingback shoes with high heels. She plonked her leather handbag down on the folded *Mail* and began to scrabble about in it.

"Here," Quirke said, offering her his packet of Senior Service, "have one of mine."

"Thanks," she said, taking a cigarette and leaning down to the flame of his lighter. "And for Christ's sake get me a drink, will you? Vodka and ice. I feel as if my head is about to burst."

She sat down opposite him on the low stool, exhaling an

angry cone of cigarette smoke. She was having trouble with the director of the play she was rehearsing. Quirke braced himself for a tirade, and went to the hatch and signaled to the barman. When he sat down again Isabel suddenly laughed. "I'm sorry," she said. "I won't start, I promise." She took another long drag on her cigarette. "But that *bastard,* honestly—that little *bastard!*"

"What's he done now?"

She opened her mouth to speak but shut it again, and again laughed. "No," she said, "I said I wouldn't, and I won't. It's a lovely evening outside, I'm going to have one drink with you, then we're going to take a taxi home and you're going to—well, you know what you're going to do, being the gentleman that you are and ever ready to lay a cool hand on a hot girl's brow. I mean a girl's hot brow. Or do I?"

She leaned across the table and kissed him. The barman, his big moonface looming at the hatch, cleared his throat pointedly.

They drank their drinks, the little fingers of their free left hands entwined on the table between them. Quirke admired the way the glowing spot of gold reappeared in the bottom of his glass each time he set it down. Where was the light coming from? He could not see. He did not care. Maybe Isabel was the one who would save him. From what? From himself, first.

To keep herself from complaining about the director, Isabel complained about the play instead. "Talk about kitchen sink, my God!" she said, throwing her eyes to the ceiling and putting on what he thought of as her comical El Greco face. "Sink, tin bathtub, chamber pot, and all. Can life really be like that?"

"Mostly it is," Quirke said.

"And the jokes! All of them seem to be about cows—the

thing is set in the bog somewhere. Is that how country people are?"

He laughed. "How do you mean?"

"Oh, you know—stupid and comical."

"We're all like that."

"I'm not!" she said indignantly. "You're not. Well"—her lips trembled on a laugh—"I'm not, anyway. You know I play the mother? The one playing the daughter, so called, is forty if she's a day. And my husband is about eighteen, and has spots."

Quirke squeezed her finger more tightly. He liked to listen to these rants of hers; they amused and soothed him. He watched her long pale animated face. She was a handsome woman, still. She worried that she might be too old to have children, she had told him so one night over an after-show dinner in the Trocadero, tears shining in her eyes and her mouth slack. She had been a bit drunk. He wondered if she remembered. They both worried about babies, but his worry was of a different order to hers.

He tried to imagine himself bouncing a damp and odiferous infant on his knee. "Have another drink," he said.

Isabel stood up. "No—I said just the one. Come on. I have to be at the Gate at half nine—I'm in the second act."

They had left the snug and were making their way towards the door among the dim forms of the early drinkers when the barman spoke Quirke's name. "Call for you, Doctor," he said, holding up the receiver of the phone that stood beside the cash register. Quirke frowned. Who would be calling him here? Who would have known where to find him?

He took the receiver and crouched over it at the bar. Isabel waited, tapping her foot. She was uneasy, feeling eyes on her from the shadows, trying to see through her clothes. She had wanted Quirke to meet her in the Gresham but of course he had insisted on McGonagle's. She could not think what he saw in the place. She imagined him sitting here like these other ones, lurking in the dimness with his drink and his cigarette, eyeing someone else's woman. She banished the image. She tapped her foot. At last Quirke handed the receiver back to the barman and turned and took her by the elbow and steered her to the door.

"Sinclair," he said. "Something about Phoebe."

HE PUT HER INTO A TAXI IN THE RANK AT THE CORNER OF THE Green. Her face at the side window was white with anger. She had wanted to know what the "something about Phoebe" was, but he had said he did not know, that it was confused, that the line had been bad and he had not been able to hear Sinclair properly and what he had heard he had found hard to understand.

All this, most of it, was a lie. He had not mentioned Mona Delahaye. She had tried to call him at the hospital and the woman on the switchboard had put it through to the pathology lab and Sinclair had answered, and then Sinclair had phoned him. Phoebe was at the Delahayes' house and was unwell, it seemed, and needed to be collected—Sinclair was working late, he was in the middle of a postmortem, he could not get away. Quirke would have to go. Sinclair gave the address. Yes, Quirke said, he knew the house. Then there had been a silence on the line. How much did Sinclair know about Quirke and Mona Delahaye? Sinclair had an uncanny knack of getting wind of things that no one else knew about. Quirke watched until the taxi with Isabel in it was out of sight, then climbed into the next car in the row.

It was Mona who opened the front door to him. "Oh, hello," she said, as if his sudden appearance were an unexpected and mildly pleasant surprise.

"I've come for Phoebe," he said.

"Yes, of course you have."

She stood there with her hand on the door, looking him slowly up and down, in that way she did, as if measuring him for something, some garment into which he might have to be fitted. She smiled. "You're the very picture of paternal concern," she said.

He took a step forward. "Where is she?" he asked. "What happened?"

"Oh, she drank too much gin, that's all." Still she had not taken her hand from the door, and seemed indeed to be considering whether or not to let him come in. Then she shrugged and stood aside. "For God's sake keep your voice down," she said. "My father-in-law is on the warpath."

She led him to the drawing room. Phoebe was lying full-length on the white sofa, her head propped on a cushion, and with another cushion under her feet. Her hands were crossed on her breast. In her black dress and white blouse with the white lace collar she looked alarmingly like the corpse of a maiden saint laid out on a bier. He went and lifted her wrist and took her pulse. It was slow. He smelled her breath.

As he leaned over her she suddenly opened wide her eyes

and stared at him in a sort of happy disbelief. "Daddy," she said softly, and her eyelids fluttered shut again. She had never called him Daddy before. She must think he was someone else.

He turned to Mona, who was standing in the doorway with her shoulder against the doorjamb and her ankles crossed, smoking a cigarette and watching him with a sardonic smile. "What happened?" he asked again.

"I told you—she drank too much and passed out."

"What was she drinking?"

"Gin. I already said. Don't you listen?"

He glanced about the room, saw the empty glasses, the open lid of the radiogram. "Who was here?"

"I was."

"Who else?"

"The twins. Honestly, Quirke, you look terribly fierce—you'll have me frightened of you in a minute."

Quirke made a dismissive gesture, chopping at the air with the side of his hand. "Why was she here?" he asked. "What was she doing?"

Mona gave an exasperated sigh, expelling hasty cigarette smoke. "*I* don't know. I arrived and here she was, knocking back gin by the bucketful and dancing. It was quite a party."

"A party? Were there others?"

"What others?"

"*Any* others."

"The twins—I told you!"

"And that's all? You and those two and Phoebe? What was going on?"

"Will you stop asking that? You sound like a broken record."

"My daughter was in your house, comatose, and I was called

to come and collect her. You made the call. I think you owe me an explanation."

She sighed again and was silent for a moment, giving him a level look and shaking her head slightly from side to side. "I know what it is about you," she said. "You think you're living in the movies." She put on a heavy voice, mimicking him. *"My daughter, in your house, what's going on?* Can't young people have a little party now and then?"

"If they harmed her in any way . . ."

He did not go on, and Mona laughed. "You mean," she said, "if they 'dishonored her'? If they 'ruined' her? Now you're playing the Victorian father—you should have mustaches to twirl."

He shook his head, as if he were being bothered by some flying thing. "Will you call a taxi for me, please?"

"I could drive you somewhere—anywhere, in fact."

"A taxi would be best. If you show me the phone I'll call one myself."

She was smiling at him with a wry expression. "You're really being a bore," she said. "Nothing happened. There were some drinks, we danced, she got dizzy."

"A taxi," he said.

She looked to heaven and turned and sauntered out, and a moment later he heard her in the hall, dialing. Then she came back, and stood where she had stood before, with her cigarette.

"Like a drink?" she asked.

On the sofa, Phoebe moaned faintly.

• • •

HE TOOK HER TO HIS FLAT IN MOUNT STREET. IT REQUIRED some effort to get her up the stairs: her legs were not working very well, and kept crossing and threatening to buckle. Once they were in the flat he walked her to the bedroom and put her to lie on his bed and drew the curtains. She spoke some unintelligible words and gave a burbling little laugh and then lapsed back into unconsciousness.

He went out to the kitchen and poured himself a whiskey—he had a bottle hidden at the back of one of the cupboards—and took it into the living room and lit a cigarette and sat down on the window seat. Late sunlight was dividing the street into halves of light and shadow. Lines of cars were parked at the curbs along both pavements, ranked side by side in two neat shoals, their roofs gleaming like the backs of dolphins. He sat there for a long time, thinking, then went to the telephone and called Sinclair.

He had finished his drink and wanted another, but instead he filled the coffee percolator and put it on the gas and watched it as it came slowly to the boil. He wondered what it was that Phoebe had taken, apart from the gin. There had been no smell of a drug on her breath. Some barbiturate, he supposed—Luminal? They would have put it in her drink and she would not have noticed. That would be their idea of fun. A nerve began to jump at the corner of his right eye.

He was at the window in the living room again, drinking a second cup of coffee, when Sinclair arrived. Quirke told of how he had found Phoebe unconscious at the Delahayes'. He said the twins had been there, and then was sorry that he had. Of Mona Delahaye he made no mention.

"What was going on?" Sinclair said, frowning in bafflement.

"I don't know," Quirke answered.

"What was she doing there, at that house, drinking?"

For a moment Quirke was silent. He was angry with Sinclair, he was not sure why. "She needs looking after, you know," he said.

Sinclair considered the toecaps of his shoes. "She's not a child," he said mildly.

"In some ways she is."

"She wouldn't thank you for saying it."

"I don't ask for thanks."

There was another silence. Quirke fetched a silver cigarette box from the mantelpiece and they lit up and stood smoking, looking at anything save each other.

"I don't know what I could have done," Sinclair said. "The woman on the phone, Mrs. Delahaye, seemed to think the whole thing was funny. I didn't realize."

You could marry her, Quirke thought, surprising himself. Did he want to see Phoebe married? Did he not have doubts about Sinclair? To whose benefit would it be if his daughter were to marry—hers, or his own? Was it not just his own peace of mind he was thinking of? Was it simply that he wanted to be rid of his daughter, rid of the responsibility of being the one nearest to her?

He turned away. In his mind he saw again Mona Delahaye standing at the door of the drawing room in Northumberland Road, in her green blouse and her little girl's puffed-out skirt. That recent afternoon, in her shadowed bedroom, he had held her in his arms and she had pressed her mouth against his shoulder to stifle her moans and he had thought himself in love. Now he cursed himself for a fool.

The bedroom door opened and Phoebe appeared, in her stockinged feet, blear-eyed, with a hand to her forehead. "I heard voices," she said dazedly. She saw Sinclair and frowned. "David? Why are you here?"

"I rang him," Quirke said.

She stood blinking. "I must have—I must have passed out. I feel really peculiar."

"I'll make some tea," Quirke said. "Tea will be good for you."

He went into the kitchen and boiled the kettle and set out cups and saucers on a tray. When he returned to the living room Sinclair and Phoebe were sitting close beside each other on the sofa, and Sinclair was holding her right hand in both of his.

Phoebe looked at Quirke as he poured out the tea for her. "They invited me for a drink," she said. "Why did I go?" She looked about herself helplessly. "My head feels as if it's stuffed with wet wool."

"Do you remember taking anything?" Quirke asked.

"What do you mean?"

"Tablets, pills—anything like that?"

"No." She frowned, trying to concentrate. She shook her head. "No, there wasn't anything. We drank gin. I don't know what I was thinking of." She put her other hand on top of Sinclair's hands. "I'm sorry," she said, and suddenly it seemed she might cry. "I'm so sorry."

Sinclair looked up at Quirke and said nothing.

"Drink your tea," Quirke said.

She looked at the cup and saucer balanced on the arm of the sofa beside her. "He told me I was his alibi," she said. Both men watched her, waiting. She shook her head again and gave an incredulous laugh. "He sang it," she said.

Again the two men exchanged glances.

"Sang what?" Sinclair asked.

"About my being his alibi. He said the Guards had questioned him"—she looked to Quirke—"your friend Inspector Hackett brought both twins in to ask them about the night when that man died, that Clancy man. So Jonas said. I think he's mad." She looked from one of them to the other. "I really think he *is* mad. They both are, both the twins."

Quirke drew up a chair and set it in front of the sofa and sat down and leaned forward with his hands clasped. "Which one was it that spoke about an alibi?"

"Jonas." She turned to Sinclair. "He was talking about the party at Breen's house, you remember? We saw them there, the twins. Only—"

She stopped.

"Only what?" Quirke said.

"Only I noticed something. You know they have a joke that Jonas wears a ring on his little finger and that's the only way people can tell them apart. But that night, at the party, they were both wearing rings, I saw them. Jonas met us when we arrived, remember, he was with Tanya Somers? And then, later, we saw James upstairs, talking to that girl in the doorway. But they both had the identical signet ring on the little fingers of their left hands."

Sinclair was frowning. "I don't understand," he said.

Quirke watched Phoebe. "How were they dressed?" he asked.

"One of them had on a black blazer, the other was wearing—I don't know—something pale, a linen suit, or jacket."

"And Tanya Somers was there, with one of them?"

"Yes."

The room had grown very quiet. Distantly in the city an Angelus bell was dully tolling.

"There was only one of them," Quirke said. "They pretended they were two, but there was only the one."

"But why?" Phoebe said. "They would have had to switch clothes. And Tanya Somers would have had to go along with the pretense."

Quirke stood up. "One of them needed to be somewhere else," he said. "That was the reason for the trick. That's why you, and whoever else was at the party that knew them, would be their alibi. There was only one twin, masquerading as two."

He walked to the mantelpiece and took another cigarette from the silver box and lit it, and drew the smoke deep into his lungs. Phoebe and Sinclair sat and watched him.

"I still don't see it," Sinclair said.

Quirke turned, and stood with his back to the fireplace, wreathed in cigarette smoke that gave him for a moment the look of a magician about to make himself disappear. "Phoebe said it. That night, the night of the party, was the night Jack Clancy died. The night he was murdered."

THE LIGHTS SHINING DOWN FROM THE BIG WINDOWS ON THE ground floor seemed to darken the twilight beyond their reach, and in the front garden, behind the railings, shadows congregated among the flowerbeds and under the boughs of the big beech reaching towards the house like tentacles from the road. At the gate Quirke hesitated. What would he say to the twins if they were there? What would he say to Mona Delahaye? Should he not have called Hackett, and told him Phoebe's story of the signet ring?

But he knew that none of this was why he was here, loitering at dusk in front of a dead man's house. He took off his hat and held it in front of him, against his breast, as if it were a shield to ward off something.

She was surprised to see him. "Back so soon?" she said, with her sly smile. She was wearing a dark green kimono—green again—and her slender pale feet were bare. Without shoes she seemed slighter and more delicate than ever, and the top of her head was barely level with his chin. In the lamplight her hair had the texture of hammered bronze. "Come through to the kitchen," she said. "I was making myself a nice hot drink." He walked behind her down the hall. It was plain to see that she was naked under the kimono. "Maid's night off," she said over her shoulder. "I'm all on my little ownsome." And she laughed.

"What about the twins?"

"Oh, they've gone off," she said lightly. "And so has my father-in-law. He's in the hospital, in fact. He had another stroke this evening. Quite serious, it seems, this time."

In the kitchen there was the throat-catching bittersweet smell of warm chocolate. A small saucepan was simmering on the stove. "Want some?" she asked. "I make it with real chocolate, not that awful powdered stuff." She took up a wooden spoon and stirred the pot, peering into the steam.

"My daughter has recovered, by the way," Quirke said. "In case you were wondering."

"She must have quite a hangover." She went to a cupboard and took down two white mugs. "A girl of her age had better steer clear of the gin. I should know."

"It must have been more than gin."

She glanced at him, then turned back to concentrate on pouring the hot chocolate into the mugs. "The boys were just playing, as usual. Your daughter isn't used to that kind of thing, I imagine. Very straitlaced, isn't she? She dresses like a nun. They tell me she has a boyfriend?"

"Yes. My assistant."

"Hmm. A Jew, isn't he?" She sniffed. "Anyway, I'm sure she'll always be Daddy's girl. You mustn't let the Hebrews make her one of theirs." She came and handed him one of the mugs, and clinked hers against it. "Here's to fun."

"What kind of drug did they give her?" he asked.

"Did they give her a drug? I told you, I only saw her drinking gin."

He looked at the steaming umber stuff in the mug. "She's had a lot of trouble in her life."

"Yes. I could tell."

"I have to protect her."

She smiled. "Not doing a very good job, by the look of it. Aren't you going to drink your chocolate? It's very soothing. I think you need soothing." She was standing very close to him. Behind the heavy fragrance of the chocolate he could smell her hair.

"Tell me what was in the note your husband left," he said.

She sighed irritably. "Oh, there was no note." She walked back to the stove and poured herself another go of chocolate and took a drink of it, clasping the mug in both hands. "I just said that to humor you, since you seemed so pleased with yourself playing the detective."

"Were you having an affair with Jack Clancy?"

"With Jack? Certainly not." She chuckled. "Jack Clancy—my God, what do you think I am? Not Jack, no."

He caught something in her voice. "Who, then?"

She gave him a measuring look, thinking. "Why do you want to know?" He said nothing. She put her mug down on the draining board. "Give me a cigarette," she said. "You know"— she leaned down to the flame of his lighter—"I've been doing a lot of thinking since Victor died. Well, you can imagine. He was such a torment to himself, I wonder if he's not better off gone. Do you think I'm terrible, to say such a thing?" She went and leaned against the sink, crossing one arm under her breasts and holding the cigarette level with her mouth. In the opening of the kimono her right leg was bared to the thigh. "People didn't know him. They took at face value the image he had of himself—the successful businessman, the expert sailor, the loving husband and responsible father. But really he was a mess. It took me a while to see that. Deep down he disgusted himself. He knew what he was, you see."

"And what was he?"

She considered. "Weak. Spineless."

"He had enough courage to kill himself."

This seemed to interest her. "Do you think it takes courage to do that?" she asked. "I think it was cowardice." She shook her head sadly. "Such a mess," she murmured.

Quirke set the mug down on the table. He had not tasted the chocolate. "Could I have a drink?" he said.

They passed through to the drawing room. Mona lit lamps, and went to the sideboard and poured whiskey into a tumbler. Quirke looked at the garden's velvet darkness pressing itself against the window.

"Are you an alcoholic?" Mona asked, in a tone of mild inquiry.

"I don't know," he said. He took the glass and drank off the whiskey in one gulp and gave her back the glass to refill. "Probably."

She seemed to find his reply amusing. She smiled at him, arching an eyebrow, and turned and picked up the whiskey bottle.

"You slept with me once," he said.

"Yes, I did. Like you, I'm curious."

"You were curious, about me?"

"I was. Now I'm not anymore." She moved to the sofa and sat down and crossed her legs. The wings of the kimono fell back on both sides to reveal one bare, glossy knee. "Remember how I said to you before that people think I'm a dimwit? They do. I mean them to." She lifted a hand and pushed her bronzen hair back from her face at the side. "When I was a little girl," she said, "I used to lie on the floor and pretend to be asleep, but I'd have my eyes open just the tiniest crack, so I could watch people, my parents, my brothers, my sister that I hated, without them knowing. Now I'm a big girl and I do the same thing, only instead of pretending to be asleep I pretend to be stupid."

Quirke sipped his whiskey. "Why have you let me in on your secret?"

"I don't know. I suppose because you're pretending, too."

"And what am I pretending to be?"

She studied him for a moment, cocking her head to one side, like a blackbird. "You're pretending to be human, I think. Wouldn't you say?"

He lit a cigarette. The flame of the lighter flickered, he noticed, for his hand was not entirely steady. "Did you know," he said, "that Jack Clancy was planning to take over the business from your husband?"

She nodded. "Yes. Victor told me."

"When did he find out?"

"The day before he killed himself."

He looked at her without speaking. She held his gaze calmly.

"Was that why he killed himself?" he asked.

"Partly."

He set his glass down slowly on the sideboard, next to the whiskey bottle. He would pour himself another drink, but not just yet.

"What else had he found out?" he asked.

"Oh!" She waved a hand. "He was impossible. So jealous."

He waited. She regarded him with a slightly swollen look, as if struggling to keep herself from laughing.

"Who was it?" he said.

"Who was who?"

"Who was he jealous of?"

"Don't you know?" Now she did laugh, giving an odd sharp little whoop. "Not *Jack* Clancy," she said. "But you were warm."

He was silent for a long moment, gazing at her. Then he took up the whiskey bottle and half filled the tumbler. He turned back to her. "The boy, then," he said. "What's his name?"

"Davy. And he's not a boy, though he's as pretty as one—

don't you think? And so—so *energetic,* with that kind of youthful vigor that gladdens a girl's heart, I can tell you."

Quirke sipped his whiskey. The glass knocked against one of
his front teeth. "Are you still—seeing him?" he asked, surprised
at how steady his voice was.

"For goodness' sake!" she said, and gave another laugh.
"I'm the grieving widow—I can hardly go about sleeping with
people."

"You slept with me."

"I told you," she said, with a sulky pout, "I was curious."

He felt exhausted suddenly. He shut his eyes and kneaded
the flesh at the bridge of his nose between a thumb and two
fingers. He had a tearing sensation in his chest, as if there
were an animal in there, raking at him with its claws.

He opened his eyes. "Jack Clancy's death," he said.

"What about it?" she asked. "I assume, since his scheme to
take over from Victor had been found out, he decided to follow
Victor's example. Rivals to the end."

Quirke shook his head. "No," he said, hearing the weariness
in his voice. "Jack Clancy didn't kill himself." She waited. "Don't
you know?" he said. "Haven't you figured it out?"

She put a finger to her chin and looked upwards, mimicking
a schoolgirl who has been asked a hard question. "Someone
did it for him?" she said.

"Yes. Someone did it for him."

"Not"—she sat bolt upright and slapped a hand on her bared
knee and laughed—"not Maverley? Not that white rabbit? He
adored Victor, I know, but I can't imagine him killing someone
in revenge for his death."

"No," Quirke said, "not Maverley."

"Then who?"

He walked to the sofa and stood over her, the whiskey glass clenched in his hand. She leaned back a little, pulling the kimono closed over her knees, and the faintest shadow of alarm crossed her face.

"Are you pretending now?" he said. "Or are you stupid, after all?" He drank the last of the whiskey in the glass and held it out to her, and she took it, and set it down on the arm of the sofa. "Where are the twins?" he asked.

"I already said, they've gone." She was watching him carefully, as if readying herself to forestall whatever move he might make. She was right to be wary. He was very angry. He put a hand into the pocket of his jacket and made a fist of it, digging the nails into his palm. "Good-bye," he said, and turned abruptly and walked from the room, and along the silent hall, and opened the front door and stepped out into the fragrance of the night. He felt nothing, only the sensation of something icy melting in his heart.

13

A LIGHT FINE RAIN WAS FALLING WHEN THEY LEFT THE CITY, but it soon lost heart and stopped, and a watery sun came out and put a blinding shine on the road in front of them. They went up by the canal, past lock after lock, the suburbs on their left becoming more tired and shabby with each mile they covered. Then they turned onto the Naas Road, and the trees on either side seemed to hold themselves averted, gazing off elsewhere.

"I wish you wouldn't smoke in the car," Rose Griffin said. "I'd much prefer to breathe."

Quirke opened the window a little way and pushed his half-smoked cigarette out through the crack. They went on for a long way in silence after that, until Rose spoke again, asking if he thought there might be somewhere they could stop to eat lunch. Quirke stirred himself and said he had not thought about lunch. There was, he said, a hotel in Cashel that might be tolerable. "Tolerable!" Rose said faintly, and sighed.

They spoke of Malachy Griffin. Rose said she was worried about her husband, about how sedentary he was becoming. "Couldn't you and he take up golf?" she asked. Quirke glanced at her sidelong. "No, I suppose not," she said. "Pity," she added, with wistful regret.

She was puzzled as to the purpose of this journey, and Quirke, it seemed, was not inclined to enlighten her. Although she would not have thought it possible, he was even more taciturn than usual today, shut far off inside himself. She had the impression that he was suffering, gnawing away at some inner hurt.

"The trouble with Malachy," she said, "is that he's just not assertive enough."

Quirke made a noise that might have been laughter. "Who do you want him to assert himself against?"

"Oh, Quirke, you know what I mean! My Mal has so much to offer, but he holds back. It's an almighty shame."

Quirke wondered doubtfully what it might be that Mal had so much of, but he said nothing.

The damp green of summer fields rolled past. It was midday and they were almost alone on the long road south. They passed through melancholy villages, ramshackle towns. More than once they were forced to slow to a crawl behind a farmer driving his cows. Outside Kildare town they met in the middle of the road a ram with elaborately curled horns and strings of matted wool hanging down on all sides. Rose sounded the horn impatiently, but the ram just stood there, head lowered, glaring at them, and in the end Quirke had to get out and wave his arms and shout before the beast would move. When he got back into the car Rose was laughing. "Oh, Quirke, you should have seen yourself!"

The road seemed endless. Fields, trees, then ragged outskirts, then long streets with pubs and drapers' shops and general stores, then outskirts again, then trees again, then fields again. They crossed a bridge over a river, a broad slow stretch of stippled silver, with bulrushes at both sides and a single swan afloat in the shallows. The huge sky over the Midlands was piled high with luminous wreckage. On a hairpin bend some small creature, rat or squirrel, ran out from the verge and under their wheels, and there was a quick bump, and Rose gave a little scream. "Oh, Quirke," she wailed, beating the steering wheel with her palms, "tell me why we're going down to Cork."

THEY STOPPED IN CASHEL, AT THE CASHEL ARMS HOTEL, WHICH even in the lobby smelled of cooked cabbage. With sinking hearts they allowed themselves to be conducted to the dining room, where they were given a table by a window looking down into a cobbled yard. "Order a bottle of wine, for pity's sake," Rose said. They ate doubtful fish with mashed potato; the cabbage they had been smelling since they arrived made a soggy appearance. But the wine was good, a lustrous Meursault that in Quirke's mouth tasted of gold coins and melons.

Rose began to feel better. "Tell me," she said to Quirke, "how is that lady friend of yours, the actress?"

"She's very well," Quirke said, but would not meet her eye. "Very well."

"Is it serious?"

Now he did look at her. "Is what serious?"

"You and your lady friend, of course."

"You make it sound like an illness."

Rose shook her head. "Quirke, Quirke, Quirke," she said, "what are we to do with you?"

"I wasn't aware that something needed to be done."

"Well, exactly."

They went on eating, in an ill-tempered silence. Then Rose tried again. "This trip, it's to do with those two men who died, yes? Maggie's brother, and then his partner? What was the outcome of all that?"

Half a minute elapsed before Quirke answered. "An outcome," he said, "is still awaited."

"That's why you want to talk to Maggie?"

"That's why I want to talk to Maggie."

"You know she's thinking of living permanently down there, in—what's the place?"

"Slievemore."

"That's it. Fishing town, is it? Sounds like Scituate." It was in Scituate, south of Boston, that Quirke had first met Rose Crawford, as she was then. "Why would she want to bury herself away down there?" She chuckled. "Maybe to get away from her family, especially that Mona Delahaye."

She stopped. At the mention of Mona's name she had felt something from across the table, a tiny tremor, and she looked hard at Quirke. Mona Delahaye. So that was it—Mona had got her talons into him. Well, that would smart, all right. Her gaze softened. Poor Quirke, he would never learn.

Outside, the afternoon had mellowed, and the air, laden with dust and midges, was the same soft gilded color as the

Meursault they had drunk. They did not want to set off and instead strolled for a while in the town's main street. The great gray ruin of the castle loomed above them on its crag against a sky of bird's-egg blue. Rose had an urge to talk seriously to Quirke—it was probably the effect of the wine—to tell him he was frittering away his life on things that were not worthy of him. But somehow Quirke would not be spoken to like that, he would not allow it, and she held her peace, and felt cross. If he had indeed got himself entangled with Mona Delahaye then he was in for a deal of heartache, and serve him right. Rose and Quirke had gone to bed together, just once, many years before. It had not been a success, yet Rose remembered the occasion with a melancholy fondness. Scituate seemed very far away, now.

In Fermoy they stopped again, Quirke having run out of cigarettes, and while he was in the tobacconist's Rose sat in the car and watched in dismay a man belaboring a cart horse with a stick. He was a coarse-looking fellow with a red face and a lantern jaw and a prominent forehead—he might have been modeled on a *Punch* cartoon—and he wore an old coat with a belt of plaited straw. The horse stood between the shafts of the cart, its head hanging, suffering the blows without flinching. *Oh, my Lord,* Rose thought, *this poor benighted country!*

Slievemore was a green hill above a turquoise bay. When they arrived, along the winding road from the north, the early-evening sunlight was tawny, and there was a breeze and the air was hazed with salt, and the blue water was flecked with ragged scraps of white. Ashgrove, the Delahayes' house, was on the far side of the hill, and they had to drive along the harbor front, and climb another stretch of winding road for ten miles. Neither of them had been to the house before, and they had trouble locating it. When at last they pulled in at the gate the house rose before them, a gray granite mansion with arched windows and a steep roof angled in many planes, and there were even turrets. All that was missing, Quirke thought, was a flag, or pennant, flapping above the chimneys on a tall pole.

The house had a deserted look. No door opened, no face appeared at any window, no voice called a greeting. "Dear me," Rose said, "it seems as if our trip has been in vain. Where can she be?"

They knocked at the front door, waited, knocked again. Then they walked along a gravel path round to the side of the house. French windows there stood open to the evening. They looked at each other, and went in.

Quirke was sensitive to the atmosphere in old houses. It was an instinctive memory, buried deep in his very bones, of Carricklea, the industrial school and reformatory in the west of Ireland where he had passed his childhood. He remembered the sounds, the thud of heels on polished floors, the hollow echoes of distant doors shutting, the whispers in the darkness.

"We should have telephoned," Rose said. "Maggie is peculiar, you know. She has peculiar ways." They went through all the rooms downstairs. Everything was so neat and tidy it seemed no one could be living here. Then they heard it, a sound, from upstairs, as of something being dragged across a wooden floor. They stood and listened. The hall around them seemed somehow to be breathing, slowly, deeply. Above the hall table hung a tall looking glass in a gilt frame, reflecting the hat stand opposite and a pair of dusty antlers mounted on a sort of plaque on the wall. Quirke understood they were not welcome here, he and Rose; houses had a way of showing their resentment.

Upstairs all was disorder. Furniture was stacked in the corridors, chairs, dressing tables, tallboys, a folding screen with painted panels, a full-length looking glass on a mahogany stand. In many rooms the beds had been stripped and their mattresses raised up and propped against the walls. Curtains too had been taken down, and thrown in untidy heaps on the bare bedsteads. Pictures had been lifted from their hooks and set on the floor against the walls, all facing inwards. A white chamber pot with a shriveled red rose leaning in it stood on top of a bureau, like a parody of a votive offering.

They found Maggie Delahaye in one of the big bedrooms at the back of the house. She wore a man's checked shirt and an old pair of baggy corduroy trousers, and a red bandanna was tied around her head. Rose had never noticed before her friend's faint mustache, or the few gray whiskers sprouting on her chin. She looked at them both with a mixture of puzzlement and alarm, as if she did not know what they were. For a moment it seemed she might dive past them and escape through the door and down the stairs and out at those open French windows. She had been pushing, with great effort, a heavy antique wooden chest across the floor, and now she straightened, and brushed her hands.

"I was just rearranging things," she said. "I was just . . . tidying."

IN THE KITCHEN SHE MADE COFFEE FOR THEM, AND PUT OUT dry crackers on a plate. There was no butter, it seemed. "I'm a bit low in provisions," she said. "I'd have gone into the village if I'd known you were coming." She had put Quirke and Rose Griffin to sit at a big wooden table; over the years the surface of it had been scrubbed to furrows and ridges, like sand at the tide line.

Rose had introduced Quirke, and he had said he was a doctor, without specifying which kind. "Oh, yes," Maggie said. "You were at my brother's funeral, I saw you there." As she moved about the kitchen she kept shooting quick, sidelong glances at him, in the way a dog would glance at a stranger it was suspicious of. Quirke wondered if she thought he had come to take her away somewhere, since he was a doctor. In fact, she had not asked them why they had come, unannounced, like this, and she behaved as if they were chance visitors whom she had little desire to see.

"Maggie, dear," Rose said, "Dr. Quirke wants to talk to you about something."

Maggie turned quickly to the stove, on which the kettle was coming to the boil. "Oh, yes?" she said. "My brother's death, is it?" She looked over her shoulder at Rose. "Has he found out something?"

"It's not about your brother's death, Miss Delahaye," Quirke said. "It's about—it's about Jack Clancy."

She poured the boiling water into the coffeepot, moving her lips silently. "That's what I was doing when you arrived," she said, "I was clearing out the Clancys' things, getting them ready for the removals men to collect. I rang up a firm in Cork and asked them to send down one of those big vans—what do you call them?—pantechnicons, is it? Odd word for something so ordinary. They were very nice on the phone. I spoke to a very

polite girl who took all the details and said I was to let them
know twenty-four hours before I want them to come. I didn't
realize there would be so much heavy work involved. I think
I shall have to call them again and ask them to send down some
men to help me. I don't think I could get all those things down
the stairs by myself, do you? There's so much—you wouldn't
think three people would have needed so much furniture."
She brought the coffeepot to the table. "Do say if it's too strong,
won't you, Dr. Quirke? Rose likes hers very strong, I know that."

"Do you mind if I smoke?" Quirke said.

"No, no, of course not—please, go ahead. I don't, myself,
but Victor used to smoke Balkan Sobranie sometimes and I
loved the smell."

Quirke tasted the liquid in his cup and to his consternation
discovered it was not coffee but some kind of beef broth or
powdered gravy. He saw Rose tasting hers. She grimaced, and
looked at him wide-eyed.

"Miss Delahaye," he said, pushing his cup away from himself
with a fingertip, "on the night Jack Clancy died, did you see
your nephews—the twins, Jonas and James?"

She was standing beside the table, holding the coffeepot.
She had fallen into a daze, and he was not sure the question
had registered, and was about to ask it again when she stirred
herself, and blinked. "Did I see them?" she asked. "How do you
mean?"

"Were you with them—did you talk to them?"

She went to the cupboard and took down a cup and saucer
for herself and filled it from the coffeepot and took a sip, and
frowned. "Oh, dear," she murmured, "this isn't coffee at all."
She looked at Rose, at Quirke. "What did I do?" she asked, in

helpless bafflement. "I must have put Bisto in the pot, instead of coffee." She giggled, and bit her lip.

Rose went and took the cup and saucer from her and poured the contents into the sink, then held her by the arm. "Come, dear," she said, "come and sit down with us. You shouldn't be here on your own, you know. It's not good for you."

"Oh, but I love it here," Maggie said. "This is my home now. I'm not going back to Dublin." She let herself be led to the table. "How elegant you look, Rose. Blue always suited you." She sat down on the chair that Quirke had placed for her opposite his own. "I was always happy here," she said to him, as if explaining something to a child. "And now I'm going to settle down. I might work the land, you know. There are fifty acres, more. It's good land, rich soil. I could keep cattle, sheep. And bees, I'd like to have bees. There were hives here once, down in the Long Meadow, I remember them. And I could grow crops." She focused on Quirke. "Do you know anything about farming, Dr. Quirke?"

"No," Quirke said. "I'm afraid I don't."

"It's no matter. I can hire someone in. There are always farmers' sons, wanting work." She saw Quirke looking about for an ashtray. "Do use the saucer," she said. "I'll be washing up later. I always do the washing up last thing. It's very soothing. I listen to the wireless while I'm doing it." She pointed to the big wooden set on a shelf beside the fridge.

"Isn't there a woman who comes?" Rose said. "A local woman, who does the housekeeping?"

"Mrs. Hartigan, yes. But I've let her go. I intend to keep house myself, from now on."

"But—but you'll need help. In the winter. There'll be fuel to get in, and—" But here Rose's imagination failed her; it was a very long time since she had tended personally to the everyday running of a house.

Quirke finished his cigarette and lit another. "Which one of the twins was with you that night?" he asked. "Because one of them was with you, isn't that so?"

She was looking at him in that glazed way again, with her head lowered. He noticed that her mouth was slack at one side, as if she had suffered a slight stroke. The red rag tied around her forehead might be a bandage.

"I always favored James," she said, smiling wistfully. "Jonas was everybody's darling, being so intelligent and charming, but I took to James. I suppose it's because he's not like the others, and neither am I." She leaned forward suddenly and set both her hands flat on the table before her and looked hard at Quirke. "Do you think there might be something wrong with my mind, Doctor? I think I haven't been right since Victor died. The strangest things come into my head, all kinds of strange thoughts. Down here, I sometimes find it hard to know whether I'm awake and having fantasies or asleep and dreaming. Do you ever have that feeling?" She turned to Rose. "Do you?"

Rose put a hand over one of Maggie's. "Yes, dear, of course," she said. "We all feel like that at times. Life can be very puzzling."

"Yes, yes," Maggie said eagerly, gazing into Rose's eyes. "That's what I think too, that life is—is puzzling. That's exactly the word. Puzzling, and so wasteful, don't you feel? Think of Victor, dying. That was a waste." She turned back to Quirke. "Wasn't it? A waste?"

Rose was looking hard at Quirke now, sending him some

signal. He supposed she wanted him not to ask any more questions, to leave this poor frantic creature in peace. But he could not do that.

"Tell us," he said to Maggie, "tell us what happened, that night."

She smiled that wistful smile and her eyes slipped out of focus again. "Dun Laoghaire," she said. "James and I had driven out there, to find him, to find Jack Clancy. Such a lovely night. There was a moon, remember? Huge—bigger than I've ever seen the moon. You could have read a newspaper by it."

She stopped, and took her hands from the table and put them in her lap and sat there smiling to herself.

"Go on," Quirke said softly.

"What?" She looked at him and frowned, as if she had never seen him before in her life.

"Tell us what happened."

"What happened," she said. "Yes." Her eyes went vague, and Quirke was about to prompt her again when she spoke. "Jonas had got it out of Mona, you see."

"Got what out of her?" Quirke asked.

She gave him a pitying look. "Why, about being unfaithful. To Victor."

"With whom?"

"She wouldn't say, but we knew, of course."

"You knew?"

"We guessed. It had to be him. You know what he was like, Clancy." She gave her head a little shake in disgust. "Jack couldn't keep his hands off any woman. And as for Mona— well."

Rose was gazing at Maggie as if mesmerized.

"Go on," Quirke said. "Go on about that night."

Maggie sat forward, birdlike, eager now to continue with her story. "James knew where Jack Clancy was, he had been following him. Clancy had been with another one of his"—she made a sour face—"of his girlfriends, in Sandycove. James had a cricket bat—" She broke off and laughed briefly. "Trust James, always the sportsman." She frowned suddenly, bethinking herself, and looked at them both apologetically. "But I promised you coffee! Oh, dear, I'm hopeless. What my mother would have said, I can't think. Mother was a stickler where manners were concerned. She used to keep a ruler in her lap at mealtimes, one of those old-fashioned wooden tubes, and would crack us on the knuckles with it, Victor and I, if we used the wrong knife, or didn't offer things around before helping ourselves. Oh, yes, a real stickler."

Quirke moved his chair closer to hers. "Please go on," he said.

"What?" She blinked.

"You were telling us about that night, in Dun Laoghaire, with the full moon."

"Oh, yes. We caught up with him at the bandstand"—she turned to Rose—"you know the bandstand, on the front? He was hiding there, I think he must have sensed James was following him. He saw me, coming towards him—I wanted to be there, when it happened. Then I heard it, the blow. It was very loud. He didn't make a sound, though, just fell straight down, like an animal under the poleax."

There was a silence, in which they could hear Maggie breathing, taking rapid, shallow breaths, like a sleeping child.

Her eyes shone, and a small, perfectly circular spot of pink had appeared on each cheekbone.

Quirke leaned closer to her. "And this was because of Mona, yes—Mona and him? That's why you—that's why James—hit him on the head?"

"That, yes. And the other business."

"What other business, Maggie?"

She looked straight into his face, again with that softly pitying expression, as if he were an idiot child. "Jack Clancy had been getting ready to take over the firm and push Victor out. Didn't you know? The boys couldn't have that. They were very cross, when Mr. Maverley told them about it. We had a little conference, the three of us, Jonas, James, and I—well, Jonas and I, really. James doesn't think the way Jonas does. He's not clever, like Jonas."

Quirke had taken his cigarette case from his pocket, but did not think his hands would be steady enough for him to light a cigarette. He was slightly dizzy, and had a strange sensation; it felt like euphoria. "And that was when you decided, you and Jonas, what to do about Jack Clancy—yes?"

"Yes," Maggie said. "That's when we decided Jack Clancy could not be allowed to go on living, not when Victor was dead."

"So you and James followed him that night, and James hit him, and then you put him in the boat, and one of you sailed it out, and the other followed, in another boat."

"Yes, yes," Maggie said, almost panting now. "James took him in his own boat—Jack's boat, I mean, the *Rascal*—and I came along with him in one of ours, the *Maggie Dear*. My father named it after me, you know. I was always so proud, sailing in it, with my name on the side. Maggie Dear."

"Was he still alive then?" Quirke asked softly.

"What?"

"Was he alive, Jack Clancy, when you put him in the boat?"

"I don't know. I didn't—I didn't look at him. James did all that. He was always very kind to me, James, very considerate. *You leave it all to me, Auntie Maggie*, he said. He sounded so cheerful, like he used to when he was a little boy." She paused, remembering. "I was upset, of course. Jack Clancy was a dreadful man, and deserved all he got, and yet—"

She put a hand up to her forehead and, feeling the bandanna there, untied it at the back and took it off. "Oh!" she said, with a wide-eyed smile. "What a relief! I'd forgotten I had it on."

"So James scuttled the boat, the *Rascal*," Quirke said, "and then the two of you returned in your boat, in the *Maggie Dear*."

She nodded rapidly. "Yes, yes, we both came back together." She looked at her hands on the table in front of her. "I can still see that moon, shining on the water, a long gold path leading out to the horizon."

Rose Griffin had lowered her head, and sat motionless, her shoulders hunched. "Oh, Maggie," she murmured.

Maggie turned to her. "Do you think we were very bad, to do what we did?" she asked. She looked to Quirke again. "Do you?"

"You killed a man," he said. "You committed a murder."

She nodded slowly, considering this. "Yes, we killed him," she said. "But I don't think it was murder, not really. It was more like something in the Bible, you know—my father was fond of quoting the Bible to us when we were little." She lifted a finger, pointing upwards. "It was an act of justice."

"No, Miss Delahaye," Quirke said. "It was an act of vengeance."

"Well," she retorted quickly, in a petulant tone, "you can think that, if you like. *Vengeance is mine, saith the Lord*—yet they say, *An eye for an eye, and a tooth for a tooth.*"

"They don't," Quirke said, shaking his head. "They say, *Love thy neighbor as thyself.* They say, *Turn the other cheek.*"

Suddenly the woman's eyes narrowed and she drew her lips together into a wrinkled bud. "You're a fool," she whispered. "Jack Clancy tried to take everything my brother had, his business, his wife—"

"No," Quirke said, "not his wife."

She drew her head back and stared at him, her pinched nostrils flaring. "He was sleeping with that woman, I know he was."

"No," Quirke said again. "Not the father."

"Not the father? What do you mean?"

"Not the father. The son."

"What?" She lifted her hands and slapped them down hard on the table once more. "What are you saying?"

"I'm saying that Jack Clancy wasn't sleeping with Mona Delahaye. His son was."

"Oh, Lord," Rose Griffin said, a sort of moan, and stood up with her cup and rinsed it at the sink and filled it with water and drank deep, then stood there with her back turned, staring out the window into the garden.

Maggie was struggling to take it in. "Davy?" she said, in a tone of disbelief. "Davy, and Mona? But Jonas said Mona had told him—"

"Whatever she told him was a lie."

Maggie was staring at him. "The boy," she said softly, "not the father—the boy . . ."

"Yes. Your brother had found out about him and Mona at the same time he found out that Jack Clancy was scheming to take over the business. That's why he took Davy out in the boat and left him stranded. That was your brother's attempt at vengeance. He meant to kill Davy, I think, but I suppose couldn't bring himself to do it. Perhaps he thought Davy would die anyway, of exposure, or that he would drown."

"You're lying."

"I'm not lying, Miss Delahaye."

"How do you know—how do you know it wasn't Jack?"

"She told me."

"Mona?"

"Yes. Mona."

She looked away. "That filthy little—! The two of them, filthy animals."

Abruptly, and as if she did not realize it, she began to cry, big shining tears rolling down beside her nose and dripping from either side of her chin onto the table. She stood up, pressing her fingertips to the worn wood to balance herself. "I must—" she said. "I feel—" She shook her head, crossly, it seemed, and turned away, and walked out of the room, stiffly, head erect, her arms rigid at her sides. Quirke looked at the blood-red bandanna on the table. Rose turned from the sink. "You should have told me," she said.

He nodded. "Yes, I should have. I'm sorry."

"Sometimes, Quirke," she said, walking slowly towards the table, "sometimes I don't understand you at all. I don't understand what goes on in your head."

BENJAMIN BLACK

He lifted his eyes to hers. "Nor do I," he said.

From somewhere off at the side of the house came the sound of a car engine starting up. Quirke rose and went to the window, in time to see a station wagon slewing across the gravel and heading off along the drive, towards the front gate. Rose came and stood at his shoulder. "It's Maggie," she said. "Look, she's gone."

"Yes."

"Shouldn't we follow?"

Quirke shrugged. "No, I don't think so."

THE LAST OF DAYLIGHT WAS A DENSE PINK-GOLD SHEEN ON THE seemingly unmoving waters of the bay. A lobster boat was coming in past the harbor mouth, and on the quayside two fishermen were gathering up nets that had been drying there all day long. A man was throwing a ball into the water for his dog. The dog would scamper down the stone steps of the jetty and dive in and paddle frantically out and snatch the ball in its jaws and then paddle back again, snorting.

In half an hour the dark would be complete. She wondered if she should wait until then. But, no, the sooner she set out, the better. What she felt most strongly now was a kind of angry impatience—an impatience to be away, to be done with all this.

The rowboat was moored at the far end of the jetty, and she had to untie it and drag it behind herself to the steps. The man called his dog, and put it on its lead, and bade her good evening. She did not respond.

She and Victor used to sail in this boat when they were chil-

dren and staying at Slievemore. Of the two of them she had
always been the stronger, and on more than one occasion had
fought bigger boys on his behalf. No one was allowed to hit her
brother. Strange to think that some trace of Victor would still
be here, the memory of his hand on the oar, the mark of his
fingers on the tiller, undetectable but real, something of him,
enduring.

When she stepped into the little boat it rocked in giddy
fashion from side to side, as if for pleasure, as if it recognized
her and was glad of her familiar weight. She sat down on the
thwart and took up the oars. She had always loved the moist
cool texture of varnished wood; it was the very feel of boats
and boating, for her. Amid soft plashings she steered out from
the jetty. Each time she lifted the oars from the water thick
strings of molten gold cascaded from their lower edges. The
man on the quayside was watching her. He wore a flat cap and
a sleeveless jerkin made of green felt; a hunter's coat. His dog
sat beside him, and it, too, seemed to watch her, one pointed
ear standing upright and the other lying flat.

Off to her right a cormorant suddenly surfaced, shaking itself,
and so quiet was the evening that she could hear its wetted oily
feathers rattling. The moon hung above the hill and, not far off
it, Venus glittered, impossibly bright. The sky low down was a
tender shade of greenish blue, and seemed as breakable as the
shell of a bird's egg. Everything was impossibly lovely. The cormorant dived again, and the ripples left by its going expanded
outwards on all sides, each ripple smoothly flowing, swift as an
eel. She pulled harder on the oars and the little boat bounded
forward eagerly.

The man and his dog were gone from the quayside; the

lobster boat had docked. She could hear faint strains of dance music—the lobstermen must have their wireless tuned to some English station. She could see the light of the lamp in the cabin, and the shadows of the men moving about. It seemed to her she had never been so vividly alive to the sights and sounds of this watery world. On she went, and on, into the gathering dark.

14

THEY STROLLED TOGETHER IN ST. STEPHEN'S GREEN, AS SO
often before. The day was warm and overcast. There was rain
coming, Hackett said, he could smell it in the air, and, sure
enough, the tip of a cloud as dark as vengeance itself appeared
behind the trees to the west.

They stopped to watch a group of children sailing toy boats
on the duck pond. Sodden crusts of bread that even the ducks
would not eat floated in the brownish water. Hackett was talking about strip lighting. He asked if that was what Quirke had
in the dissecting room, and how did he find it. Quirke said it
was hard on the eyes. Hackett nodded. "The wife has me tormented about the bloody lights in the living room," he said.
"Now she's thinking of strip lighting. Is that, like, neon, those
long bulbs with gas in them?" Quirke said he was not sure how
they worked, but he supposed it was gas. "I think there's a kind

of filament in them," Hackett said, "that makes the gas glow." He shook his head. "I'll tell her it's not good for the eyes."

The children had begun to squabble—someone had capsized someone else's boat, and mothers had to intervene. The two men walked on. They crossed the little humpbacked bridge. The fragrance of flowers, wallflowers, mostly, came to them from the numerous beds roundabout. A terrier had got into the concrete basin of the fountain and was swimming about in circles, snapping at the water cascading around it and barking madly. In the bandstand the army brass band had finished a recital. The players were packing up their instruments, and the audience was drifting away, scattering in all directions across the grass.

They came to two empty deck chairs beside a bed of asters, and Hackett suggested they might sit. As soon as they did, the park attendant popped up out of nowhere, with his leather purse and his roll of tickets, and took thruppence from each of them. "We'd have been better off on a bench," Hackett grumbled. He squirmed his bottom against the canvas, making the joints of the chair legs groan. "I can never get comfortable in these things."

The cloud was a quarter way up the sky by now.

Marguerite Delahaye's boat had been found the previous morning adrift in Slievemore Bay. Of the woman herself there was still no trace. Missing, presumed drowned. "Isn't it a queer thing," Hackett said, "the three of them, Delahaye, Clancy, and then Delahaye's sister, all of them gone in boats? Do you ever sail, yourself?"

"No," Quirke said. "I'm nervous of the sea."

"As any sensible man would be. I don't much care for it

myself, either." He paused. "Would you say she jumped?" Quirke did not reply. He was keeping a wary eye on the cloud. They both had their hats in their laps. "A tragic waste of lives," Hackett said.

Quirke offered him a cigarette, but Hackett was a Player's man, and preferred his own. They smoked in silence for a while. The smoke would rise a little way and then the breeze would catch it and whip it off at an angle to the side.

"What about the Delahayes?" Quirke asked. "The twins."

"Oh, a fine pair of rogues. I should have paid more attention to those boys from the start. They were thrown out of school— Clongowes Wood, you know—when they were lads, for tying one of the junior kids to a tree and leaving him all night. The poor little fellow was asthmatic, and had an attack and died. The grandfather got them off that particular hook."

"How did he do that?"

"The Commissioner was a Freemason. No charges were pressed."

Quirke nodded; such things happened. "They drugged my daughter."

"Did they?" Hackett turned in the chair to look at him. "Why did they do that?"

Quirke shrugged. "As a warning, maybe, since she was supposed to be their alibi. But more for fun, I think. They're fond of fun." He squinted at the darkening sky. "Where are they now?" he asked.

"One of them, the one we're particularly after—James, is it?—skedaddled down to Cork, to his auntie. Too late, though, his auntie being gone. He's still in the house—the boys down there spotted him, and I've asked them to pick him up."

"And the other one?"

"Not a trace. I imagine he's in England somewhere, or maybe America." He chuckled. "I'm thinking of getting Interpol on the job. Wouldn't that be a thing, now."

"And the girl—what's her name? Somers?"

"Aye—Tanya Somers. I had a word with her. Nothing there."

"But she had to be in on it. The night of the party, when there was only one of them but they pretended it was two, she played along with them."

"She says they told her it was for a bet. She's not the brightest ticket, the same Miss Somers. A grand-looking girl but"—he tapped his forehead—"not much up top."

"And she doesn't know where Jonas is."

"If she does, she's not saying."

"You think she does know?"

Hackett shook his head. "No. He wouldn't have told her. He would have been planning it—he knew your daughter suspected. He took a load of money out of the bank and had a ticket booked to London. That's the last trace we had of him." He shifted again awkwardly in the chair, swearing under his breath at the discomfort. "He'll turn up, sooner or later," he said. "Clever as he is, he didn't think far enough ahead. It's no life, being on the run. He'll get careless, and make a mistake, and then we'll have him. Or he'll just get lonely, and come back—you'd be surprised how many do." He paused, and looked sideways at Quirke, and gave a small cough. "The widow, Mrs. Delahaye, is selling up, I hear."

Quirke was still looking at the cloud. "Selling up?" he said.

"Getting rid of the house—the *houses*—and moving to South

Africa. I believe it's where she's from, originally." He paused again, coughed again. "A cool customer, that lady."

Quirke said nothing. It was starting to rain; they felt the first stray drops.

"Well," Hackett said, struggling up from the chair, "that's three good pennies wasted." He put on his hat. Quirke remained seated. He steepled his fingers and tapped them against his lips. "A bad business," Hackett said.

"Yes," Quirke answered.

The detective looked down at him, his head tilted. "Are you all right?" he asked. Quirke lifted his head.

"I'm all right," he said. "I'm fine."

Hackett nodded, smiled lopsidedly, and touched one finger to the brim of his hat. "I'll be seeing you, then," he said, and turned away.

Quirke stood up and walked off in the opposite direction. The rain was falling harder now.

IT WAS A SUMMER DELUGE. IT BEAT ON THE ROADWAY AND drummed on the roofs of cars, and the gutters raced. By the time he found a phone box he was drenched—the water had even soaked through the shoulder pads of his jacket, and he could feel the chill damp on his skin. He took off his sodden hat, but there was nowhere to set it down so he put it back on. He lifted the receiver off the hook and fumbled in his pockets for change. The park attendant had taken his last coppers. He dialed zero and the operator came on, and he gave her Isabel Galloway's number. "I'm sorry, caller," the woman said, not sounding sorry at all, "please insert three pennies or I can't connect you." He told her it was an emergency, that he was a doctor and that she must put him through. "I'm sorry, caller," she said again, in her singsong voice. "Look," Quirke said, thumping his fist softly against the phone's big black metal box, "please, I'm telling you, it's an emergency—it's life or death." But it was no good, the operator did not believe him, and broke the connection.

He stood for a long time listening to the pips sounding on the empty line. The rain beat against the small glass panes all around him. He hung up the phone and blundered out into the storm.

ACKNOWLEDGMENTS

My warmest thanks to Gregory Page and Fiona Ruane.

ABOUT THE AUTHOR

BENJAMIN BLACK is the pen name of the Man Booker Prize–winning novelist John Banville. The author of the bestselling and critically acclaimed series of Quirke novels—*Christine Falls, The Silver Swan, Elegy for April,* and *A Death in Summer*—he lives in Dublin.

CPSIA information can be obtained
at www.ICGtesting.com
Printed in the USA
LVHW050216040523
746009LV00002B/137